Old Books, New Technologies

As we rely increasingly on digital resources, and libraries discard large parts of their older collections, what is our responsibility to preserve old books for the future? David McKitterick's lively and wide-ranging study explores how old books have been represented and interpreted from the eighteenth century to the present day. Conservation of these texts has taken many forms, from early methods of counterfeiting, imitation and rebinding to modern practices of microfilming, digitisation and photography. Using a comprehensive range of examples, McKitterick reveals these practices and their effects to address wider questions surrounding the value of printed books, in terms of both their content and their status as historical objects. Creating a link between historical approaches and the emerging technologies of the future, this book furthers our understanding of old books and their significance in a world of digital technology.

DAVID MCKITTERICK is Fellow and Librarian of Trinity College, Cambridge. His books include *A History of Cambridge University Press*, 3 vols. (1992–2004) and *Print, Manuscript and the Search for Order, 1450–1830* (2003). He is also a general editor of *The Cambridge History of the Book in Britain*.

Old Books, New Technologies

The Representation, Conservation and Transformation of Books since 1700

DAVID McKITTERICK
Fellow and Librarian, Trinity College, Cambridge

CAMBRIDGE
UNIVERSITY PRESS

CAMBRIDGE
UNIVERSITY PRESS

University Printing House, Cambridge CB2 8BS, United Kingdom

Cambridge University Press is part of the University of Cambridge.

It furthers the University's mission by disseminating knowledge in the pursuit of education, learning and research at the highest international levels of excellence.

www.cambridge.org
Information on this title: www.cambridge.org/9781107470392

© David McKitterick 2013

This publication is in copyright. Subject to statutory exception
and to the provisions of relevant collective licensing agreements,
no reproduction of any part may take place without the written
permission of Cambridge University Press.

First published 2013
Paperback edition 2014

Printed in the United Kingdom by TJ International Ltd., Padstow, Cornwall

A catalogue record for this publication is available from the British Library

Library of Congress Cataloguing in Publication data
McKitterick, David.
Old books, new technologies : the representation, conservation and transformation of books since 1700 / David McKitterick.
   pages   cm
ISBN 978-1-107-03593-5 (hardback)
1. Publishers and publishing – Technological innovations.   2. Book industries and trade – Technological innovations.   3. Books – Conservation and restoration – History.   4. Book industries and trade – History.   5. Publishers and publishing – History.   I. Title.
Z280.M35   2013
070.5–dc23

2012038444

ISBN 978-1-107-03593-5 Hardback
ISBN 978-1-107-47039-2 Paperback

Cambridge University Press has no responsibility for the persistence or accuracy of URLs for external or third-party internet websites referred to in this publication, and does not guarantee that any content on such websites is, or will remain, accurate or appropriate.

Contents

List of illustrations [*page* vi]
Preface [ix]

1 The past in pixels [1]

2 Restoration and invention [27]

3 Conservation, counterfeiting and bookbinding [57]

4 Representation and imitation [72]

5 From copying to facsimile [94]

6 The arrival of photography [114]

7 Public exhibition [139]

8 The Caxton exhibition of 1877 [159]

9 A bibliographical and public revolution [183]

10 Conclusion [204]

Notes [214]
Select bibliography [245]
Index [278]

Illustrations

2.1 Cicero, *Epistolae ad Atticum* etc. (Venetiis: Paulus Manutius, '1548') [*page* 38]

2.2 Lodovico Ariosto, *Orlando furioso* (Venetia: Nicolo Zopino and Vincentio Copagno, 1524) [40]

2.3 *The castrations of the last edition of Holinshed's Chronicle, both in the Scotch and English parts... Printed with the old types and ligatures, and compared literatim by the original* (London: Printed for William Mears, Fletcher Gyles and James Woodman, 1723) [44]

2.4 Instructions by a member of staff of Cambridge University Library for the removal of leaves from one of the Library's copies of Caxton's *Recuyell of the historyes of Troye*, and their insertion in the other [48]

3.1 Giovanni Guerra, *Varie acconciature di teste usate da nobilissime dame in diverse cittadi d'Italia* (Rome?, c. 1589) [68]

4.1 William Shakespeare, *Mr. William Shakespeares comedies, histories, & tragedies. Published according to the originall copies* (London: Printed by Isaac Jaggard and Ed. Blount, 1623) [74]

4.2 William Shakespeare, *Mr. William Shakespeares comedies, histories, & tragedies. Published according to the originall copies* ('London: Printed by Isaac Jaggard and Ed. Blount, 1623'). Type facsimile by R. and J. Wright, 1807 [75]

4.3 Giovanni Boccaccio, *Il decamerone*, 'Firenze, 1527', type facsimile [Venice: Pasinello, 1729] [78]

4.4 Raoul Lefèvre, *The recuyell of the historyes of Troye* (Ghent?: William Caxton, 1473 or 1474) [81]

4.5 *The destruction of Troy, in three books*, 8th edn (London: Printed for T. Passenger, at the 3 Bibles on London-Bridge, 1670) [82]

4.6 *The most delectable history of Reynard the fox, newly corrected and purged from all grossenesse in phrase and matter* (London: Printed by H. B. and are to be sold by Edward Brewster at the Crane in St. Paul's Church-Yard, 1662) [83]

List of illustrations vii

4.7 Desiderius Erasmus, *A playne and godly exposytion or declaration of the commune crede* [London, 1726?]. A reprint of the edition printed by Robert Redman in 1533   [86]

4.8 *The solempnities and triumphes doon and made at the spousells and marriage of the Kings doughter the Ladye Marye to the Prince of Castile Archeduke of Austrige* (London: Wright and Murphy, and Ackermann, 1818). Reproduced lithographically after a copy of the original   [92]

5.1 Joseph Ames, *Typographical antiquities* (London: Printed by W. Faden, and sold by J. Robinson, 1749)   [103]

6.1 *The Bookworm* (Elliot Stock, 1893)   [116]

6.2 William Shakespeare, *A reprint of his collected works as put forth in 1623* (London: Lionel Booth, 1862–4)   [127]

6.3 Jacobus de Cessolis, *The game of chess* (London: William Caxton [1483])   [132]

6.4 *The game of the chesse*, by William Caxton. Reproduced in facsimile by Vincent Figgins (London: J. R. Smith, 1855)   [133]

6.5 John Milton, *Paradise lost* (1667)   [134]

6.6 John Milton, *Paradise lost, being a facsimile reproduction of the first edition* (London: Elliot Stock, 1877)   [135]

7.1 Statue of Gutenberg erected at Mainz, August 1837   [143]

7.2 The printing exhibition at Haarlem, 1856, in honour of the memory of Lourens (or Laurens) Janszoon Coster   [157]

8.1 Daniel Maclise, *Caxton shewing the first specimen of his printing to King Edward IV and the royal family in the abbey of Westminster, 1477*   [172]

Figures 2.1–2.3, 4.1, 4.3–4.8, 5.1, 6.3, 6.5 and 6.6 are reproduced by permission of the Master and Fellows, Trinity College, Cambridge, and Figure 3.1 is by permission of the Syndics, Cambridge University Library. Others are from a private collection.

Preface

Any new technology, just like any new idea, requires some understanding not just of what is new, but also of what it replaces. The current revolution in printing and publishing is no different. It offers new ways of doing things, and new ways of thinking. It offers opportunities for creativity and imagination on a scale and by routes of which we are so far scarcely aware. During the past few years there has emerged a considerable literature about the effect on conventional publishing of what is sometimes called the digital age. While we have moved on from early simplistic announcements that the book is either dead, or dying, to more considered – and better informed – assessments of an increasingly complex world, on the other hand it is perhaps not surprising that less thought has been given to the structures and details of relationships between past, present and future.

The following pages are about attitudes, and about practices. They are about those whose professions or other interests have made them responsible for the care and preservation of older printed books, about those who have sought to explain and understand their manufacture and their alteration at the hands of subsequent generations. They are about both private and public knowledge of objects which are simultaneously so familiar, as books, and yet, by their increasing age or by their monetary or other values, so apparently alien. They are about the dissemination and enhancement of public understanding. By addressing these kinds of evidence over a long period, the revolution in our reading of older books, and the ease with which we can now download – and often manipulate – texts and images, can be better comprehended.

In turn, this raises questions about how books should be valued and preserved so that future generations can understand features of the world of print that are – at present – well within living memory of most people.

In writing this book, I have been encouraged and helped by a wider than usual range of friends, colleagues and audiences in four continents. I am grateful to publishers as well as librarians, printers as well as authors, booksellers as well as book collectors, lawyers as well as historians, journalists as well as archivists, and people from several different backgrounds well beyond academia who have shared with me some of the topics addressed in the following pages. But, as always, I have been helped most by my wife Rosamond who watched and nurtured the project as the book gradually took shape.

David McKitterick

1 | The past in pixels

In what shape or form do we read old books? In what shape or form may we expect to read them within the next few years? As the demand for e-publication and hand-held readers accelerates and follows the pattern of rapid adoption that has characterised other major breakthroughs in everyday consumer technology, for most people the answer is probably that they will increasingly be read in scanned versions on various hand-held screens, mostly at various scales of reduction. That will make old books immensely more accessible, in larger numbers, over a greater range of dates and genres and to more people in more regions of the world than ever previously. Even if the concept of universal availability will remain no more than that, a concept, we may still assume that the opportunity to read books from the past, in something approximating their original appearance, will be open to immeasurably more people than was possible when they were available only in libraries or to collectors. The decreasing stocks of older books available in antiquarian and second-hand shops have been replaced by this new kind of wealth – not material in a physical sense, but nonetheless immediately available, as virtual recreations.

In one respect, old books have never been so easily available. But they are available only at several removes from the form in which they were printed, published and sold before being read by generations of readers for whom paper was the natural vehicle. We now confront a world where knowledge of books in the form they have been known for five and a half centuries is declining. The angle of this decline will increase; the only questions are the speed at which this will happen in the near future, and how printed books will relate to the possibilities of electronic media.

For all the immense advantages that scanned images of books present, in widening access and enabling different ways of reading, there is one obvious and fundamental difficulty about reading and assessing images on screen. They generally require some prior knowledge of the physical form of the original object. This is the weakness in the position of any reader seeking more than the most superficial understanding of the past when he or she faces a book – or any kind of printed or manuscript document – that has been recast in two dimensions, stripped of its physical and material characteristics, and scaled to a uniform size. Books and manuscripts are not unique in this, but because the words and images that they contain can be reproduced on screen in a way that creates an appearance of reality – more or less the same shapes of letters and images – this reincarnation is tolerated. The elements of meaning conveyed in a book by its physical properties are suppressed, and in the absence of comparative knowledge of what books of a particular period look and feel like – their weight, their bulk, their colour or other features – it cannot be assumed that a reader will properly understand what is presented on screen. No amount of magnification, colour adjustment, page-turning software or other screen facilities can alter this. And even as use of large databases of images increases, so the proportion declines of people possessing any experience of handling originals.

As we face, and exploit, these changes, so we need to ask all the more carefully what we mean by old books, and what others have meant by them in past generations. Comparatively few early printed books survive in exactly the same form that they were received by their first readers, at the conclusion of a series of compromises reached between author, printer, publisher, bookbinder and bookseller consummated in what were called new books. The forms in which they were originally published were usually not only very different from what we now search for, and see, on screen. Often they have been physically adjusted several times over in the interval. We may gain much in our modern computer-aided search strategies, and in our ability to compare texts, copies and all kinds of physical properties of books in numbers unimaginable only a generation ago, but how much have we lost? And how much is this process of loss a new phenomenon?

As this book will seek to show, it is not a straightforward or speedy translation from original to screen. Material properties and their appearance have always been subject to change, to manipulation, to revaluation and to reinterpretation.

Over the last few years there has been increasing anxiety amongst scholars, teachers and book historians concerning the relationship between books as physical objects, artefacts, and their presentation in different media, as surrogates and similitudes.[1] In a damning indictment of the world of scholarship and librarianship alike, the late D. F. McKenzie spoke of 'a theft of evidence' in reproductions.[2] This is not a new issue, even if it has been given a new urgency by library managers faced with difficult decisions about budgets, space and the uncertain sustainability of electronic files. There is now an ever-growing tension between different kinds of reading and the realities of library costs. Unable or unwilling to provide the space, staffing and other supports for books on paper, and beguiled by the promise of liberal access, librarians are faced with daily temptations to turn to electronic versions of past and present publications.

Since long before the nineteenth century, every generation has sought new visual means to harness the past. In the early 1870s, the New England bookseller and bibliographer Henry Stevens put forward ideas for the microphotography of parts of books as a means of bibliographical control.[3] In 1931 the Anglo-American conference of historians heard a paper by the Tudor historian G. B. Harrison comparing the advantages of collotype with the Replika process for the full-size reproduction of manuscripts and early printed books.[4] In the 1930s, Eugene B. Power, based in Michigan, began a programme of mass microfilming of early printed books and, even more importantly, publishing the microfilms so that any library with the necessary money could buy them.[5] It was useful in saving rare originals from wear, or saving library storage space, or saving expensive research trips. But it was not a panacea, as the Harvard rare books librarian W. A. Jackson explained in a vigorous paper delivered in Cincinnati (well away from the obvious major collections of early printed books on the east and west coasts of America) in 1940.[6] The microfilms that he castigated then were in the same programme that has since become the basis of much of EEBO, *Early English Books Online*, the essential resource today for anyone working on British and North American books before 1701. The faults remain. With the move of books from paper to celluloid began the process of recreation of which today's scanned books, read on a computer screen rather than as light cast on a white screen, are direct descendants. The questions, opportunities and implications of surrogates are not new.

What is new is the immensely greater, more varied and cheaper accessibility that is now available to readers. So too are questions of escalating costs in maintaining the world's libraries, the repositories of human memory. This is a challenge that affects everyone: not just readers or library managers, and not just everyone who contributes through taxes or charitable giving to the maintenance, rebranding, development or destruction of institutions that share a history in recognisable form dating from the ancient world. The costs of libraries in our own world, with all their complexities and challenges, are still only partly grasped. The present book is indirectly about these questions that need much better contextual understanding than the usual ones that are advanced. It is concerned with bibliographical values more than financial ones. By taking contemporary questions as its starting point, it attempts to be more than another history of book collecting, though many figures familiar in this genre also make their appearance in the following pages.

It has been written in the years immediately after several large libraries disburdened themselves of collections that had been assumed to be in safe hands.[7] The New York Public Library had a seemingly undiscriminating drive to reduce its research collections, in a programme that showed little or no knowledge of what was being discarded. It was far from alone among American research libraries which, led by the Library of Congress, had since the Second World War developed a belief in the replacement of originals by microfilms, as the only feasible means of preserving fragile originals, and incidentally saving expensive shelf space. Where America led, others followed. The British Library advertised dozens of runs of newspapers dating from the mid-nineteenth century onwards, and offered them free to any library, in any country, willing to take them. The defence for this dispersal was that these newspapers were all on microfilm. Despite a great deal of special pleading, it remains that neither filmed nor scanned images are adequate substitutes for original documents. Their format does not mimic the experience of opening up a newspaper, and seeing a double-page spread, all legible at a glance. They do not reflect the ways in which newspapers are put together, the stories carefully graded in prominence so that what seems most important to the editorial team is noticed first. They do not capture the quality of photographs – black and white or colour – that have been selected, cropped, placed and printed with considerable thought and care.[8] Much of this is true also of printed books. Put briefly, the two-dimensional screen cannot illustrate adequately a three-dimensional object that constantly changes shape as its leaves are turned. Nor (to repeat) can it provide a sense of weight, or of materials. It would be pleasant to be confident that these destructive practices are matters of the past. While microfilming is now out of date as a technology, scanning presents an even bigger temptation to librarians pressed for space, money and other resources. There will be further similar cases in the future. For this reason, it is imperative that librarians and the committees that govern them understand more clearly not only what is gained, but also what is lost by the disposal and dispersal of evidence in its original form. Librarians caring for research collections (a term that encompasses far more than just what is held in departments of special collections) are trustees for the past. It is a betrayal of trusteeship to assume that a surrogate will answer sufficiently not just for the immediate present but also for the future.

Most of the themes raised in this first chapter concern current or quite recent changes in the ways that books are published, sold and managed. Like all changes, they are partly defined by what happened previously. And like all changes, they also affect attitudes in the present. They affect the ways in which the past is viewed, and the ways it is valued. We can only see the past through our present experiences. The following pages offer an enquiry into how various kinds of old books, as distinct from new ones, have been presented, viewed, evaluated and often changed, from the early eighteenth century to the development and application of photography in the late nineteenth century. By that date, most of the technologies that are of most relevance to this discussion were in place. The audiences include scholars and the book trade, and what we might, somewhat hesitantly, call collectors and ordinary readers. These and other various groups of readers and possessors of books are not discrete. There has always been substantial overlap. How have old books been brought before the public at various times? How has public interest in old books changed, and how have different publics changed? Given that most people's attention is drawn constantly to new books (a preoccupation reflected in dozens of studies in book history), these questions might seem divergent, but there is a pattern in changing attitudes to older books that offers much common ground. The following pages are mainly concerned with 'old' as defined by those published before the nineteenth century, and the historical thread of the chapters ends in the first years of the twentieth century. That is partly the accident of where much work has been focussed by some kinds of recent scholarship. It is not meant to be exclusive. Indeed, very similar threads can be found in later periods. The questions are the same for more recently published books and for periods since.

If there is a common theme, it is one of time. The computer screen suppresses a sense of time. It is not just that it is quicker than going to a library. Because everything is available at much the same speed, on the same screen, in a universal format defined not by the materials or shapes of original manufacture but by software that has been deliberately written to be as widely applicable as possible, all images possess common qualities that are actually designed to suppress chronological relationships. On the other hand, in viewing or handling artefacts, we bring visual and tactile accumulations of knowledge and experience to make judgements over the relative age and status of what is before us. We may be more or less adept at this, and it can be difficult to appreciate shorter or longer historical periods: many people tend (for example) to have a more nuanced understanding of a recent life-span of, say, eighty years than they do of a usually shorter life-span in, say, the fifteenth century. But the uniformity and near immediacy of the computer screen do not, in themselves, contain the values and experiences that enable us to judge time with anything like the same ease.

The values we set on any object depend on the meanings we attach to it or draw from it, on the extent to which we value or ignore its history, on the content as it is appreciated by the world at large. Further, while it is generally accepted that an original artefact, be it book or painting, has a value bearing only a distant relationship to any reproduction of that same object, nonetheless our understanding of either original or reproduction depends on what we have learned, or can learn, from the other. Reproductive engraving has ensured this since the sixteenth century, and photography has strengthened the relationship since the mid-nineteenth. But what happens when an object becomes universally accessible – also in two dimensions – on the computer screen? There is substantial evidence that wide public availability on screen not only extends awareness and opportunities. It also generates its own extra interest in original artefacts.

Hence the importance of trying to understand why and how we have come to our present assumptions and beliefs, concerning what we consider important when faced with an object in either its original or its surrogate form. Hence, also, the importance of recognising the fragility of digitised texts dependent on software that (as the short history of computing has repeatedly shown) may not be maintained.[9] Hence, too, the importance of recognising even some quite basic inadequacies and differences in digitisation programmes.

A new world

This book has been written partly as a companion to my earlier study *Print, manuscript and the search for order* (2003). During the brief period between the appearance of that book and today, attitudes to books, the means whereby we acquire them and the economics underlying their production and circulation have undergone profound changes. Paper is no longer necessarily the most obvious way for an author even of a straightforward novel or monograph to reach the market. What formerly would have been marketed first on paper and then electronically is often now presented in the reverse order. As for paper, on the one hand books have met a large-scale welcome in non-traditional places of sale such as supermarkets, while on the other hand the large stock-holding bookshop of a kind that has existed since the eighteenth century has gone into a probably permanent decline. Many of the latter have closed. Whether small independents or large chains, and whether offering new books or old, none seems to be immune. While it is not always clear how far their demise is due to poor management decisions, how much to an overburdened trade structure, how much to the manipulation of credit arrangements or – in the case of new books – how much to competitive discounting, and how much to broader commercial pressures from trade rivals, publishers or suppliers, the rise of major web booksellers has undoubtedly contributed massively to this shift. Some of this was foreseeable, but much has happened more quickly than was anticipated. In Britain, the demise of the Net Book Agreement in 1997 obliged independent firms dealing in new books to come to urgent decisions, and some moved quickly to establish themselves in different parts of the book market. Yet, more recently, many firms and their shareholders have been taken by surprise even while overall sales remained buoyant for some kinds of books on widely popular subjects sold through non-traditional classes of shops such as supermarkets. This same period of what is widely perceived as a crisis, and by more sombre observers even as a juddering finale, has also witnessed some of the most remarkable publicity campaigns and best-selling phenomena in the history of bookselling.[10] It remains to be seen how publishers will react to changes in consumer habits, and the saturating effects of social media, that will inexorably influence the kinds of books that can be most easily published. Meanwhile, the number of titles published each year increases. In 2009 the UK publishing industry produced over 133,000, up 3.2 per cent on 2008 and up about 33 per cent on fifteen years previously.[11]

On another hand, publishers have responded with programmes for e-publishing, both for new books and for their backlists. To this 2009 figure needs to be added a further 24,000 digital titles.[12] Some publishers are turning to a mixture of non-commercial Creative Commons licences,[13] alongside print-on-demand for paper copies. For paper, the development and improvement of print-on-demand technology and of digital printing for extremely short runs have transformed new publishing, stock control and the ways in which backlists can be exploited. The economics of publishing are changing, and no model has yet proved ideal. There is almost as much confused activity amongst authors and readers as the world comes gradually to terms with multiple arenas of paper and screen, print and an increasing range of electronic forms of delivery.

Amidst all this, long-held and deeply ingrained attitudes to the place of print and manuscript are being modified. Print-on-demand is changing the market for old books. Whether or not books will continue to be published in the form that they have been known for centuries (and so far there is no evidence to suggest that they will not), attitudes to books of all kinds, new and old, are being irreparably altered.

Ever since the work of Gutenberg in mid-fifteenth-century Mainz, most printed books have been generally published according to a pattern. An edition of so many copies was printed, in one place, and if all went well it paid for itself and sold out within a reasonable time. That is no longer the case. In about the last twenty years, not only have most print runs shrunk dramatically; it is now widely expected that editorial, manufacturing and selling costs should be recovered within a very few months, not years. In their own turn, booksellers have been forced – often by the banks on whose loans they depend – to seek to sell books within a very few weeks. The bookshop that could once afford to hold stock for months or years on end is now in a diminishing minority. The most obvious changes in the manufacture of books include: the advent of digital printing, making extremely short runs economically feasible; the concept – learned from long-standing practices in newspaper publishing, where printing has been distributed in different cities and countries for many years – of printing to market (and thereby no longer incurring very heavy transport costs); and, perhaps most importantly, the advent of print-on-demand. These and other new procedures both offer benefits and pose challenges to publishers. Subject to technology and customer bases, for some booksellers they might offer an opportunity. Niche bookselling has become possible at negligible risk. Again, the wholesale and retail price structures need to be re-thought. At least in theory, books – on paper – need no longer be considered as being out of print. Quite apart from the disagreements between publishers, authors and literary agents that have resulted from this, as each group has sought to grasp at new 'rights', the advent of such a restructuring entails still greater changes for the traditional bookshop. It also poses questions about ways in which libraries might be further exploited, restructured and brought within the book trade.

The downloadable e-book, so long talked of by journalists, publishers and trade analysts, is only a small part of the story of the last few years. As its sales represent an ever-increasing part of all book sales (a majority in some parts of the market), its full impact has yet to be felt. One thing is clear: it will drive the market into further segments both with respect to customers and with respect to the kinds of books that are published. It does not need a management consultant to advise that any large or middle-size firm must invest, with some imagination, in e-publishing in order to survive. Realistic pricing policies have yet to be established, for the true cost centres for such publishing are very far from clear, and market opinion has yet to be measured in more than the most preliminary ways. Furthermore, e-books are well suited to some kinds of publication and reading, but much less so to others. Whatever the pattern, they will further affect the ways in which books, whether paper or electronic, are written, chosen, designed, presented, understood and considered. The current lack of a trade standard for downloadable books and for the devices on which they are read immediately affects choices for buying, and is unsustainable if e-books are to be properly developed as they deserve. It dominates much current discussion, but it is unlikely to be a long-term issue. It should take less time to settle than, for example, the arguments some years ago over different voltages offered by different power companies within a single national boundary, a world even in Britain still easily within living memory, or the somewhat older arguments about railway gauges, still unresolved in some countries and leading to economic inefficiencies.

All these changes in the book trade are affecting the ways in which books are regarded, as well as the ways in which they are used.

Loss and gain

It is improbable that there will ever be a time when all the books that have ever been published, and that survive, will be available electronically. But very large numbers have been scanned already, and not only in the major western languages.[14] Like the microfilming programmes of early English books that were set in place in the United States in the 1930s partly so as to ensure that books would survive in some form even if Britain's major libraries were destroyed by war, some of the more recent – and vastly larger – scanning programmes are built on weak foundations. They are hugely beneficial, and have transformed the ways in which we access and read books. But despite millions of pounds or dollars of investment, the goods offered to the world too often show lamentable quality control. Not all of them confess to their imperfections with quite such candour as the following warning that accompanies the *Edinburgh Review* digitised from film and published online:

Vol.173 wanting. Best copy available for photographing. Pagination is irregular, some pages are missing. Several pages are torn or stained and have print faded with some loss of text. Several title pages are misdated. Cols. [sic: presumably Vols.] 1 and 169 lack title page. Vol.18: p.274 is bound and photographed out of order. Vol.173: January-April, 1891 is missing.[15]

The sense of editorial exhaustion is palpable. It is also misplaced. This is certainly not the 'best copy available for photographing', for many libraries possessing this widely held title were not asked. It is also not clear how one page can be bound out of order, for single pages cannot be bound, whereas a single leaf (two pages) can. The danger is not so much in these misstatements as in the fact that the existence of an easily purchased digital copy of an otherwise space-hungry run of a journal will lead to the discarding of hard copy – in favour of this inferior and incomplete digitised version. Entirely unnecessarily, and thanks to the publisher, readers are placed in a situation worse than that enjoyed previously. The evidence on which any serious scholarship depends is being taken from them.

For the early microfilming projects some of the difficulties were technical (the film stock has not always survived well), and some were bibliographical (sometimes the wrong edition was chosen, sometimes an incomplete copy). Pages were sometimes cropped in order to fit in the screen, exposure – especially in the early years – was variable. The resolution was deliberately set low. Notwithstanding constant attempts to monitor photography in dozens of libraries on both sides of the Atlantic, and the insistence on attention to specified standards, the images that result – perhaps especially in the transition from film to scan on screen – can be of disappointingly limited use. This is especially noticeable in the reproduction of many engraved illustrations and decorations, which cannot be studied in any serious way. Originals are compromised in other ways as well. Colour printing becomes black and white. Paper quality is indeterminable. In a reversal of history, the codex is turned into a scroll as volumes filmed or scanned opening by opening, or page by page, are set out side by side. Nonetheless, despite such difficulties and despite the most obvious fact of all, that a three-dimensional product was turned into one of two dimensions, the publisher of *Early English Books Online* (EEBO) has claimed to provide 'cover-to-cover full-page images that show the works exactly as they appeared in their original printed editions', so that modern readers can see 'exactly what the original readers saw, back when the Wars of the Roses still raged'.[16] The files, which perfectly understandably have concentrated on the printed texts ever since the first microfilms were made in the 1930s, certainly do not provide cover-to-cover images in the sense that has become familiar in some more recent – and current – scanning programmes. Nonetheless, problems persist in more recent projects. Missing pages, wrong editions, missing volumes from sets, and hands intruding in front of the lens are all familiar to even casual users of non-copyright material that is, at present, mostly free on screen. There is no reason why in the future it – good and bad – should not incur a financial charge. Indeed, and quite apart from any unavoidable charging régimes for in-copyright material, this will become a necessity as the world gradually recognises that, somehow, what is delivered to the screen must be paid for. Scanned publications cost money to make, just like any other publication; and, unlike paper publications that are out of print, they cost their publishers appreciable sums to maintain. One of the greatest of all public challenges, little considered for many years, lies in the transfer of on-costs, from libraries holding out-of-print books on paper to publishers holding computer-based files. Since this involves patterns of library budgets, which have to be agreed, it is a social challenge, not a technical one; and being social, it is more difficult because it involves private investment and charges to libraries or individuals for continuing access to what has been usually assumed to be free.

While there are very considerable practical benefits in linking large-scale microfilm programmes first to digital delivery and then (more recently) to print-on-demand agreements, it remains that these increasingly distant links to the originals provide a world of reading ever more loaded with ambiguity. The Nabu Press, for example, makes books available on a print-on-demand basis, but their publicity printed at the front of their books carries a warning:

This book may have occasional imperfections such as missing or blurred pages, poor pictures, errant marks, etc. that were either part of the original artifact, or were introduced by the scanning process.

The copy of the eighteenth-century book from which this is taken, scanned in the New York Public Library, was also missing the ends of lines on many pages because the original could not be sufficiently opened for scanning. It may be doubted whether adequate notice had been taken of how far conservation needs and the scanning process had been matched. Whatever the hopes of the library or the publishers, the reproduction was certainly not adequate preservation. Other reproductions include parts of operators' hands, half-turned pages and other features that betray inattention and poor quality control. *Caveat emptor*, and perhaps all the more so because the publishers are clearly not interested in the true origins of any faults in what they are offering in return for money. Or, to take another example: a print-on-demand publisher offers a copy of a book from the English Faculty Library at Oxford. It is certainly not the best copy available, for this one is defiled by ink blots and stains on several of the pages. The root of the problem in these and hundreds of other poor-quality and incomplete reproductions is the hurried scanning programme, on whose files many print-on-demand publishers draw for their images. Much of the work is invaluable. Much of it should never have passed quality controls, yet these are the images forced on readers. No doubt the libraries that have been drawn into the various commercial agreements would prefer matters to be otherwise, but they have in effect turned their backs on questions of public responsibility. The University of California libraries have their own series, based on copies in their own collections. Understandably, these copies bear library ownership stamps and other marks of use, what are termed in the blurbs on these particular reprints as 'artifacts'. But

in addition to these artifacts, the work may have additional errors that were either in the original, in the digital scans, or introduced as we prepared the book for printing. These errors may include missing pages, upside down pages, obscured pages, cropped or missing text, and/or other errors.[17]

It does not add that the page size and type size of the original may bear no relation to the reprint. Another site, much used by anyone wishing to read early books, is more detailed. The series of print-on-demand books derived from *Eighteenth Century Collections Online* (ECCO) is 'made possible' by the much larger and more wide-ranging Bibliolife network, which has the praiseworthy aim that 'every book ever published should be available as a high-quality print reproduction'. Each book comes with a warning:

While we have attempted to accurately maintain the integrity of the original work, there are sometimes problems with the original work or the micro-film from which the books were digitized. This can result in minor errors in reproduction. Possible errors include missing and blurred pages, poor pictures, markings and other reproduction issues beyond our control . . .

In an online database, page images do not need to conform to the size restrictions found in a printed book. When converting these images back into a printed bound book, the page sizes are standardized in ways that maintain the detail of the original. For large pages, such as fold-out maps, the original page image is split into two or more pages.[18]

Thus the limitations of the reproduction process are turned into a benefit: page images and sizes 'do not need to conform', and yet they are 'standardized in ways that maintain the detail of the original'. In fact, the process ensures that the 'detail of the original' is exactly what is ignored. Current print-on-demand equipment limits the range of page sizes, with the result that some books appear grotesquely larger than the originals, and others appear much smaller. Quite apart from faults in the original filming, that can themselves include distortions, a sense of scale is lost in a technology where there can be little oppportunity for accurate reproduction of size.

The second fallacy, in filming or in digitisation programmes, is a more insidious one because it makes an assumption about the nature of what is being captured. It assumes that a single copy of an edition will serve. There are very good economic reasons for this assumption, for it is clearly impracticable to scan multiple copies of everything, stabbing at the possibility that such a scattershot approach will hit all the necessary targets.

In thousands of cases multiple copies have been scanned and published, frequently because of accidental overlap in large projects. One of the very few books of which multiple copies have been made publicly available on a more organised and scholarly basis is the Gutenberg Bible. Copies have been scanned from the British Library, Cambridge, Tokyo, Göttingen, Washington and Texas. While this book has no equal in the history of printing, or in public esteem, Shakespeare attracts similar attention, both in the first folio (1623) and in the early quarto editions. Again, there are several different copies consciously planned so as to be available online. But it cannot be expected that many other books will command such planned multiple investments not just of capital, but of ongoing costs. While these and numerous other specialist digitisation projects (one might offer as an example the incunabula project at Munich)[19] have produced scans of a quality that permits unprecedented study and comparison in some respects, they share many of the same assumptions and characteristics as more comprehensive and less-detailed scanning programmes.

Few of the large and more general digitisation sites acknowledge detailed imperfections in the originals that have been scanned. Besides this, it has long been established that in an edition of almost any early printed book no two copies will be precisely the same. Printed books are assumed to be uniform from one copy of an impression to the next, but this has by no means always been the case. In words that have become celebrated, Falconer Madan summed up the position with respect to early printed books in 1911: 'There is no such thing as a duplicate.'[20] His words were no less true of eighteenth- and even nineteenth-century books. The processes of printing and binding offered repeated opportunities for changes of mind, for correction, for alteration and for rearrangement. Authors, editors, proof-readers, printers and publishers all took advantage of this. Readers were constantly warned of differences between copies, and advised to correct their copies accordingly, by hand.[21] Unannounced differences are frequent in many books printed since the early nineteenth century – the beginning of the machine age in the book trades.[22]

Furthermore, where once the emphasis was on manufacturing differences (this was the impetus behind the several digitised versions of the Gutenberg

Bible), more recent work on printed matter (not just books) of all ages has pointed to the differences that arise as a result of use. Each copy holds its own history in this respect.[23] Readers are as important as writers. If we are to try and understand what is meant by the printing revolution of the fifteenth century, a period that ushered in five and a half centuries where print and manuscript were the main means of alphanumeric and pictorial recording and communication, then we need also to understand the implications of variance and multiplicity in reproduction and uniformity. This in turn places a very considerable responsibility on the future of our libraries: that they consult carefully and widely before casting out paper because the same texts are seemingly available electronically. In this, all libraries are accountable to the footsteps of time. Physical books are physical evidence, and no electronic or photographic surrogate is an adequate or a responsible replacement. As records of knowledge and of ways of thought we hold books in trust for the future, as well as materials to be mined in our own generation.

Since this affects our choices in what we are prepared to pay to keep, it is essential to understand the relationship of what we see on screen to the original from which it is ultimately derived. This is usually presented as a problem of interpretation, primarily a concern for scholars and researchers. Since such people are those most able to judge matters, this is sensible enough. But there is also a question that affects any reader, skilled or not, historically minded or not. What exactly is seen on screen? Quite apart from the more obvious questions concerning the presentation of physical reality mentioned above, the relationship of the capturing of an image of a book to its re-presentation to a reader is an essential part of understanding. As printers, publishers, booksellers, advertisers and readers have all been aware since the fifteenth century (and it was not a new concept then), form and meaning are inseparable. Many of the following pages are concerned with the rise of facsimile-making, from manuscript imitation to tracings to the early days of photography.[24] Ever since the fifteenth century – and in the wholly manuscript environment before then – there has been a demand for copies that represent originals. And ever since the fifteenth century those who have made facsimiles have been at pains to stress how close they are to their models. The claims of modern e-publishing are not new.

The process has sometimes been called remediation, the recreation of an artefact through different media. For early English books this recreation is at several removes. First, a library was asked to provide a negative microfilm of a book, filming from start to end of the printed pages, in the order they stood. Then (during this programme, before ProQuest took on the project)

University Microfilms created a duplicate negative, retaining the original as archive. From this duplicate negative, multiple copies were made in positive (i.e. black print on a white/grey background) for sale to libraries. In these libraries, readers read the films with the help of microfilm readers of various models and qualities and in various states of repair. Not surprisingly, quality varied, of the film when it was originated in libraries across mostly Britain and North America, through to the various copying processes, right through to delivery on screen, where soiled lenses and scratched film were commonplace. Yet, understandably, researchers welcomed these surrogates, imperfect though they were. Many more books were made accessible than even the most dedicated traveller to the libraries of the world could hope to see. Time and money were saved, and the database of knowledge for innumerable projects was increased. The difficulty was the same as for anyone working with the scans of the negative films that have largely replaced the microfilm versions of English books down to 1700. The original books, as three-dimensional physical objects of varying thicknesses and sizes, had been suppressed. Often there was not even a scale on the reproduction to show the size ratio. Illustrations had been coarsened in the process of filming, and thus they remained inescapably so in the subsequent digitisation.

EEBO, with (by the standards of the industry) a long ancestry and developed during many changes in technology, presents an admittedly extreme example. But it is also one of the most widely used corpora of its kind, and in principle it presents exactly the same general challenges as the most recent scanning programmes, whether large general ones or the high-resolution ones that have featured particular treasures in major libraries. The technology has improved. The principle of remediation remains the same.

For many readers – and taxpayers whose money supports libraries – facing trends in the contemporary book trade and revolutions in communication, these are not always easy concepts to grasp. The number of books published grows. Yet e-knowledge is more accessible than paper knowledge, and authorial responsibility on innumerable websites seems to matter little even where it can be ascertained. As a reading mechanism, the codex was a measurable advance on the scroll, bringing new possibilities of textual organisation and reference, quite apart from a new portability and convenience for reading and storage.[25] While most books in the last few years – both codices and e-books – have changed very little in the ways in which they are conceived by their authors, and the most obvious physical change for the delivery of some books is from codex to screen, it has become more difficult to conceive how books were viewed in the past.[26] The obvious obstacles to grasping this historical dimension used to be broadly educational and social, demanding the ability to measure and understand chronological, spatial and other relationships. With the advent of universally available electronic communication, the past has become remote in further ways – not just chronologically but also conceptually. Books and printed matter no longer hold monopoly positions, or even dominate in some activities and areas of knowledge. A knowledge of the use of books, and how the codex both offers opportunities and sets limits to ways of reading, can no longer be assumed, save at a quite elementary level. The subtleties of the organisation of section arrangements and of typography, features that have made the codex such a supple and advanced mechanism for reading, are becoming less understood. For those who read older – or even most existing – books, this will become more difficult again, as authors increasingly take advantage of computer-based structures that can be delivered on screen just as easily as a conventional sequence of pages.

Whatever unforeseen changes the future holds for what we are still pleased to call books, and whatever the speed of these changes, there remains an essential and closely related question. It concern how books have been viewed in the past by authors, publishers, booksellers and readers, and hence how, today, we can recover and understand our past. There is a copious literature on the manufacture and use of new books at various times, whether in the fifteenth or the twentieth century. This is the general basis of the several national histories of the book that have recently appeared. For the most part these histories have concentrated on new books in their periods under review, and this despite the fact that at any time the number of old books in circulation will always have been many times greater. The history of book collecting also has its several chroniclers. But as soon as one moves away from a few antiquarian issues, there is much less literature available concerning attitudes at different periods to old books as physical objects. What criteria were important, and how did they change? When did people outside antiquarian circles begin to value old books, and for what reasons? Who were the leaders in public opinion and education? How successful were they? How far and to whom did this matter? How did the concept of an old book, often popularly taken to be synonymous with rare book, develop? Why were some kinds of old books kept, and others ignored? To what extent were these matters for various élites, and to what extent did the wider reading public care?[27]

These and other questions lie, often hidden, behind our current debates concerning the relationship of old books to new ones when they are made available on screen. In these debates, mostly inspired by programmes of mass digitisation, the relationship commonly emerges as a distinction between copyright and non-copyright material. This is only a small fraction of the questions involved. It simply defines books according to commercial criteria, for the argument centres on costs and on compensation to copyright holders. The challenges to comprehension, as opposed to the challenges of commerce, are rather more important for the ways that we will in the future interpret and measure our past. In a computer environment it can be extremely difficult to grasp chronological relationships, where everything is presented two-dimensionally, scaled to the same screen and equally accessible without regard to geography or rarity. In seeking answers to questions about how old books have been viewed in the past, in a world of paper, we may place ourselves better to take advantage of the current changes in the presentation and dissemination of books new and old alike.

Cheap print transformed

There is one obvious shortfall in much of the evidence adduced in the following pages. Inevitably, thanks to the extra attention that is always paid in different generations to what is regarded as more valuable, expensive, rare or otherwise interesting, the focus is mostly on what might be called the upper end of the market: incunabula, the better-known early printers, early editions of classical texts or of major authors in modern languages. There is much less evidence concerning the lower end, what has generally been discarded and disregarded as the detritus of ordinary life. Yet it is exactly this detritus that now commands special attention among historians of all kinds.[28] Though interest in ephemera can be traced back at least to collectors such as Samuel Pepys and John Bagford in the late seventeenth century, and there is evidence of selective interest before then, it has only become a serious subject of study, accompanied among dealers by a gradual establishment of scales of commercial values, since the 1960s. John Johnson's collection of such material assembled a few decades earlier at Oxford University Press was appreciated only by a few people. The collection assembled by the typographer John Lewis, and now housed in the University of Reading, proved a wake-up call when in 1962 he published (not through any established London publisher but through the printing firm for which he worked) a large album of colour reproductions dating from the fifteenth century onwards.[29] This generally disregarded material was shown to have a major relevance to historical study and – not least – to the history of design. Valuably, it set well-known genres in context.

Street ballads, for example, collected for their own sake since the early seventeenth century, were just a part of the assortment of printed matter to be met in social environments ever more dominated by the printed word and image.

As such ephemera were among the cheapest of all forms of publishing, their digital presentation on screen today serves as a useful foil to the databases of more established kinds of literature. One of the most ambitious projects, the English Broadside Ballad Archive based at the University of California, Santa Barbara, offers an up-to-date and carefully planned entry for cheap printed popular ballads. The website is explicit in its claims, and makes clear the extent to which the digitised images relate to originals. But they are also alarmingly frank about what has been done in this process – not just in a series of transitions among different computer files, but also in the deliberate visual manipulation by human intervention:

Ballad facsimiles are digital approximations of what the original printed ballads would have looked like when they originally came off the press. They are created by the EBBA team in Adobe Photoshop from raw TIFFs of individual, usually trimmed ballads or – as is more often the case – of the album page(s) onto which the broadside ballads had been pasted by collectors ... When a ballad sheet has been trimmed, as is typical, we recreate an outer border. When the ballad sheet has not only been trimmed but also pasted onto an album page, we trim away the album page before recreating a border around the ballad sheet.[30]

In other words, by ordinary standards these cannot be said to be facsimiles of the original documents in all their untidy and raw states. The question is inescapable: at what point does the process move from the representational in the sense of some form of facsimile, to one that is primarily editorial, even intrusively recreative? Readers face a sequence of operations designed to destroy bibliographical evidence, and by imposing an 'artificial standard' also to destroy important aspects of bibliographical individuality and identity:

For the cut apart ballads, we also put the two parts of the ballad back together and provide an inner margin dividing the two parts. In determining the size of the borders and inner margins, we surveyed 23 uncut, two-part ballads: 10 from the Pepys ballads and 13 from the Wood ballads (Wood 401) at the Bodleian Library. What we found was that both outer margins and inner divides between two-part ballads varied enormously. The space between the two parts of the uncut ballads, for instance, could be as small as 2 mm and as large as 51 mm. Given the wide range of variation, we decided on an artificial standard for the outer margin of 10 mm and for the inner margin or divide between two parts of 20 mm. These proportions were chosen in order to give the viewer a sense of the ballad as an independent, whole sheet without creating too much white space when the ballad is viewed in large sizes in EBBA.

There follows a process of editing and transcription, in a modern typeface using (so far as possible) a similar range of types as the original, though in fact the range is reduced.

Once a modern transcription is made, the ballad facsimile is opened as a PSD in Adobe Photoshop by a member of the EBBA facsimile transcription team and blocks of the original text are cut out and replaced with the modern transcription. Line breaks and text size conventions in the original are observed as closely as possible so that the resulting facsimile transcription will resemble the layout of the original ballad. All ornaments and woodcuts adorning the ballad are left untouched, thereby creating a version of the ballad that is easily read, even by those untutored in black letter or other forms of early modern print, without losing the ballad's aesthetic impact. A readable print-out of the ballads on 8 x 11 (or larger) paper is thus also produceable for independent study or classroom instruction.

Among several remarkable phenomena, one is readily observable to anyone who reads later chapters in this book.[31] While careful attempts are made to copy and reproduce images, all typographical material is translated into currently available typefaces; Times Roman is quoted as a standard. The same procedure was followed by the many printers in the first half of the nineteenth century who aped old editions by producing type facsimiles of more or less conviction. The difference lies perhaps in the somewhat depressing fact that modern readers are apparently either reluctant or unable to read black-letter or old-style typefaces. It all has to be visually translated so as to be 'readable', though it might be questioned how far the 'aesthetic impact' has in fact survived, to offer any kind of historical sense to the classroom.

If it is true today that we cannot be sure what exactly we are reading on screen, the same was often no less true in the past, with hard copy. Moreover, readers from the fifteenth century onwards faced books that were not necessarily what they seemed. They faced forgeries, fakes and facsimiles, often of very high quality. They faced copies made up from several different ones, even as can happen today with digitised books and microfilms, and they were told nothing of it. Indeed, such creations were to be encouraged for exactly the same reasons as today: that they made imperfect copies perfect. Just as today there is a gulf between the carefully crafted and expensive facsimile and the mass-production methods of the many large digital scanning programmes, so in the past there was very frequently a desire to save public or private money. Results could be indifferent, as they can be today.

From private interest to public access

Aside from the bibliographical matters in which this book is couched, there are two major themes that accompany every chapter, sometimes unspoken and often explicit. First, we shall be concerned with the transition from private to public responsibility in decisions concerning the preservation and presentation of what has been inherited from the past. This phenomenon, familiar in the history of museum studies and partly expressed in the well-known transition from private *Wunderkammer* to public museum,[32] has its parallels in the world of books. In the seventeenth century there were no national libraries. Those who saw the need for them looked to the Bibliothèque Royale in Paris, as the nearest to such an institution.[33] It was privately owned, and accessible to those who could claim some scholarly interest. In England, the Bodleian Library was the nearest equivalent.[34] The lack of a national library was a matter for lament among some scholars.[35] In practice, both in France and in England – as elsewhere in Europe – most responsibility for preserving the written and printed inheritance was a private matter, undertaken by individuals with their own money and according to their own tastes. The situation did not change with the British Museum Act in 1753, which was designed to bring into national ownership several private collections – a very different concept from accepting public responsibility for actively building on them with a disciplined and publicly funded programme for further accessions from the past. In Germany, the new library founded at Göttingen in 1734 developed under its directors Johann Matthias Gesner (d. 1763) and Christian Gottlob Heyne into a major research collection; but it could not claim to be a national library.[36] In Britain, as in most of the rest of Europe, national public responsibility had to wait until the nineteenth century, and the flow of ideas following the institutionalisation of knowledge in the aftermath of the French revolution, the campaigns for centralisation under Napoleon, and the unprecedented release of millions of books into the European antiquarian and second-hand markets as a consequence of the dispersals of ecclesiastical and secular libraries.

The idea of what was meant by the public itself changed. It was defined and limited differently almost generation by generation. It was certainly not the population at large, where literacy rates varied in town and country and among different social classes. It was not even the educated public, in the sense of those who had received education into their teens or at university. Many (or, more precisely, most) such people had neither access to nor interest in antiquarian books. For seventeenth-century collectors, access to their books depended on social networks, not on any kind of wider claim. This remained true in later centuries. A private sense of trust and responsibility for artefacts from the past did not imply a duty to make them generally available. But as private collections were dispersed, regrouped and then dispersed again in a process that by the mid-nineteenth century was seeing a systematic removal of private property into public collections, as the British Museum and other major libraries either bought or were given or bequeathed books, so the sense of the public and of public responsibility metamorphosed.

Yet, throughout the nineteenth century, it was still far from clear what these terms might mean. We shall see later some of the tensions experienced in the major London museums as those responsible for their development disagreed fundamentally about how far a much larger part of the general population should be allowed access.

If some of the noisiest discussions about free access to museums and galleries were to be heard in the capital cities, there was a no less committed web of discussions taking place in the provinces. The provincial museums established in Britain and France in the nineteenth century were part of this wider debate, to be seen not only – in Britain – in the pursuits of mechanics' institutes with their joint aims of education and entertainment, but also in the growing numbers of cheap, secular publishers who supplied light reading and useful knowledge alike. It was seen, eventually, in the movement for free public libraries leading to the Act of 1850, and in the Education Act of 1870, both with subsequent legislation. If we seek to understand how attitudes to old books changed, then we must look beyond the obvious boundaries of bibliographical or antiquarian scholarship, and consider also a mixture of political, educational, publishing, consumer and cost opportunities reflected in, and enabled by, legislative and commercial guidance. As a partial answer, this holds true today.

Boundaries and perspectives

Beyond this lie questions of interpretation that bear repetition. How can people be brought to understand what is old? How can people understand relative differences in age? The computer screen makes no distinction, and requires visual knowledge that is beyond the capacity of most people. In the nineteenth century the best route seemed to be via museums and exhibitions – of classical sculpture, of old master paintings, of the works of early printers, of manuscripts. Old and new achievements and inventions were frequently exhibited side by side. For printing, the last and greatest occasion in this nineteenth-century tradition linking past and present, and epitomised in the writings of Charles Knight (1791–1873), was the exhibition 'Printing and the mind of man', held at Earl's Court and the British Museum in 1963 and setting old and modern equipment alongside printed books, newspapers and pamphlets from over five centuries.[37] That exhibition was half a century ago. Underlying all this, in the past just as today, is a sense of change. The pace of that change was assuredly slower in the past, but it is readily detectable: in the search for terminology in describing books; in the ways that booksellers presented their goods differently over the years and in different markets to putative customers; in changing price structures; in the changing reasons for valuing one kind of book over another; in changing priorities concerning what was thought worthy of preservation for the future. The present book is mostly about the past, and about how we have come to understand old books. It carries questions that are no less concerned with what we are – and are not – passing on to future generations.

Limits of this book

Four limits need to be delineated. First, this book is mostly about the history of the study and evaluation of printed books, not about manuscripts. Compared with the literature on manuscripts (modest as it is), that for printed books scarcely exists. A proper account of the evaluation of manuscripts is urgently needed, for although there has been much scattered work since the appearance of A. N. L. Munby's pioneering *Connoisseurs and medieval miniatures, 1750–1850* in 1972, this was concerned only with illuminated medieval manuscripts; there is still nothing for the subject as a whole, and he was also most concerned with the subject in Britain. On the one hand, a further study would include systematic investigations of such phenomena as the nineteenth-century revival of creating medieval illumination.[38] On the other, it would deal with the development of palaeographical knowledge, with attitudes to post-medieval manuscripts, and with forgeries. Nonetheless, manuscripts make occasional appearances, for many of the issues concerning them apply also to printed books. Ever since Mabillon in the late seventeenth century, their serious study has been advanced by their reproduction, copies that are accurate enough to sustain comparison with scripts or decoration. Their exhibition has also often depended on copying, either photographically or by hand, or more recently by digital scans. The manuscript *Très riches heures* at Chantilly is rarely shown to the general public; facsimiles are displayed instead. The same is true of the most celebrated drawings by Dürer in the Albertina, in Vienna. Surrogates can never wholly replace originals, but they have their various functions.

Second, while this is about attitudes to old books, it cannot be about attitudes to all kinds of old books equally. That would be impractical, or would at least require a very different approach. The gulf between a copy of the Gutenberg Bible and an old book on a market stall is immense, in financial, bibliographical, social and educational terms. Their circumstances bear no relation to each other. The following pages are not about what may be called the ordinary second-hand trade, but about attitudes to books that, for the most part, already possess some status. There exist comparatively few studies of the trade in old rather than new books.[39] Perhaps understandably, the various national histories of the book – on France, Britain, etc. – have concentrated on new productions, and not linked these to the contemporaneous much greater numbers of old books in circulation at any time. Old books have, moreover, a peculiar status. Despite the fact that some are saved and some are discarded when worn out, they are not like most old household effects, to be replaced generation by generation.[40] The frequency with which they do not figure in more than general terms in post-mortem inventories of the sixteenth and seventeenth centuries has tended to lump them with the bric-a-brac of history; yet their physical and textual complexities endow them with evidential value far beyond ordinary hardware. It would be fruitful to study trends in what is disregarded or discarded: only occasional remarks are made here, where we are concerned mostly with what has survived, and been noticed.

Third, rather than bring the present study down to the second decade of the twenty-first century, and so risk doubling its length, I have chosen to end in the last decade or so of the nineteenth. By then, many of the principles were in place that were to remain familiar pillars of the antiquarian trade, of library collecting, of personal collecting and of bibliographical scholarship until the development of powerful and cheap computing tools in the late twentieth century. Even the collaborative structures that were so vital a part of the presentation and management of older printed books were by the 1890s in existence in an embryonic form.

Fourth, the principal focus of this book is on Britain and her nearest continental neighbours, France and the Low Countries. Ever since the fifteenth century, when John Russell bought printed books in Bruges in 1466, and Caxton worked in the southern Low Countries, and then in 1487–8 commissioned service books from the Parisian printer Guillaume Maynal, cross-Channel and cross-North Sea links in printed books have been instrumental in the book trade, in reading and in taste.[41] Links were strengthened by political, religious or economic exile – of (to recall only some of the most obvious) English royalists in the Low Countries and France in the mid-seventeenth century, French Huguenot families in England at the end of the century, or French refugees after 1789 and again in the mid-nineteenth century.

For a person in Britain buying or reading anything beyond the most ordinary book, it was impossible to be unaware of imports, whether of new or old publications. Thanks partly to the costs of paper, seventeenth-century books could be printed more cheaply overseas, and especially in the Dutch Republic. Moreover, until the lapsing of the last of the Licensing Acts in 1695, and the subsequent national expansion of the printing trade, there was simply not enough capacity among printers to provide for the country's increasing needs. With respect to old publications, Britain's longstanding dependence on overseas printers and publishers became even more pronounced as demand grew for books from the past. Books both new and old (not necessarily very old) were as important as furnishings to many more people than those who accounted themselves collectors or scholars in a more organised sense.

For about half the period between the accession of William and Mary in 1688–9, and the accession of George III in 1760, Britain was at war. Wartime conditions disrupted trade in different ways during the war of the League of Augsburg (1689–97), the War of the Spanish Succession (1701–13), the wars of Jenkins's Ear and of the Austrian Succession (1739–48) and the Seven Years' War (1756–63); but they could often be countered. During the War of the Spanish Succession, for example, French books were imported through the Low Countries, and exports were traded to France by the same route. The revocation of the Edict of Nantes in 1685, and the subsequent dispersal of French Huguenot bookselling families especially to the Low Countries and to Britain, created a network able to exploit and build international trade.[42] Migrants from both northern and southern Germany settled in London sometimes for economic reasons and sometimes also to escape persecution.[43] With close trade and family connections, booksellers and auctioneers in countries separated by war contrived to co-operate. Both in printing new books and in selling older books, the trade became increasingly centred on Amsterdam and The Hague, London and Paris. They did not have a monopoly. Copenhagen, Hamburg and Frankfurt all played major parts; and as increasing numbers of northern Europeans made their way to Italy in search of the classical and renaissance past and more modern musical, literary and artistic taste, so further links in the book trade were established and strengthened.[44]

Booksellers in England imported old books, often entire libraries, from at least the early seventeenth century onwards, on such a scale by the early nineteenth century that many thoughtful Frenchmen realised that their patrimony was being removed on a disastrous scale. The history of French institutional and private book collecting in the nineteenth century is partly of attempts to recover it. As communication became ever easier and cheaper, English and French collectors and booksellers mingled increasingly. French and British tastes in collecting remained noticeable as much for their contrasts as for international competitive spirit, but friendships were important. The Société des Bibliophiles François, founded in 1820, included English members from its early days. When in 1853 Richard Monckton-Milnes and a small group of like-minded enthusiasts founded the Philobiblon Society, members included the Duc d'Aumale (exiled in Twickenham) and the Anglophone Belgian ambassador Jean Sylvain van de Weyer. By the nineteenth century, the antiquarian trade had become international not just on a scale far larger than previously. The existence of well-financed, knowledgeable and cosmopolitan booksellers in most major European cities, corresponding and collaborating with each other, gave a new character again to the trade.[45] Family connections often strengthened their position, as they had in the sixteenth century. Aided by ever more extensive and faster postal systems, their catalogues circulated internationally month by month. In the 1850s the Parisian bookseller Anatole Claudin issued a monthly bulletin, a mixture of bibliographical gossip and lists of books for sale, and it had a wide circulation in England. He reported English auctions and thought it worth printing for his readers a translation of Samuel Johnson's celebrated letter of 1768 addressed to the Librarian of George III on how the royal library might be developed by what would now be called a buying trip to the continent.[46] Meanwhile, by the early 1820s firms such as Bossange & Masson in Great Marlborough Street, and Dulau and Treuttel & Würtz, both in Soho Square, provided England with easy access to French books old and new. In the mid-century, Baillière and Barthès & Lowell provided similar resources. Anglo-French rivalry was demonstrated season after season in the auction rooms of Paris and

London, as dealers crossed the Channel to secure prize lots. In 1878, for example, the fine private collection of the bookseller J. T. Payne (former partner in Payne & Foss) was sold at London in April, much of it to France. In June, Quaritch, Ellis and others from England were in Paris, buying at the Firmin-Didot sale. It was a pattern repeated with variations, as booksellers from Berlin, Amsterdam, The Hague and elsewhere also shared a network where sale-room alliances could be as important as sale-room rivalry.

It is the persistence of personal and geographical links such as these that contribute to the perspectives in the following pages on questions respecting the presentation and understanding of old books that have become universal. More generally still, we face not a series of mutually exclusive alternatives, paper versus screen. Rather, we face questions of how these complement each other not just in their meanings and in their content, but also in the ways that, increasingly, we understand one only by reference to the other. How has this situation come about?

2 | Restoration and invention

One of the greatest difficulties confronting anyone who reads old books lies in being certain that what is being read is what it seems. It is none the less a difficulty for being often unrecognised. How far is the information provided on the title-page and in the colophon reliable, or accurate? Was the text printed when it is alleged? Was it printed at the same time as the rest of the volume? Has the volume been restored, or even assembled from several disparate places? Is the volume entirely composed of the same sheets that its first readers saw? These are all questions of evidence, an essential part of confidence in reading quite apart from historical probity. And yet for most people they are among the least understood questions of all. To answer them often requires considerable experience and knowledge, but even these cannot always provide conclusive answers. When books are in turn scanned, turned into computer files and then read on screen, it can be all but impossible to tell what exactly confronts a reader. The evidence is distorted. It is simply impractical to see and judge the often complicated nature of the printed or manuscript marks on the page, and it is completely impossible to see how leaves might have been replaced, and the structure of the book – with its contents – thereby altered. For these reasons, in this and some of the later chapters in this book, we shall be much concerned with alterations and repairs, imitations and facsimiles, as well as, to some extent, with forgeries.

In the last chapter, we explored some of the expectations people may, or may not, have concerning the appearance of early printed books. What is required or expected of old books? While there are dozens of possible answers to such a generally phrased question, depending on circumstance as well as both people and books, it is possible to identify some preoccupations that have directly affected the books that we have inherited. In this chapter, we shall be looking at two topics in particular: cleanliness and completeness. Both have repercussions in later chapters, but it is convenient to gather some of the principal strands together here. In doing so, it is important to bear in mind that the craftsmen and others who attended to the repair or improvement of books were drawing on generations of experience, and that while some of them preferred to keep their skills to themselves (and thus enhance their reputations and their incomes), many more were ready to share them; some wrote manuals on the subject.[1] New processes and methods were discovered, but not everyone was equally able to apply them. The binding trades have always represented a range of skills, from masters of their craft to others who were little more than botchers, and the results are to be seen today in millions of surviving volumes.

As elsewhere in this study, it is useful to look also beyond the ordinary boundaries of books and the book trade.[2] Art historians and bibliographers have engaged all too seldom in conversations on a subject having directly relevant mutual interests, but the values, preoccupations and practices in the treatment of other kinds of artefacts reveal much common ground. In particular, the fortunes of paintings and sculpture at the hands of restorers and owners suggest parallels that enable a better understanding of why particular courses of treatment of books were followed. All three media were valued for their age and for their creators. All three deteriorated with age. All three required compromises with contemporary values in the way that they were to be preserved and presented. Visual qualities were important to all three. Finally, the history of their collecting embraces a common world of connoisseurship.

Cleaning and alteration

In 1879, the London printer William Blades contributed to a trade periodical, *The Printer's Register*, a series of articles on 'The enemies of books'. The series was assembled into a book in 1880, and further editions appeared in 1880, 1881, 1888, 1896 and 1902. It was translated into French in 1883. Apart from obvious enemies such as fire and water, insects and dirt, he adduced modern problems such as town gas. Children were added as a further threat in one of the later editions. Neglect was regarded as an enemy, but the beneficial effects of benign neglect did not figure. Among the enemies were bookbinders and collectors.

The temptation to have old books rebound was always a strong one, and was born of necessity. All but a handful of the hundreds of incunabula collected by Lord Spencer in the early nineteenth century, and now at Manchester, were rebound by the fashionable workshops and craftsmen of the day – Kalthoeber, Baumgarten, Walther and others. Many of them had their pages washed, in more or less successful attempts to remove all traces of early use. Old books were forced to look like new ones, or at least as if they had come fresh from the press. Most of their individual histories were destroyed in the process.[3] It is only comparatively recently that bindings other than the oldest have been appreciated for the information they can preserve concerning the insides that they protect, and Blades himself recounted the story of the modern owner of some books printed by Caxton who had them rebound – thereby considerably reducing their cash value as well as their bibliographical value.

Blades did not mention readers or others who scribbled on books or who caused books to be inappropriately or inexpertly decorated. But he was cautious about cleaning. By the 1870s the antiquarian book trade, and dozens of libraries, were homes to books that had been cleaned with more or less vigour and knowledge. There were published collections of recipes for cleaning or bleaching paper, for use by amateurs and professionals alike. For many people, it was assumed that books should be cleaned: white paper was preferable to greyish-brown. While some ownership marks were of value, these were in practice restricted to the names of comparatively few, notably members of royal families and celebrated collectors or other figures of the past. Names, coats of arms and other marks on title-pages or elsewhere in books, not obviously recognised and celebrated, tended to be regarded as blemishes, to be removed.

The proprieties of cleaning, restoration and conservation have rarely been agreed. But it is possible to trace some of the course of changing historical appreciation and sensitivities in surviving books and in the papers of a few bookbinders. In 1664 Samuel Pepys went to his binder to arrange for the repair of his copy of the 1602 edition of Chaucer: 'to the binders and directed the doing of my Chaucer, though they were not full neat enough for me, but pretty well it is – and thence to the clasp-makers to have it clasped and bossed'. Such furniture on a binding, frequently used on Bibles in the early seventeenth century, was distinctly unusual for a secular book by the 1660s. Pepys was clearly aiming at an antiquarian style, but it was far from authentic.[4] For his parchment copy of Lydgate's *Hystorye of Troye* (1513) he retained the early sixteenth-century blind-stamped binding, and added a modern decorated spine.[5] It was a rare early survival in his library.

Few large libraries have enjoyed the kind of benign neglect visible until the 1970s in the books belonging to White Kennett (1660–1728), who bequeathed much of his library to Peterborough Cathedral.[6] As a result of this neglect, in a library that was only lightly used between the mid-eighteenth century and the late twentieth, the books still offer a representative sampling of what such volumes looked like in an ordinary library in the seventeenth century – some in simple wrappers fashioned out of cut-up medieval manuscripts, some in rough parchment wrappers, some in cheap calf bindings. There was nothing here of the money spent by men in the late seventeenth century such as Pepys, John Evelyn or, in France at the beginning of the century, de Thou, on their books.[7] For them, books were not only to be read. They were also to be displayed, and for this the appearance of the spines and covers on the shelves was as important as the content of the volumes. In the eighteenth century this became assumed as a part of collecting, whether in the expensive bindings sought out by the Harleys or in tidiness sought for the shelves in lesser private libraries in town and country.[8] In Dublin, the physician Edward Worth paid almost as much attention to the bindings for his books as he did in their selection. The lavish Turkey leather coverings on his early books are testimonies both to his pride in possessing early editions from respected printers, and to his wish that his library should have a distinguished appearance. It was a far cry from the plain coverings on most of the books in Archbishop Marsh's library, kept in another part of the city as a public collection and assembled by a man of no less erudition but one less concerned with outward appearance.[9]

In the eighteenth century, the activities of the bookbinder Roger Payne (1739–97) have become celebrated partly because of the high quality of his work and also because of the unusually detailed, often idiosyncratic, bills that he was liable to present to his customers. When, for example, he was faced with a rather poor copy of Euripides printed at Cambridge in 1694, he detailed not only the forwarding and finishing, but also his treatment of the leaves:

Some Sheets was of a very bad Colour & had gott the dry rott these are all put to rights & refreshed NB not any Aqua Fortis has been used in the washing Some leaves had been broken by the printing Types these took also a good deal of time to mend them very neat and some Wrinckles which took a great deal of time one Leaf for instance page 47 took a full days Work the Weak Leaves was also very neatly sised, strong and Clean.[10]

On the invoice for dealing with a copy of Petrarch, he reported

To Washing their was a great deal of Writing Ink and the bad stains, it required several washings to make the paper of the Book quite safe, for, tho the Book with one or two washings would look as well as at present, it will not stand the test of Time without repeated washings. Carefully and quite Honestly done	9.0
To Sise-ing very carefully and Strong	7.6
To Sise the Book	1.6[11]

Payne's work was valued, but he was not the only binder who also offered specialist skills. In his own workshop he relied for paper repairs on his assistants, Mr and Mrs Weir. Others were elsewhere in London. Richard Dymott, for example, 'Bookbinder to his Royal Highness the Duke of Gloucester', in Vere Street, advertised that he would take out 'Stains or Interlineations from old scarce Books'.[12]

The skills needed in cleaning paper in books were not dissimilar from those needed in cleaning prints. Stains were to be removed, dirt washed away, and if necessary old inscriptions removed. The needs of the print connoisseur and the bibliophile coincided in this, and bookbinders advertised their ability to cope with both.

In 1751 the French engraver Robert Hecquet published at Paris a *Catalogue des estampes gravées d'après Rubens*. At the end he added a brief 'sécret pour blanchir les estampes'. He was concerned to show how connoisseurs could recover the 'premier éclat' of prints. His method depended on exposing prints to steam and to sunshine (the work was best done in high summer), in a process designed to eliminate or reduce spots and oil stains.[13] Hecquet was one of several who proffered such recipes to a world increasingly occupied with print-collecting; as the context of his remarks made plain, the problems of dirty or imperfect prints could apply even to quite recent ones. The point about 'premier éclat' was a revealing one. It assumed that such a condition was recoverable, and that it was desirable. It sought to set aside the intervening years. Similar standards had been the target of restorers of other works of art for generations, the aim being to recover what first saw the world. If the aim was understandable, it was frequently a vain one. Physical changes in materials, whether paint, pigment, ink or paper, prevented such recovery.

Meanwhile a succession of chemists and bookbinders strove to discover a safe and reliable way of cleaning paper and leather, seeking to accommodate the wishes of connoisseurs who prized volumes that bore little or no signs of use. As had been known for generations, oil and grease could be tackled with a thin solution of potassium. Pigments and writing ink were more difficult. The possibilities were transformed with the discovery of chlorine in the early 1770s by a Swedish chemist named Carl Scheele. At first, chlorine was known as dephlogisticated muriatic acid air, muriatic acid being the term then used for hydrochloric acid. It was not to be recognised as an element until Sir Humphry Davy did so in 1810, but its properties were quickly exploited for their manufacturing applications. In the 1780s the French chemist Claude Louis Berthollet used it as a bleach in his tapestry factory. Then, at the end of the decade, Jean-Antoine Chaptal (1756–1832), professor of chemistry at the University of Montpellier, pointed out its applications for cleaning old prints and books in a paper to the Académie Royale des Sciences, published in the first number of a new journal, *Annales de Chimie*. By immersing sheets of paper,

non-seulement les livres sont rétablis, mais le papier en reçoit un degré de blancheur qu'il n'a jamais eu.[14]

Through a surgeon named Robert Kerr, Chaptal's work was published in Dublin (at the behest of the Trustees of the Linen and Hemp Manufacture) and Edinburgh; the impetus came from the cloth trade, not from the book trade. His translation of a work by Berthollet on bleaching was published first in 1790, and included a translation of the summary of Chaptal's ideas.[15]

Having bound the book, and separated its leaves, he provides a wooden frame, upon which they are laid, having thin slips of wood interposed between every two leaves; and these are fastened together by means of small wooden wedges, which are driven in between the slips and leaves. The whole being properly disposed, is immersed in the oxygenated liquor, and kept there for two or three hours, according to circumstances. After this, the frame and its contents are taken out of the oxygenated liquor, and plunged into cold water. By this process the books are not only restored to their original appearance, but the paper acquires a degree of whiteness which it never possessed before, even when new. The liquor has, besides, the valuable property of obliterating any blots, or other marks of common ink, which frequently injure the value of books or prints. It has not, however, power to cleanse any stains of oil or grease; but then, we have long known that these may be removed by means of a weak solution of caustic fixed alkali.[16]

Chaptal was given a further airing in his four-volume *Chimie appliquée aux arts*, published in Paris in 1807, as the new techniques moved out of the specialist literature and into more general manuals. In England, the new edition in 1803 of a popular compilation originally by John Imison included a brief summary, and – in an entirely different part of the work – noted that grease spots could be removed from books by the application of turpentine, and that leaves could be restored to their former whiteness with the help of 'rectified spirit of wine'.[17]

After having gently warmed the paper that is stained with grease, wax, oil, or any other fat body, take out as much as possible of it by means of blotting paper; then dip a small brush in the essential oil of turpentine, heated almost to ebullition (for when cold it acts only very weakly), and draw it gently over both sides of the paper, which must be carefully kept warm. This operation must be repeated as many times as the quantity of fat imbibed by the paper, or the thickness of the paper, may render necessary. When the greasy substance is entirely removed, recourse may be had to the following method to restore the paper to its former whiteness, which is not completely restored by the first process. Dip another brush in highly rectified spirit of wine, and draw it in like manner over the place which was stained, and particularly round the edges, to remove the border that would still present a stain. By employing these means with proper caution, the spot will totally disappear, the paper will resume its original whiteness, and if the process has been employed on a part written on with common ink, or printed with printers' ink, it will experience no alteration.

In 1819 the articles in Abraham Rees's *Cyclopaedia* on bleaching and on 'Books, whitening of' dealt with Chaptal's invention, noting that engravings could also be cleaned by this method, while Deschamps of Lyon suggested warm turpentine to remove spots of grease. The articles drew partly on the *Bibliothèque économique*. Thus bookbinders and book restorers, in France and England alike, were increasingly well armed in meeting wishes for books in supposedly pristine condition.

The fact that it was possible to clean books led to widespread demand; and with that there also seemed to come an increased public urgency. In 1802 Gabriel Peignot included in his *Dictionnaire raisonné de bibliologie* a section on 'Bibliuguiancie', which he summarised as a 'nouveau terme imaginé par les citoyens Vialard et Heudier, pour signifier l'art, inventie par eux, de restaurer les livres précieux qui ont été endommagés'.[18] It further marked a new emphasis in the treatment of old books. The process could involve an alarming sequence in which volumes could be cleaned, oil stains removed, wormholes repaired, paper restored to its original strength or even made stronger. Vialard and Heudier had been invited to pursue their calling in the national libraries of the Département de la Seine, an appointment that clearly signalled interest from central government. According to their remedy, the cinders of vine stems were to be mixed in river water and boiled for several hours, then left to sit for seven or eight days for the mixture to settle. This could then be applied to paper to wash away everything except the printing ink itself: it was unsuitable for cleaning books that had been decorated in colours or in ordinary ink. For books, once the covers had been removed the entire text block could be suspended in the mixture which was then boiled for a quarter of an hour. After this, the text block was pressed to expel the water, before being re-immersed in the boiling mixture, pressed again and then immersed in clean boiling river water. The paper was finally resized by suspending it in a solution of alum. But the structure of any book that included glue would also have been damaged in the prolonged boiling. Almost the only advantage to the process was that it did not require books to be completely taken down, and then resewn afterwards.

Cleaning by these more vigorous methods was not universally admired. In 1819 Antoine-August Renouard, the most learned of his generation of Parisian booksellers and author of an already authoritative bibliography of books printed by the Aldine dynasty in Venice, wrote of 'la désagréable équivoque résultant de l'usage assez moderne, et souvent nuisible, de laver et nettoyer les vieux livres'.[19] For him, the word *lavé*, much used in the trade, carried all kinds of unwelcome connotations, and he tried to avoid it – at least during this part of his life. In truth, there was a world of difference between older methods and the over-enthusiastic application of modern chemicals. Most of the book trade, and most collectors, preferred clean books to soiled ones, and it was not necessary to damage a book irrevocably. But, as Pie Namur, University Librarian of Leuven, pointed out (needlessly, since he had just given a graphic summary of some of the more extreme methods), 'en général il faut de la prudence et de la patience dans ce genre de travail'.[20] By the time that Sébastien Lenormand issued his *Nouveau manuel complet du relieur* in 1840, as part of the popular series of *Manuels-Roret*, the bookbinder was expected to have an arsenal of cleaning skills at his command. Referring now to several other authorities as well, Lenormand divided his discussion between paper that was to be whitened and paper that was stained with grease or other matter. In describing techniques in considerable detail, Lenormand emphasised the need not just for chemical knowledge, but also for practised skill: 'il faut un peu d'adresse et une certaine habitude, pour réussir complètement et avec facilité'.[21] Namur as a librarian and Lenormand as a binder were making a similar point.

What of the books themselves? If some of these methods seemed brutal, and endangering for original materials, the following years saw ever-growing inventiveness. Book cleaning became an occupation for amateurs as well as for professional bookbinders: there was little suggestion of the modern distinctions between conservators and binders.[22] Lenormand pointed out the advantage of some of Imison's methods, which did not require a volume to be taken apart. For most cleaning, books had to be dismembered, thereby disturbing and usually destroying the former binding. It is further striking that among the many recipes for cleaning paper how little account was sometimes taken of the materials and processes of paper-making. Paper could indeed be washed, but if it was washed in acid, and then not properly rinsed, it was left brittle. If it was washed in ordinary water, and not further treated, it was left soft and pulpy, having lost the size that had been added in the manufacture to give it a hard surface. Thousands of amateur or unskilled efforts have left fifteenth-century books with margins displaying extensive brown stains, and with portions of old handwriting still partially visible. It was difficult to strike a balance between very bad work and overkill. Moreover, it was not enough to remove stains, ink marks and unwanted decorations. Unless the paper was properly resized after cleaning it was left in a worse physical state than before, even if it appeared – for the moment – to be restored to some kind of earlier condition.

It is perhaps not irrelevant that the most dramatic advances in the chemistry of cleaning were made at the same time that increasing attention was being paid to the manufacture of new paper: several patents related to the bleaching of paper during manufacture. The development of wove paper by Baskerville and James Whatman in England in the 1750s and by Johannot and others in France in the 1780s was accompanied and followed by various experiments to produce smoother paper, both for printing and after printing.[23] High-quality writing paper was as much in demand in its own sphere as was good printing paper. Further public interest was generated by the search for new materials with which to manufacture paper, in the face of a growing shortage of rag, the ordinary raw material. Straw, nettles, jute, thistles and bark were only some of the most celebrated of fibrous plants that were the subjects of experiments to make paper from alternative and cheap sources.[24] More usefully as it proved, with the discovery of a means to bleach second-hand paper, the trade in waste took on a new meaning.

The trade in waste paper was always a lively one. It was advertised in newspapers – by the ream or in much larger amounts.[25] When a quantity of unbound popular books was stolen from the London bookseller James Lackington in 1790, he advertised for its return, pausing also to warn that it might have ended as wrapping for cheese.[26] Bookbinders were heavy users of waste, and printed waste was also sometimes damasked, obscured by marbling, so that it could be employed as cheap decorative covering for books.[27] There was a duty on imported waste, so as to protect the domestic trade; but as shortages became apparent in the early years of the Napoleonic wars, there were calls for its repeal. The matter was brought before the House of Commons in June 1800.[28] That summer, a company was established in London to produce pulp from used paper, even that which had been written on or printed. This had been done for some time abroad, by a process adopted by Madame Masson. One news report remarked that this would be 'the grand defence of posterity against superfluous and tedious books',[29] but there was a more fundamental purpose as the country faced shortages:

Whereas the scarcity of Rags has greatly increased the Price of every kind of Paper, which has occasioned a Company to establish a manufactory, by His Majesty's Letters Patent, for extracting printing and Writing Ink out of printed and written Paper, and converting the same into perfect white Paper, fit for Printing, Writing, and other Purposes, which is the first Establishment of that nature.

They flatter themselves, that such a useful Undertaking, so beneficial to the Country, and which, of course, will reduce the Price of Paper, will meet with the approbation and support of the Nobility, Gentry, and Public at large. It is requested they will save all Waste Paper, for which they will be paid the full value.

Public Offices, Gentlemen of the Law, Merchants and others, who have always quantities of Waste Paper and old Books unsold, and which are often burnt, not wishing to have them exposed to the Public, find now an opportunity to convert them into Money, being certain that they will be torn to pieces, and re-manufactured.

If every Family would save their Letters and old Writing-paper, which are generally burnt, and not regarded as of any consequence, it would annually produce such a quantity, that very few rags would require to be imported, and thereby save considerable Sums of Money which now go to Foreign Countries.

Stationers, if they consider this Establishment in its true light, will be guided by self-interest to support it with their Waste Paper, at a just price, because the Exportation Trade must be lost to this Country if the high price of Paper continues.

Printers have already experienced, that many Presses have stopped working, on account of the high Price and Want of Paper, which, most certainly, has operated on the commerce of Booksellers and the business of Bookbinders; it is therefore hoped that the Trade in general will prefer selling their Waste Paper to this Manufactory, many of them having, with patriotism, rendered their assistance to this Concern.[30]

There were many similar notices in the newspapers at this time. In all these ways – debates over import duties, the search for new materials, the invention of ways to recycle old matter, the development of wove paper with a smoother surface and the invention of hot-pressed paper with a glossy finish – paper was a topic of public importance. A material that was on the one hand so much assumed in its everyday familiarity was on the other hand one that commanded attention. The price of new paper climbed steeply between the 1790s and 1810.[31] In all this, the development of a method of restoring whiteness to old paper, and removing marks that had hitherto resisted attack, was yet another further technical advance, where science offered benefits. The fundamental difference was that this time it was for the restoration of old books, not for the manufacture of new ones.

Washing and cleaning were only two of the dangers faced by old books. The temptation for binders to reduce volumes to objects that would look well on the shelves, regardless of their content, was an ever-present threat.

Copies were cut down, their margins thereby reduced or even eliminated. While a few binders took care to turn in any leaves that bore text or annotation which would thereby disappear, many ignored the question and cut away these as well. Though there were some writers who were ready to criticise provincial binders especially, whether in England or in France, in fact the dangers were as great in the large cities. Meanwhile, old bindings continued to be discarded as they had been for centuries. Whether internally or externally, old books could be made new. On the one hand, their restoration could be presented as the recovery of original, or at any rate early, appearance – a state clearly admired by Hecquet in speaking of 'premier éclat' and by Chaptal. On the other, old books could be given a modern guise, dressed to a status that accorded with their seniority in age.

Mixing, matching and completing

More positively, missing parts could be restored, though there do not seem to have been many books like the copy of *The tragedie of Claudius Tiberius Nero* (1607), described rather whimsically in the twentieth century as having 'the blank leaves A1 and N4 ... supplied in facsimile'.[32] It was no new thing to insert leaves in manuscript where printed leaves were missing: this had been the practice even for new books ever since the early days of printing.[33] But books losing their leaves later on had also to be adjusted, such as a copy of a book printed in Venice in 1549. This later lost its title-leaf, and an ingenious owner or binder subsequently replaced it with a colophon leaf, adding the title and other details in manuscript – and incidentally also changing the date of the book in the process (Fig. 2.1).[34] Other repairs or improvements might be less extensive. Namur explained that wormholes could be filled, and where they coincided with a printed area the judicious use of a piece of type could restore the text.[35] In Paris in the eighteenth century, Jacques le Clabart advertised his skills as 'écrivain pour les Généalogies, & pour l'entretien des vieux livres'.[36] His note explained that he 'imite l'impression en toutes sortes de Caracteres tant pour les Manuscrits gothiques ou imprimés'. 'Il racommode les Livres défectueux, copie les Vignettes', and further makes good what is lost or damaged.[37] Le Clabart (or Léclabart or l'Esclabart) was by no means the only person to provide such skills. In 1847 a library offered at auction in Paris included a copy of Politian (Florence, 1489) 'parfaitement lavé par M. Abry et retouché, en quelques points, avec le plus grand succès par M.Vigna'. In

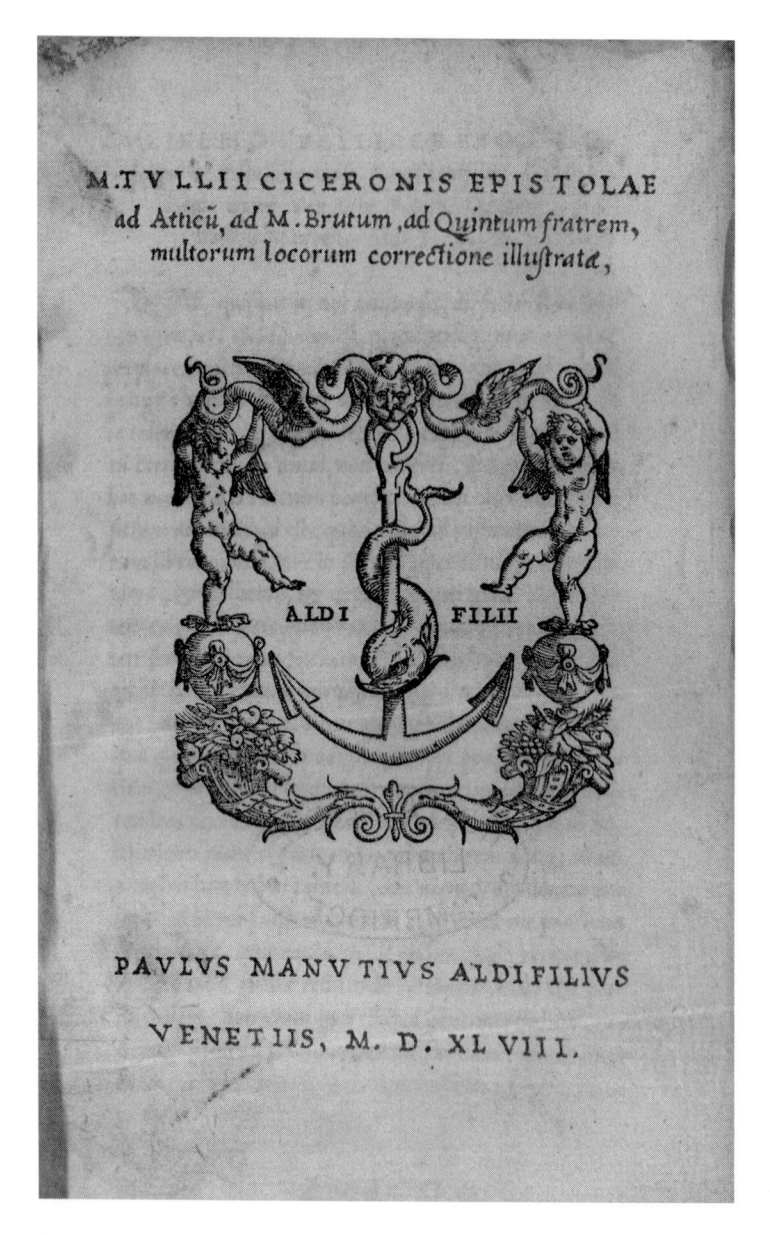

Figure 2.1 Cicero, *Epistolae ad Atticum*, etc. (Venetiis: Paulus Manutius, '1548'). In fact this is a copy of the 1549 edition. The title-page has been faked, using a colophon leaf (with the Aldine anchor) and with the title and imprint written in by hand. Trinity College, Cambridge M.12.178.

the same sale there was also a copy of *Orlando furioso* (1524), with four leaves 'admirablement faites à la plume par M.Gobert, d'après le fac-simile que le marquis Trivulzio a eu la bonté d'envoyer au possesseur de ce livre' (Fig. 2.2).[38]

It was not a skill restricted to the French. Nor was the pen the only means for making good missing parts of books. In 1817, John Whittaker was described by the arbiter of bibliophile taste Thomas Frognall Dibdin as 'a modest, unassuming, indefatigable, and singularly-successful artist'. His reclusive nature could not obscure the considerable value of his skills. 'Give him your imperfect Caxton, and, within a few days thereof, you shall receive it so perfected, that the deficiencies cannot be discovered.' Dibdin went on to describe the method used for these 'reparations':

He has caused to be engraved, or cut, at a great expense, four founts of Caxton's letter. These are cut in the manner of binder's tools for lettering, and each letter is separately charged with ink, and separately impressed upon the paper. Some of Caxton's types are so riotous and unruly, that Mr. Whittaker found it impossible to carry on his design without having at least twenty of each such irregular letter engraved. The process of executing the text, with such tools, shall be related in Mr. Whittaker's own words: 'A tracing being taken with the greatest precision from the original leaf, on white tracing paper, it is then laid on the leaf (first prepared to match the book it is intended for) with a piece of blacked paper between the two. Then, by a point passing round the sides of each letter, a true impression is given from the black paper, upon the leaf beneath. The types are next stamped on singly, being charged with old printing ink, prepared in colour exactly to match each distinct book. The type being then set on the marks made by tracing, in all the rude manner, and at the same unequal distances, observable in the original, they will bear the strictest scrutiny and comparison with their prototype: it being impossible to make a fac-simile of Caxton's printing in any other way – as his letters are generally set up irregularly, and at unequal distances, leaning various ways, and altogether so rude and barbarous, that no printer of our time could set up a page, or even a line, to correspond with the original by any other means...

Mr. Whittaker also informs me that he has 'types engraved to correspond with those of WYNKYN DE WORDE' and others of various description, by which he is enabled to complete ANY book, printed before the sixteenth century, so exactly, that the most able judge of old printing cannot discover the restoration from the original.

Dibdin went on to draw attention to the copy of the 1457 Psalter in the Royal Library, with one of the leaves copied in this way from the Spencer copy, and the vellum copy of the 42-line Bible then in the stock of the bookseller George Nicol, having two leaves in facsimile.[39] We shall return to the topic of making good in Chapter 5.

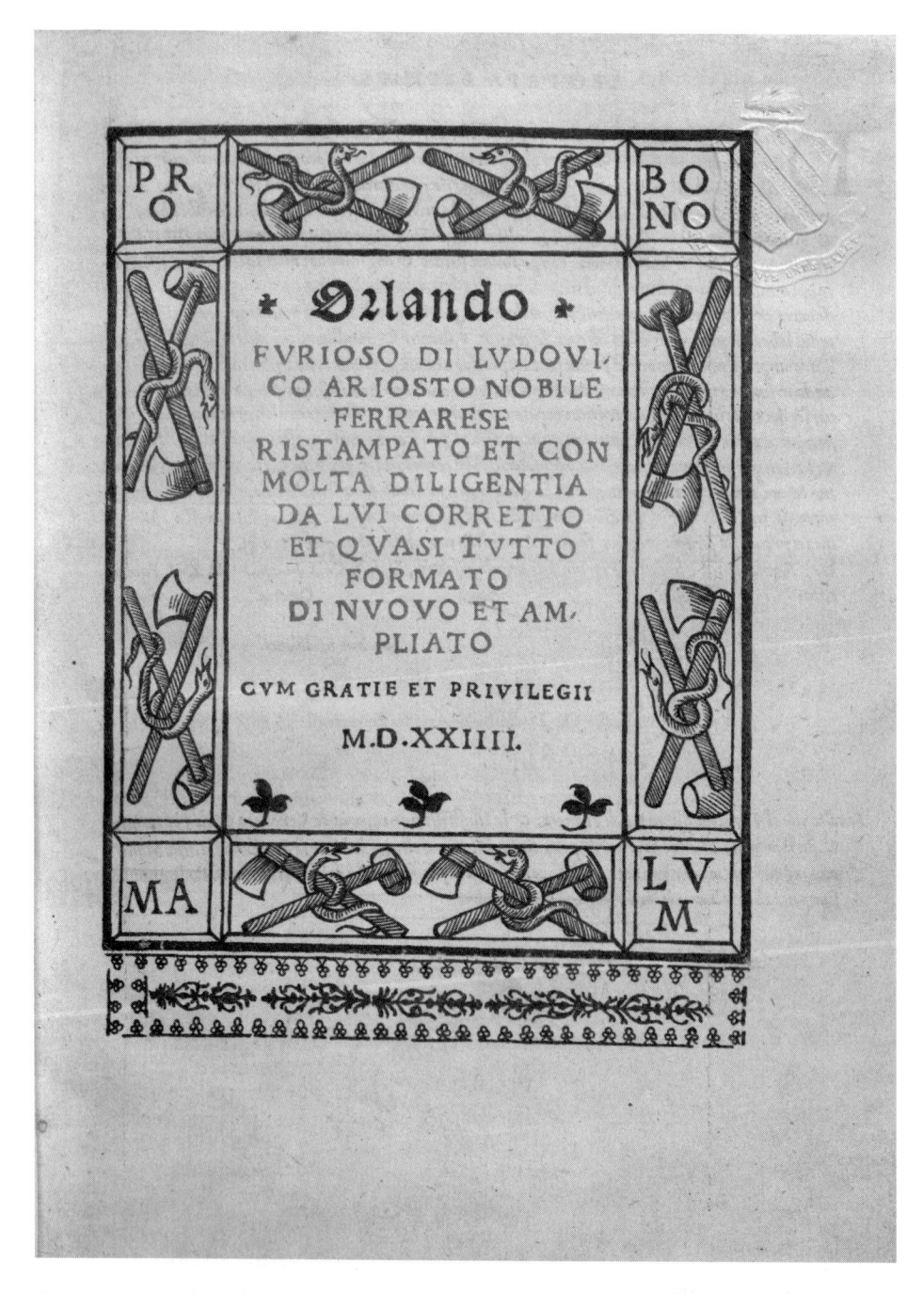

Figure 2.2 Lodovico Ariosto, *Orlando furioso* (Venetia: Nicolo Zopino and Vincentio Copagno, 1524). The title-page is in pen facsimile. Trinity College, Cambridge Grylls 11.325.

To read an incomplete book is to risk missing some crucial part of its content. Collectors, scholars and ordinary readers alike all require that by preference the book in hand should be entire, at least insofar as its text is concerned. Or that it should appear to be entire; there is plenty of room here for fraud as well as willing self-deception. For printed books, the idea of completeness is inextricably linked with ideas of consistency between copies of an edition.[40] That is the way that completeness is defined.

On the other hand, while completeness is self-evidently absolute in its meaning, in practice it can vary substantially both in the hands of publishers and of readers. So, many other readers, more carefree if not more careless, may be less concerned with the presence or absence of paratextual matter such as contents lists, indexes, prefaces, odd illustrations or even title-pages, let alone dedication leaves or advertisements for other books. For most purposes, for example, there is no need to be aware that the student crib edition of Juvenal's *Satires* published by the Cambridge bookseller John Nicholson in 1777 contains on the verso of its half-title a priced list of books offered by Nicholson for the same student market. Nonetheless, the presence of such a list is a reminder of the context in which this book was conceived, edited, manufactured and sold. It helps our reading, and no doubt it helped sales in the 1770s. Booksellers and printers have used spare pages or inserted extra leaves to include advertising for their further publications ever since the late sixteenth century.[41] In the nineteenth century, revenue for advertisement sheets became an essential contribution towards publication costs, whether on the covers of cheap yellow-backs or bound up with the separate monthly parts of novels by Dickens and others. For periodicals as well, they became necessary sources of revenue. While books and periodical articles alike are not dependent on the reader's also absorbing accompanying advertising, it is impossible to understand the circumstances of publication without taking it into account as part of the contemporary reading environment. That it is only a part is underlined by the equally obvious fact that most editions of most books do not contain advertising. There is, in practice, no absolute.

Nevertheless, it is reasonable to contemplate what is meant by completeness, if the term is taken as applicable to whatever form is published originally. With the widespread publication of scanned copies during the last few years, the question – of material importance for anyone wishing to understand a printed book or a periodical – has proved to be of minor interest, or no interest at all, to most uncomprehending major suppliers.

Some of the same questions concerning completeness in the past apply to works of art, save in one important respect. Whereas printed books are produced in quantity, and therefore on most occasions it can be assumed that, if not in the present then at least at some point in the past, there were many identical copies, for paintings, drawings, manuscripts and frequently for sculpture there can be no such expectation. Each is unique. This contrast – between the multiple but nonetheless shared identities of the printed book and the individuality of works of art – has meant that study of the two broad groups, the one manufactured and the other created individually, has not always been alert to their similarities. In the history of books more specifically, the triumph of print was founded on the fact that many copies of the same text could be produced and circulated at the same time. The earliest observers of printed books noted this feature in particular, and marvelled at it. It was both printing's main asset, and its most obvious threat. Authors and readers were encouraged to believe this; and they did so readily. The fact that in practice there were frequently – perhaps even usually – many minor variations in typesetting between different copies of the same book was of secondary importance. The myth of the uniformity of print was a powerful one.[42]

It was difficult to police. Since printed books were uniform, those that were imperfect in some way had to be made good. New books that were imperfect could be exchanged with the bookseller for a complete copy. That was not possible for old or rare books. 'In the purchase of old books,' wrote Samuel Johnson in 1768, 'let me recommend to you to examine with great caution whether they are perfect. In the first editions the loss of a leaf is not easily observed. You remember how near we both were to purchasing a mutilated Missal at a high price.'[43] Moreover, to make good a mass-manufactured article such as a printed book was not the same as repairing a damaged painting or piece of sculpture. For printed books, one method was to replace a missing page with an approximate type facsimile. Leaves might be missing for many reasons, but two broad categories define themselves: books that had been censored or withdrawn for other reasons, and books that had become worn and damaged through use.

We may take two celebrated examples of the former first. A few months after the initial volume of Richard Hakluyt's enlarged *Principal navigations*, containing an account of the Earl of Essex's Cadiz expedition, was published in the winter of 1598–9, Essex returned from Ireland in disgrace. The title-page and the pages describing the Cadiz expedition were removed from many copies. Subsequently, in order to make up complete copies, various repairs were made, with reset title-pages and with the missing pages reset in a near-matching type, these replacement campaigns dating from about 1720, or perhaps a little later, and about 1795. Further replacement leaves were made in about 1850 under the auspices of the bookseller Henry Stevens, so that he could meet American demand for this work. As a result, copies survive in several mixtures, with or without various revised title-pages, and with or without various replacements for the Cadiz pages.[44]

The enlarged edition of Holinshed's *Chronicles*, published in three volumes in 1587, was a much more complicated affair. Again, it involved recent history. Following intervention on the orders of the Privy Council, large numbers of leaves were cancelled in the first and second volumes, and further leaves were cancelled after November 1590. The effect is a work of unusual bibliographical complexity. As with the Hakluyt, the result was that there were in circulation many imperfect copies. Again, the early eighteenth century brought attempts to make them good, with facsimile inserts. In 1723–8 no fewer than three rival series were printed. The first was printed almost entirely by William Bowyer, and published by a consortium of booksellers composed of William Mears (a bookseller with a particular interest in publishing historical works), Fletcher Gyles and James Woodman, priced expensively at 5 guineas for the 44 replacement sheets. They considered that there was market enough to absorb 250 copies (including 50 on fine paper), 'printed with the old Types and Ligatures, And Compared Literatim by the Original', in the words of an advertisement on the back of one of Fletcher Gyles's catalogues. A rival set was quickly published by Christopher Bateman (the leading antiquarian bookseller of the day) and Benjamin Cowse: this was priced at just £2.10s. Then yet another appeared in 1728. All three were printed in black letter, to match the original, and the first at least was provided with a magnificent title-page (a rare phenomenon for such enterprises) announcing that the new pages had been printed 'with the Old Types and Ligatures, And Compared Literatim by the Original' (Fig. 2.3).[45]

Books with damaged or missing leaves are vastly more common. In Cambridge, both the University Library and the St Catharine's College copies of Thomas Cooper's Latin *Thesaurus* (1584) are imperfect, and were made good with different type-facsimile title-pages in the late seventeenth and early eighteenth centuries. Unlike a painting, there were other examples to which any need for repairs could be directly referred. Thus, the concept of perfection, or completeness, involved a directly comparative exercise. Moreover, and often crucially, the existence of other imperfect copies from which leaves could be taken meant that the process of making-good was actually one that could be readily justified by reference to the processes and ordering of printing and binding.

THE
CASTRATIONS
OF THE
LAST EDITION
OF
HOLINSHED's Chronicle,
Both in the
SCOTCH and ENGLISH PARTS,
Containing Forty Four Sheets;
PRINTED
With the Old TYPES and LIGATURES,
And Compared LITERATIM by the Original.

LONDON,
Printed for WILLIAM MEARS without Temple-Bar, FLETCHER GYLES over against Grays-Inn in Holbourn, and JAMES WOODMAN in Bow-Street Covent-Garden.
M.DCC.XXIII.

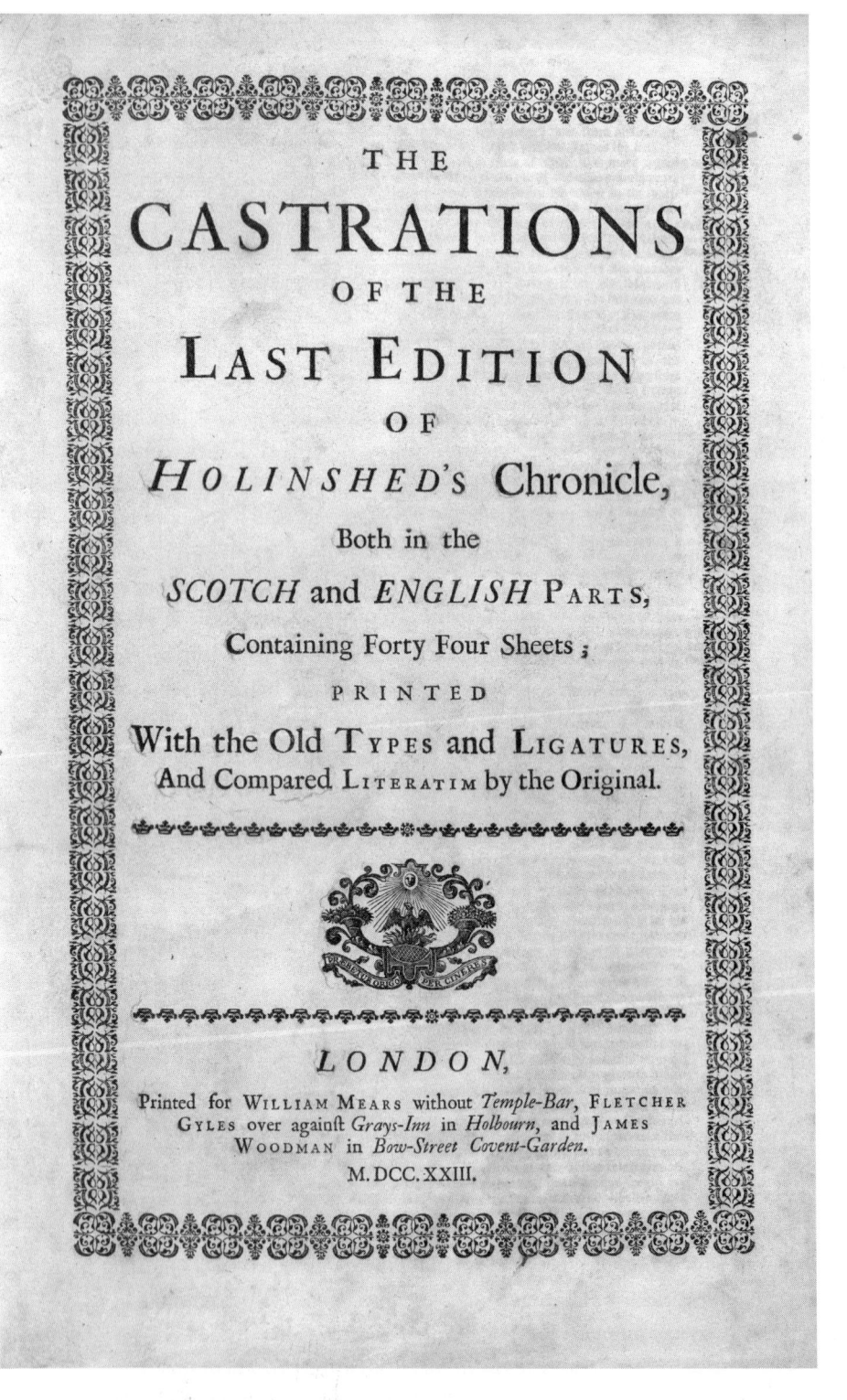

Figure 2.3 *The castrations of the last edition of Holinshed's Chronicle, both in the Scotch and English parts... Printed with the old types and ligatures, and compared literatim by the original* (London: Printed for William Mears, Fletcher Gyles and James Woodman, 1723). Trinity College, Cambridge X.4.8.

While booksellers and most collectors preferred to deal in books that were perfect (or had been made perfect), there were always some people for whom the printed book was a quarry, to be rearranged and cut up so as to provide more conveniently for private interests.[46] In the sixteenth century, Archbishop Matthew Parker rearranged several of his manuscripts and printed books in this way, so as to collocate texts that related to each other in his scholarly and historical work.[47] Printed books lent themselves readily to anthologising, where passages were cut out and mounted in albums. The so-called Little Gidding concordances are among the best-known examples of how the Bible was cut up for reading – in this case the synoptic Gospels.[48] These were not albums in the sense that developed in the early nineteenth century, where assortments of texts and pictures were intended either as mementoes or merely as entertainment for Sundays or wet days. Both of these tactics for reading and study were generally private affairs, but the re-ordering of the Bible or the assembling of chronologies involved a much better defined approach to the possibilities of printed books. Books could be made perfect in different ways, whether by restoration or by reorganisation, and of these the second was either a matter of individual taste or (as in the case of Little Gidding) of communal preference.

To make an imperfect book good for the purposes of sale or bibliophile satisfaction involved sophistication of a different kind. At its best, it was a question of matching, so that the separate parts of the new artefact would be indistinguishably joined. In 1789, the abbé Jean-Joseph Rive commented on the duplicates that had been assembled in the library of the Duc de la Vallière for the purpose of completing imperfect copies.[49] Major booksellers, even until after the Second World War, kept large stores of such books, so-called hospital copies that could be cannibalised in order to make up perfect examples.[50] It is a practice that has fallen out of general favour only very recently, though it is still to be found in some parts of the trade. The heyday of making up copies was in the nineteenth century, but it was practised long before then. By 1911, A. W. Pollard, the most respected bibliographer of his generation in Britain, felt able to say that 'Few collectors even now are educated enough to prefer copies in the condition in which the ravages of time have left them to those which have been "completed" by dealers; hence many old books have been "made up" with leaves from other copies, or not infrequently from other editions.'[51] The practice of inserting leaves from other editions was made all the easier when successive editions had been reset page for page. It was not always the earlier editions that were made up by quarrying later ones – the most obviously desirable procedure.

In a copy of the 1545 edition of the *Hypnerotomachia Poliphili*, for example, leaves were taken from apparently two copies of the first – and usually much more highly prized – edition of 1499 and inserted to make good the later edition.[52] Ignorance and deliberate deception could wreak havoc for anyone seeking to recover bibliographical evidence of early texts or early printing practices. We shall never know how many books were made up by this method, but hundreds of examples have left trails of evidence. There was no disgrace in making up copies. Quite the contrary, to improve a copy was better than leaving it imperfect. In 1868, for example, the London bookseller Bernard Quaritch – already a leader in the trade – had an imperfect copy of the 1488 Homer ('extremely rare') on his hands, and he advertised for a remedy:

Any gentleman possessing an imperfect copy will please to communicate with Mr. Q., as they might make up a perfect copy between them. My copy wants Vol. I. prel. leaves A-E, margins of 1, 3 and 4 cut, sheet M, N; leaf O1; Q1 soiled; V1 soiled: & 2: Vol.II. AA1 damaged: PP3 and 8.[53]

In the same catalogue he advertised a seriously imperfect copy of the First Folio, useful possibly either as a specimen 'or for supplying leaves wanting in other copies'. Amongst his desiderata in the same catalogue he sought to make good Foxe's *Actes and monuments* (1563) with:

1. The small woodcut at p.25, complete. I have half of it (the right hand portion). 2. A good title page. [I have a title of the second and third edition, possessing the same woodcut borders] . . . the cut on folio 25 (not the one of the Pope putting his foot on the Emperor's head).[54]

It was in this spirit that in the late nineteenth century Lea Wilson and Francis Fry assembled their remarkable collections of English Bibles, Fry in particular making up as many copies as he could either to trade or to keep for himself. Bibliographically, the consequences were disastrous, most obviously but by no means exclusively when he tackled the two 1611 folio editions of the King James, or Authorised, Version. For the second edition, the type had been reset page for page, so that shortfalls of any one sheet could be easily made up from another setting; this was a common practice in Bible printing. Failing to realise that there were not, as he called them, two issues, but in fact two quite separate editions, Fry mingled sheets without concern for the editions. The matter was further complicated by the fact that some 1611 sheets had been used for the edition of 1613.[55] Fry's own bibliographical descriptions were further adulterated by his mistaken choice of a copy dated 1611 against which to compare all others.

Made-up copies of all kinds of books, which exist in their thousands, can be very difficult to detect. It was only some time after the late Lord Rothschild bought from an American bookseller in 1937 a copy of the first edition of Fielding's *Tom Jones* that the leaves inserted from another edition were spotted by a bibliographical friend.[56] On many other occasions the composite nature of a volume is all too visible. Sometimes the inserted leaves are of a different size compared with the rest of the volume. Sometimes, as in the case of the Crevenna copy of the first edition of Petrarch (1470), formerly in the possession of Consul Smith, the difference was such that Crevenna had to have the inserted leaves inlaid. In book after book, leaves might be cut down, or remargined so as to line up with the fore-edges of the rest of the volume into which they were inserted. Bibles lacking a general title-page (a not infrequent occurrence) could be made good by moving the New Testament title-page to the front of the volume, inserting the necessary changes in the wording by means of carefully executed facsimile lettering on paper then let into the leaf. Always, the aim was to create a copy uniform in its presentation, which would appear to be complete, at least to a casual glance. Nonetheless, in early books differences in rubrication or other manuscript marks can provide clues as to what once happened. The Pierpont Morgan copy of the *Recueil des histoires de Troyes* (c. 1476), for example, lacks thirty-four leaves, two of them blank. It was formerly in the Roxburghe collection when several leaves were removed to perfect a copy in the King's library.[57] The fortunes of a broken-up copy of the Delft Old Testament (1477) can be followed through its early annotations: the core of it is in Ghent University Library, but it was used as a quarry in the nineteenth century, the evidence for the dismantling pointing to the Belgian collector of incunabula Senator Frans Vergauwen.[58] Two leaves once in the Cambridge University Library copy of Caxton's *History of Jason* now in a copy held by the British Library were probably transferred in the eighteenth century; the evidence for the transfer rests not on any document but on the patterns of rubrication.[59] More recently, and in a well-documented case, in 1960 Cambridge University Library disposed of one of its two copies of Caxton's *Recuyell of the historyes of Troy*, after leaves from the less complete copy had been abstracted and added to make up the better one that was then retained by the Library (Fig. 2.4).[60] The present study is concerned with the treatment of volumes often several generations following their original publication – in these last cases hundreds of years. But books are just as liable to adjustment and alteration as soon as they reach their first readers, as volumes are assembled from different quarters for convenience's sake, or because of acquisition opportunities, or because of

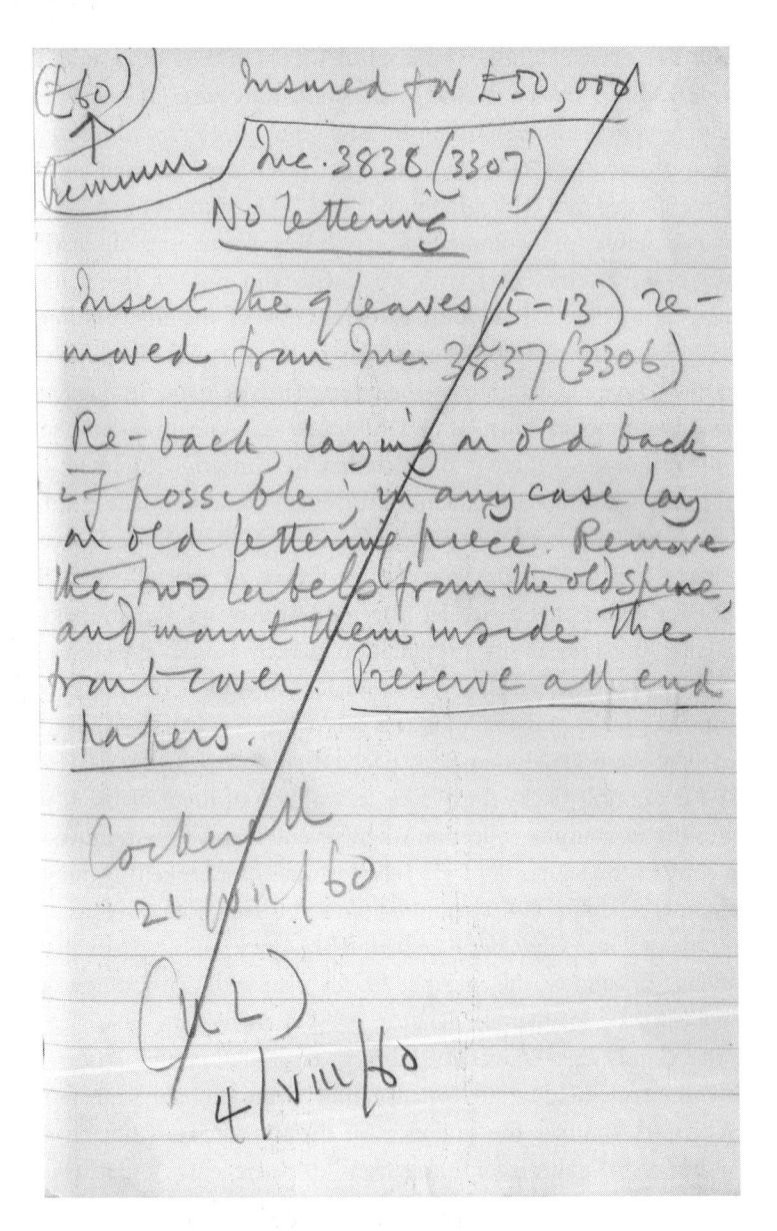

Figure 2.4 Instructions by a member of staff of Cambridge University Library for the removal of leaves from one of the Library's copies of Caxton's *Recuyell of the historyes of Troye*, and their insertion in the other. The work was executed by S. M. Cockerell in July 1960. A note at the head of the page records the insurance valuation. Private collection.

simple misuse. Major changes can take place within a very short time-frame, and although this study is focussed on the period since the late seventeenth century, plenty of earlier books had by then long since been altered.[61]

Just as in sculpture, painting and furniture restoration, the matching and assembling of one part of a printed book to another was a highly skilled operation. It involved resourcefulness and abilities drawn from binding, paper repair and printing. Again, it is worth looking over the shoulders of those working in related fields. Dealers in old prints were familiar with such tricks as the staining of paper with tobacco juice, to make it look older, or with the insertion of missing pieces of pictures so carefully that only the most careful inspection would detect a repair.[62] These were skills equally applicable to printed books. For bindings, one method was to remove a covering from one book and re-use it on another. If done well, this process of *remboîtage* could be very difficult to detect.[63] It assumed a hierarchy of values in bindings, a recognition that some were of more interest than others, either because of their decoration, their marks of distinguished ownership or because of their age. The last – age – was also the last to be much valued. The re-use of bindings – or rather, parts of bindings, since it is impossible to transfer every part – dates from centuries before the invention of printing. Its practice for purposes of deception seems more recent, though it is still often difficult to judge whether economy, or the desire to preserve something for aesthetic or sentimental reasons, determines the transfer of a covering from one volume to another. Certainly the intent has frequently been to deceive, often for financial gain.[64] One celebrated instance, not recognised for some years, concerned a copy of the Shakespeare first folio, acquired by the London bookseller and binder James Toovey. In about 1887 he replaced the then existing binding with one bearing the Sidney arms, taken probably from a volume given by Philip Sidney, Earl of Leicester, and subsequently discarded by the Bodleian Library. The Sidney connection made the copy much more attractive, and it was sold to John Pierpont Morgan with many other books from Toovey's library in 1899, when it was valued at the high price of £1,000. It was misreported in Sidney Lee's census of surviving copies in 1902, and then quickly corrected.[65] The process of *remboîtage* was described quite late, in a short book by Alfred Bonnardot, *De la réparation des vieilles relieurs*, published in 1858. Bonnardot's larger work, *Essai sur l'art de restaurer les estampes et les livres*, was first published in a small edition in 1846 and quickly went out of print. An enlarged second edition appeared in 1858. Most of this useful and widely read work was concerned with the cleaning and repair of prints. A German translation appeared in 1859 and the book was studied in London as well.[66] The briefer work on *réparation* was written partly in response to a reviewer of his earlier book on prints.

Again, analogies are helpful. Copies, fakes and facsimiles were endemic in the world of connoisseurship, whether paintings, coins, prints, sculptures, ceramics, manuscripts – or printed books.[67] Many of the same collectors who came to possess books that had been restored, or even composites assembled from several different sources, were the same who took an interest in antique sculpture, old master paintings or other antiquities.[68] Few pieces of classical sculpture were complete when recovered from the ground, and the inclination to restore them to what was envisaged as their original shape or beauty became a powerful one. Collections of antique sculpture formed in late fifteenth- and early sixteenth-century Rome reveal few examples of restoration at that time.[69] Taste, and the skills accompanying it, changed rapidly during the next few generations with invention and imagination. Workshops in seventeenth- and eighteenth-century Rome were able to create illusions of completeness. There were hundreds of sculptures where missing limbs were supplied, or heads were attached to unrelated other fragments, or else set on new shoulders, in order to make them more acceptable to collectors – and more exhibitable in museums or in private houses.[70] These restorations were not necessarily the work of second-rate artists, and they sometimes involved not so much restoration as alteration and even, on occasion, imaginative recomposition from several sources. Cosimo I de'Medici commanded Benvenuto Cellini to restore a statue and to add an eagle, in order that it could be called Ganymede.[71] In Rome, Bernini added to the Ares Ludovisi (1633), and Algardi to the statue of Hercules and the Hydra.[72] In France, many of the pieces in Mazarin's collection were restored in Rome by Matteo Buonarelli and Baldassare Mari so as to appear more complete, and they remain today in the Louvre, as much monuments to seventeenth-century taste and ingenuity as to those of ancient Rome.[73] The exiled Queen Christina of Sweden exerted considerable energy in surrounding herself with classical pieces, arranging for them to be restored as necessary. In the Vatican, the pieces of Laocoön were reassembled, invented and reinterpreted several times over between the sixteenth and twentieth centuries, as artists and critics sought what they believed to be the best composition.[74] When the Warwick vase was discovered, it was what has since been called 'a porridge of fragments'. After reassembly under the guidance of Piranesi, it was brought to England by Sir William Hamilton in 1774 and was much copied.[75] In Rome, Bartolomeo Cavaceppi (c. 1716–99), friend of Winckelmann, provided restorations, copies and fakes from his large studio to collectors both in Rome and from overseas; Carlo Albacini restored and sometimes adapted sculptures for Charles Towneley's collection; and Joseph Nollekens learned some of his skills in Cavaceppi's workshop. Canova was trained in the same way, though he later spoke out against the restoration of the Parthenon marbles, and was hostile to copying.[76] When Nollekens's workshop was sold in 1832, it included various adaptations of antique sculpture, 'by Mr Nollekens in lieu of the antique'.[77] Restoration, even to the extent of providing new and more saleable identities, was a part of the relationship between archaeologists, middlemen and collectors.[78]

In the nineteenth century, the recovery from Melos in 1820 of the Vénus de Milo presented a problem to which people with several different skills returned. It was originally made in two pieces, divided across the hips. The missing arms invited debate. But at some point early in the statue's history four pieces had broken off near the hips, and these were recovered to be brought back to Paris. At the Louvre, they could not all be set back exactly in place, and so the restorers there resorted to chisels and wedges before reattaching them with plaster, so as to achieve a compromise that both removed stone from the statue and then set it up at the wrong angle.[79] The demand for antique sculpture fuelled the business of restoration, additions and recreation. For those who wished to sell or to possess a statue of a well-known figure from the past, pieces could be altered to suit. Lysimachus, a bodyguard of Alexander the Great, was changed into Achilles.[80] In order to meet sensitivities, the statue of a hermaphrodite belonging to Henry Blundell was dismembered in the early nineteenth century and changed into a less challenging sleeping Venus.[81] Ancient work could be adapted to still more modern needs: in 1809 Vivant Denon, in his capacity as Director of the Musée Napoléon, ordered that an ancient torso should be converted into a statue of Napoleon.[82] For works at more mundane levels, noses and chins were restored, head-dresses re-cut, and it frequently happened that a part of one statue was attached to another. The recent discovery that the large sculpture of Hadrian in the British Museum, gathered from fragments found at Cyrene, north Africa, in 1861, consisted of a body from one statue attached to a head having no previous relationship to it, was a reminder of what is frequently all too readily visible in the crude agglomerations constituting pieces in museums and private collections alike.[83]

The trade in antiquities was organised by those who excavated (legally or illegally), the agents who paid them, the dealers who traded in them, the restorers who met the expectations, hopes and requirements of those prepared to pay, and, at the end of this sequence, the collectors who bought them. Amidst all this there was ample room for disagreement at every stage.

While it was widely assumed in the seventeenth and eighteenth centuries that imperfect pieces would be restored or perhaps adapted in some way, by the early nineteenth century there were voices raised who were less willing to countenance what had become accepted practice. The example of Edward Daniel Clarke, widely talented, a bold traveller, Professor of Chemistry at Cambridge as well as University Librarian and a copious author, has been quoted in connection with the top of a colossal statue of what he named Ceres that he acquired during his sojourn in Greece in 1802. He was determined that it should not be 'degraded by spurious additions',[84] but his observations on contemporary practice are worth quoting more extensively, bearing always in mind that England and France were at war for most of this time. They point not only to national differences that were visible in other kinds of collecting as well, but also to distinctions between the wishes of collectors and the requirements of university learning. The distance that Clarke perceived between the two with respect to survivals from the classical world was – as we shall see – also to be seen in the world of books. This piece and his other sculpture had, he explained, been set up in the vestibule of the University Library:

It is believed, the Public will not dispute the good taste of the University, preferring a mutilated fragment of Grecian sculpture, to any modern reparation. Had Ceres gone to Paris, she would soon have issued from a French toilet, not only with a new face, but with her appropriate insignia, her car, dragons, and decorations, until scarce any of the original marble remained visible. Some of the Statues in the French Collection have not a cubic foot of antique marble in their composition. Even the famous Belvidere Apollo (a circumstance little known) was degraded by spurious additions, when placed in the Vatican.[85]

In painting, as in sculpture, the boundaries between restoration, conservation, renewal, repairs and alteration are not always clear. Subjects could be changed, sometimes quite drastically, and canvases could be cut to fit different spaces – as happened to Rembrandt's so-called 'Night watch', which was severely cut down probably in 1715 so as to be accommodated in the town hall in Amsterdam.[86] Paintings deteriorate naturally as well as because of accidents, and again there was a wide diversity of practice and skills. By the seventeenth century some craftsmen specialised in what may be broadly designated restoration.[87] Major artists including Sodoma in the early sixteenth century, Van Dyck in seventeenth-century London, Rubens in early seventeenth-century Spain, Guercino in seventeenth-century Bologna and Carlo Maratta in seventeenth-century Rome were all called on to restore work.[88] Sir Joshua Reynolds frequently remarked the botched efforts of cleaners and restorers, and was himself called on for help.[89] During the eighteenth century, restoration developed into a separately organised trade. In Venice, Pietro Edwards (1744–1821) was an unusually thoughtful restorer in a programme of work on both public and private collections temporarily halted with the French occupation in 1797. He had a large business in his studio at the church of San Giovanni e Paolo, and in 1798 there were about fifty works under his care.[90] In France, Robert Picault (1705–81) and the Godefroid family were among those employed on the royal collection.[91] After the Revolution, vandalism in Paris and in the rest of the country was countered by official awareness that many pictures were in urgent need of attention.[92] But, through most of western Europe, such was the demand for restoration, cleaning and adaptation that there were many more practitioners possessed of only modest skills, or even no skill at all.

Again, some of the most celebrated of alterations make the point: that interventions are an inescapable part of the history of connoisseurship and scholarship. If the drapery added to Michelangelo's Last Judgement for reasons of modesty offer one example, there were innumerable other early paintings that were victim to what has been called 'devotionally inspired overpainting',[93] to the sensitivities of the Counter-Reformation and to anxiety concerning overt sexual representation. The original overpainting on Bronzino's Allegory with Venus and Cupid in the National Gallery perhaps dated from when the painting was given to François I. It was removed only in 1958.[94]

A letter from the Grand Duke Cosimo of Tuscany to his restorer, written in 1698, has been quoted elsewhere, but it sums up many of the issues:

A painting has fallen into my hands which appears in good taste as far as the animals and the rest are concerned; it only seems lacking [in taste] in the figure, which I would like covered with a tasteful tint, but keeping the same attitude. The drapery, shirt and head-dress you may repaint to your taste; I should also like that the two heads of the cadavers to be covered, both the woman's and the man's, but I should like you to paint everything from nature, because it is this that I ask you, that will make a fine picture.[95]

Alterations to subject matter and to size were commonplace. But these and changes to composition were only one part of the myriad arguments surrounding conservation, including such matters as the extent to which repainting and overpainting were justified, the deterioration and darkening of varnishes, changes in binding materials, changes in the colour of pigments over time, and methods and materials of cleaning. Age brought browning, and a patina that was widely valued but on the other hand was imperfectly understood.[96] In England, Dryden wrote to Kneller of how time would 'Mellow your colours, and imbrown the tint'. Addison, in *The Spectator*, wrote of 'an old man' (Time) who by working imperceptibly yet incessantly 'wore off insensibly every little disagreeable Gloss that hung upon a figure. He also added such a beautiful Brown to the Shades, and Mellowness to the Colours, that he made every Picture appear more perfect than when it came fresh from the Master's pencil.'[97] Copal varnish, which dries hard and provides the old master effect so admired by Addison, was especially in vogue in some circles in the eighteenth century. But Hogarth, famously, defended modern painters and derided those who believed that time, or shades of brown, improved pictures. For him, the question was about modern values, not about former practices.[98] Nevertheless, in the nineteenth century visitors to the National Gallery admired the glowing effects of the 'gallery varnish' invented by the restorer William Seguier.

It was less clear how paintings were to be cleaned and restored to their earlier colours. The restorer's agents included sulphuric acid and warm beer, besides urine and lemon juice.[99] But opinions were always divided, and the many recipes and other advice, either published in books, offered in letters or recorded in private notebooks, some harmless, some destructive and some effective, reflect an activity that was widespread, necessary and often ill-founded.

Thanks to their materials and to the differing practices of those who had created them, paintings presented peculiarly complicated problems. Works on paper in some respects presented fewer challenges, even if they were not always straightforward. Many of the skills and techniques that were applied to books were equally relevant to works of art on paper, but two underlying issues need to be held in mind. First, much of the impetus for the cleaning of books emerged from the same ideas that encouraged the cleaning of works of art. Just as sculptures could be restored by additions, and the composition and colouring of paintings could be changed, so too with books. All these different artefacts could be subjected to cleaning processes that not merely sought to remove ordinary surface grime, but also to return the object to what was taken to be its pristine condition. On the other hand, paintings could be quite radically altered. So could books, set in new bindings, supplied with new pictures, their pages cleaned and even bleached, and provided with leaves from elsewhere to make up imperfections. Professionally, those who repaired pictures or restored statues had nothing in common with those who restored books. But frequently the issues were closely related. Moreover, the overlap in collecting these various media meant that many of the people who sought this kind of revision approached books, sculpture and painting alike: that they attended to a greater or lesser extent to historical criteria, and made decisions, with very similar expectations. The past could be saved and made accessible, but it was a past that was reinterpreted and often literally reshaped to meet modern needs or expectations of cultural or even national identity.[100]

Finally, a modern note. While informed taste in our own times tends to incline against intrusive restoration of missing parts, or over-restoration of paintings, and the term 'honest copy' is to be found in the book trade signifying a worn or imperfect copy that has not been restored, the issue resurfaces insistently. In 2010 it was reported that the Prime Minister of Italy, Silvio Berlusconi, had caused offence in Rome by arranging for missing parts of two antique statues of Venus and Mars in his official residence to be restored.[101] While this was an extreme instance of its kind, even less obvious conservation or restoration measures involve decisions that are not only potentially controversial but also destructive of some kind of history. It is not necessary to think very long about the moral judgements and causes involved in the book trade's choosing to describe some books as 'honest' copies to reach conclusions about such self-recognition. More generally, intrusions in any object, whether sculpture, paintings, old buildings, archaeological sites or old books, are inescapably interpretative. In practice, original condition is irrecoverable, and authenticity without further definition is a chimera.[102]

As we saw earlier in this chapter, Antonio Canova, widely admired and arguably the greatest sculptor of his generation, held views about restoration that changed during the course of his career. In 1818, his friend Antoine Quatremère de Quincy visited London, so as to see the marbles from the Parthenon. His reflections to Canova were applied to the contemporary debate concerning the restoration of antique sculpture. But they could be as well applied to the restoration of books, a discussion that had not yet happened:

I am convinced that the antique would never have had the effect that it has had on public taste over the last fifty years if all the monuments of sculpture had been left in the mutilated state in which artists often prefer to see them, the better to study their detail. When restoration does not damage the original workmanship, when it does not mislead, when it falsifies neither the subject nor the composition by mendacious addition, why should we refuse to allow works to be seen in their own ensemble? They often drew much of their value from that ensemble and cannot hope to please the eye unless the destructive accidents of time are repaired.[103]

This chapter has been mostly concerned with the treatment, alteration, restoration and copying of works of art. With these debates and practices in mind, formed and nurtured amongst connoisseurs who also frequently had to care for large libraries of early printed books, in the following chapters we turn more specifically to books.

3 | Conservation, counterfeiting and bookbinding

We have seen in the last two chapters how the appearance of books can be changed so as to meet the needs and expectations of different audiences; how the material composition of books can be altered; and how changes whether to paper, make-up or bindings can be employed for both honest and occasionally nefarious purposes. In other words, quite fundamental alterations in the ways that books are presented to the reading public, and in the ways that they are preserved for the future, are not unique to the digital environment. They have existed for hundreds of years.

From this, we can move on to other kinds of adaptation. Again, we are looking at a spectrum of difference, not a sharp edge. Digitisation involves editing, the choice of what to present and how to present it. It can involve editing in the sense of reassembly. It represents a form of facsimile-making: visual in that the images captured and edited for the screen are adaptations of what an original document looked like, both in its three-dimensional form and page by page, where the computer screen distorts shape and either suppresses or misrepresents colour. Such images may be of high resolution, and they may be of acceptable quality, but they are representations. Apart from such obvious visual issues are those respecting use: the ways in which images are accessed, and then summoned up as a series of screen shots, rather than turned over leaf by leaf, as in a codex.[1] The process of reading is different. Different demands are made on readers, as they adjust to the standards of what is before them. Further, to read an old book in a modern typeface is not the same as to read it in supposed facsimile; but to read it in some kind of facsimile involves compromises of different kinds again. Partly for this reason, it is pertinent to look at earlier forms and purposes of facsimile, the assumptions that they entailed and the range of their relationships to different degrees of verisimilitude.

The nineteenth-century attention to the past that characterised so much in literature, pictorial arts, politics and religion alike has long been remarked, and much studied. It was manifested in innumerable ways, including the formation of local archaeological and antiquarian societies, in the reinterpretation of elements of medieval buildings using modern materials and construction methods, in the taste for historical themes in novels, drama and poetry, and in the scholarly and liturgical interest by the later part of the century in some kinds of medieval music. Nostalgia played a large part, though disciplines from engineering to the study of the history of liturgy demanded rather more than this term alone suggests. The link between modern skills and antiquarian pursuits was rarely better illustrated than in the work of Robert Willis (1800–75), Jacksonian Professor of Natural and Experimental Philosophy at Cambridge and author of what became a standard work, *Principles of mechanism* (1841), who also wrote about the architectural history of the Middle Ages. A keen book collector, in his historical writing he joined an engineer's professional eye to detailed reading of medieval documents. Though he published much during his lifetime, his pioneering approach to architectural history was best shown in the three carefully documented volumes on the architectural history of Cambridge and of Eton, published posthumously in 1886 and completed by his nephew J. W. Clark.[2] Similar links between ancient and modern are to be seen in the work of William Blades (1824–90), a printer who wrote the standard study of Caxton, and Talbot Baines Reed (1852–93), a type-founder who wrote the still indispensable account of his predecessors in England. Charles Enschedé (1855–1919), of the old type-founding family, was to do the same for the Low Countries in 1908.[3]

In other words, and as in most periods, the pursuit and examination of antiquarian books or other matters was – and is – often informed by a context of apparently divergent activities and interests in the contemporary world. There thus lay behind the Caxton exhibition of 1877 much more than a taste for old books, or an appeal to England's printing history, or even to Caxton as a representative hero. We shall return in more detail to this exhibition in Chapter 8. In spring 1877, the year of the Caxton exhibition but a few weeks before it opened, William Morris founded the Society for the Protection of Ancient Buildings, 'to awaken a feeling that our ancient buildings are not mere ecclesiastical toys, but sacred monuments of the nation's growth and hope'.[4] The society's manifesto sought support from other media in appealing to a more conservative approach to old buildings:

Of all the restorations yet undertaken, the worst have meant the reckless stripping of a building of some of its most interesting material features: whilst the best have their exact analogy in the Restoration of an old picture, where the partly-perished work of the ancient craftsmaster has been made neat and smooth by the tricky hand of some unoriginal and thoughtless hack of today. If, for the rest, it be asked us to specify what kind or amount of art, style, or other interest in a building makes it worth protecting, we answer, anything which can be looked on as artistic, picturesque, historical, antique, or substantial: any work, in short, over which educated, artistic people would think it worth while to argue at all.[5]

This was no sudden conversion. Morris had been restive about the treatment of ancient buildings for some years. In 1874, A. J. Beresford-Hope had drawn attention to the extent of damage done to old churches, and to how little remained.[6] It was thus as a part of a rapidly developing public discussion that in 1877 Sir John Lubbock contributed to the newly founded magazine *The Nineteenth Century* an article entitled 'On the preservation of our ancient national monuments'. He opened by noting the remarks often made by English travellers abroad concerning the neglect, in Middle Eastern countries especially, of the remains of antiquity. In support of his observation, he further quoted William Stokes in his recent biography of Sir George Petrie: 'The number of ancient remains that even during the last century have been wantonly destroyed is so great that their enumeration would be tedious.'[7] Lubbock was one of several people thus concerned. The summer number of *Macmillan's Magazine* included an attack by the antiquary and journalist W. J. Loftie on the over-enthusiastic restoration of churches in England. His words were as applicable to architects and buildings as they were to bookbinders and books: 'It becomes then a question of how far an architect is justified in meddling with this delicate charm. Once destroyed, it cannot be replaced.' Not surprisingly, his article immediately provoked a defensive riposte from Sir George Gilbert Scott.[8]

The debates concerning ancient monuments[9] were relevant to the treatment of old books. In both cases, many of the arguments and practices were polarised, some arguing for intervention and wholesale restoration to the point of replacement, others for a more restrained approach that respected what had survived. The invasive and creative restorations of buildings by Viollet-le-Duc in France and of Scott in Britain had their parallels in the treatment of books, in the vigorous washing and cleaning of pages, the discarding of old bindings regardless of whether they could still be made to function, and the neglect of key aspects of the history of individual copies. More conservative approaches to book repair were paralleled by the caution expressed by John Ruskin in England and by Ludovic Vitet in France concerning intervention in buildings. Books and buildings alike were subject to long processes of neglect, and long processes of sometimes ignorant if well-meaning restoration, even to the extent of intrusive replacements.

Like good examples of early buildings, many books were also rare. The Caxton exhibition of 1877[10] drew attention to them in an environment independent of the great national museums and libraries of London, Oxford, Cambridge, Paris, Munich and elsewhere. But it did not have anything to say about preservation or repair, let alone conservation. Indeed, some of the most aggressive and destructive repairs to old books were made in the last two decades of the nineteenth century, most of them in order to meet the demands of collectors. While a few binders such as Francis Bedford (1799–1883) or Robert Rivière (1808–82) were careful about the materials they used, their work was expensive. In others' hands, often the materials used were shoddy or poorly manufactured, so much so that by 1905 the Royal Society of Arts and the Company of Leathersellers in the City of London took alarm at the quality of leathers used for bindings, and issued a report on the subject.[11] The materials and conditions even in the British Museum were demonstrably poor.[12] Conditions in which books were kept were impaired by expectations of warmer and drier environments in private houses. Coal fires and town gas, comforting to people, were enemies of books, and overheated institutional libraries added further to the damage. Improving standards of private comfort meant that books printed and bound in entirely different environments were placed under life-shortening stress.

The history of conservation treatment for bindings remains unwritten, but it involved a change of attitude that emerged most clearly in the late nineteenth century, and applied mostly to bindings in leather rather than those in cloth or paper. It coincided not only with concern for the quality of recent work and materials, but also with an interest in the study of books as individual copies. As always, opinion ranged from indifference to considered and knowledgeable care.

While hundreds of binders cut vigorously, glued liberally and used poor paper and leather, more in the interests of presentation than of any long-lasting repairs, by no means all books reached their hands. Quite simply, not all collectors wished or could afford to restore their books. Either out of choice or by circumstance, these other enthusiasts bought imperfect or battered and well-used copies, and left them as they were. Besides this, there was a growing respect for old bindings not just for the sake of the marks they bore of celebrated owners, or for the sake of their gilt decoration, but also because they were in themselves witnesses of past skills and tastes. The present book is not primarily concerned with the history of the study of bookbinding, which deserves much more attention, but it is to some extent inescapable.[13] The books bought by William Morris in the 1860s and 1870s offer their own comment on his views on other antiquities. During those years he assembled a small group of incunables, a slightly larger group of sixteenth-century books and a working collection of Icelandic books. At this stage (this was well before he took a serious interest in the design of typefaces), his interest in books illustrated with woodcuts was already apparent. He acquired a few very grand books, but as Paul Needham has pointed out, it would be excessive to call him a bibliophile.[14] Morris occasionally spent a lot on a book, such as £26 paid to the bookseller F. S. Ellis in the mid-1860s for a copy in a stained vellum binding of Boccaccio *De claris mulieribus* printed at Ulm in 1473, or the £30 spent on *Lancelot du Lac* (Paris, 1533). Generally the prices he paid were much lower, and this early library contained many imperfect books which he did not seek to have improved. In this respect, his approaches to old buildings and to old books had several features in common. In his letter of March 1877 to *The Athenaeum*, he wrote protesting 'against all "restoration" that means more than keeping out wind and weather'. There was an equivalent for books: bindings were necessary protections, but repairs and replacements to the pages were not prerequisites.

Morris's own views on bookbindings were eventually to be shaped by T. J. Cobden-Sanderson,[15] but they are most obvious in the presentation of the books printed at the Kelmscott Press. For these he chose the simplest of materials. His treatment of his own collection of early printed books and, increasingly, of medieval manuscripts reveals something of the principles which guided his tastes. Cobden-Sanderson was trained by a London binder, Roger de Coverly, a man described by Morris in 1882 as 'not a man of any taste... but is careful, & will do what you tell him'.[16] Though Morris gave some of his books to Cobden-Sanderson for binding, including his copy of the Dupré *Missale Parisiense* (1489), bound in half pigskin to Morris's design,[17] he used the firm of Leighton much more. From them he obtained simple bindings in limp vellum. His interests were firstly in woodcuts, in decoration and in type designs.[18] They were not in bindings. In 1880 he sold many of his books, and while the collection he subsequently assembled is in many respects consistent with the first, he was able to spend more money. The results were very similar in his lack of interest in having his books restored or improved with facsimiles to replace missing leaves, or new bindings to replace those that were old and worn.

Though photographs of bindings were used to illustrate some copies of the catalogue of books from the library of Guglielmo Libri in 1859,[19] booksellers' interest in old bindings was led by the Techeners and Antoine Bachelin-Deflorenne in Paris, and by Quaritch in London. Their publications introduced new reference works on which study could be based. In 1868, Bachelin-Deflorenne issued an auction catalogue of the library of the book agent Giovanni Gancia in two forms, with or without three-dozen-odd mounted photographs. But as a Quaritch catalogue of 1883 pointed out, with one possible exception there was still no good work on the subject. The exception was the recent work on French bindings by three members of the Marius

Michel family. Even this was written from the point of view of finishers: 'Their opinion is that nothing merits mention in connexion with the art of bookbinding beyond the process of decorating the sides and back of leather with ornaments in gold.'[20] This catalogue predated by six years the first catalogue to be issued by Quaritch devoted solely to bookbindings and other books from celebrated owners. It was unillustrated, and usefully divided the bindings according to countries and names of owners or binders. It offered opinions and information, not all of it accurate. Many of the notes on the books were speculative, the word 'probably' appearing dozens of times.

The timing of Quaritch's catalogue was prompted partly by the work on French bindings and partly by the two series of sales held in London on overlapping dates in 1881–3 of what were briefly referred to as the Sunderland and Beckford libraries, though in fact both sales owed much to books gathered by generations subsequent to the original eighteenth- and early nineteenth-century owners.[21] The Sunderland library, sold over several months by Puttick & Simpson from December 1881 onwards, had been mostly formed by Charles Spencer, third Earl of Sunderland (1674/5–1722), politician and opponent of Harley. In 1749 the books had been removed to Blenheim on his son's succeeding to the title of second Duke of Marlborough. The second Duke of Marlborough added further to it, but by the time it came to sale the library had been little attended to for many years. Like the books of Lord Harley sold in the 1740s, many were in red Turkey leather, many were on large paper and many bore on their covers the insignia of former owners. With special credit arrangements, Quaritch bought almost 60 per cent of the sale by value, and he and his staff were thus in the best possible position to assess the library outside the auction room. His assistant Michael Kerney summed up its condition in as balanced a way as he could, but his conclusion about the quality of the bindings was withering in its comparisons with English and French collectors alike. Of the probably 40,000 volumes, he estimated that two-thirds had been bought by Sunderland. They were

> either in their original (or early) covers, or else in bindings executed for him – nearly always a cheap morocco, red, blue or citron, unadorned even with his arms. He was evidently not so much a fancier of bindings as many who had gone before him, and some who have followed. He does not seem to have employed the best binders of his time, although occasionally some books reached him in fine coverings. Even in the case of volumes which he thought worthy of special ornamentation, the gilding was more elaborate than tasteful, and the materials to which it was applied very inferior, not only to the leather in which contemporary French books were drest, but even to that which was used for Robert Harley and others in England.[22]

While accurate enough, Kerney's candour is remarkable in that these were the very books that he was expected to sell, 'a great encyclopaedic library, weak only in the department of English incunabula and poetic literature'.

William Beckford (1760–1844) had had many of his books bound by the most fashionable craftsmen of the day. After his death they passed into the hands of his son-in-law, the bibliophile tenth Duke of Hamilton, and were hence included in the sales of the Hamilton heirlooms; the books were sold by Sotheby's, beginning in June 1882. The simultaneous appearance in the London sale rooms of two enormous libraries naturally excited comment and comparison in the newspapers. In reporting on the first day of the Hamilton Palace sale, *The Times* drew attention to the fundamental differences in appearance between the two. In Sotheby's galleries, the reporter found

> a splendid library, redolent with the incense of Russia leather and morocco, so precious in the nostrils of the devotee to book worship. It is this air of courtly attire so lavishly and with such admirable care and taste bestowed upon volumes that shine out in crimson, purple and gold, like fine pictures from the walls, which distinguishes the Hamilton Palace Collection from those heaps of dusky tomes – jewels in the rough, it is true – which were seen in the same rooms in the late Dr. Laing's library, and from those tattered regiments of revered veterans of the Sunderland Collection which we saw ranged round the spacious walls of Sir Joshua's old studio in the Leicester-square book sale-rooms. In this Hamilton and Beckford library the heart of the book lover is not touched with regret at the neglectful decay of the precious volumes, but with the warmest respect and gratitude that they have been thus religiously preserved like the pictures of the palace, now also being dispersed, in all their pristine beauty.[23]

With bindings in the Beckford sale by Le Gascon, Kalthoeber, Staggemeier, Padeloup, Lewis and other much sought-after names, prices were often high. There had not been so many seen at once in the auction rooms for many years, and it is perhaps little wonder that the writer in *The Times* suffered from a kind of Dibdinesque flatulence. Quaritch dominated the sales, buying more than half the lots by value and again helped by special credit arrangements. His principal opponent was Techener of Paris, the others including Ellis in London, Morgand of Paris, Cohn of Berlin and Frederik Muller of Amsterdam. Techener was thought to be buying for the Duc d'Aumale.[24] The newspapers enjoyed the jousting, without really understanding the difficulty of releasing so many old books into the market at once with all the consequent dangers of a collapse of prices: out of self-protection for the rest of his vast stock, Quaritch needed to see prices maintained. In order to recoup some of his money he had to sell quickly, and in the catalogues that followed immediately after the sales he marked some of his purchases up by 10 per cent or even less.

Many remarked on the differences in physical condition between the two libraries. The Sunderland books were in good if not always outstanding condition, but they were old-fashioned beside the Beckford books. Moreover, while they included many fine bindings, there were few binders' names that could be attached to these books. In book-buying, as in most markets, a name counted importantly towards price and status. While the Beckford books averaged an unusually high £10 per lot, the Sunderland books included many that proved difficult to sell. It was not just that the Beckford books were in expensive covers, many by celebrated craftsmen. In details that were presumably circulated informally in the auction rooms as part of the publicity, the press commented on the conditions in which these books had been kept:

> To those who possess valuable libraries it will be of importance to know that the books, the beautiful condition of which has been the admiration of all the connoisseurs and dealers, have been specially protected by excluding all direct sunlight, the lighting of the room in the palace built for the Beckford collection being entirely from the ceiling and with double ground glass windows. From the time of Mr. Beckford himself no gas has ever been permitted to be used, neither was the library ever lit up, being rarely entered but in the daytime. The book cases were not glazed or closed up having only brass wire trellis in front to admit of proper ventilation, the air of the room being carefully regulated as to temperature and dryness.[25]

These sales, of libraries formed several generations previously, presented both difficulties and opportunities to the trade and to customers alike. In many ways they both represented a kind of collecting that had long past. The extensive series of *editiones principes* of classical authors in the Sunderland sales excited attention, and the best of them fetched appropriately respectful prices. There was much in this library that roused next to no interest. On the other hand, there was a strong interest in illustration. The series of illuminated books by William Blake in the Beckford sales was mostly shared between Ellis, Bain, Pickering and Quaritch, Quaritch soon charging £170 for a copy of the *Songs of innocence and of experience*. He did not manage to sell it – at the same price – until 1895.[26] In November 1882, the Sunderland library produced one great surprise: a copy of Petrarch printed at Venice in 1488, which was found to contain six engravings besides the ordinary woodcut illustrations. It fetched the extraordinary sum of £1,950. Compared with it, the well-known 1481 Dante, with engravings associated with Botticelli, had fetched just £35 the previous April. Quaritch, Ellis and Thibaudeau all wanted the Petrarch, and it was knocked down to Quaritch. He devoted over a page to it in his 1883 catalogue of works on the fine arts, attributing the plates firmly to Botticelli and referring to the available authorities: Bartsch, Ottley, Passavant and Nagler (all of them inadequate on the subject), besides Vasari.[27] For once he omitted to state the Sunderland provenance, and he asked £2,225 for the volume.

The Sunderland books were efficiently and observantly catalogued by John Lawler, who was later to become the senior book cataloguer at Sotheby's and in 1898 to write the first modern account of seventeenth-century English book auctions.[28] Since the more important volumes had been periodically annotated by the Rev. Vaughan Thomas, the Duke of Marlborough's librarian, and also bore the marks of other scholarly members of the household including the knowledgeable bibliophile Jacob Bryant (1717?–1804), his task was made lighter.[29] Both Lawler, working for an auctioneer, and Quaritch's cataloguers had to work fast: they could not afford the luxury of many scholarly detours. But they were working for slightly different audiences. It could be expected that most of the bidders in the sale room would be booksellers, professionals in their own right. For Quaritch, the audience was among collectors and librarians. He was also acutely aware of an increasingly active American market, what he called 'the ever-increasing prosperity and bookish tastes of English and American society'.[30] The differences in descriptions of the same volumes are therefore of some interest. One of the more anticipated lots in the first series of sales from the Blenheim library was the Valdarfer Boccaccio (Venice, 1471). The record price of £2,260 in the Roxburghe sale, for a perfect copy, was part of book-collecting folklore, and the Sunderland copy was well-known by repute. Puttick & Simpson's catalogue (lot 1604) concentrated on a careful description of its condition, its few missing leaves and its repairs. It gave exact measurements of the size of the volume, and referred readers to William Clarke's *Repertorium bibliographicum* (1819), an easily available reference work. The catalogue alluded to the Roxburghe copy (in the possession of Earl Spencer) almost in passing. Quaritch took a quite different, and more promotional, approach: 'the famous Valdarfer Boccaccio', 'the largest copy in the world', 'excessively rare'. Compared with the auctioneer's, his notes about imperfections were incomplete and perfunctory. Most of the half-page or so in his catalogue was taken up with an anecdote about the volume involving two bibliophiles in the eighteenth century, and it finished with a prod at the British Museum: 'The authorities of the British

Museum to-day resemble the two baffled bibliophiles: they wished to buy the Sunderland Boccaccio, but they thought the price too high.' Quaritch asked £650.[31]

The Sunderland and Beckford sales brought onto the market books in fine bindings in quantities rarely seen in such numbers. Their prominence, their huge scale and their timing in the wake of changes to inheritance laws helped bring the subject to the attention of the general public, not just to bibliophiles. Apart from Quaritch's pioneering catalogues, by the time the Burlington Fine Arts Club organised an exhibition on the subject in 1891, a succession of popular books was beginning to develop, led in Britain by Joseph Cundall in 1881. Other similarly targeted books soon followed: some general, such as J. H. Slater's *Library manual* (1883; 3rd edn 1892), Percy Fitzgerald's *The book fancier* (1886) and Henry Wheatley's *How to form a library* (1886). Further, more focussed, summaries followed on such matters as royal English bookbindings (by Cyril Davenport, 1896) and on English embroidered bindings (also by Davenport, 1899). France was led by the publisher Edouard Rouveyre's *Connaissances nécessaires à un bibliophile* (Paris, 1877; 5th edn 1899) and by a series of short works on books, bookbindings, illustrations and bookplates from the hand of Henri Bouchot, of the Cabinet des Estampes in the Bibliothèque Nationale, from 1886 onwards.

We saw earlier how Samuel Pepys took unusual care to preserve some of the late medieval characteristics of his copy of Lydgate.[32] While he was unusual in his interest in keeping them, rather than following the more normal course of wholesale replacement with a modern binding, awareness of the past could also be expressed in other ways. In Paris, at the end of the seventeenth and the beginning of the eighteenth centuries there was a workshop producing bindings deliberately retrospective in style, on books printed much earlier.[33] This workshop seems to have worked with a small group of connoisseurs, or *curieux*, but the taste for such work later became widespread. It expressed not just different vogues for different decorative styles, nor even a sense of revival of past artistic achievements, but also a way of judging and accommodating the past.

Like the printed page, bindings too could be imitated and copied, generally in their more obvious outward decorative appearance than in their structures, and not always in the same materials as earlier versions. They were subject to many of the same misdirections as the pages they contained. The tools used for their decoration could be copied; indeed, the art of repair sometimes required such replacements. As we have already noted, bindings having some known provenance, or elaborate decoration, were – at least until the late nineteenth century – of more interest than those merely decorated with blind-tooling, even when this was on early books.[34] Meanwhile, in all periods, up to the present times, they could be revised, adapted and faked, almost always with a view to increasing value of some kind. It was but a short step from *remboîtage*, the re-use of covers appealing for their provenance and transferred from dull books to more interesting ones, to full-scale pastiche or forgery. Some sections of the book trades chose not to comprehend the various gradations of deception. The Paris bookseller Anatole Claudin noticeably did not apply specific words of censure to the practice of *remboîtage* when he wrote in 1891 of the several forgeries on the market, created by those in the same paragraph whom he described as 'industriels malhonnêtes'.[35] It was a revealing omission. It did not only reflect the mores of the antiquarian book trade. It also represented one outcome of a world where copies and imitations were parts of everyday bibliographical life, in facsimiles and other kinds of copies of printed books and of manuscripts. The world of copying became bibliographically and morally confused with the world of forgery, whether in bookbinding, autograph manuscripts or (as in the internationally celebrated cases of forged Columbus letters) in printed books.[36]

While many alterations and forgeries were easy to detect, many others seem to have deceived collectors. Many more remain undetected today. It is sometimes as difficult to say how far they deceived the booksellers who sold them as they duped guileless or over-eager customers. As demand rose during the second half of the nineteenth century for decorative bindings, or bindings with notable provenances, so craftsmen and dealers came forward to meet it. Some of the consequences are to be seen in the collections formed by imperfectly informed amateurs. Samuel Sandars (1837–94), the benefactor of Cambridge University Library,[37] relied for a great deal of his knowledge about early printing on his Cambridge mentor, Henry Bradshaw. But Bradshaw was no expert on bindings, and Sandars's unaccompanied excursions into assembling this part of his collection from the London trade and from auctions resulted in an accordingly confused assemblage. Perfectly genuine bindings were mixed on his shelves with volumes that had been made up, covers that had been re-used and bindings that were modern fakes covering perfectly good sixteenth- or seventeenth-century books. He was an enthusiastic supporter of the Burlington exhibition of bookbindings in 1891, lending two dozen exhibits. Not all were what they seemed. Despite its Tudor covering, a thirteenth-century manuscript *remboîtage* (bought from Quaritch in 1884) had never belonged to the royal library. A printed sixteenth-century collection of engravings of hair styles was in a faked Grolier binding created in Italy in the 1870s (Fig. 3.1).[38] It is

Figure 3.1 Giovanni Guerra, *Varie acconciature di teste usate da nobilissime dame in diverse cittadi d'Italia* (Rome?, c. 1589). Grolier's arms and motto were added to a genuine sixteenth-century binding in the 1870s. Cambridge University Library SSS.36.22.

frequently difficult to determine how far collectors cared about such enforced marriages. There was always a market for bindings aping or copying originals.[39] While on the one hand Sandars' collection, and dozens more like it, illustrates late Victorian taste for the highly decorative, it also confirms the more enduring assumption that printed or manuscript texts are quite literally tied to the manner in which they are presented to readers.

Like most of his generation of bibliophiles, Sandars was a client of Quaritch, not on the scale of his more wealthy contemporaries but a respected member of a large customer base. Quaritch's catalogue of 1889 was preceded by a summary history of decorated bookbindings that was self-consciously exploratory. 'The reading public,' it stated, 'is almost wholly ignorant of what is meant by "book-binding".' The utility, aesthetic appeal and 'sentimental aspect' of bookbindings were combined in a catalogue 'devoted to the service of the Holy Church of Bibliophily'. Religion apart, its tone of voice, the emphasis on gilt decoration and the choice of starting date (there were no bindings before the fifteenth century) all spoke of a subject and tastes that had scarcely developed since the late seventeenth century. At the end, the preface spoke of Cobden-Sanderson, 'an amateur binder, who has already produced some fine work in flat contradiction to the précieuseté of his theories'. More ominously, it also praised 'a young Frenchman named Hagué', trained in London by Zaehnsdorf and 'who ought rather to have lived late in the sixteenth century than in the second half of the nineteenth century'.

Théodore Hagué's reputation as a forger has long been established.[40] He had been the restorer for books belonging to the duc d'Aumale and his work had been known since the 1860s. Quaritch became his London agent in selling to unsuspecting customers. But in essence he was doing – at a highly skilled level – what many other leading binders of nineteenth-century France and England were doing. Some of the most sought-after decoration on bindings was imitative of earlier periods, in particular of sixteenth-century France. 'Grolieresque' was a term intended to invite admiration. Books bound for Jean Grolier (1479–1565), bibliophile and statesman, had been principal desiderata for William Beckford.[41] Following the publication in 1866 of Le Roux de Lincy's *Recherches sur Jean Grolier, sur sa vie et sa bibliothèque*, they were wanted by dozens of serious collectors, and parts of the book trade were happy to oblige with fakes: Samuel Sandars has already been mentioned in this respect. For Quaritch, the 'grand age of bookbinding' was in France, 1530–75, the period of Grolier, Henri II and Diane of Poitiers. By 1889, Hagué's activities as a forger were known to enough people for some care to be needed, but the catalogue did not identify with complete candour what was genuine and what was imitation or fake.

While Hagué has become the most notorious, he was by no means the only person creating bindings *à décor rétrospectif* in the nineteenth century. Many perfectly honest collectors encouraged such work, and the French collector Joseph Barrois (1785–1855) sought vigorously to invent bibliophilic confections partly by disguising or improving the provenances of books that had been stolen from the Bibliothèque Nationale.[42] In his celebrated article of 1891 already referred to,[43] Claudin alluded to forged bindings circulating in France, England, Germany, Belgium, Austria, Italy and the United States. He claimed that the more responsible booksellers held back from buying such objects, but that others, less scrupulous and perhaps seeking a ready profit, supported the forgeries. No doubt partly to avoid professional embarrassment, and partly to avoid charges of libel, he gave no names. Further fearful, even pusillanimous, he also wrote his article under a *nom de plume*.

Among the leading booksellers in other countries, at least Quaritch had continued to profit from Hagué's work. Quaritch's own position was at best ambiguous. In 1889, thinking of modern preferences among binders and their clients for imitating older styles and patterns of bindings, rather than exploring new ones, he referred to 'the stigma of secular thraldom to old models'.[44] That was no reason to stop him selling hundreds of books bound in this way. It has been suggested that he may have been in a weak position to identify what he was selling as modern forgeries. It has reasonably been pointed out that such reproductions of genuine early bindings as were available, even those based on photographic processes, had been so touched up prior to printing that they did not provide an adequate point of comparison. Certainly his great catalogue of bookbindings completed in 1889, with its colour pictures printed by Griggs in a mixture of lithography and letterpress, did not provide anything like a sufficiently informative guide to the realities of what was represented. But Quaritch was in touch with the major Paris booksellers; and like his chief assistant Michael Kerney, he did not need to rely always on reproductions. He possessed one of the largest stocks of antiquarian books in the world; his staff were handling early books every day of their lives. He was in a perfect position to compare volumes and to evaluate their status. Many forgeries and fakes are indeed extremely difficult to detect, and no doubt many more – of all kinds of goods – remain undetected. But for an eye attuned to genuine sixteenth-century bindings it required a lack of suspicion amounting to willingness not to perceive that there were a remarkable number of otherwise unprovenanced books from Grolier, Maioli, Henri II and Diane de Poitiers on the market.

We return to contexts, with which this chapter opened. Past and present strained at each other, sometimes constructively and sometimes in unrecognised or inexplicable ways. In a quite different context, and in a phrase that has since been much adopted for other activities, Coleridge had written of the willing suspension of disbelief.[45] The acceptance of forged bindings represents an extreme example of this in the world of antiquarian books. But the same response is to be seen in tastes for such books as a whole. Bibliophiles, booksellers, scholars and readers negotiated their variously informed positions between the genuine, the counterfeit, the faked, the facsimile, the imitation and the pastiche. Money, knowledge and circumstance all played their parts, and in the following chapters we shall explore some of the manners in which this happened. One matter was clear. By the end of the nineteenth century, almost ever since, the existence of surrogates – real or false, partial or complete – had created not always a better informed world but one where it was vastly more difficult for many people to comprehend what they were seeing, let alone evaluate it in an historically responsible way. Thanks to exhibitions and to library displays, thanks to a book trade better organised than ever previously, and thanks to a burgeoning popular literature on old books and on book collecting, antiquarian books had become familiar. That did not mean that they were understood.

4 | Representation and imitation

Readers of all kinds can be misled by fake information concerning the dates and places of printing or publication. This affects private and public interests alike, those of collectors, scholars and booksellers as much as those of institutions or government. Appearances can deceive even the most wary. In this and the following two chapters, we shall examine how the past came to be manipulated on sometimes considerable scales, and was presented in artificial forms to ever wider audiences. We begin with printing type.

Charles Knight, born in 1791, was the son of a bookseller and printer in Windsor. In his autobiography he relates that when he was a late teenager he was given a very imperfect copy of the First Folio of Shakespeare, which he decided to make complete. Using the recently published type facsimile printed by John Wright of St John's Square as his copy, he tells us that he set the missing pages using an old fount of type in his father's shop that seemed to him to match that of 1623. These he printed off on sheets of old paper – abundantly available from seventeenth-century books – and then had the whole handsomely bound. 'I was in raptures at my handiwork.'[1] In his own way, Knight was doing what others in far more exalted positions had been doing for centuries: making good what was missing. The border between making good old books, and perfecting incomplete books only just printed, is not an obvious one, and is not one of time alone. It was common practice from the fifteenth century onwards to use sheets from one edition to make good another – sometimes simply using the nearest reprint. And not only single copies. Many editions, especially of popular and much reprinted works, are partly made up of sheets bound from different settings of type, creating so-called 'mixed editions'. This book is not concerned in detail with this normal and widespread publishing practice.

A question of integrity

The development in the nineteenth century of ever more ingenious – and often very convincing – methods of completing books that had only partially survived responded to the demands and hopes of owners or customers.

It also prompts questions having greater implications concerning the values set on the integrity of what was previously created, and what was received by each generation, as books became damaged or altered over time. If a copy or facsimile was not an original, to what extent could it be said to be representative? How far was it admissible as textual or historical evidence? How far was it a reinterpretation, as distinct from a copy? How far do concepts of verisimilitude alter with changes in technology, whether manual, mechanical or chemical? Some of the assumptions implicit in the acceptance of copies created by the several different processes employed at various times in the nineteenth century have their direct descendants in the presuppositions of early twenty-first century viewers of scans on computer screens. Sometimes willingly, sometimes out of ignorance, readers accept a replication of an original, frequently not just at one but at several removes.

Wright's reprinting of the First Folio, the first effort at reproducing the whole of this book that has since been so much copied by various methods, was an extraordinary achievement. He ignored the decorative head and tailpieces, but had a copy made of the engraved title-page portrait and set the text almost entirely line by line, following spelling and punctuation carefully. He used paper specially made by Whatman, watermarked 'Shakespeare' and dated 1807; the date helped make precise the time of appearance. There was not to be any confusion about originals and modern printings (Figs 4.1, 4.2).

In principle, the idea of a type facsimile was not new. We shall return to eighteenth- and nineteenth-century examples later in this chapter, but there were parallels with the modern book trade in any period. In the early sixteenth century, the forgeries of Aldus Manutius's editions, for example, depended on acceptable imitations of his italic type. The success of his innovative octavo editions at Venice bred a new kind of literature: the piracy. He was active in seeking legal protection for his work, including his typefaces, but these attempts met with only limited success even in Venice. He had little protection against counterfeiters in Lyon and elsewhere, who aped his format and his italic typefaces and copied his texts. The facts that (as he noted in a rejoinder to the Lyon printers, in 1503) the texts were inaccurately printed, and the paper used was inferior, made little difference.[2] Several dozen of these forgeries appeared, usually without date, and further ones appeared in other towns.

The type-founding trade was not constructed on a one-to-one relationship with any single printer. It was diffuse. Most typefaces could be bought by anyone. Typefaces could be copied, as Aldus realised all too well but as also can be seen elsewhere in the fifteenth century and especially from the sixteenth century onwards.[3] Forgery, copying and imitation were

THE TEMPEST.

Actus primus, Scena prima.

A tempestuous noise of Thunder and Lightning heard: Enter a Ship-master, and a Boteswaine.

Master.

Bote-swaine.

Botes. Heere Master: What cheere?

Mast. Good: Speake to th'Mariners: fall too't, yarely, or we run our selues a ground, bestirre, bestirre. *Exit.*

Enter Mariners.

Botes. Heigh my hearts, cheerely, cheerely my harts: yare, yare: Take in the toppe-sale: Tend to th'Masters whistle: Blow till thou burst thy winde, if roome enough.

Enter Alonso, Sebastian, Anthonio, Ferdinando, Gonzalo, and others.

Alon. Good Boteswaine haue care: where's the Master? Play the men.

Botes. I pray now keepe below.

Anth. Where is the Master, Boson?

Botes. Do you not heare him? you marre our labour, Keepe your Cabines: you do assist the storme.

Gonz. Nay, good be patient.

Botes. When the Sea is: hence, what cares these roarers for the name of King? to Cabine; silence: trouble vs not.

Gon. Good, yet remember whom thou hast aboord.

Botes. None that I more loue then my selfe. You are a Counsellor, if you can command these Elements to silence, and worke the peace of the present, wee will not hand a rope more, vse your authoritie: If you cannot, giue thankes you haue liu'd so long, and make your selfe readie in your Cabine for the mischance of the houre, if it so hap. Cheerely good hearts: out of our way I say. *Exit.*

Gon. I haue great comfort from this fellow: methinks he hath no drowning marke vpon him, his complexion is perfect Gallowes: stand fast good Fate to his hanging, make the rope of his destiny our cable, for our owne doth little aduantage: If he be not borne to bee hang'd, our case is miserable. *Exit.*

Enter Boteswaine.

Botes. Downe with the top-Mast: yare, lower, lower, bring her to Try with Maine-course. *A plague——*
A cry within. Enter Sebastian, Anthonio & Gonzalo.
vpon this howling: they are lowder then the weather, or our office: yet againe? What do you heere? Shal we giue ore and drowne, haue you a minde to sinke?

Sebas. A poxe o'your throat, you bawling, blasphemous incharitable Dog.

Botes. Worke you then.

Anth. Hang cur, hang, you whoreson insolent Noysemaker, we are lesse afraid to be drownde, then thou art.

Gonz. I'le warrant him for drowning, though the Ship were no stronger then a Nutt-shell, and as leaky as an vnstanched wench.

Botes. Lay her a hold, a hold, set her two courses off to Sea againe, lay her off.

Enter Mariners wet.

Mari. All lost, to prayers, to prayers, all lost.

Botes. What must our mouths be cold?

Gonz. The King, and Prince, at prayers, let's assist them, for our case is as theirs.

Sebas. I'am out of patience.

An. We are meerly cheated of our liues by drunkards, This wide-chopt-rascall, would thou mightst lye drowning the washing of ten Tides.

Gonz. Hee'l be hang'd yet,
Though euery drop of water sweare against it,
And gape at widst to glut him. *A confused noyse within.*
Mercy on vs.
We split, we split, Farewell my wife, and children,
Farewell brother: we split, we split, we split.

Anth. Let's all sinke with' King

Seb. Let's take leaue of him. *Exit.*

Gonz. Now would I giue a thousand furlongs of Sea, for an Acre of barren ground: Long heath, Browne firrs, any thing; the wills aboue be done, but I would faine dye a dry death. *Exit.*

Scena Secunda.

Enter Prospero and Miranda.

Mira. If by your Art (my deerest father) you haue
Put the wild waters in this Rore, alay them:
The skye it seemes would powre down stinking pitch,
But that the Sea, mounting to th' welkins cheeke,
Dashes the fire out. Oh! I haue suffered
With those that I saw suffer: A braue vessell
(Who

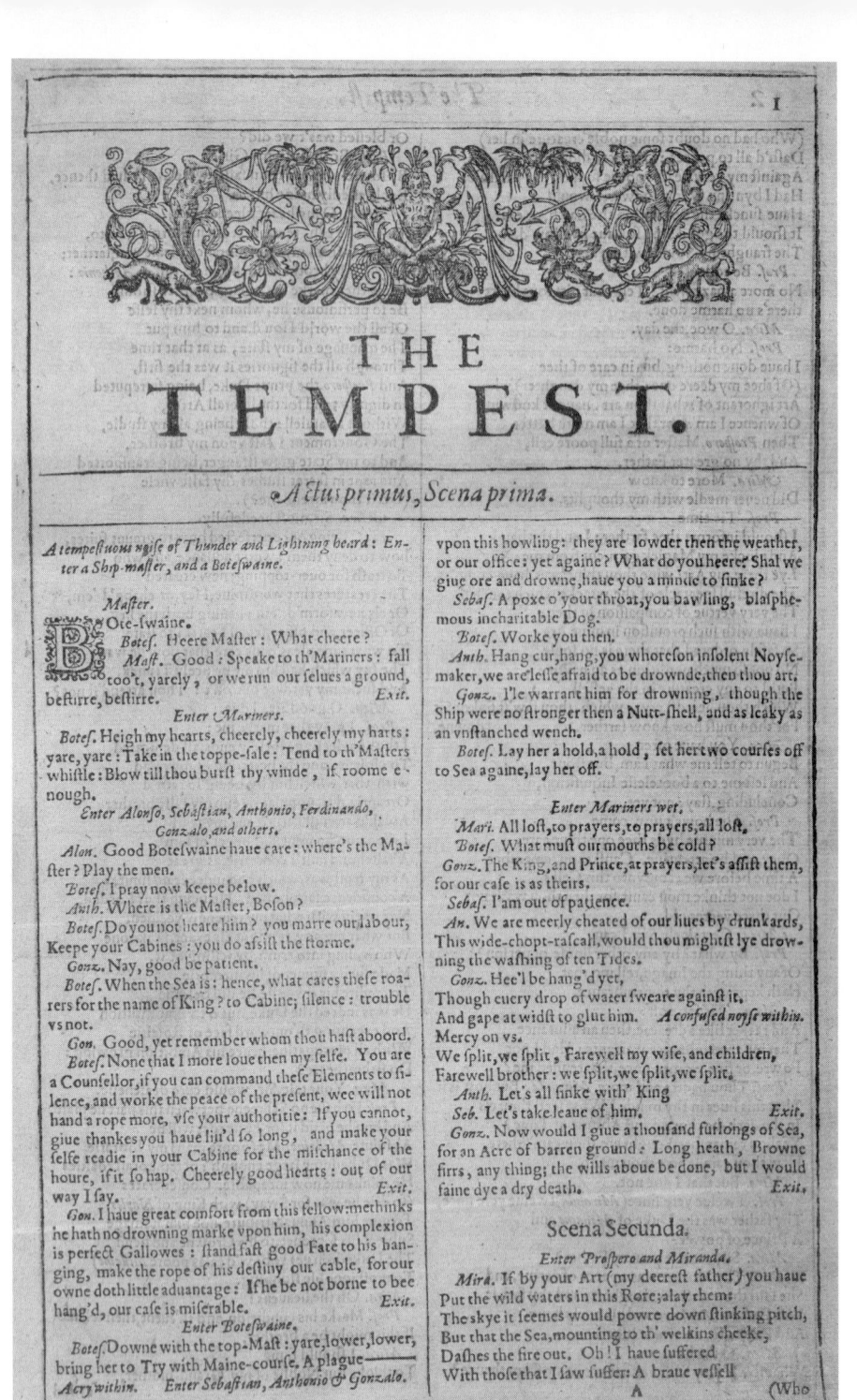

Figure 4.1 William Shakespeare, *Mr. William Shakespeares comedies, histories, & tragedies. Published according to the originall copies* (London: Printed by Isaac Jaggard and Ed. Blount, 1623). Trinity College, Cambridge Grylls 10.229.

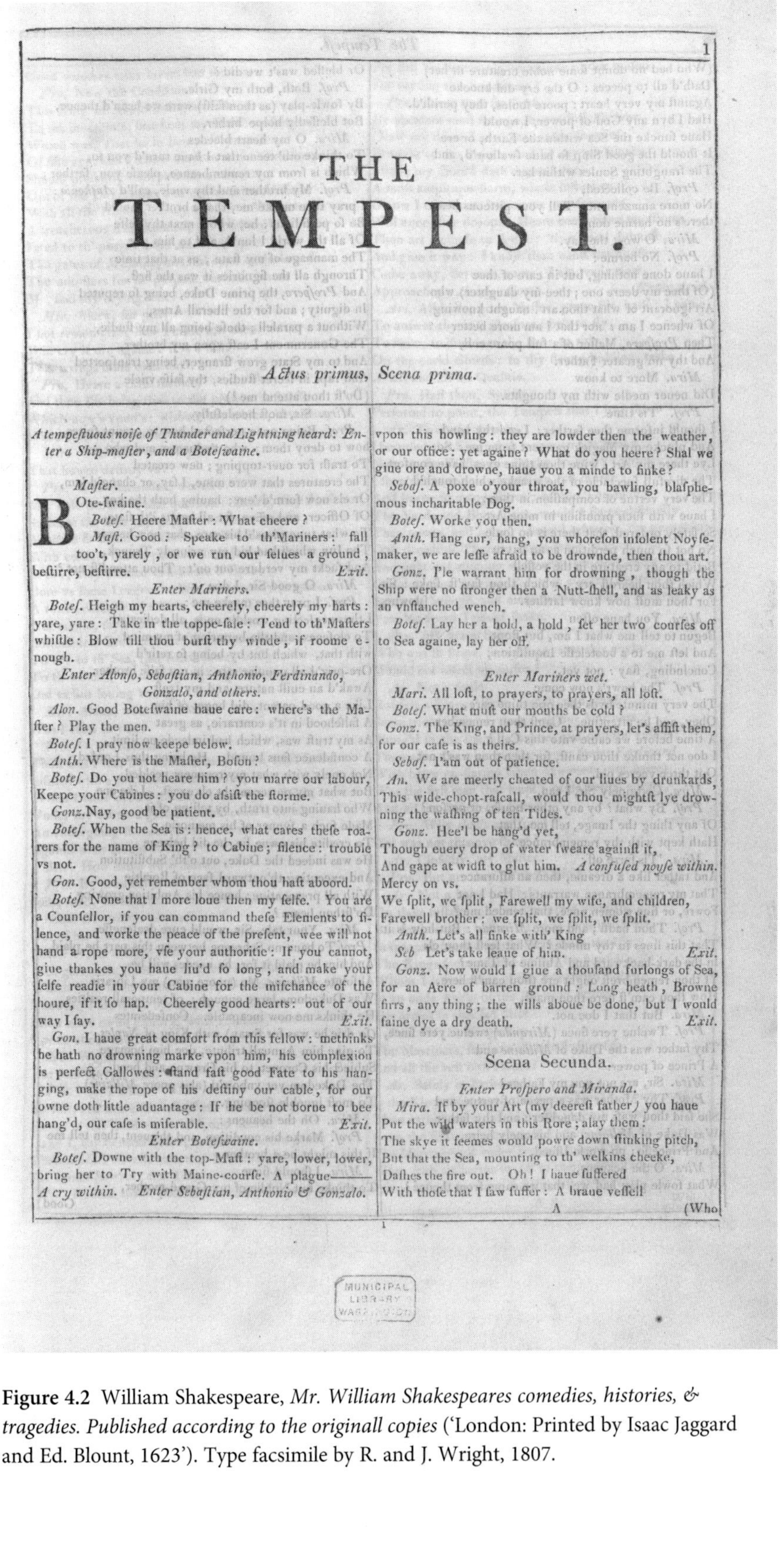

THE TEMPEST.

Actus primus, Scena prima.

A tempestuous noise of Thunder and Lightning heard: Enter a Ship-master, and a Botefwaine.

Mafter.

Bote-fwaine.

Botef. Heere Mafter: What cheere?

Maft. Good: Speake to th'Mariners: fall too't, yarely, or we run our felues a ground, beftirre, beftirre. *Exit.*

Enter Mariners.

Botef. Heigh my hearts, cheerely, cheerely my harts: yare, yare: Take in the toppe-faile: Tend to th'Mafters whiftle: Blow till thou burft thy winde, if roome enough.

Enter Alonfo, Sebaftian, Anthonio, Ferdinando, Gonzalo, and others.

Alon. Good Botefwaine haue care: where's the Mafter? Play the men.

Botef. I pray now keepe below.

Anth. Where is the Mafter, Bofon?

Botef. Do you not heare him? you marre our labour, Keepe your Cabines: you do afsift the ftorme.

Gonz. Nay, good be patient.

Botef. When the Sea is: hence, what cares thefe roarers for the name of King? to Cabine; filence: trouble vs not.

Gon. Good, yet remember whom thou haft aboord.

Botef. None that I more loue then my felfe. You are a Counfellor, if you can command thefe Elements to filence, and worke the peace of the prefent, wee will not hand a rope more, vfe your authoritie: If you cannot, giue thankes you haue liu'd fo long, and make your felfe readie in your Cabine for the mifchance of the houre, if it fo hap. Cheerely good hearts: out of our way I fay. *Exit.*

Gon. I haue great comfort from this fellow: methinks he hath no drowning marke vpon him, his complexion is perfect Gallowes: ftand faft good Fate to his hanging, make the rope of his deftiny our cable, for our owne doth little aduantage: If he be not borne to bee hang'd, our cafe is miferable. *Exit.*

Enter Botefwaine.

Botef. Downe with the top-Maft: yare, lower, lower, bring her to Try with Maine-courfe. A plague—— *A cry within. Enter Sebaftian, Anthonio & Gonzalo.*

vpon this howling: they are lowder then the weather, or our office: yet againe? What do you heere? Shal we giue ore and drowne, haue you a minde to finke?

Sebaf. A poxe o'your throat, you bawling, blafphemous incharitable Dog.

Botef. Worke you then.

Anth. Hang cur, hang, you whorefon infolent Noyfemaker, we are lefse afraid to be drownde, then thou art.

Gonz. I'le warrant him for drowning, though the Ship were no ftronger then a Nutt-fhell, and as leaky as an vnftanched wench.

Botef. Lay her a hold, a hold, fet her two courfes off to Sea againe, lay her off.

Enter Mariners wet.

Mari. All loft, to prayers, to prayers, all loft.

Botef. What muft our mouths be cold?

Gonz. The King, and Prince, at prayers, let's affift them, for our cafe is as theirs.

Sebaf. I am out of patience.

An. We are meerly cheated of our liues by drunkards, This wide-chopt-rafcall, would thou mightft lye drowning the wafhing of ten Tides.

Gonz. Hee'l be hang'd yet, Though euery drop of water fweare againft it, And gape at widft to glut him. *A confufed noyfe within.* Mercy on vs.

We fplit, we fplit, Farewell my wife, and children, Farewell brother: we fplit, we fplit, we fplit.

Anth. Let's all finke with' King

Seb Let's take leaue of him. *Exit.*

Gonz. Now would I giue a thoufand furlongs of Sea, for an Acre of barren ground: Long heath, Browne firrs, any thing; the wills aboue be done, but I would faine dye a dry death. *Exit.*

Scena Secunda.

Enter Profpero and Miranda.

Mira. If by your Art (my deereft father) you haue Put the wild waters in this Rore; alay them:
The skye it feemes would powre down ftinking pitch, But that the Sea, mounting to th' welkins cheeke, Dafhes the fire out. Oh! I haue fuffered With thofe that I faw fuffer: A braue veffell

A (Who

Figure 4.2 William Shakespeare, *Mr. William Shakespeares comedies, histories, & tragedies. Published according to the originall copies* ('London: Printed by Isaac Jaggard and Ed. Blount, 1623'). Type facsimile by R. and J. Wright, 1807.

ready by-products of the structures of the printing trades, but they were not always inspired by a wish to defraud. Aldus was by no means the only printer whose books were faked in this way. So were books from the Elzevir presses in the seventeenth century. So were early editions of the classical French dramatists. There were plenty of collectors ready to believe.[4]

On a much smaller scale, not necessarily involving entire editions, manuscript erasures and alterations were made by booksellers and publishers for all manner of reasons.[5] Often they were simple misprints. On other occasions there was something more serious. In William Painter's *Moorning diti vpon the deceas of the high and mighti prins Henry Earl of Arundel* [1580] it was perhaps politic to overwrite 'high and mighti' with 'most nobl'.[6] Dates were not always changed in manuscript so as to make a book appear older – a by-no-means uncommon fraud. They might be changed simply for better accuracy: the date on the title-page of Roger Ascham's *Apologia* (1577) was changed to 1578 in manuscript. Or they might be changed so as to make a book appear more recent – and new – than it was. The poet and playwright Elkanah Settle made some of his living from selling his books to people who were made to believe they were being treated specially, and some copies (for example) of his *Eusebia triumphans*, a poem on the Hanoverian succession, have the date altered in manuscript from 1702 to 1703.[7] On the other hand, the date on Thomas James's *Bellum papale*, altered in pen in some copies from 1600 to 1606, had perhaps more to do with sales than with more private hopes.

Beyond handwritten changes in individual copies lie deliberately misdated books;[8] and beyond these lie facsimiles. The latter are dealt with in the following pages, though it is worth noting here that at least one publication has been offered as a faked facsimile: an imperfect copy of an advertisement issued by the Augsburg printer Anton Sorg in about 1483 was copied at some point and the missing lines were wrongly reconstructed, so that the faked facsimiles, printed on old paper, could be sold as rarities.[9] In the most obvious sense, of a reproduction of an entire book, facsimiles can serve various purposes – scholarly as well as nefarious. The boundary between a fake and a forgery can often be expressed in economic terms, though this is not adequate for all circumstances: history offers a wealth of examples of fraud for theological, political or scholarly purposes. Facsimiles can include both fakes and forgeries, though neither may necessarily be a likeness of something else.

For these reasons it is not always easy to detect the purpose of books that are deliberately misdated. The first edition (Salamanca, 1492) of Nebrija's *Gramatica castellana* is a rare book. In about 1775 a counterfeit edition was printed. It was set in a roman type, rather than the round gothic that had been used in 1492, though in view of the rarity of the original it is unlikely that many people would have been aware of any difference unless they possessed some rudimentary knowledge of early Spanish typography. The text was set line for line, and the page layout was retrospective, not of fifteenth-century Spain but not obviously of the late eighteenth century. In view of the small number of copies now surviving, it seems probable that the edition was also small; and as there was no modern imprint it would have been easy to pass it off as the original edition.

More obviously intended to mislead was *Il decamerone* printed at Venice in 1729, a copy of the rare edition printed at Florence by the Giunta press in 1527 (Fig. 4.3).[10] It was made at the instance of Joseph Smith, but it was not the first reproduction. In 1725 a verbatim reprint of the 1527 text was printed in London, in roman type and including some copies on large paper. By the early nineteenth century the 1729 edition fetched no less than 15 guineas, though the price later moderated. No doubt Smith's timing of his reprint was due in part to the recent description of the original as 'edizione rarissima e migliore di ogn'altra'.[11] For this new printing, the printer's mark was inexpertly copied, and the type was chosen so as to be as close to the original as was possible with the modern materials to hand. We shall return below to the related question of allusive typography.

The production of imitations, fakes and forgeries has always depended on opportunities. On the one hand was what might be called the opportunity of demand – rarity of original editions combined with demand from collectors. On the other was the opportunity of materials. With sufficient investment, type can be copied. The existence of very large type-founders by the nineteenth century, selling to multiple printers often in different countries, provided further opportunities. By 1911, A. W. Pollard of the British Museum could note in no less a place than the *Encyclopaedia Britannica* the existence of what he called 'type-facsimile forgeries' of short works by Tennyson, George Eliot and Swinburne.[12] It was a very public statement, which both avoided the possible private embarrassments to be associated with coteries reading a learned journal, and yet also was a warning to a much wider audience. Suspicions about the origins of these pamphlets seem to have been restricted to a small circle until as late as 1934, and further investigations since have pointed to the most likely perpetrator.[13] One mistake in their making was to have originals reset in what appeared to be the same type from the same type-founder, whereas small changes had meanwhile been introduced to the design. Differences in paper and the existence of a documented original edition, for example, made it straightforward to distinguish the original – and extremely limited – printing for copyright purposes of Swinburne's poem *Siena* (1868) from the later resetting.[14]

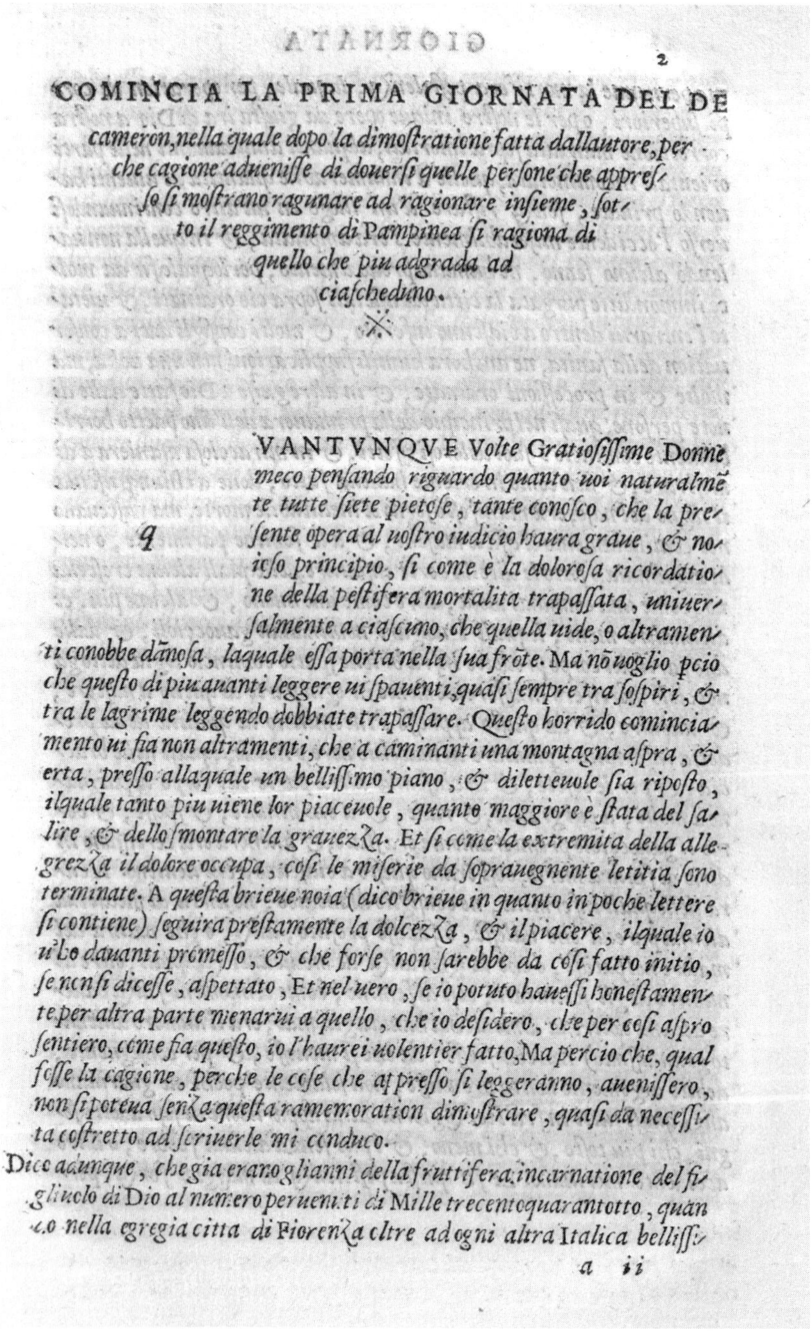

2

COMINCIA LA PRIMA GIORNATA DEL DE cameron, nella quale dopo la dimostratione fatta dallautore, per che cagione adueniſſe di douerſi quelle perſone che appreſſo ſi moſtrano ragunare ad ragionare inſieme, ſotto il reggimento di Pampinea ſi ragiona di quello che piu adgrada ad ciaſcheduno.

q VANTVNQVE Volte Gratioſiſſime Donne meco penſando riguardo quanto uoi naturalmẽte tutte ſiete pietoſe, tante conoſco, che la preſente opera al uoſtro iudicio haura graue, & noiſo principio, ſi come è la doloroſa ricordatione della peſtifera mortalita trapaſſata, uniuerſalmente a ciaſcuno, che quella uide, o altramenti conobbe dãnoſa, laquale eſſa porta nella ſua frõte. Ma nõ uoglio pcio che queſto di piu auanti leggere ui ſpauenti, quaſi ſempre tra ſoſpiri, & tra le lagrime leggendo dobbiate trapaſſare. Queſto horrido cominciamento ui ſia non altramenti, che a caminanti una montagna aſpra, & erta, preſſo allaquale un belliſſimo piano, & diletteuole ſia ripoſto, ilquale tanto piu uiene lor piaceuole, quanto maggiore è ſtata del ſalire, & dello ſmontare la grauezza. Et ſi come la extremita della allegrezza il dolore occupa, coſi le miſerie da ſoprauegnente letitia ſono terminate. A queſta brieue noia (dico brieue in quanto in poche lettere ſi contiene) ſeguira preſtamente la dolcezza, & il piacere, ilquale io u'ho dauanti promeſſo, & che forſe non ſarebbe da coſi fatto initio, ſe non ſi diceſſe, aſpettato, Et nel uero, ſe io potuto haueſſi honeſtamente per altra parte menarui a quello, che io deſidero, che per coſi aſpro ſentiero, come ſia queſto, io l'haurei uolentier fatto, Ma percio che, qual foſſe la cagione, perche le coſe che appreſſo ſi leggeranno, aueniſſero, non ſi potеua ſenza queſta ramemoration dimoſtrare, quaſi da neceſſita coſtretto ad ſcriuerle mi conduco.

Dico adunque, che gia erano gli anni della fruttifera incarnatione del figliuolo di Dio al numero peruenuti di Mille trecentoquarantotto, quando nella egregia citta di Fiorenza oltre ad ogni altra Italica belliſſi-

a ii

Figure 4.3 Giovanni Boccaccio, *Il decamerone*, 'Firenze, 1527', type facsimile [Venice: Pasinello, 1729]. Trinity College, Cambridge Grylls 6.212.

Whether of the fifteenth century or the late nineteenth, the results of all these confusions were manifold. Some were straightforward mistakes. Most were intended variously to confuse government or other authorities, to defraud owners of true copies, to give comfort to those who possessed some modest knowledge, to mislead book collectors or historians, to add value to books, or simply to manipulate sales. The result was the same. Books were misrepresented and were not necessarily what they seemed. Old books were made older, and new books were both rejuvenated and equally mendaciously aged.[15]

Typographical survivals

There was a difference once an attempt was made to imitate the past rather than simply redate or rename it. Typefaces were not ageless. The ordinary processes of fashion and taste, quite apart from wear and tear on the punches and matrices from which type was manufactured, ensured that only a few typefaces survived more than very few generations. There were, of course, exceptions. In the twentieth century, Enschedé at Haarlem, Drugulin at Leipzig, the Imprimerie Royale at Paris, Caslon at Sheffield, Plantin-Moretus at Antwerp, the royal printing office at Stockholm and Oxford University Press all, for example, possessed early materials of typefounding, some dating back to the sixteenth and seventeenth centuries.[16] The 1768 specimen of printing types from the Enschedé foundry, designed not least as a showpiece for the punchcutter J. M. Fleischman (d. 1768), included many faces dating from the sixteenth century.[17] In the London trade, the sale of the James type-foundry in 1782 brought into the market a collection of punches and matrices including some dating from the same period.[18] Punches (made of steel) and matrices (made of copper) lasted better than type, which was made largely of lead and was subject to the most wear. But there were still cases of type several generations old in many early twentieth-century printing houses. In other words, there was no shortage of materials for facsimile printing of a kind, and for printing in suitably allusive antiquarian styles.

This long tradition of re-use is at several points inseparable from ordinary everyday printing practices. There was a world of difference between the careful maintenance of prized historic material and the ordinary everyday need in lesser printing houses to make the best use of what was available. The typographical antiquarianism evident, for example, in a fresh edition of Caxton's account of King Arthur, printed by William Stansby in 1634, was very different from that evident in many other cheap editions of old tales.[19] Stansby employed roman type for the new historical introduction. He then turned first to italic and then to roman to reprint (in an adapted arrangement) part of Caxton's prologue of 1485 – incidentally changing Caxton's original and now addressing the book to gentlewomen instead of gentlemen. Only with the story proper did he turn to black letter, itself a typeface that bore only the most generic relationship to Caxton's original. Typographically as well as textually, the book had been re-edited. There was a similar mixture of roman and black letter in the chapbook adaptation of Raoul Le Fèvre's history of Troy, repeatedly published in the seventeenth century (Figs 4.4, 4.5). It was just one of several other histories printed in the 1660s and 1670s for Thomas Passinger, who supplied chapmen with such titles as *Valentine and Orson*, *Palmerin of England*, *Don Juan Lamberto* and *Amadis de Gaul*.[20] A closer relationship to old forms is more evident in some other popular printing in the late seventeenth and early eighteenth centuries. In 1662, for example, a cheap quarto edition of *The most delectable history of Reynard the Fox* was printed at London for the bookseller Edward Brewster. This was set in a worn black-letter type, and the woodcuts had been in use for many generations (Fig.4.6). The story had long been a popular seller. By the 1660s, the blocks were all but worn out, and though editions of the story remained at the cheapest end of the market, it later became necessary to cut new ones. Edward Brewster, whose imprint At the sign of the Crane in St Paul's Churchyard was still appearing on books in the eighteenth century, arranged for a new series of woodcuts, copying the old and worn-out ones. To these were added his initials. But the books were still carelessly printed: an edition of 1701, for example, has one large woodcut printed upside-down.

In these traditional tales, priced at a few pennies for distribution as much by chapmen and other itinerants as by bookshops, lies the strongest visual relationship between old and new. While it cannot for a moment be pretended that Caxton, Wynkyn de Worde or their immediate successors would have seen much other than innovation in these pamphlets of several generations later, these publications are the closest typographical link to England's earliest printers – printers whose work was by the second half of the seventeenth century beginning to exercise a fascination for collectors. The link lay curiously unacknowledged, and when these pamphlets attracted the attention of collectors it was for quite different reasons. Samuel Pepys, the best documented English collector of his generation, collected both early English printing and later cheap popular literature.[21] But the two seem to have been quite separate enthusiasms.

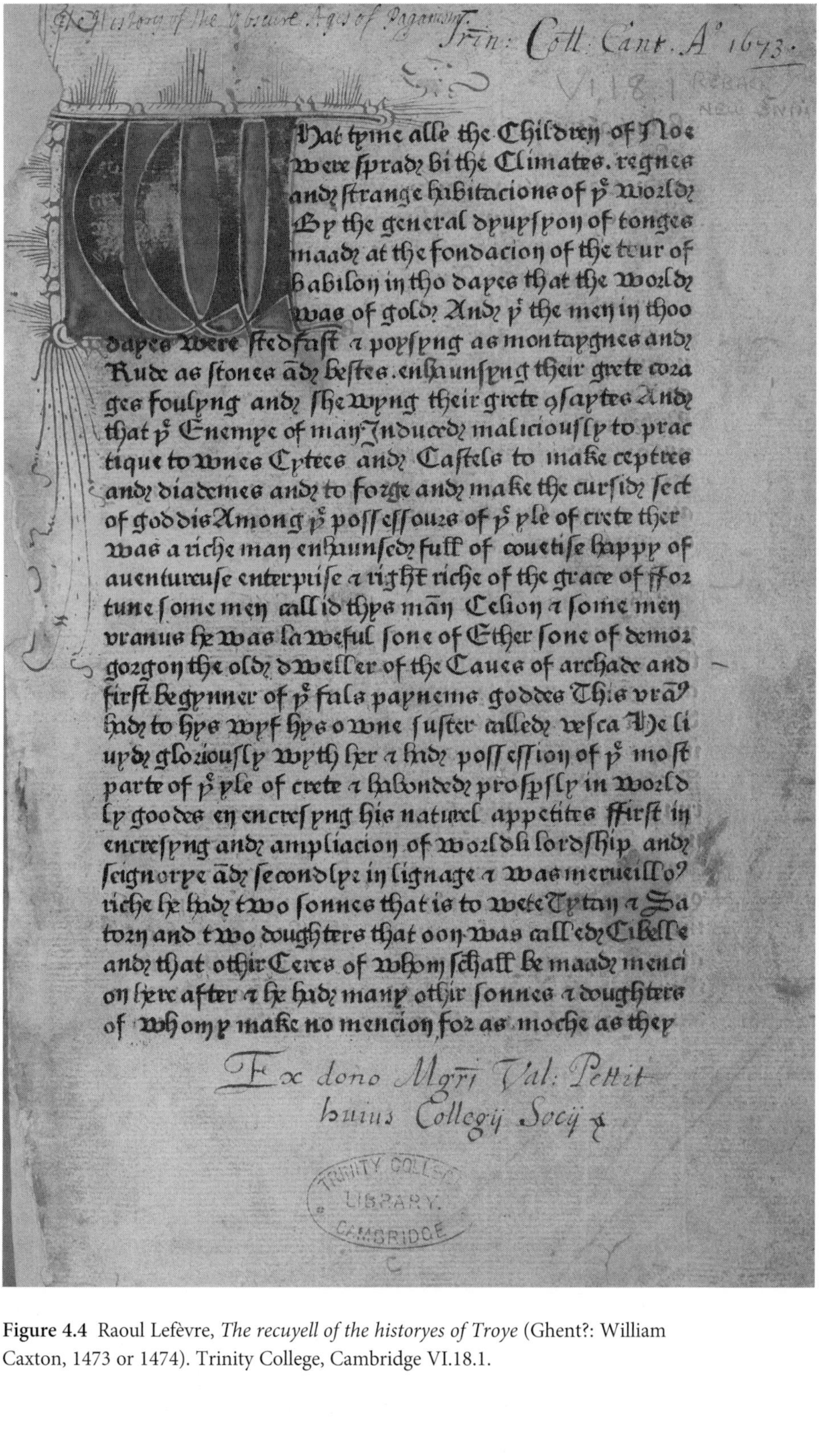

The History of the Obscure Ages of Paganism
Fran: Cott. Cant. A° 1673.

Hat tyme alle the Children of Noe
were sprad bi the Climates. regnes
and strange habitacions of þᵉ worldᵉ
By the general dyuysyon of tonges
maad at the fondacion of the tour of
Babilon in tho dayes that the worldᵉ
was of golde And yᵗ the men in thoo
dayes were stedfast a poysyng as montaygnes and
Rude as stones and bestes. enhaunsyng their grete cora
ges foulyng and shewyng their grete ysaytes And
that þᵉ Enemye of man Induced maliciously to prac
tique townes Cytees and Castels to make ceptres
and diademes and to forge and make the cursid sect
of goddis Among þᵉ possessours of þᵉ yle of crete ther
was a riche man enhaunsed full of couetise happy of
auentureuse enterprise a right riche of the grace of ffor
tune some men callid thys man Celion a some men
vranus he was laweful sone of Ether sone of demor
gorgon the old dweller of the Caues of archade and
first begynner of þᵉ fals payneme goddes This vra
nus to hys wyf hys owne suster called resca He li
uyd gloriously wyth her a and possession of þᵉ most
parte of þᵉ yle of crete a habonded prosply in world
ly goodes en encresyng his naturel appetites ffirst in
encresyng and ampliacion of worldli lordship and
seignorye and secondlyᵉ in lignage a was merueillo⁹
riche he had two sonnes that is to wete Tytan a Sa
torn and two doughters that oon was called Cibelle
and that othir Ceres of whom schall be maad menci
on here after a he had many othir sonnes a doughters
of whom y make no mencion for as moche as they

Ex dono Mgrī Val: Petit
huius Collegij Socij

Trinity College Library Cambridge

Figure 4.4 Raoul Lefèvre, *The recuyell of the historyes of Troye* (Ghent?: William Caxton, 1473 or 1474). Trinity College, Cambridge VI.18.1.

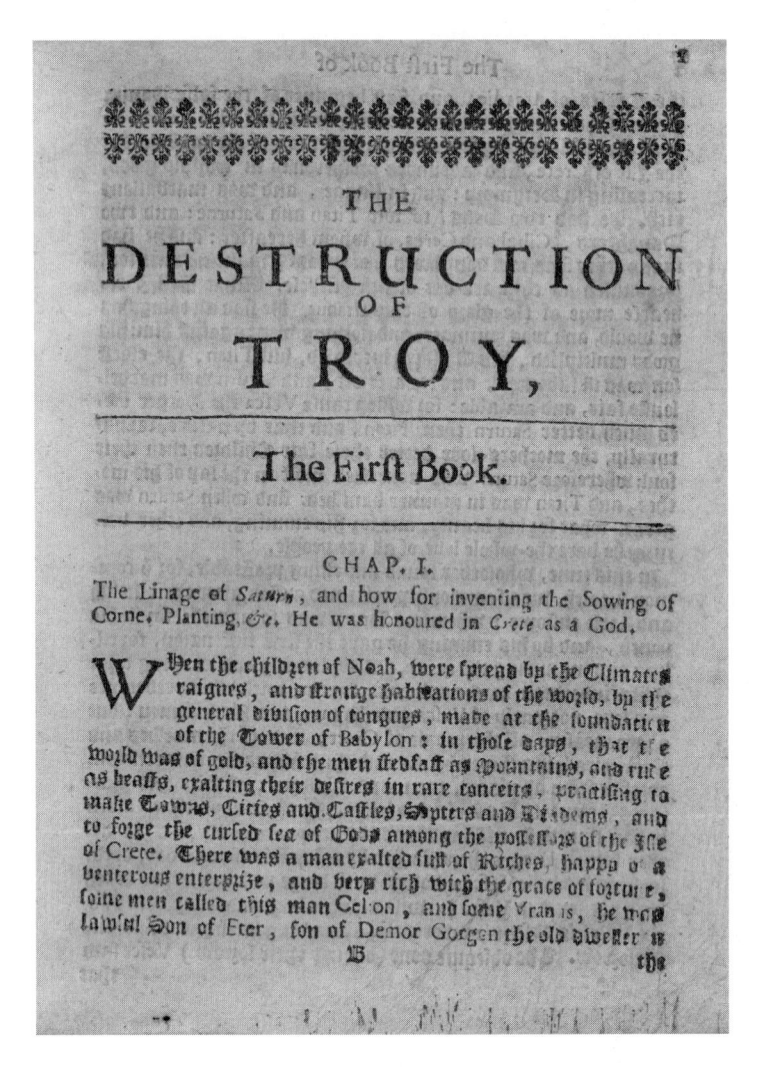

Figure 4.5 *The destruction of Troy, in three books*, 8th edn (London: Printed for T. Passenger, at the 3 Bibles on London-Bridge, 1670). Trinity College, Cambridge Grylls 3.385.

Imitation and revival

Here we must distinguish typography that is merely allusive, such as the several reprints edited by Anthony Sparrow of the crucial printed documents for the Edwardian, Elizabethan and early Caroline church. These gathered royal injunctions and various liturgical texts, set mostly in black letter (like the originals), but did not seek otherwise to reproduce the typography of the originals. The first edition of Sparrow's collection appeared in 1661, and was

Figure 4.6 *The most delectable history of Reynard the fox, newly corrected and purged from all grossenesse in phrase and matter* (London: Printed by H. B. and are to be sold by Edward Brewster at the Crane in St. Paul's Church-Yard, 1662). Trinity College, Cambridge Grylls 3.387.

addressed to Convocation: 'to vindicate the Church of England and to promote Uniformity and peace in the same'. It was part of the debate on what became the new *Book of common prayer*, attached to the Act of Uniformity (1662). Black letter stood not only for antiquity but here more importantly for ecclesiastical authority.[22]

Among the earliest conscious attempts at a type imitation of a substantially older English book was an edition of *The primer set furth by the kinges maiestie*, printed originally by Richard Grafton in 1546.[23] The new edition, in red and black and with the black-letter, roman and italic passages all carefully echoed, was printed in about 1710, possibly for non-jurors. But it cannot be described as a type facsimile. Most obviously, it lacked any representation, or even imitation, of the original woodcut border on the title-page. Though the text was set in a black letter of similar design, and the pages generally followed the typographical hierarchies of the original, the resetting was neither line for line nor page for page. The decorative initials used by the anonymous printer were from old stock, not from recent eighteenth-century designs, but they were not copies of those of 1546. As an exercise in allusive typography, the new printing had many merits. Although it became a typographical curiosity, it was not intended for any bibliophile market. A different kind of antiquarianism is to be seen in Thomas Baker's edition of John Fisher's funeral sermon for Lady Margaret Beaufort, founder of two colleges at Cambridge.[24] The original was printed in quarto by Wynkyn de Worde in 1509, and contained two woodcuts. Fisher took as his text the passage from the Gospel read just previously in the service, about Martha's conversation with Jesus. Baker provided a long historical introduction, and arranged for the accompanying new edition of the sermon itself to be set in black letter. It was not a type facsimile in the manner of the *Primer*. A few side notes were added, and as Baker's edition was a small octavo, there was no question of its following the former pagination, let alone the lineation. The text was heavily edited, introducing different spellings, punctuation and capitalisation, and new archaisms. The title-page, likewise printed in black letter apart from the name of the modern bookseller A. Bosvile at the foot, was a confection partly invented and partly copied from the colophon of the original; the edition of 1509 had no title-page. It was a new edition mimicking the old style. A comparison of the opening sentence shows Baker's early eighteenth-century approach to the early sixteenth century: the original is printed first, albeit without the decorative initial capital.

This holy gospell late red / conteyneth in it a dyalogue that is to saye a comynycacyon betwyxt the woman of blessyd memory called Martha and our sauyour Ihesu / whiche dyalogue I wolde applye . . .

  This holy Gospel late red contayneth in it a Dyalogue, that is to say a Commynication betwixt the Woman of blessyd Memory, called Martha, and our Savyour Ihesu. Which Dyalogue I would apply . . .

Baker's edition was no forgery. Its antiquarian allusiveness supported the text. The purpose was to claim authority from the past. It did not seek to deceive. Nor did an edition of another book that came from the London book trade at about the same time. Erasmus's *Playne and godly exposytion or declaration of the commune crede* had originally been published in 1534, and a new edition was published in the 1720s. While its typography could in no way be described as modern, neither could it be called sixteenth-century (Fig. 4.7). The original was set in black letter, and the new edition was in roman. The 1534 title-page had been set within a decorative border made up of rules and woodcut ornament, and the new was surrounded by cast fleurons. The typographical hierarchy of the 1534 title-page had been of the simplest, continuous prose in gradually diminishing type sizes. In the 1720s the printer set it out so as to emphasise the chief words of the title and give prominence to Erasmus's name. Similar visual liberties were taken in the text, and occasional explanatory side notes were added.

Other mid-eighteenth-century exercises, also directed at a general interest in the English past, proved to be sometimes alarmingly successful deceits. They are difficult to date precisely. Matthew Walbancke's *Annalia Dubrensia*, an account of the so-called Olympic games in the Cotswolds, was originally published in 1636. Perhaps to mark the centenary, a type facsimile was published that accurately aped the original, so much so that it narrowly escaped inclusion in Pollard and Redgrave's *Short-title catalogue* (STC) in 1926. But this eighteenth-century printing did find its way into the standard bibliography of English poetical miscellanies (1935), and on this basis thence to its purchase, as a 1636 edition, by Cambridge University Library in 1950.[25] Cambridge is by no means the only large library to have been deceived by eighteenth- and early nineteenth-century reprints of early books.[26] The most celebrated of all such exercises was the so-called *English Mercurie*, an account of the Armada and purporting to have been printed by Christopher Barker in 1588. So widely has it been quoted as genuine that it has merited an entry in the revised STC with a warning note that it is a forgery. The first person to have alluded to it, believing it to be genuine and therefore the first English newspaper, seems to have been George Chalmers in his life of the Edinburgh librarian Thomas Ruddiman, in 1794.[27] It was referred to again – and still as genuine – by John Nichols in the *Gentleman's Magazine*, by Nichols again in his *Literary anecdotes* (1812), by Isaac D'Israeli in his *Curiosities of literature*, by the *Encyclopaedia Londinensis*, by Brockhaus's *Conversations-Lexikon*, by the *Encyclopaedia Americana*, by Hone's *Year book* and many others. Its career as a reputable document collapsed in 1839 when Thomas Watts of the British Museum wrote a pamphlet setting out typographical, historical, orthographical and literary

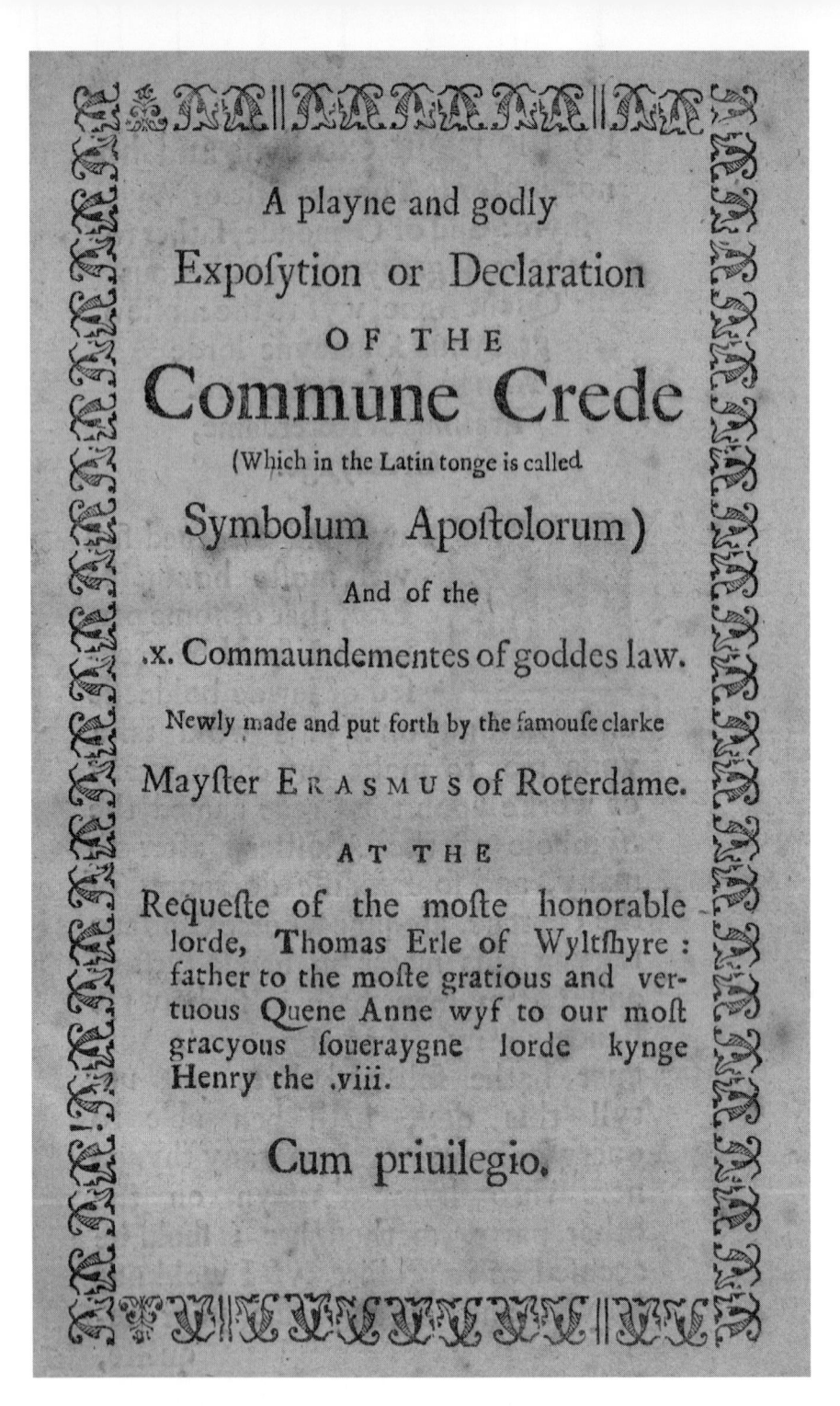

A playne and godly
Expofytion or Declaration
OF THE
Commune Crede
(Which in the Latin tonge is called
Symbolum Apoftolorum)
And of the
.x. Commaundementes of goddes law.

Newly made and put forth by the famoufe clarke
Mayfter ERASMUS of Roterdame.

AT THE

Requefte of the mofte honorable lorde, Thomas Erle of Wyltfhyre: father to the mofte gratious and vertuous Quene Anne wyf to our moft gracyous foueraygne lorde kynge Henry the .viii.

Cum priuilegio.

Figure 4.7 Desiderius Erasmus, *A playne and godly expofytion or declaration of the commune crede* [London, 1726?]. A reprint of the edition printed by Robert Redman in 1533. Trinity College, Cambridge C.32.20.

reasons why it could not be genuine. One of his central points was the design of the typeface:

Instead of being that of two centuries and a half, it is that of about a century back, the 'English fount' in fact, bearing a strong resemblance to that in Caslon's Specimens of Type, published in 1766.[28]

Unlike almost all of those who had written about the pamphlet in the past, Watts and his colleagues looked at the original rather than taking their predecessors' word for granted, and they brought to it an alertness that had perhaps been trained by the antiquarian revival of interest in Caslon's type during the 1830s. They saw with modern eyes, but with eyes that had – subconsciously or otherwise – been educated.

Allusive printing and editorial resurrections

It remained for Capell Lofft (1751–1824) to recognise the potential in printing an edition of earlier literature in an allusive way. Lofft was the nephew of Edward Capell, a pioneering editor of Shakespeare who recognised the crucial importance of collating the earliest editions: Edward Capell gave his exceptional collection of early editions of Shakespeare and his contemporaries to Trinity College, Cambridge. Lofft himself, Cambridge-educated, radical in his politics, nonconformist in his religion and diffuse in his interests, inherited his uncle's estate near Bury St Edmunds, in Suffolk.[29] In 1792, without any previous experience of editing, he issued a specimen of a new edition of *Paradise lost*, 'printed from the first and second editions collated', and with 'the original system of orthography restored'. His printer in Bury St Edmunds, John Rackham, could not command the same range of types as some of the large printers in London, but the layout of Lofft's edition made the point sufficiently. He repeated the box lines and line-numbering on each page of the original edition, as well as following the original pagination. The opening initial of the original was replaced with a factotum decorated initial – presumably the best Rackham could offer. This was no mere transcription. Notwithstanding the promise of his title-page, Lofft changed the spelling, capitalisation and italicisation. He explained his reasons in his preface, where he nonetheless added that the edition 'should be a likeness of the revered original in every permanent, expressive, characteristic feature; but not in every freckle, scare or casual blemish'. Here, in other words, was a compromise. It was a compromise whose core strategy heralded a typographic movement that was to command the respect of bibliophiles, scholars and more everyday readers for well over a century.

All this was not inspired solely by bibliophily, or by anxiety to arrive at some half-understood textual authority. In their awareness of some of the relationships between past typographic practice and present possibilities and limitations, there was a parallel to be seen in others' interests in the past and in other disciplines: in, for example, James Wyatt's remodelling and restoration of gothic buildings, in the inspiration Sir John Soane found in classical antiquity for his new buildings, in the baronial creativity of Sir Walter Scott's Abbotsford.[30] In France, Napoleonic building campaigns and the prolonged programme for the completion of Orleans cathedral offered their own related parallels.[31] As with the restoration and associated alteration of books, over-intrusive architectural innovation was not universally welcomed: Wyatt faced candid opposition from contemporary antiquaries including John Milner and Horace Walpole.[32] In so essentially conservative an occupation as reading, where inherited traditions and the requirements of readers placed limits on innovation by printers, there was an in-built tendency almost always to look back. Invention was countered by the need for familiarity. Wyatt's aggressive alterations and restorations of Salisbury Cathedral date from 1787 to 1793, and Abbotsford was completed in 1824. It is a long period, and further parallels might easily be suggested beyond even these limits, for many of the same issues were at stake as much in the mid-eighteenth century as in the mid-nineteenth. Enthusiasm for type facsimiles, the conscious typographical reconstruction of the distant past, became an ordinary part of the book trade for the first time in the last years of the eighteenth century and the first years of the nineteenth.

With the work of the London printers Joseph Smeaton (or Smeeton) and his son George, the world of type facsimiles entered a new phase. Their premises were in St Martin's Lane. After Joseph and his wife died in a fire in 1809, George re-established the business further down the road, near St Martin in the Fields. He later became known for his association with the Cruickshanks' book illustrations. Both father and son produced close typographic imitations of early English books. For this, Joseph was employed by Joseph Haslewood. Among his most successful productions was a reprint of the scarce account of the battle of Flodden, printed probably in 1513 and sometimes accounted the first newsbook to be printed in Britain: one copy survives of the original, in the British Library.[33] The woodcut was copied, the type chosen was a modern black letter, the text was reset line for line with the punctuation and spelling carefully reproduced. As required by law, Joseph Smeaton set his name to it, but in very small type and low on the page in order that it could be cut off if an owner so wished. The later series of Historical and Biographical Tracts, comprising sixteenth- and seventeenth-century historical and popular literature printed by George Smeeton from 1817 onwards, were less deliberately faithful to the originals, often set in modern-face type and with title-pages made up of confections of open capitals and modern and old faces.

The Smeetons were not the only people in the book trade who worked in this way. It is not clear who in about 1820 printed a facsimile of Thomas Coryate's pamphlet of 1616, *From the court of the Great Mogul*; the difference between the original and the facsimile can easily be seen in the different cuttings of the large woodcut of an elephant on the title-page. Similar type facsimiles were available from J. Sturt, a bookseller a little to the north of Smeeton's premises, in St Giles's, who published various pamphlets dating originally from the 1620s to the 1680s. His printer, usually James Barker of Covent Garden, used Caslon type, occasionally Fry's type and occasionally even early nineteenth-century fat faces.[34] On these books, likewise, the imprints were placed so that they could be easily cut off if wished. The semblance of age was sometimes furthered by the use of old paper.[35]

While the work of the Smeetons, Sturt and others like them has occasionally misled booksellers, librarians and collectors, there is little evidence that their primary intention was to deceive. The fact that imprints could be removed presented an opportunity to purchasers: legally the imprints had to be there. Sturt advertised his reprints openly. The same range of approaches, from close facsimiles to allusive typography to pastiches with grossly inappropriate modern faces, characterised the fashion for reprints of sixteenth- and seventeenth-century English and Scottish literature that flourished during the next several decades. These reprints were how more people were able to see representations of early printing. While some work was published in the ordinary commercial way, much other was circulated in very restricted numbers of copies. The demand was not great, and costs of publication could be contained within small editions. Publishers and enthusiasts were supported by printers led by Thomas Bensley, R. & A. Taylor and Charles Whittingham in London, and James Ballantyne in Edinburgh, whose stocks of archaic type enabled them to meet the needs of antiquarian tastes of enthusiasts such as William Upcottt, S. W. Singer and others. Alexander Boswell, son of Johnson's biographer and promoter of Scottish literature, used his private Auchinleck Press to print typographically imitative editions of authors including Richard Barnfield and Thomas Churchyard between 1815 and his death following a duel in 1822.

These and other books were reprinted because they were not just scarce. In many cases only a single copy was known to survive. This also could present difficulties. The English translation of Damiano da Odemira's *Ludus Scacchiae; chesse-playe*, published in 1597, was known in the early nineteenth century only in a single copy, which was imperfect at the end. So the last few lines had to be invented. Further copies of the original have since come to light, so the original lines can be read:

Requesting you with all my hart,
To take my verses in good part;
And to remaine my louing friend,
For this time thus I make an end.

Whereas the type facsimile read:

Requesting you with all my hart
To take the same] on the good part;
[Of your louing] friend.   G. B.

Some of these type facsimiles achieved perhaps more than was intended. As we have seen, Smeeton placed his imprint in places where it could be cut off. When in about 1815 he printed a new edition of *Soliman and Perseda*, using the edition of 1599, he set his name at the extreme foot of the verso of the title-page. The facsimile later confused its twentieth-century editor F. S. Boas, and it was itself used as the basis of a facsimile allegedly of the original for the Tudor Facsimile Series published by John Stephen Farmer in 1912.[36]

The market for most of these books was strictly limited by social circumstance. Thus, in 1814 the Taylors printed for Upcott an edition of Andrew Borde's *Boke of the introduction of knowledge*, originally published in the early 1560s and comprising linguistic and other practical help for those travelling overseas. The Taylors reset it in black-letter type facsimile, but this was an amalgam of imitation and new editing. Upcott explained that 'the orthography has been strictly preserved, except in a very few instances, where an evident error of the press occurred'. Facsimiles of most of the original woodcuts were provided, with two further ones of a Scotchman and a Frenchman copied from the *Recueil de la diversité des habits* published at Paris in 1562. It was not for wide circulation. Just 120 copies were printed, plus 4 on vellum. In the same year that Upcott's edition of Borde appeared, the Bristol book collector John Fry addressed another restricted, and partly overlapping, audience when he published an edition of *Pieces of ancient poetry* gathered from manuscripts and early printed books. He had 102 copies printed, including 6 on blue paper. The edition itself, partly by the use of asterisks, presented carefully expurgated versions of some of the poems.

He also printed a circulation list. Of those who received copies, five were members of the Roxburghe Club.

While this was the generation that witnessed the founding of the Club in 1812, the Club was not identical with those who took an interest in such literature. Its limitation to thirty-one members ensured one kind of exclusivity. While the Club – some of whose members dominated the most remarkable saleroom prices over the next few years – has come to define an age of book collecting, it was only part of a larger movement whose roots can be traced well before the Roxburghe sale of 1812. The circles of friendship among those who promoted these various facsimiles and imitations ensured the founding of other bibliophile publishing societies. The Bannatyne Club, founded by Sir Walter Scott in 1823 for the study of Scottish literature, consisted originally of just 31 members, a figure later raised to 100. The Maitland Club, founded for similar purposes, was limited initially to fifty.[37] The Bannatyne Club was responsible, for example, for a type facsimile of *The buik of the most learned and vailzeand conquerour Alexander the Great*, presented to the Club's members by the book collector W. H. Miller in 1831. The following year members received Alexander Hume's *Hymns and sacred songs*, including a type facsimile (with stop-press corrections) of the edition published at Edinburgh in 1599.

Some of the closest imitations of early printed books were attempted in the more obviously commercial world, where the London printer Charles Whittingham possessed an unusually wide repertoire of older types to produce allusive typography such as William Roy's *Rede me and be not wrothe For I saye no thynge but trothe* printed in 1845.[38]

Amidst excitement over the prices fetched for early printed books, bibliophily in the early nineteenth century took a new turn. While people mocked or even lampooned the Roxburghe Club for its members' foibles and its dinners, there was a more serious purpose: the publication of rare early books that had become so rare as to be almost lost.[39] Members were to present copies of their publications to each other. Among them, an old-style type facsimile of Thomas Bancroft's *The glutton's feaver*, a book originally published in 1633, was notable for the care that its printer Thomas Bensley took over its fidelity to the original. It was presented to members in 1817 by John Delafield Phelps, a lawyer and a collector with an especial interest in Gloucestershire. Other Roxburghe books were more occasionally allusive, but in them a convention was established that led as early as 1818 to the use of lithography (for a facsimile of *The solempnities and triumphes at the marriage of Ladye Marye to the Prynce of Castile*, printed by Ackermann, (Fig. 4.8)) and, later, to a valuable tradition of scholarly facsimiles of all

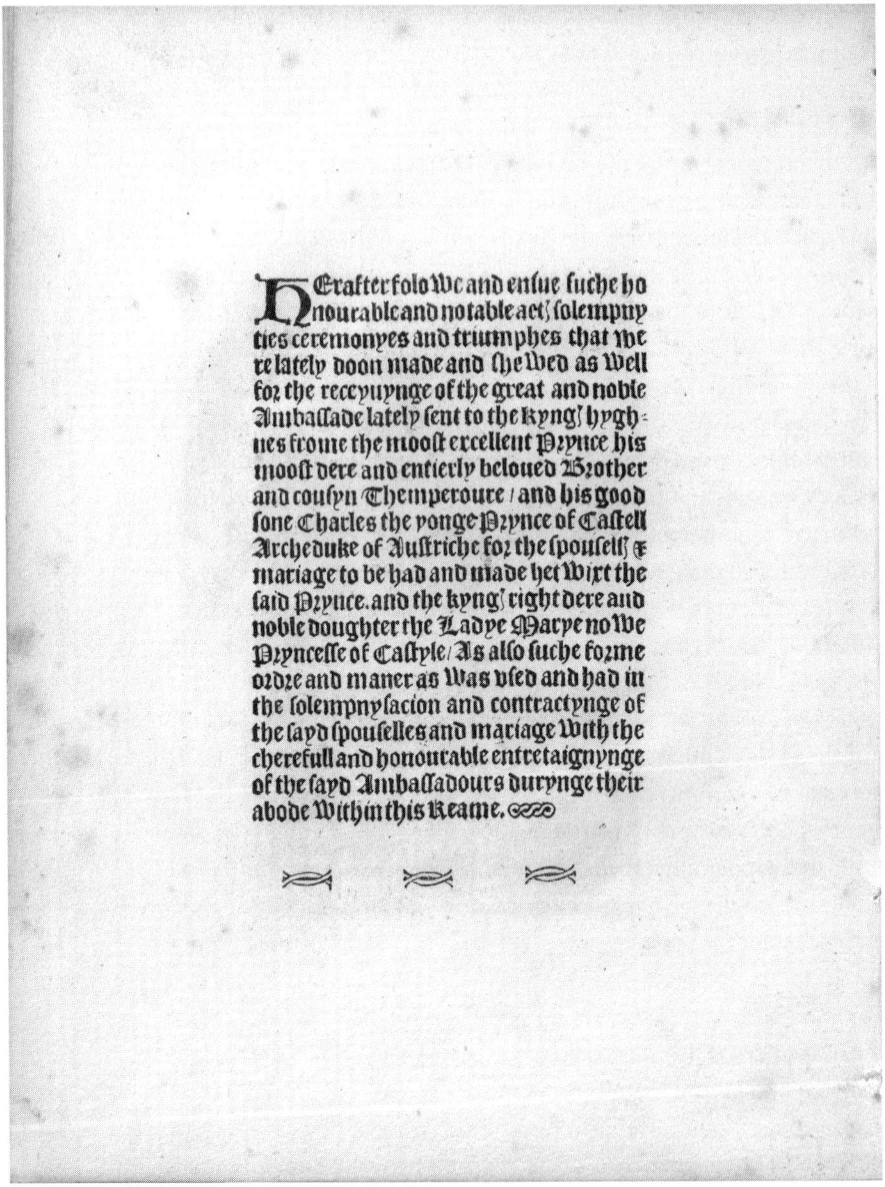

> Hereafter foloweth and ensue suche honourable and notable actys solempnyties ceremonyes and triumphes that were lately doon made and shewed as well for the receyuynge of the great and noble Ambassade lately sent to the kyngs hyghnes frome the moost excellent Prynce his moost dere and entierly beloued Brother and cousyn Themperoure / and his good sone Charles the yonge Prynce of Castell Archeduke of Austriche for the spousellys & mariage to be had and made bet wixt the said Prynce. and the kyngs right dere and noble doughter the Ladye Marye nowe Pryncesse of Castyle / As also suche forme ordre and maner as was vsed and had in the solempnysacion and contractynge of the sayd spouselles and mariage with the cherefull and honourable entretaignynge of the sayd Ambassadours durynge their abode within this Reame.

Figure 4.8 *The solempnities and triumphes doon and made at the spousells and marriage of the Kings daughter the Ladye Marye to the Prince of Castile Archeduke of Austrige* (London: Wright and Murphy, and Ackermann, 1818). Reproduced lithographically after a copy of the original (London: Richarde Pynson [1509]) in the British (Museum) Library. Trinity College, Cambridge.

kinds. Here as in some other, less limited, circumstances, the ideas of allusive typography spread further: to the editing of manuscripts. In 1819, George Hibbert presented to the Roxburghe Club an edition of the Pepys manuscript of Caxton's translation of *Ovid moralisé*. He had it printed, red and black, in black-letter type by William Bulmer, and he provided it with illustrations taken from the French text printed by Colard Mansion in 1484. The two-colour reproduction of the first page of the manuscript was a woodcut, after a copy by Triphook. Not surprisingly the edition bore no visual relation at all to the original manuscript.[40]

We began this chapter on a theme of adaptation, using available materials – in Knight's case of old paper and old type – to assemble what was missing. That implies not only a considerable range of skills, but also the means and stimuli to adapt. Typographically, and into the twentieth century, there was no shortage of means. Old cases of type remained half-forgotten in the backs of printing houses, on a scale that has become difficult to comprehend following not only determined searches for old metal as contributions to the prosecution of two world wars, and the great rise in the price of type metal in the twentieth century, but also the wholesale clearances of the 1970s and 1980s as letterpress printing came to an end as a large-scale commercial proposition. As for stimuli, a mixture of antiquarian eagerness to revive the past, and increased interest amongst bibliophiles and scholars especially in early literature, brought inspiration, opportunities and challenges.

Typographical revivalism was not copying. It was a reinterpretation, whether for scholarship, bibliophily or convenience. In the next chapters we turn to new kinds of verisimilitude, and the growing attention paid to what, eventually, was to develop into the modern idea of the facsimile.

5 | From copying to facsimile

Themes of copying, imitation and facsimile have recurred in earlier chapters. In particular, Chapter 2 examined the replacement of missing or damaged leaves by facsimiles. This chapter takes us into later generations, and onto larger scales. The mid-nineteenth century made the concept of the facsimile familiar to mass audiences. In plaster and in metal, from large-scale sculpture to the smallest ornaments and knick-knacks, the traditional and long-established markets for works of art were extended to a rapidly growing number of people with leisure, opportunity and money, prepared to be educated in the possibilities of reproduction. Casts and copies of three-dimensional originals, readily available from growing numbers of museums and commercial suppliers, were ever cheaper. For works on paper, including manuscripts, traditionally copied by hand as engravings, mezzotints, aquatints, etchings or lithographs, photography gave a new meaning to representation. Colour printing, and in particular chromolithography, brought reproductions of paintings out of the black and white world of engraving and mezzotint, and into fresh interpretations available to ever larger markets.[1]

Customers seeking medicines or foodstuffs were exhorted to look for the facsimile signature on the packaging as a sign of authenticity and quality, much as they had on some books since the previous century. The architect James Wyatt was reported to have substituted 'facsimile plaster' for the original over-heavy stone groining in Lichfield Cathedral in the late eighteenth century. Even whole buildings were copied. In 1864 the directors of the Crystal Palace at Sydenham, where part of the 1851 exhibition building had been re-erected, busied themselves with a facsimile of Shakespeare's birthplace so that visitors could admire not only the building but also the hundreds of signatures that had been added to the walls in Stratford-upon-Avon by visitors.[2] The word 'facsimile', perhaps derived from *per factum simile*, had borne its modern use since the late eighteenth century, but now it was extended. Frederick Netherclift, whose skills made him also an expert on identifying handwriting, was described in 1862 as a 'facsimilist'.[3] The noun was adopted as a verb. It was even applied to political events when in 1876 *The Times* reported of Hanover's plight in the face of Prussia that 'The Guelphian tragedy is an exact fac-simile of the one enacted a few years ago at

Naples.'[4] In all this, the exact meanings may have been usually clear enough from the contexts, but in fact the word had come to mean something between imitation and copy.

Everyday and long-standing perceptions of copying and imitation remained. The distinction was that these concepts were increasingly exploited, introduced to new markets and sold to groups of people both of different wealth and of different interests. The concepts took physical form as sculpture, pictures, furniture and ornaments, engravings and other prints – and manuscripts and printed books. The scientific discoveries that lay behind the new possibilities of facsimile possessed popular appeal, and were presented to a public increasingly eager to listen to chemists, physicists and biologists who were willing and able to respond to audiences thirsty for novelty. Science brought entertainment as well as intellectual, social and economic benefit. While the Royal Institution, founded in 1799, was the best known, there were many other places where science was presented in appealing experiments, and expounded by lecturers to paying audiences. Throughout the country, a thriving local newspaper trade carried advertisements for lectures directed at both professional and more general needs. Most large towns, and many small ones, had their literary, philosophical or scientific institutions that provided platforms for professional and amateur scientists alike. Popular magazines such as the *Mechanics' Magazine* (founded 1823), the *Mirror of Literature, Amusement and Instruction* (1822) and the *Penny Magazine* (1832), circulating in their tens of thousands, supplemented and stimulated public discussions. If much of this was at a quite elementary level, it made little difference to the enthusiasm of those who attended the lectures, or who read the journals.

Three-dimensional copying

Casts of sculpture and other three-dimensional objects such as the cameos and coins that formed part of the core of the study and appreciation of classical antiquity had been familiar for generations.[5] Tourists brought back from Rome fake as well as genuine coins, and casts of early sculpture.[6] Plaster casts, sometimes made in the studios of the artists themselves, and sometimes from secondary suppliers such as John Cheere (1709–87) in London, formed a part not just of training in draughtsmanship but also of furnishing. They could be of very high quality, such as some of the work that adorned Sir Francis Dashwood's house at West Wycombe in the late eighteenth century.[7] More workaday busts representing ancient and modern figures decorated interiors and open grounds alike, such as the Wren library in Trinity College, Cambridge or the gardens at Stowe in Buckinghamshire.[8] Sometimes they were coloured, such as the patinated black busts at West Wycombe; others, more cheaply, were plain plaster. Copies played an honoured – indeed central – role in the understanding of antique sculpture as well as in the celebration of modern work. They also had much more modest places in quite ordinary collections, such as those offered for sale in the 1740s by Christopher Cock amongst the chattels of a watch-chaser and an artist alike.[9] In 1758, Robert Dossie had included an account of how to take casts 'from figures, busts, medals, leaves, &c.' in his comprehensive *Handmaid to the arts*. Casts were also used in medical teaching.[10]

Just how universal the phenomenon had become was made clear in legislation introduced in 1798 to try and control the unauthorised copying of casts.[11] In future, anyone who made a new cast or copy was to add his name and the date. Such legislation was impractical, however powerful the need for protection. In 1734 similar legislation had been passed, with more success, to control the copyrights in engraved plates,[12] and the inspiration for 1798 was derived mainly from this.[13] But if there was little that the law could do with casts, the debates preceding the Act of 1798 exposed a universal issue. The public wanted, and understood, copies as distinct from original works of art. These issues were part of the art world long before they became part of the world of books, but they were by no means dissimilar insofar as markets were created and developed for surrogates where the originals were unattainable.

Until the 1840s, the only means of making an exact copy of a three-dimensional object was by casting.[14] The British Museum offered casts from both stone and metal objects, mostly from the Parthenon sculptures but also including the Rosetta Stone and the Cellini cup. Prices varied from 2s.6d. for a cast of a lamp to £47.10s. for the whole of the Phigaleian frieze.[15] The development of stereotyping for print, and its successful application on a large scale in the first years of the nineteenth century in Britain and France, depended at first on plaster casting just as much as did the market for reproductions of sculpture. All this was changed radically with the application of electrolysis to the creation of metal copies. In 1840, John Wilson and Thomas Spencer obtained a patent for 'engraving metals by voltaic electricity'.[16] Because it derived from work by Luigi Galvani at the end of the eighteenth century, the process was at first sometimes known as Galvanism, before the more lasting term electrotyping was adopted.

Electrotyping caught the public imagination. Scientific journals were full of it. Lectures on the subject, much advertised in the newspapers, were offered on this amongst other scientific entertainments at the Polytechnic Institute in Regent Street.[17] It was soon pointed out that a similar discovery had been made at St Petersburg by Moritz Jacobi, who had presented his findings to the St Petersburg Academy of Science in 1838[18] – at much the same time as Spencer was first sharing his work with audiences in Liverpool. Jacobi's work was further reported in the *Annales de Chimie* in October 1840.[19] The process was ideally suited to copying coins and medals, and even busts, though attention also quickly focussed on its application to printing, to copying plates for illustration and more generally to making electrotype plates rather than stereotypes. In autumn 1840, Spencer published a pamphlet, *Instructions for the multiplication of works of art in metal, by voltaic electricity*.[20] In it he rehearsed some of his early work, and showed how coins and printing plates could be copied with the utmost accuracy.

Much of the public interest in electrotyping also remarked the recent discovery of the daguerreotype, which allowed the copying of drawings – a two-dimensional rather than three-dimensional application. Inevitably there were difficulties. In America, the notes of the Cincinnati Bank were illegally daguerreotyped, and the coins were electrotyped.[21] By 1842 the process so clearly published by Spencer, who had first demonstrated it with the use of farthings, was widely available, for legal or illegal use. There were articles in the *Literary Gazette*, the *Athenaeum*, the *Philosophical Magazine*[22] and elsewhere. Details were presented in publications ranging from Charles Walker's shilling *Electrotype manipulation* (7th edn, 1841) to the much fuller *Elements of electro-metallurgy, or the art of working in metals by the Galvanic fluid* (1841) by Alfred Smee, who described himself on his title-page as Surgeon to the Bank of England but who also supplied electrotyping apparatus, including the means to copy a number of medals simultaneously.[23] A whole section of his book related to printing processes, including the multiplication of type, the multiplication of steel plates, the multiplication of woodcuts and the multiplication of daguerreotypes. Smee alluded especially to the firm of De la Rue, 'one of the most complete specimens of the union of art and science', and specialists in electrotyping for printing. In Aberdeen, a firm advertised that it possessed the 'electrotype apparatus', 'which will enable any one to make fac-similes in Copper of Medals, Seals, Casts and Engraved Plates, in various forms and at different Prices; together with every article required for the very interesting operation of Electrotyping, including a great variety of Plaster and Wax Casts, Fusible Metal, Plumbago, &c. Solutions of Gold and Silver for Gilding and Plating as well as for taking Impressions'. Prices were low, at 1s.6d. upwards.[24]

With the opening of the South Kensington Museum, the opportunities were legion for simultaneously educating the public and exploiting a now well-established market. In 1859 the Museum issued its first priced lists of works of art reproduced by means of photography, electrotypes and casts, an initiative whose direct descendants are to be seen in museum shops today throughout the world.[25] Museums were proud of their own collections of copies. As Secretary of the South Kensington Museum, Henry Cole suggested in 1864 that copies should be exchanged internationally, an idea that was taken up in the aftermath of the Paris exhibition in 1868. The first of the cast courts (also known as the Architecture Courts) in the South Kensington Museum was opened to the public in July 1873, though the collection had by then been growing for some years. It astonished visitors facing a growing and ever more crowded assembly of ambitious full-size versions including Pisano's pulpit at Pisa and Trajan's column,[26] both acquired in 1864, and dozens of other large medieval and renaissance works of art.

Across Britain, casts and electrotypes became an accepted part of museum-going. In 1867 the Museum published a priced *List of the electrotype reproductions in the Art Division of the Museum at South Kensington*. Copies could be finished in copper, silver, gilt or parcel gilt, as appropriate either to the object or to customers' means. An enlarged edition appeared two years later, explicitly presented 'for the use of schools of art, for prizes, and generally for public instruction'. By 1873 the catalogue had grown in format and in thickness, and now contained pasted-in photographs of eighty electrotype selected reproductions available from 2 shillings upwards.

Meanwhile in 1868 Henry Cole and Henry Scott, Director of the new buildings for the museum, had been on a tour of inspection in Italy, seeking out works of art that would be suitable for reproduction.[27] Basing their work on Murray's guidebooks and a few standard works including Cicognara's *Storia della scultura* and Crowe and Cavalcaselle's recently published history of painting in Italy, they reached Palermo in their search for sculpture to be cast or electrotyped, paintings to be copied and objects to be photographed. The miniatures in the Grimani Breviary at Venice had been published in photographic facsimile in 1862,[28] and they now suggested that a selection of pages should be further copied. It was the only book to reach their recommendations. The Museum paid little attention to the copying of books, save that book covers counted as sculpture, and a few crept in this way: the first were two early covers from Byzantium, copied in 1855 from originals in the Louvre. By 1876, their number had grown. The price list of casts in 'fictile ivory' available either from the main London supplier Elkington & Co. of Regent Street, or from the Arundel Society, numbered almost a hundred. By the late 1870s, the business of supplying casts and electrotypes had grown enormously. Apart from Elkington, other firms in London having connections with the Museum included Franchi in Myddelton Street EC and W. Johnson in Ledbury Road. In Paris there were Lionnet frères, Gueyton and Lefevre; in Vienna Haas; in Nuremberg Rotermund; in Dublin Waterhouse and West; in Florence Pellas; in Milan Pirotti; and in Rome Castellani. Many more names appeared in the local directories. By 1887, Elkington's illustrated retail catalogue ran to 120 pages. Skills in electrotyping meant that it was possible to copy as large an object as a silver wine cistern made in England in 1734–5 and now in the Winter Palace at St Petersburg: it measured 3ft 4ins high and 5ft 6ins long, and the price for a copy was £400.[29]

There was a lively export market from Europe. Elkington had a branch in Sydney, and in Melbourne the museum attached to the new Public Library of Victoria worked vigorously to assemble a collection of casts of statues, busts and smaller sculptures from Rome, Naples, Florence, Paris, London and elsewhere; many of the ivory objects were in private collections. Alongside these sat prints, tracings and photographs. By 1865, more than £800 had been spent on the collection, and donors had added much more, 'furnishing means of enlightened gratification and material instruction in the practical branches of art-manufacture and design'.[30]

As the South Kensington Museum developed its educational role, it assembled a circulating collection that mingled originals and copies. This travelling exhibition could be booked for suitable local venues. By March 1862, when the scheme had been running for 7 years, it had been seen in 37 towns including 5 each in Scotland and Ireland, and had been visited by 639,672 people. Sales of the catalogue numbered 39,962.[31] Extending its role further, in 1864 the Museum published a further list of photographs for sale, the germ of museum postcards everywhere.[32]

Copying and print

It is a commonplace that a series of inventions in the nineteenth century brought a new visual awareness in most walks of life. Illustration on all scales became widespread as never before.[33] The discovery of lithography at the end of the 1790s and its introduction across Europe during the next decades made the manufacture of pictures easier. Thomas Bewick's innovative work as a wood-engraver, and its adoption by the fashionable world, prompted a host of more or less skilled followers. His reputation spread to continental Europe, but the principle of letterpress printing remained unchanged. For our present purposes, the key innovations were in lithography and, later, photography. Where an engraved copper plate took sometimes many weeks to prepare, a lithographic stone could be prepared as quickly as an artist could draw. Lithography did not immediately displace intaglio prints. Inventions such as steel plates for engraving, and dozens of new techniques for preparing plates, meant that the market for intaglio images remained strong. But it shifted towards an art market for high-quality reproductions and it was increasingly appreciated as an artistic medium in itself. Its place as a medium for reproduction was modified accordingly.[34] Meanwhile lithography also found a dual market, as a medium for reproduction and as a medium for artists. Its reputation sometimes suffered from this ambiguity.[35] It was capable of being used very cheaply, and it was a medium of great versatility. The development of chromolithography not only multiplied its possibilities. It also for the first time made high-quality, cheap colour printing possible.

Pages or portions of pages from both manuscripts and printed books had long been presented in facsimile, either as engravings or as lithographs. Some were interpretations, such as the engraved plates for Grotius's edition of the ninth-century Leiden manuscript of the Aratea, published in 1600. Jacob de Gheyn copied the stars from the manuscript accurately enough, but reinterpreted the figures and gave them faces of noticeably modern appearance.[36] The earliest published engraved reproduction of a substantial part of a manuscript, and that of considerable quality, was of an eighth-century Echternach manuscript of Jerome's *Martyrologium*, now in Paris. It was fitted onto twenty-five engraved plates, and at first just nine copies were printed. On this occasion the script was copied carefully, and the lineation of the original was followed almost entirely; but the pagination and the original page size were ignored. The plates were prepared in 1627–33 at the instance of Héribert Rosweyde for the printer Balthasar Moretus at Antwerp, early in the project that became the *Acta sanctorum*, but they were not published until 1660.[37] A further pioneering exercise came in 1655, when Franciscus Junius included an engraving of a page from the Oxford manuscript in his edition of Caedmon. Mabillon used engraved facsimiles of manuscripts copiously in his *De re diplomatica* (1681); they were employed by Daniel Papebroch in the *Acta sanctorum* in 1701; and Montfaucon used them in his *Monumens de la monarchie françoise* in 1729–33.[38]

The reproduction of pages from printed books, using engraved plates, had a shorter history. Since printing is not usually classed as one of the fine arts, the history of it in facsimile has been less studied. But the needs and principles were the same: to compare examples in order to further the history and understanding of the subject in question.

Something of the difficulty can be seen if one compares the reproductions from the same book in two studies published almost a hundred years apart. In 1765, Gerard Meerman included in his *Origines typographicae* a reproduction of a page from what he described as the first edition of the *Speculum humanae salvationis*, a book having a woodcut at the head of the page and text underneath. It is a book that continues to attract attention, being one of the earliest books printed in the Low Countries. In 1858, Samuel Leigh Sotheby included a reproduction of the same page from another copy in his *Principia typographica*.[39] Yet the two were very different, as Sotheby pointed out with some asperity when he introduced his own version. The edition, he explained,

was considered by Meerman and others as the *first* Dutch edition, and, as such, to take the precedence of all the rest. Meerman has given, in Plate III., what professes to be a fac-simile of the first page; but altogether so unworthy of the name, that we have been induced to make a fac-simile of the same page, in order to afford the opportunity of comparison. His fac-simile can, indeed, be regarded in no other light than as a deliberate attempt to confirm, at all hazards, his own hypothesis, and only shews how far a zealous partisan may be led to compromise his veracity in the defence of his views. The type in the original (throughout the copy) is by no means so defective in the way it has been there represented; while, on the other hand, the wood-engraving exhibits symptoms of decay, which, in the fac-simile in question, has been altogether overlooked.[40]

Though *Principia typographica* was published in 1858, the plate used by Sotheby had been made some years previously, in 1826, as a part of his father's assembling of plates that were eventually to be published in the *Principia typographica*. The original of this copy was in the Pembroke library at Wilton; that used by Meerman was in the Netherlands. Meerman's facsimiles were engraved; Sotheby's were lithographed. But while there could be no doubting the inadequacy of Meerman's version, that offered by Sotheby was far from perfect, and Sotheby himself was confused. Neither man offered an accurate facsimile, and both compared poorly with the plates in J. W. Holtrop's later *Monuments typographiques des Pays-Bas* published in 1868, just a little after Sotheby. Both Holtrop and Sotheby were working at the point where the application of photography to the reproduction of old books was beginning to be acknowledged, but where it had not won general acceptance. Sotheby's hand was also prevented by the fact that he was including old stocks of printed leaves, though he did include one photographic print of a block-book.[41]

The difficulty of reproducing on a copper plate the regularity of printing types was universal. In serious writing on the history of printing, it was rarely more dramatically demonstrated than in the successive editions of Ames's *Typographical antiquities*. For his original edition in 1749, Ames turned to the writing master George Bickham when he required a full-page plate to show six different types. He dedicated the plate to the type-founder William Caslon. It is unlikely that Caslon admired the quality of the reproduction, which showed lines straggling in far from straight or parallel lines across the page, letters supposedly of the same fount in noticeably different sizes, and variant forms of characters even within a single line (Fig. 5.1). William Herbert was able to use the same plate, with all its misrepresentations and disadvantages, for his revision of Ames in 1785–90. It was not available to Dibdin, whose much more generously illustrated edition of the work appeared in 1810–19. Apart from the many woodcut copies showing parts of early books, Dibdin also inserted several plates reproducing pages of type. He employed engravers including James Basire and Bartholomew Howlett.[42] Only occasionally did any of them achieve any kind of verisimilitude, but that did not prevent Dibdin from criticising Herbert's parsimony in re-using Ames's plates. By the 1820s, lithography was replacing engraving and woodcuts. This was the process used by Joseph van Praet for the plates in his study of Colard Mansion published at Paris in 1829, and by Johann Wetter in his account of Gutenberg, published at Mainz in 1836.[43]

It was one thing to create facsimiles or replacements of one or two leaves. It was quite another to recreate a complete book. When in 1817 Rudolph Ackermann produced the series of lithographed copies of the Emperor Maximilian's prayer-book decorated by Dürer, it was an achievement and a labour justified by the exceptional interest of the original.[44] The labour was reflected in the high price. Such books raised expectations, in that it was seen to be possible to copy complete books. The multiplicity of processes for copying that were developed especially in France and Britain between the 1840s and the 1870s brought opportunities for publishers, booksellers and new classes of collectors. They also brought increased scholarly understanding of manuscripts and early printed books. With the application of photography, different manuscripts housed hundreds of miles apart could be compared in ways impossible in a world dependent on drawings and prints. The same was also true of printed books. For both, as J. W. Holtrop of the royal library in The Hague remarked in 1861, the existence of facsimiles meant that it was no longer essential to have sufficient wealth to travel in order to see distant books.[45] Bibliographical studies and the history of art

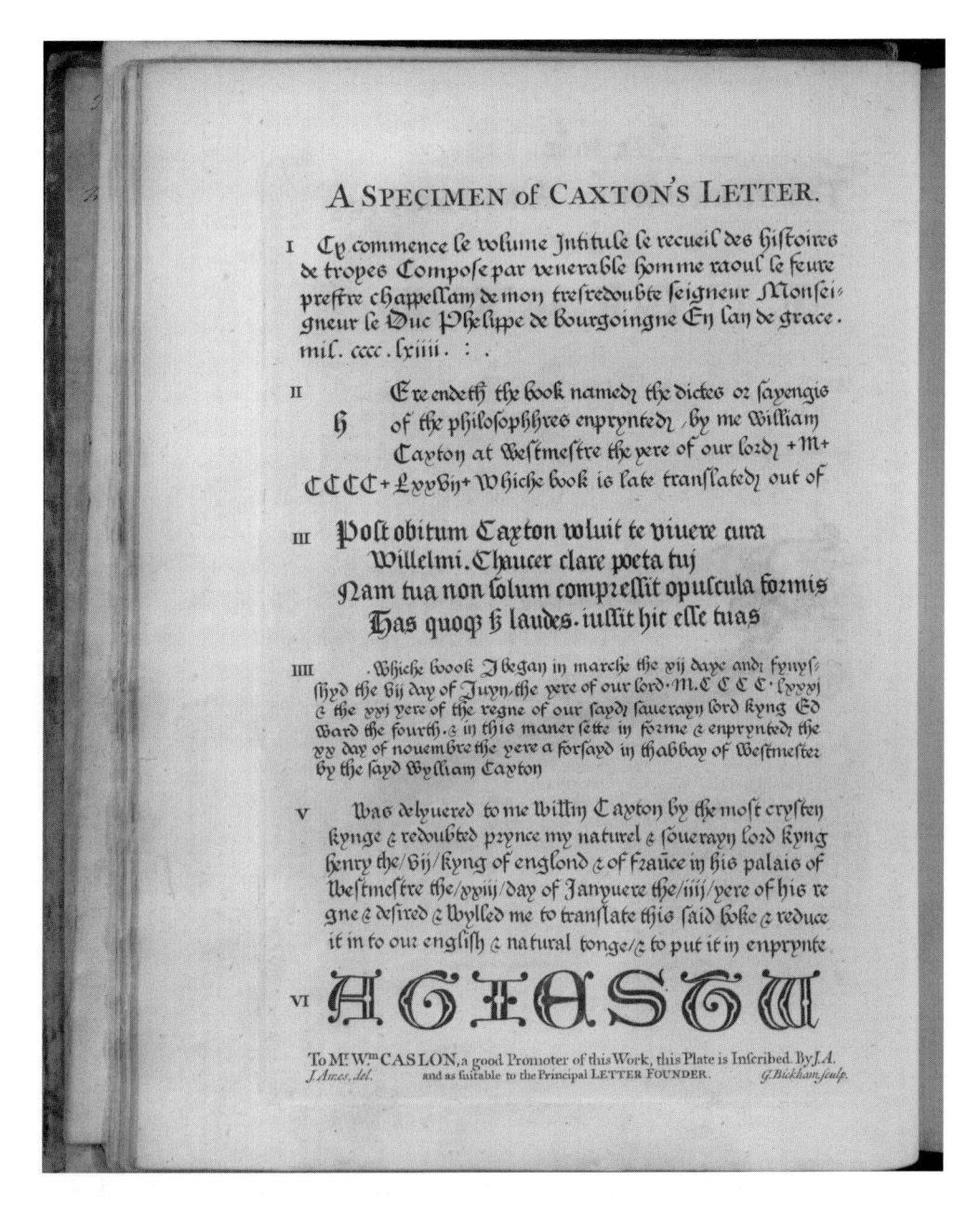

Figure 5.1 Joseph Ames, *Typographical antiquities* (London: Printed by W. Faden, and sold by J. Robinson, 1749). Engraved plate by George Bickham, with representations of Caxton's types. Trinity College, Cambridge V.14.15.

were not simply given a stimulus. As disciplines they were fundamentally transformed, in a world where comparison and analysis were now possible on a scale and with a confidence without precedent.

Apart from the difficulties facing anyone who wished to compare types precisely, all these inadequacies and ambiguities made early printed books seem even more antiquated and crude or, to use a word much loved by nineteenth-century bibliophiles, curious, than was sometimes the case. It was almost inevitable that early printers would thus be called 'rude', in the sense of unsophisticated or unskilled. It was thirty years, and another generation, before the bibliographical study of early printing took a new turn. More importantly, with the notable exceptions to whom we shall return, of Holtrop on the early printers of the Low Countries and Blades's work of the early 1860s on Caxton, few people possessed a sufficiently commodious and analytical memory to allow serious work on analysing the types of early printers. And outside the large libraries, few people had access to sufficient numbers of early printed books. Henry Bradshaw in Cambridge and Holtrop in The Hague, both benefiting from working in such libraries, were wholly exceptional in their analytical and observational abilities. Most people had to wait until the application of photography to the subject.

The process of photozincography, or photolithography, is discussed in the next chapter. It proved to be the best at combining accuracy, cheapness and respect for original objects, but it followed other efforts. At the Paris exhibition in 1839, Paul Dupont of Paris and his brother Auguste of Périgueux exhibited a process reported as *litho-typographie*, a means of reproducing copies of printed works. This held considerable potential for everyday commercial printing, since it offered a way of avoiding having to store large quantities of type metal either as standing type or as stereotype plates. It could also be used to reproduce old books. The report on the invention in the *Revue Française* provided no details of exactly what was involved, but it did emphasise the possibilities for reproduction: it included an example of a facsimile taken from an edition of Theocritus printed at Venice in 1539.[46] In commenting on the applications to old books, it added a slightly sardonic note to the effect that 'Cette découverte va sans doute dérouter un peu les bibliomanes.' In 1842 Dupont produced a facsimile of an early seventeenth-century book, *L'estat de l'église du Périgord*, by a process that he called *typo-lithographique*, later made familiar in England by Cowell's of Ipswich, who called it anastatic printing. The process was invasive – not to say destructive – of originals, since it involved damping the original with dilute acid, or sometimes soaking it for up to ten days in dilute nitric acid. The image side of the paper was then pressed firmly against a metal plate, so creating an etched reverse image which could be printed.[47]

In fusing art and industrial manufacture, the Great Exhibition of 1851 addressed a concept fundamental to printing ever since the fifteenth century. The sections pertaining to books were divided between two classes: one concentrating on industrial manufacture, the other on the plastic arts. As a result, remarks on bookbindings were divided between the two. Few printers in Britain were among the exhibitors, thanks to a misunderstanding that led local commissioners to indicate that printed books were inadmissible.[48] Some, nevertheless, crept in, and the jury (which included the London printer Charles Whittingham, now a senior figure in the trade) made a point of lauding much of this work. In fact, with 212 out of a total of 559 exhibits in their class of machinery, printed matter, bookbindings and paper-making, Britain was a far larger presence than any other country. But in a display where Tasmanian and Australian lithographic printing were better represented than America, which sent no books but only newspapers, the jury could only repeat its dismay at the unevenness of the class as a whole, 'for printing is a gift almost as necessary to man as speech, for the manifestation of his thoughts'.[49]

One theme that emerged was that of techniques for copying, and the reproduction of manuscripts or early printed matter. Among the French exhibits, the anastatic reproductions of early books by Paul Dupont called for especial mention, and were awarded a Prize medal.[50] The Comte Auguste de Bastard, of Paris, received Honourable Mention for his facsimiles of ancient manuscripts printed from woodblocks, and he might have been more generously rewarded had his work not been finished by hand. It ought, in the opinion of the jury, 'not to have been admitted'.[51] The London lithographer Rudolph Appel was commended for his development of a process that used a special ink to apply images to zinc, rather than stone. 'The advantages of such mechanical means of multiplying rare and costly prints are too obvious to need remark', noted the jury.[52]

John Harris

Of all the facsimilists who made tracings from early books in England and on the continent in the mid-nineteenth century, none had a higher reputation than John Harris (1791–1873).[53] He came from a family of artists, and by 1820 he had established a growing reputation for his outstanding ability at making traced copies to make good imperfect copies of early printed books. By the 1840s, his work was to be found on the shelves of almost any major collector, and booksellers relied on his exceptional skills to perfect copies that would otherwise have remained unsightly in their incompleteness. For booksellers and collectors alike, his facsimiles replacing lost leaves were the counterparts of new bindings that further made worn books good. For the British Museum, where he was employed to make substitute pages, his skills were alarming in their invisibility, so much so that he was required by the Trustees to sign his work.[54] When in 1855 the New York book collector James Lenox wished to have some of his recent purchases of early Bibles improved, he wrote to his bookseller Henry Stevens in London that they were to be bound 'in Morocco, in the last style of Henry VIII'. They were to be 'original and generous leaves as far as possible', and he specified that Harris was to prepare the missing title-pages.[55]

The best account of his methods is in his own words, provided for the Great Exhibition in 1851:

> In the history of mankind there are few things so remarkable, as that the press and the easel have been the means of producing works of art which have most conspicuously tended to the civilization of man and the unity of nations. The avidity with which these productions are sought after, up to the present time, is fully proved by the process given either for early printed books or ancient paintings, of which the former especially are often imperfect. From this latter circumstance the collector has been induced to seek the means of having ancient and valuable works in typography and painting completed by fac-similes, and thus restoring to the present generation works which most probably in a few more years would have been buried in oblivion.
>
> It was about the year 1815 that I was first employed by the late Mr. John Whittaker, of Westminster, an eminent bookbinder at that period; and I believe the idea of having ancient books of the early printers, &c., perfected by fac-similes, was first suggested to him by the late Earl Spencer, for whom many books were so done; and numerous specimens are preserved of some of the rarest productions of the press in the library at Althorpe. Specimens are also to be seen in the King's Library, which were done in the lifetime of His Majesty King George III., the art of imitation by fac-simile being patronized by him, also by the late Earl Fitzwilliam, the Hon. Thomas Grenville, and many others. I continued to work for Mr. Whittaker till about 1820, when I was sent for by Lord Spencer, for whom I completed a Pentateuch in Hebrew and Chaldee, and several other works; also I was employed by the late Mr. Grenville, in whose library are numerous specimens of various works completed by me, as there are also in the libraries of many other noblemen and gentlemen by whom I have been employed during the last 30 years. It now only remains to give a brief sketch of the process employed. Formerly I made an accurate tracing from the original leaf, and afterwards retraced it on to the inlaid leaf by

means of a paper blacked on one side; this produced an outline lettered page, which, by being gone over carefully and imitating the original, produced the desired leaf. This process was found to take up much time, and was consequently expensive, but it was the method I adopted when I was employed by Mr. Whittaker; and he, to carry out the deception still further, had two sets of tools cut of the large and small letters generally used by Caxton, with which he has often been at the trouble to go over the pages after my work was done, to give the appearance of the indentation of the type. The process afterwards adopted by me was to make the tracing in a soft ink, to transfer the same to a thin paper, and to re-transfer on to the intended leaf: by this means I saved one-third, or one tracing of the work, which was a great saving both in time and expense. I pursued this process for some years; but I have within the last 10 or 12 years had recourse to lithography, producing the tracing on to the stone, and finishing up the letters on the same: this has been beneficial, particularly when more than one copy was wanted; but I occasionally find even this process irksome and uncertain, and frequently at this present time have recourse to my own, or the second method described, and execute fac-similes by manuscript process. I have thus endeavoured to give a concise and clear statement of the method employed in producing fac-similes. With respect to early printing, the specimens produced by me are entirely done by hand, and are specimens of a style now little in use in water-colour painting.[56]

By his mid-sixties, Harris was blind. His stock of facsimiles was his main asset, and in August 1857 this was auctioned by Sotheby & Wilkinson without reserves. 'It is to be hoped, for Mr. Harris' sake,' wrote the author of the catalogue, 'that the collectors of books and engravings, as well as whatever is curious in art, will not fail to secure specimens of the extraordinary skill of a man who leaves us without any one to supply his place.'[57]

Both the trade and private buyers recognised the opportunity, and sought to acquire work of a standard that they did not expect to see surpassed. Among the booksellers, Toovey paid £3.12s for a facsimile of the title-page of the 1535 Coverdale Bible, and £2.12s for one of the 'earliest specimens of printing with moveable Types', an indulgence issued by Pope Nicholas V in 1455. Though Harris had been as well known for his work with foreign books of the fifteenth and sixteenth centuries, most of the sheets were from English books. Naturally, they were of title-leaves or other leaves near the beginnings and ends of volumes, where the demand for replacements was greatest. Most facsimiles went for a few shillings, their value depending usually on the value of the books into which they could be inserted. Some of the best early books from the stock of the bookseller Henry Stevens in the main part of the sale offered a context for prices. A copy of the Coverdale Bible (lot 223) was bought by Lilly for £190. The map, all the preliminary leaves and eleven other leaves had all been supplied by Harris. But according to the sale catalogue there was only one copy anywhere still with its original title-page, in the library of Lord Leicester,[58] and the most recent authority on early English printed Bibles, Lea Wilson, was said to have offered £100 to anyone who could find him another. Chaucer's *Canterbury tales* (Pynson, c. 1490) was rather cheaper, at £51, with three – only – of its missing leaves by Harris. It sold to the same buyer who bought the Caxton *Polychronicon* (1482) for £70.

In the wake of Harris

In all this, it is striking that there was no suggestion that Harris's copies were forgeries. Like his slightly younger contemporary in Paris, the Polish-born Adam Pilinski (1810–87), he was offering a service – to the British Museum amongst others, as Pilinski did to the Bibliothèque Nationale. Pilinski likewise thought of himself as an artist, and he had a fine reputation in that respect. By the end of his life his name was also more readily visible, on the facsimile series *Monuments de la Xylographie Française du XV siècle* (Paris, 1882–3), where he was both copyist and publisher. It was the public *comble* of his career.[59]

Though auctioneers and booksellers lamented the passing of Harris's skills, and there were buyers at his sale, the book trade was on the verge of a technological change that was to make the hand-traced facsimile redundant. For a while his son, also called John Harris, followed him;[60] but it was a career with no future. Rightly, Harris regarded himself as an artist. His allusion to the techniques of water-colour painting, and his mention of the press and the easel in neighbourly influence, made clear his own assessment of himself. In his use of lithography he looked to the future. Appel's work with zinc plates did the same. Though both men concentrated on single leaves (Harris for books and Appel for prints), there was no technical reason other than cost as to why their techniques should not be applied more widely. This was part of the point of the note by the 1851 jurors of Appel's work being 'too obvious to need remark'.

Harris did not die until 1873. In September 1858, just over a year after the sale, John Payne Collier issued forty copies of a facsimile of one of two extant copies of the 1603 quarto of *Hamlet*. It was lithographed after tracings made from the Duke of Devonshire's copy. In the following summer, the 1604 quarto followed, also in forty copies. The choice of book – a short text, one of the best known works in English literature, and of demonstrable absolute rarity – reflected some of the preoccupations of those involved. No doubt it also helped that the books were out of reach to most people, in a private library. Collier was well in the public eye. He had published his edition of Shakespeare in 1842–4, and had been given almost free rein in the Chatsworth library. More recently, his sensational announcement in January 1852 of a copy of the Second Folio, with hundreds of textual emendations, had met a mixed reception: there were many prepared to scoff. But when in January 1853 he published his *Notes and emendations to the text of Shakespeare's plays*, there were plenty of ready customers, and a new edition was quickly called for.[61] Collier's name was not on the Devonshire reprints, though he wrote in presentation copies.

As facsimiles, the Devonshire Hamlets had several faults. In the originals, the block depicting the device of Nicholas Ling, one of the publishing booksellers, had been the same in both. In the facsimiles it appeared slightly larger in 1603 than in 1604. Textually, the hand-tracing had resulted in some minor textual changes. Missing running heads, cut off by the binder, had been restored. Some of these faults were mistakes in tracings; the restored running heads were matters of taste and judgement. What appeared to be a facsimile was in fact a recreation for a modern audience seeking antiquarian succour. So, too, was the more ambitious series issued by James Orchard Halliwell and Edmund William Ashbee, who published forty-seven facsimiles of the quartos between 1861 and 1871. Like Collier's, their editions were strictly limited, to fifty copies.[62] And, like Collier, they depended on hand-tracings. At 5 guineas each, they were very expensive. Ashbee was a determined provider of facsimiles. The occasionally published facsimiles of Kemp's *Nine day's wonder*, *Thersytes*, *Tarlton's jests* and others, all privately published, cost about 13 shillings each. His separate series of Occasional Fac-simile Reprints opened in 1868 with a traced facsimile of *Bartholomew Faire* (1641), priced at 3 shillings for just six pages of text. Printings of these and others were limited to a hundred copies of each: the project ended in 1872, with a thirty-sixth pamphlet, the rather more substantial *Historia histrionica: an historical account of the English stage* (1699) priced at 9 shillings for 37 pages.

At their best, tracings could achieve remarkable results. Harris had made them his career, and had deceived knowledgeable connoisseurs. In 1858, the year after the sale of Harris's remaining work, the printer William Blades issued a facsimile of a short book printed by Caxton, *The governayle of health*, after an original copy in the Earl of Dysart's collection. Just fifty-five copies were printed. The text was printed in type facsimile with a new casting of type copied from Caxton's original, but the frontispiece was after a tracing by G. I. F. Tupper, a facsimilist scarcely less skilled than Harris.[63] As a professional printer, Blades had more than ordinary interest in the materials he was using:

> An Effort has been made by the Use of Types very similar to those employed by Caxton, to give this Reprint something of the Appearance of the Original. To effect this still further, the Types were cast expressly in Pewter, which from its Softness, yields an Impression resembling more the Productions of the early Printers, than could be obtained from a harder Material ... Not only has the Orthography been strictly adhered to, but it is printed Page for Page, Line for Line, and Word for Word, with all the Peculiarities and Variations of contracted and double Letters.[64]

With his capitalised nouns, Blades was harking back to out-moded customs by printers in setting copy. But he had no illusions. While the new type could be close to the original, it could not reproduce it with absolute fidelity. It was 'very similar'. For the facsimile itself he used handmade paper, in sharp contrast to that employed in the rest of the volume. Yet the edition could only approximate the 'appearance' of the original. These were distinctions that were all the more pertinent in the brief interval between the end of Harris's career and the beginning of facsimiles based on photography. In 1861–3, Blades again employed Tupper for the representations of type in his magisterial biography of Caxton, the first work to subject his work to serious typographical analysis.[65]

The most obvious disadvantage of tracing was that it was time-consuming of highly skilled labour, and therefore expensive. But that did not discourage Francis Fry, of Bristol, from launching a series of entire books. His passion was the English Bible, and he focussed his attention on works either concerning, or representative of, the earliest printed translations. He began ambitiously in 1862, with the first edition of Tyndale's translation of the New Testament, using the then only-known near-perfect copy in the Baptist College at Bristol. His claims were familiar: 'a faithful representation of the original; and will be valued not only as a Version, but as shewing the state of the English language, the style of the printing, the orthography (which is very irregular), the punctuation, the divisions of the words at the ends of lines (even to a letter), and the contractions used'. Here, too, the paper had been carefully chosen:

> The paper on which this Testament is printed has been expressly manufactured to imitate the colour and appearance of the original. It is *hand-made*, the fine and cross wires being placed in the paper-maker's mould so as to produce the same wire marks as appear in the paper used by Schoeffer. The large paper copies are printed on the same paper, made thicker for the purpose.[66]

Some copies were printed on old paper, and a few on vellum. For those who wished, copies could be illuminated after the colouring in the original. In an introduction, Fry summarised the life of Tyndale, and advanced his reasons for attributing the printing of the book to Peter Schoeffer, at Worms. He added drawings of the watermarks, and a specimen coloured leaf so that some idea could be gained of the appearance of the original. As a textual document, and as a re-presentation of a sixteenth-century book, it had many merits, practical and bibliophilic. But it was no facsimile in the sense that it accurately represented the original. Closer examination of the tracings of the type reveals many inconsistencies and assumptions about sixteenth-century type forms: the tracings were adequate for their purpose, but they did not live up to the accuracy Fry suggested. The water-colour illuminations that open the principal books were poorly translated into black and white line, and the black and white version of the facsimile did not attempt to reproduce the rubrication of the original. Fry's insistence on paper and authenticity could still only produce an interpretation limited by human skill and cash investment.

The small editions of most of these reprints reflected reality: demand for such productions was small. If Collier's facsimiles of *Hamlet* from the Devonshire library were for a coterie audience, a scattering of bibliophiles, scholars and fortunate libraries, the more ambitious selection of texts by Ashbee showed how tiny the market for even the rarest seventeenth-century pamphlets really was. The originals of such publications might fetch high prices at auction, but there was little general interest for over-priced and artificially rare reproductions. The first of Ashbee's series of Occasional Facsimile Reprints were on sale through John Tuckett – a bookseller opposite the British Museum specialising in antiquarian and heraldic books – and were marketed separately. But with the seventh in the series, published only the year after the first had appeared, change was necessary. In an effort to ensure a continuing income, purchasers were limited to subscribers. When the series halted in 1872, there were still copies left over to be bound up and offered in complete sets. As a publishing venture it does not appear to have been a financial success. It was only with the series of Shakespeare quartos in facsimile, edited by F.J. Furnivall and prepared from photographs by William Griggs – 'for 13 years photo-lithographer to the India Office' – and Charles Praetorius that there was any wider interest in such projects. Where Halliwell had charged 5 guineas each, Griggs charged just 6 shillings to subscribers, and provided brief introductions as well.

While some differences between original and modern surrogates were, despite assurances, in practice unavoidable, on occasion publishers behaved as if their readers would appreciate very little of what was being offered. One of the most enthusiastic publishers of facsimile reprints of all kinds was Elliot Stock, in Paternoster Row. As we shall see, the firm issued a number of type facsimiles of well-known English books.[67] The notion of type facsimiles of much earlier books was well established: we have already noted its origins in the late seventeenth century. Before turning to the application of photography in large-scale facsimile-making, it is appropriate to allude briefly to the assumptions and hopes of type-founders and printers even while a battle was being fought between old and new methods of more faithful facsimile-making.

Until about 1840, the practice in preparing type facsimiles was to use type drawn from existing stock. While this restricted the choice of printers, it avoided the need for investment in re-cutting punches, making new matrices and casting new type. There was a sufficiency of old cases of type available. But at about that date a new mood set in. It was to be seen at its most acute in a book celebrating the anniversary of Gutenberg. In 1840 Eugène Duverger's *Histoire de l'invention de l'imprimerie par les monuments* was printed in Paris, and published also in Strasbourg by Treuttel & Würtz. The celebratory tone of what was little more than an album was established by the limited number of copies printed, including 150 with polychrome colouring. Historical significance was incidental, though the bibliophile Charles Nodier for one was full of admiration for the way in which Duverger led his readers through the processes of printing.[68] Mainly a collection of reproductions from early books, it has gained some notoriety thanks to the series of fictitious letters claiming to have been written by Gutenberg and full of detail about printing.[69] More significantly, it included facsimile resettings of an early edition of Donatus, one of the earliest of all printed books, and of the 36-line Bible. These resettings were not in existing type approximating the original, but in newly cut copies by Charles Desriez, cast by Charles Mesnager. By using two qualities of paper, a softer and darker one for the Donatus, the printers were able to show off Desriez' considerable achievement, though they could not hide the fact that his types – both that for the 36-line Bible and the smaller quantity cast in imitation of B-42 – were of different sets, or widths, from the originals.[70]

This chapter began in the eighteenth century with questions of reproduction having little obviously to do with books. It has encompassed three-dimensional copying in plaster and in metal. It ends with techniques of two-dimensional copying that had by the third quarter of the nineteenth century been partially overtaken by photography. These various techniques had a common purpose: to reproduce and to preserve the past.

Some of them were expensive; others were startlingly cheap. While some of them (such as plaster casts, or traced copies) had long histories reaching back even to classical times, in the eighteenth and nineteenth centuries they became vastly more familiar to ever-increasing numbers of people, by no means all of whom accounted themselves either collectors or connoisseurs. They made possible a new commonwealth of learning. It was by such substitutions, of more or less authority and of more or less verisimilitude, that knowledge of the past was not only made accessible. They also provided a physical framework of knowledge within which each person, with or without access to early books, could assemble his or her own historical understanding. In the next chapter we turn to a still greater change, with the advent of photography.

6 | The arrival of photography

So far, apart from some brief remarks on the South Kensington Museum, we have been principally concerned with copies of books made by hand, usually as tracings, and with type facsimiles. It is now necessary to retrace our steps for a few years, and consider the ways in which photography was gradually brought to bear on the copying and preservation of early books. This work, at first essentially intended to meet demand for study, became confused in some public discussions with the application of electrotypes for printing engraved plates in numbers far beyond what had previously been possible. To copy in this latter way was to reduce the price – and the value – of what had been created at considerable expense. Such an issue did not arise with photography. No connoisseur of early engravings would consider a photograph, however good, an adequate substitute for an original.

The changes in practice and taste did not happen in an instant. Public and scholarly interest in type facsimiles persisted, and indeed was to remain a serious option for some kinds of books even in the twentieth century.[1] For the moment, interest centred on a debate between those who trusted traced facsimiles printed by lithography, and those who were attracted by the new process of photozincography. Each had its industrious advocates, and competition between the two for public support was not settled for many years. Photographs of complete printed books were unusual; one exception was a series of eight photographs of woodcuts, published at Augsburg in 1873.[2] Pen tracings continued to be much more widely employed. As late as 1881, the Holbein Society was to publish a facsimile of an edition of the the blockbook *Ars moriendi* in the British Museum, introduced by George Bullen, Keeper of Printed Books. It had been bought at the Weigel sale in 1872 for the exceptionally high price of £1,072.10s., and it may be confidently supposed that considerable thought was given to the manner in which it should be shared with the public. The preferred method was pen facsimile:

> As a specimen of *fac-simile* art it is a perfect marvel, and shows at once the superiority of this kind of reproduction to the photographic process; as any one may see by comparing it with the photographic reproduction of the present work, published by Weigel himself in 1869.[3]

The Society itself was not averse to photolithography. In 1871, with some difficulty thanks to the original, it had published a facsimile of Alciati's *Emblemata* by this method. But by 1881 pen facsimiles were distinctly old-fashioned. They had many qualities that made them especially useful for work where some interpretation of a damaged original was necessary; but thanks partly to increasing wage levels they had become expensive to produce, and photography seemed to offer a much better quality of reproduction.

Photolithography and photozincography, the two processes differing in little more than that one employed stone for the printing surface and the other employed zinc, were not suitable for every kind of work. The effect could appear crude. It was partly for this reason that Jean Philibert Berjeau preferred tracings, which he made himself.[4] His lithographed facsimiles of editions from the British Museum of the *Biblia pauperum* (1859) and of the *Canticum canticorum* (1860) were followed by the *Speculum humanae salvationis* (1862), which he dated to about 1435. Berjeau was a journalist exiled in London after vigorously opposing Louis-Napoleon's claim to rule France, and he became a valued writer on bibliographical matters – 'almost the first in this country to popularize bibliography', in the words of his obituary. Not everyone approved of his interpretations of the earliest Dutch printing, but the two men who knew most about the subject, J. W. Holtrop in The Hague and Henry Bradshaw in Cambridge, seem to have preferred not to offend a person who was so obviously amiable and eager to promote their subject.[5] The small numbers printed of his facsimiles[6] meant that they had little influence in themselves on the wider public, but they presaged a new development in the ways that early printed books were presented and explained. In founding a succession of periodicals devoted more or less to early printed books, Berjeau identified a new kind of market. *Le Bibliomane* appeared briefly in 1861, and was little more than a promotional publication. It was followed in August that year by another French title, *Le Bibliophile Illustré*, more ambitiously produced and heavily illustrated with woodcut facsimiles of early illustrations and typefaces. This in turn gave way to a further short-lived monthly *Le Bibliophile* in 1863. English speakers were eventually provided with Elliot Stock's publication *The Bookworm*, a mixture of news, gossip, reviews and historical articles and that enjoyed a much wider circulation (Fig. 6.1).

Berjeau's example in publishing his facsimiles was of only limited comfort to J. W. Holtrop as he contemplated the method he should use for the long series of facsimiles of pages to be included in his study of early Low Countries presses, *Monuments typographiques des Pays-Bas au quinzième siècle*. This was published in parts between 1856 and 1868, and the plates

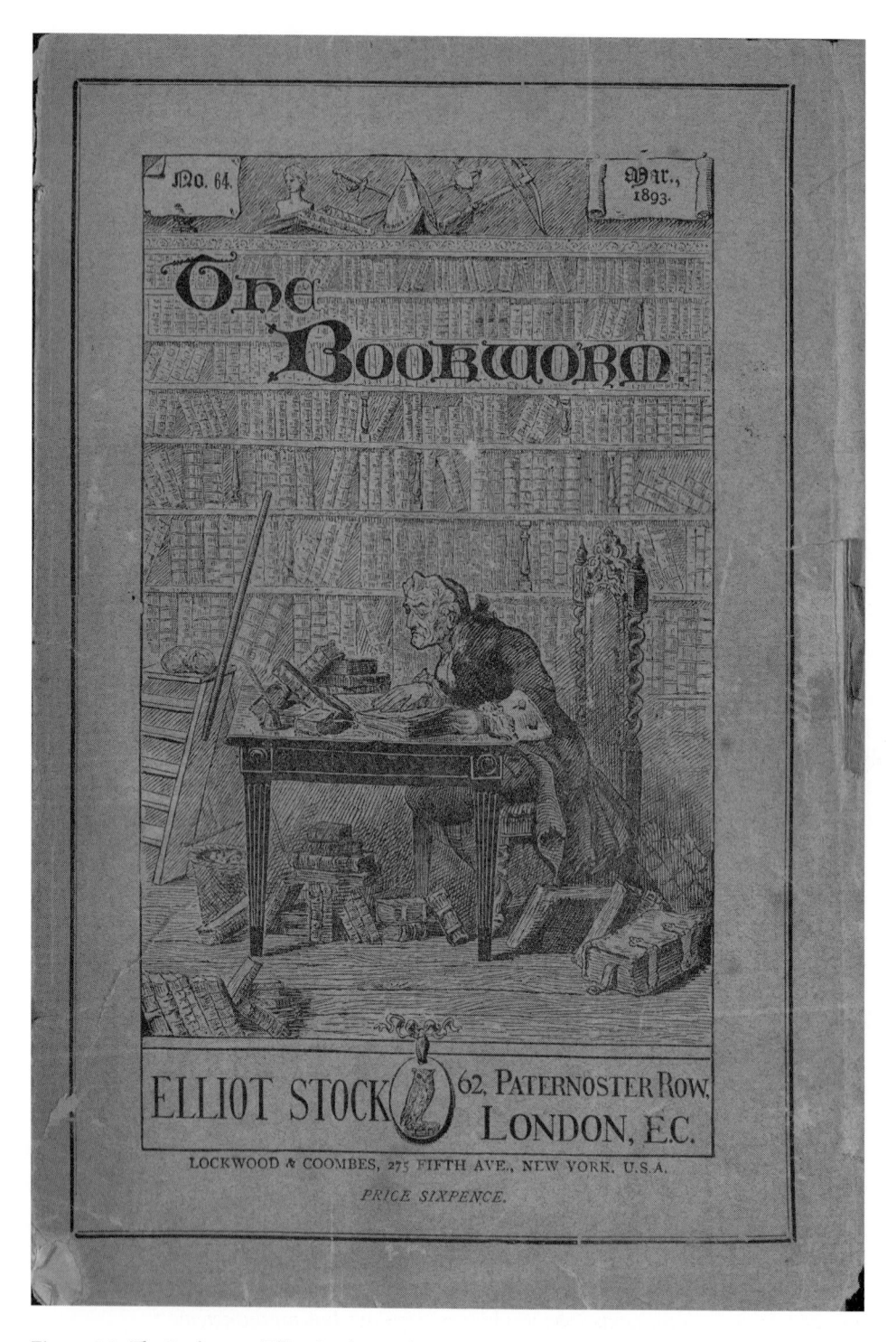

Figure 6.1 *The Bookworm* (Elliot Stock, 1893).

(lithographed by E. Spanier in The Hague) were to remain the standard reference for a century.[7] Holtrop used the same printer for a facsimile of a well-known and unique edition of the *Confessionale* in the Museum Meermanno-Westreenianum in 1861.[8] While a process based on handwork rather than the camera may seem to be at a disadvantage, and Holtrop himself seems to have had qualms as his own project proceeded and he saw other methods in use,[9] in fact the quality of Holtrop's plates and of Tupper's rather better copies of early English printing in Blades's study of Caxton, published in 1861–3, proved to be vindication of a method that was only displaced when photography itself offered both a cheap method of recording complicated matter and, most importantly, the method of their reproduction carried an assurance of longevity.

The beginnings of photography

The invention and development of photography involved many of the same tensions, but its value lay in its stronger claims to reproductive quality, of verisimilitude. Lithography brought a quiet revolution. Photography brought one that was much more obviously dramatic, as scientific curiosity merged with public enthusiasm. In 1844–6, W. H. Fox Talbot explored different kinds of subject matter in his *Pencil of nature*, but public attention at first focussed mainly on two: the human form and landscape. It was perhaps no accident that these were also the most frequent topics addressed by artists. The reproductive potential of photography was exploited rather more slowly, though it is probable that the high cost of producing prints in quantity may have discouraged art historians from using them in their publications, even as they used them in their private research.[10] Sir Frederic Madden and others in England, Léopold Delisle in Paris, and Theodor von Sickel in Vienna were among the many who applauded and used the new methods in their publications.[11] By the time that Edward Maunde Thompson, Principal Librarian of the British Museum, wrote his *Handbook of Greek and Latin palaeography* (1893) he was merely reporting what was by then generally acknowledged: that the existence of facsimiles brought together what previously had been possible only by travel,

And more than this: these facsimiles enable us to compare, side by side, specimens from manuscripts which lie scattered in the different libraries of Europe, and which never could have been brought together. There is no longer any lack of material for the ready attainment of palaeographical knowledge.[12]

In 1894 the art historian Emile Mâle remarked the same for his own field:

L'histoire de l'art, qui était jusque-là la passion de quelques curieux, n'est devenue une science que depuis que la photographie existe ... La photographie a permis de comparer, c'est à dire de faire une science.[13]

Even while the second quarter of the nineteenth century was assimilating the principles of electrotyping and skilled hand-copying, it was simultaneously discovering how the world could be recorded two-dimensionally with the help of the sun.[14] Niépce had succeeded in making a heliographic copy of an engraving in 1822, and within a few years succeeded in etching the image onto a metal plate, from which it could be printed. But he died in 1833, four years after entering into partnership with Louis Daguerre; and though he brought his work to England, it aroused no interest. Unlike the retiring Niépce, Daguerre was a consummate publicist, and made full use of the press to share his work with others.[15] In January 1839, Talbot read a paper on photogenic drawing to the Royal Society, and later in the year he sent out a pamphlet to friends and others interested.[16] Daguerre did more. Between September and December that year several editions of pamphlets by him appeared in London, some said to have been published by order of the French government.[17] He saw his own invention of a quicker and more effective process take Paris and London by storm, so much so that for several years the word daguerreotype became applied to photographic processes having nothing to do with his invention. But despite its popularity, it was limited in that the images were on metal, and therefore could not be repeated. By 1835, Talbot had succeeded independently in creating negatives on paper. Both his experiments and those of Niépce included copies of engravings.

In January 1839, Talbot was prophetic: 'I propose to employ this for the purpose more particularly of multiplying at small expense copies of such rare or unique engravings as it would not be worthwhile to re-engrave, from the limited demand for them.'[18] So he encapsulated two principles that, three decades later, were to absorb those making facsimiles of printed books: replication and cheapness. He followed this with a presentation at the British Association in summer 1839, and another at Edinburgh in the following winter. Photogenic drawing, for which apparatus was soon on sale to the public, was only one small part of the development of photography. But whether in just this, or in the development of preserving images of three-dimensional subjects (landscapes, objects or people), the conception of the copy had been transformed. Even more fundamentally, these few years had witnessed the kindling of popular enthusiasm for an idea that was to take fire.[19]

Photography and books

How did all this affect the study and appreciation of old books – printed books as well as manuscripts?

Among the assortment of subjects chosen to exhibit the range of possibilities with his equipment, Talbot included images of both a lithograph and an early printed book in *The pencil of nature* (1844–6). 'All kinds of engravings may be copied by photographic means; and this application of the art is a very important one, not only as producing in general nearly fac-simile copies, but because it enables us at pleasure to alter the scale, and to make the copies as much larger or smaller than the originals we may desire.'[20] The lithograph, Boilly's well-known 'Réunion de trente-cinq têtes diverses', was reduced; but the printed book, a page from a fifteenth-century edition of early English statutes, was printed same-size, by what Talbot called 'super-position'.[21] Though he was naturally determined in his search for possible applications (he had quickly seen the possibilities of using photography as a medium for typesetting, a process that was not to be applied in the commercial world until after the Second World War),[22] his remark on the nineteenth-century image of the printed page presaged not just a new technique but a wholesale change in attitude. 'To the Antiquarian this application of the photographic art seems destined to be of great advantage.'[23] But compared with the excitement that had greeted the development of the earliest photographs in the 1830s, the application was slow. It was only in 1856 that the British Museum published photographs by Roger Fenton of pages from the Codex Alexandrinus. This was a laborious album to produce, containing twenty-two salt prints from collodion negatives, a process recently developed and that allowed particularly high resolution of detail. For the Codex Alexandrinus, the impetus came both from theologians and from the Keeper of Manuscripts at the Museum, Sir Frederic Madden. It was not least a question of conservation:

The fragile state of the vellum leaves containing these Epistles, the damage done to them by the injudicious use of galls, and the unavoidable effects of time, which since the edition of Junius [1633] has left its traces on the manuscript, have all combined to render it very desirable to secure so interesting a relic of the earliest Christian antiquity from the risk of further injury or of future accident.[24]

Three years later, a much reduced photograph of a manuscript from Trinity College, Cambridge was included in F. H. Scrivener's *Exact transcript of the Codex Augiensis*, this time an ordinary commercial proposition. The ability of the camera to capture works of art – whether pictures, manuscripts or printed books – transformed their study, enabling much more accurate comparisons than had been possible hitherto. It also had a further application. The first extended photographic facsimiles of later manuscripts appeared in the early 1860s. First of all seems to have been a series of sixteen photographs of a manuscript in Turin by Francesco Filelfo on rhetoric, written in 1467 and reproduced as the *Manuscrit Sforza*. The reproduction was the work of Camille Silvy, 'libraire photographique' in London in 1860. Silvy's preface explained the advantages of photography for such purposes, and also for restoration.[25] Then in 1862 the early sixteenth-century Flemish Grimani breviary was photographed and published by Antonio Perini in Venice, with commentaries in Italian and French; the market for facsimiles of manuscripts was always to be international. Perini had already won medals at exhibitions in Paris and Brussels, and had become a trusted photographer in the Venetian archives. His 110 albumen prints were laid down on thick card, and a commentary was provided in an accompanying volume – a division that was also to be familiar in such productions a century and a half later. These photographs were not just for art historians. They had, again, a further purpose of conservation. As Perini explained, a photographic selection might also reduce demand:

L'espérance que cette reproduction, devenue vraiment nécessaire depuis que l'existence du Bréviaire Grimani s'est en quelques années répandue partout, dispensera les artistes, les antiquaires et les hommes de goût qu'attire maintenant à la Bibliothèque st. Marc la renommée du manuscrit, et préservera cet inestimable bijou de visites qui lui deviendraient inévitablement dommageables. N'oublions pas, en effet, que si ce splendide volume, que l'on croirait exécuté d'hier, est parvenu sain et sauf jusqu'à nous, dans toute la fraîcheur de ses pages et de sa reliure, c'est qu'il a été gardé par nos devanciers avec la plus jalouse surveillance.[26]

It was a necessary precaution. In 1861 Baedeker published the first edition of the German version of their guide to northern Italy; an English version appeared in 1868. Murray's *Handbook* had been established as the guide for English speakers since 1842.[27] The Grimani breviary was a stopping point for casual and serious tourists alike. It was in such danger that the authorities eventually had to revise the arrangements dating from more relaxed and less threatening days:

The Library of San Marco, Venice, has a manuscript, glorious with illuminations, which may fairly lay claim to the title of the most beautifully illustrated book in the world. Very few persons ever look upon it, because its examination is so hedged about by red tape that it is easier to see the Grand Llama of Tibet than this picture book, this edition de grand luxe, which is, after all, only a breviary for prayers…

While looking at this wonderful book a visitor has to stand four feet off. The attendant, when he turns the pages, averts his face. Guards are present to see that no surreptitious Kodak clicks during the interview.[28]

In this context, there was no need to worry at the concerns expressed by Baudelaire in reviewing the Paris Salon of 1859: that the camera was being used to the disadvantage of artistic creation. But Baudelaire was clear about photography in one respect:

It is time, then, for it to return to its true duty, which is to be the servant of the sciences and arts – but the very humble servant, like printing or shorthand, which have neither created nor supplemented literature ... Let it rescue from oblivion those tumbling ruins, those books, prints and manuscripts which time is devouring, precious things whose form is dissolving and which demand a place in the archives of our memory – it will be thanked and applauded.[29]

The full reproduction in 1875 of the ninth-century Utrecht Psalter was a further milestone that heralded a new approach to the study of manuscripts not simply according to a small selection of images, but in their entirety. The manuscript, with its close links to English art, was of as much interest to theologians as to art historians, circumstances that encouraged its publication in full.[30] Controversy over the Athanasian Creed, of which the Psalter provided a well-dated early example, and the appropriateness or otherwise of including it in the Church of England liturgy, ensured wide general discussion: the letters column of *The Times* returned repeatedly to it in 1872–3.[31] The manuscript invited reproduction if only on the grounds of public interest, but the tonal range of its writing and illustration made it unsuitable for the cheaper reproduction processes. Photography, on the other hand, provided good detailed pictures, and it promised a long-lived image. In its range of tonal qualities it was also vastly superior to the facsimiles of printed books that were available at the time.[32] It marked a departure that leads directly to modern times.

Of obvious use in the reproduction of works of art, photography was applied to all manner of educational purposes. It became almost as familiar for this as it was for the cheap portraiture that became an essential feature of middle-class families. The Arundel Society pioneered a market beyond a privileged few when in 1856 it published a lecture by Matthew Digby Wyatt on ivory sculpture, and added nine albumen prints as illustrations.[33] With the development of the South Kensington Museum's loan collection, photographs came into their own as a medium for sharing knowledge with audiences for whom the photographically illustrated book was too expensive. Between 1870 and 1874, a total of 1,408 loans were made to schools of art. Subjects ranged from Indian architecture to musical instruments. These loans were supported by a further programme, the publication between 1868 and 1871 of a series of photographic albums ranging, again, across most of the Museum's interests.[34] Both projects were notable for not including illuminated manuscripts, quite apart from early printed books; this was notwithstanding the fact that both featured in the Museum's own collections. But the projects enforced what had by the end of the 1860s become familiar: the use of photography for representation of inanimate objects.

The development of the South Kensington programme coincided almost exactly with the parallel popularisation of photography as an aid in the cheap facsimile reproduction of printed books in the wake of the development of photozincography and photolithogaphy, to which we now turn. The advent of photography, and more particularly its application to lithographic printing, heralded a fresh approach. The marrying of the two brought new possibilities, and for the first time it brought the cost of reasonably accurate reproductions (as distinct from copies) within the range of a public consisting of much more than a *côterie* of wealthy bibliophiles. It was not an immediate revolution. For many years the two processes were developed – and marketed – independently. Nor did their combination in itself ensure low prices for customers. Moreover, and quite apart from pricing, the markets for these new kinds of reproductions had to be created, nurtured, educated and only then exploited.

Photozincography and photolithography

Whatever the very considerable skills that were applied to the making of facsimiles, whether single specimens such as those made by pen, by Harris and a few others, or for multiple reproduction as lithographed tracings, or for separately printed photographs mounted in books, it remained that all were expensive to create. The process of hand-copying was inevitably slow. It was also a rare skill:

Only those who have endeavoured to obtain a real facsimile, – one which, for identity of types and exactness of measurement will bear the closest examination by the side of the original, – know the excessive difficulty of procuring an Artist clever and patient enough to execute the tracing, and workmen skilful enough to print it, without clogging or some worse distortion.[35]

When William Blades wrote this in the preface to his study of Caxton in 1861, he had copper engravings and woodcuts in mind, as well as his preferred method of lithographed tracings.

There is no suggestion either here or elsewhere in his book that Blades was aware of a revolution that was developing even as he wrote. In France,

England and Australia, several people were working at the same time to link photography with lithography. By far the most self-promotional was Colonel Henry James of the Royal Engineers, Director of the Ordnance Survey. In this position, supported by a publicly financed staff, he was ideally placed to ensure the largest possible and most influential audience. He was able to claim that large sums of public money would be saved. He automatically had the ear of Parliament in the annual reports that he was obliged to make. He gained the interest of the Chancellor of the Exchequer, William Gladstone. And he had ample printing resources at his disposal. Parliament first heard formally about the experiments that had been conducted under his aegis in the Topographical Department of the War Office when it received James's annual report for the year ending December 1859. He had already been working to save money in the long task of reducing maps from larger to smaller scales, and after explaining the principles of how the photographic process had been improved, he moved to his next section:

We have also tried a method, which is still more valuable, and by which the reduced print is in a state to be at once transferred to stone or zinc, from which any number of copies can be taken, as in ordinary lithographic or zincographic printing, or for transfer to the waxed surface of the copper plates.

After explaining the process, he continued,

This new method of printing from a negative is extremely simple and inexpensive, and promises to be of great use to us ... From the perfect manner in which we are able to transfer the impressions to zinc, we can, if required, print any number of faithful copies of the ancient records of the kingdom, such as 'Doomsday Book,' the 'Pipe Rolls,' &c., at a comparatively speaking very trifling cost ... I have called this new method Photo-zincography, and anticipate it will become very generally useful, not only to Government, but to the public at large, for producing perfectly accurate copies of documents of any kind.[36]

To demonstrate his point he included a specimen of the new process taken not from a map but from 'an ancient manuscript on parchment in the Records Office'. It was the first published example. Not for the last time, a process developed from the military budget was found to have applications of much wider use for civilian applications. Eager to make the process as widely available as possible, in 1859 James announced the discovery of a new method of making cheap and accurate facsimiles.[37] By this method, images were photographed down onto zinc plates, which could then be treated in a way very similar to the lithographic stone. In the following year he produced another brief pamphlet giving details of the methods employed by his staff. In this, his opening words alluded only to 'copying ancient manuscripts or any outline engravings'. It is not clear from this whether he forgot about printed books, or whether he thought them not worth pursuit, but it is very clear that he wished to make available to the public documents that were usually locked away from sight.[38]

James was not alone in the invention for which he took credit. At Melbourne, James Osborne was experimenting with similar methods at the same time and also for map-making. But having met with jealousy, he left for America, again to work on the reproduction of plans. Unlike James, who saw the possibilities of applying the process to other kinds of documents, Osborne was not quick to exploit his invention.[39] A decade later in Spain, the Cervantes enthusiast Francisco López Fabra produced a lavish facsimile of the first edition of *Don Quixote*, and unlike James he made no attempt at cheapness: the price in London was 4 guineas.

Over the next few years, James worked hard to ensure that photozincography became familiar not just to government and those who read parliamentary papers, but also among the population at large. He returned constantly to his central theme: that it was cheap. In his report for the following year, he reported that reduced copies could be transferred to copper plates for engraving, or onto stones or zinc plates for printing – 'and thus have the means of saving a very large sum annually by it'. The Treasury ordered him (presumably he was a willing listener) to make a facsimile of the Cornwall section of the Domesday Book. Copies were sold initially for 4s.6d., bringing a rapid profit.[40] By the time he came to report on activities in the year 1861, he was able to announce that arrangements had been made for facsimiles of almost all the counties to be published, mostly at 8s. or 10s. The previous example of Domesday had been published in type facsimile in 4 large folio volumes in 1783–1816, and by 1862 the set was commanding about 10 guineas.[41] James's productions were cheaper, in photo-facsimile, and could be bought as individual counties:

Any one can now procure, at a trifling cost, an exact fac-simile of the part of the original MS. in which he may be more particularly interested, and whilst the public is gratified by this, Her Majesty's Government will not be put to the cost of a single shilling for the production of the work.[42]

With Gladstone's encouragement, he embarked on a series of large-scale facsimiles of national manuscripts, first of England, then of Scotland and finally of Ireland.[43] While James received enquiries about the use of the process in India and Canada, and from various European governments, he also recognised its value as a conservation tool, relieving use of fragile or awkward originals. And as others were free to use it, so it was applied to further projects.

In 1861 it was employed by John Earle – formerly Professor of Anglo-Saxon at Oxford and now Rector of Swainswick near Bath – to print facsimiles of fragments of Anglo-Saxon manuscripts. Perhaps his comparative remoteness from the Oxford libraries (a circumstance to which he alluded in his book) enabled him to see further than James, to the opportunities the process offered for comparing different manuscripts and for a much wider study than was possible when it was limited by opportunities and strength to travel:

> A multiplication of trustworthy facsimiles, enabling the student in every region, without a toilsome pilgrimage, to have immediate access to originals, or, at least, the true picture of the original forms – this would be the greatest stride made by literary appliances since the invention of printing. Hitherto, if entire works have been reproduced in facsimile, it has been only by rare and chivalrous efforts of lithography or type-founding, such as Woide's *Codex Alexandrinus*, Mr. Babington's *Two orations of Hyperides*, and Professor Bosworth's *Orosius*. A taste for the acquisition of such books has not yet been generally cultivated, because their price has rendered them inaccessible. But that there is a desire for a pictured reproduction of ancient books may be proved by the many partial attempts which have been made to publish representations of the chief manuscripts of the New Testament. Photozincography may produce a change.[44]

Constantly in James's mind, and by extension those of others as well, the emphasis was on cheapness, and therefore on markets never before possible. Shakespeare's *Sonnets* of 1609 followed in 1862, reproducing a copy belonging to the Earl of Ellesmere; once again, Shakespeare was the most promising target. Following the Ellesmere copy of the *Sonnets*, in 1864 Howard Staunton supervised the production of a photo-lithographed facsimile of *Much ado about nothing*.[45] Here, the photographer R. Preston was named on the title-page. More promisingly still, in view of what was to happen to this market in the coming years, the facsimile was commercially published by Day & Son, one of the largest lithographic publishers in London. Over the following two years, Staunton became the first to oversee a photographic facsimile of the First Folio (1623). This too was published by Day & Son, who had acquired two of James's staff in 1863.[46] The facsimile was issued in 16 parts at 10s.6d. each, or bound as a single volume for 8 guineas. Publicity emphasised the low price, comparing it with that of originals: 'A single quarto play has been estimated at the value of £350, and the finest copy of the First Folio known would probably fetch £1000.'[47] It also alluded to the error-ridden attempt of 1807 and to the limitations of traced facsimiles. Staunton's work was greeted with enthusiasm, and the remarks that struck the publishers as especially judicious were incorporated into an advertisement in *The Times*:

But the grand condition of a certain text – a trustworthy reproduction of the original – is here obtained. All other things are of lesser importance. A critic can use this with undoubting faith in its literary accuracy, untroubled by his recollection of the several hundred blunders which were found by Upcott in the reprint of 1807. The reproduction is not made from a single copy, but from the best pages of the two best copies of the folio known – the one in Bridgewater House, the other in the British Museum... In so far as we have seen, it is a miracle of accuracy.[48]

It was possible at the same time to buy a copy of the original, with the title-page and the poem by Ben Jonson in facsimile, for as little as £53.[49] The difference in price between reproduction and original (frequently and mendaciously described as being of 'excessive rarity') can never have been closer. Meanwhile the anniversary year of Shakespeare's birth was producing a further quasi-facsimile, alluded to in the advertising for Staunton's work. This was a modern resetting in small type. Published by Lionel Booth in Regent Street, it was planned in three parts, and in three sizes, 'one to range with all good Octavo Editions ... another to range with Knight's Pictorial, and similar Editions, the third being uniform with the original Folio' (Fig. 6.2). The smallest cost 10s.6d. for each part.[50] A further reduced version, this time edited by J. O. Halliwell-Phillipps, was published by Chatto & Windus in a single volume in 1876. It was an extraordinary bargain, and at 10s.6d. offered a genuinely popular price for the first time. The price was substantially less than Ashbee was charging for just one of his slim pamphlets.

Photolithography had a better claim to accuracy than hand-tracing, even if there was some well-justified anxiety about the degree to which a lithograph could reproduce an original. Nonetheless, the photolithographed facsimile of a Sealed Copy of the Book of Common Prayer, published in 1870 and printed at the Ordnance Survey office in Southampton, was described as an 'exact counterpart',[51] and James's process certainly introduced much higher standards of accuracy. But, as a process allowing improvement and emendation, it did not necessarily mean absolute verisimilitude. In 1864, the *Publishers' Circular* was careful to note of a new reproduction of Shakespeare's Will that 'the publishers are about to issue a pure photograph (not a lithograph)'.[52] Photolithography was a process better suited to the sharp contrasts of black and white in printed texts than to the reproduction of different densities of ink in manuscripts. Though both publications were very considerable technical achievements in their own right, this was apparent in the facsimiles of Great Domesday (1861–3) and of the autograph score of *Messiah*, then in the Royal Collection (1868).[53] Perhaps understandably, *The Times* was enraptured about the latter, 'peculiarly the property of England':

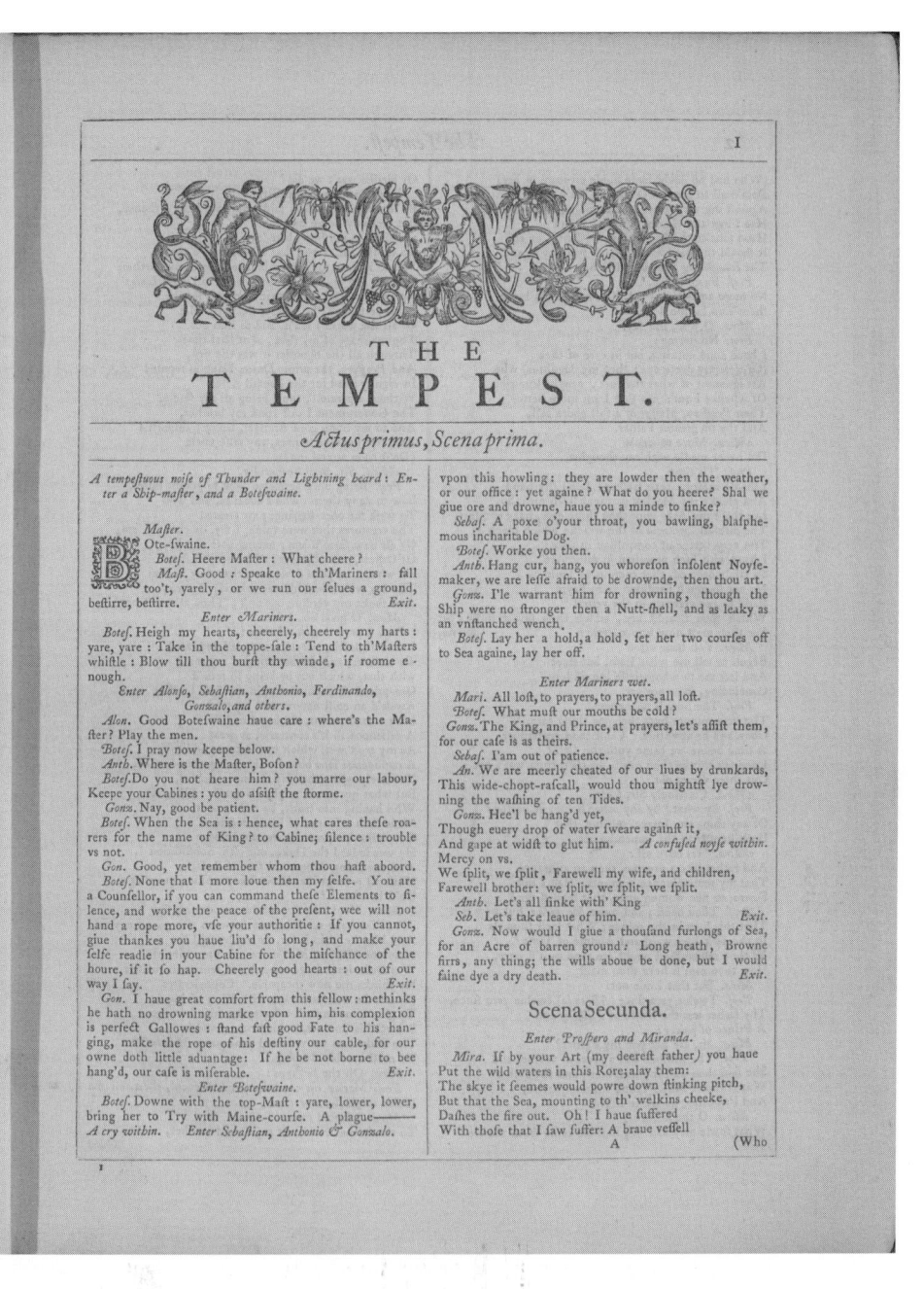

Figure 6.2 William Shakespeare, *A reprint of his collected works as put forth in 1623* (London: Lionel Booth, 1862–4). Reduced type facsimile.

The facsimile is made by the same unerring process of photolithography that has already reproduced the first folio of *Shakespeare* and the *Domesday Book*, and contains every blot, every smear, every erasure, every false start, every correction of the author exactly as they stand in the original manuscript at Buckingham Palace.[54]

Enthusiasm blinded the writer to faults such as pages omitted, inadequate reproduction of many of the erased passages and background marks that represented show-through in the original.

By the time of the Paris exhibition in 1868, photolithography was being practised to a high standard by firms such as Lemercier in France and Simonan & Toovey in Belgium, while the Heliotype Company in the United States exhibited photographic reproductions from *Punch*.[55] There was a rapid change from a world where photographically illustrated books involved laborious pasting-in of images to one where images could be cheaply and fairly quickly reproduced by photolithography.[56] Insofar as the appearances and possibilities of reproduction were concerned, it was the greatest change since the invention of lithography itself sixty or so years earlier. And with technical change, and changes in price, came also changes in attitudes to images and in expectations. Photography, with its promise of verisimilitude, engendered assumptions. By seeming to withdraw one of the veils between original and reproduction, replacing human intervention by chemical and mechanical processes, photography offered a new kind of reliability, and even a new kind of truth.

As for printed originals, they could in fact be readily enhanced. When in 1871 Edward Arber presented a photo-lithographed facsimile of the first edition of Tyndale's St Matthew's Gospel (1525) from the unique but imperfect copy in the Grenville Library in the British Museum, he reassured his readers that on the one hand he had sought absolute accuracy, but on the other had improved on the original:

In the original, as might naturally be anticipated, some of the lines and letters are faded and broken. With the view of facilitating their perusal, all these rotten letters have been made perfect, and the text printed black and sharp. After which the Fragment was again read with the original, so as to ensure absolute accuracy.[57]

The Collier and Ashbee facsimiles, expensive and printed in very small numbers, had never been intended for the ordinary market. The Ashbee volumes were marketed at 5 guineas each. Fry's facsimile of the Tyndale New Testament cost £8.0.0. for the ordinary edition. Photography, allied to lithographic methods, changed this, and in 1880 F. J. Furnivall, founder and director of the New Shakspere Society, launched a new series of Shakspere Quarto Facsimiles. Furnivall's enthusiasm for Chaucer, Shakespeare, philology, Browning, sculling and a host of other interests had brought him a mixed reputation, complicated by his willingness to enter into bitter personal arguments.[58] The new series was to be prepared under the supervision of William Griggs, whose experience as photo-lithographer to the India Office was now transferred from maps to books. The price to subscribers was to be 6s. each, rising to 10s.6d. on publication. Volumes were described as being 'half-bound in calf, in Roxburghe style'. The appeal to bibliophily was straightforward enough, but actually the books were only quarter bound, and in much cheaper leather than that used by members of the club.

If in some ways these facsimiles seemed to combine bibliophile antiquarianism with scholarship, there were other parts of the same markets that appreciated a more interpretative approach. Halliwell issued one of his privately printed pamphlets in 1860, using facsimiles by Ashbee and Dangerfield from the British Museum and the Capell collection at Trinity College, Cambridge to show that the edition of *Hamlet* dated 1605 was no more than a variant or reissue of that of 1604, with the date changed. This time just twenty-six copies were printed.[59] Others were less scrupulous in seeking out bigger audiences. Furnivall's facsimiles were clearly stated to be in photo-lithography, a reassurance on each title-page that seemed to promise accuracy. In fact they gained a justified reputation for imperfections. Cropped titles were replaced, and in the first quarto of *Hamlet* a handful of manuscript alterations to the printed text were reproduced as if in print.[60] The facsimiles sold widely and remained the most readily available until W. W. Greg commenced his series of collotype facsimiles in 1939.

As we have seen, the unwary could be led into error, whether as readers or as paying customers. Sometimes the sums involved were large. Among the most valued of all Americana are so-called Columbus letters, printed accounts published in the 1490s reporting the discovery of the western hemisphere by Columbus and his companions. Copies have been keenly sought since the mid-nineteenth century, when the market for the literature of American discovery became widely established and it was the hope of every collector to possess one. Inevitably the existence of only a few rare originals led to a market in forgeries.[61] The early bibliographer of the Columbus letters and their imitations had in mind a more general point:

No kind of fac-simile is so baulking to bibliographic comparison as the photographic. The respective sizes of the letters are altered, and the outline is rendered broken and rotten. A fac-simile of this same letter... done by hand, was published in Milan in 1863, in the sixteenth volume of the *Biblioteca Rara* of G. Daelli, and gives the type a far firmer appearance than that in the photograph. It is obvious that an opportunity is afforded of correcting the mistakes in the Ambrosiana text from the other texts which we possess. This has been done with great skill and judgment by Senor de Varnhagen.[62]

The extreme rarity of originals made the temptation to copy all the greater. The copy of the Spanish version in quarto, kept in the Ambrosiana library at Milan, was the only one known, and therefore not easily available for collectors to check when questions arose. A further copy of the 1860s version made in the 1880s (now at two removes from the original) brought trouble to a bookseller and profits to lawyers when it was sold in 1890 as a genuine piece, and then questioned; the eventual case in the American courts between the London booksellers Ellis & Elvey and the New York collector General Brayton Ives began in 1895, and after appeal it ended only in 1902. Forgeries of Columbus letters occasionally dog the market today, but most of the confusions created in the late nineteenth century by a series of forgeries were finally set to rights when in 1891 Quaritch published an edition of the unique copy of the folio *Letter to Santángel* (1493) – otherwise known as the Spanish Columbus letter – with a facsimile and an introduction by Michael Kerney. While there remained some reluctance (mostly on the part of those with vested interests) to believe Kerney's conclusions, the edition was accepted by most people, and Quaritch's copy was sold to James Lenox, from whom it passed to the New York Public Library.[63] There it rests, a testimonial not only to the history of the Americas, but also to the occasional confusions in understanding bibliographical evidence of the past.

Type facsimiles

Yet, amidst all this emphasis on accuracy, cheapness and faithfulness to originals, traced or photographic facsimiles did not displace demand for editions in archaic typography, often referred to as type facsimiles. The Duke of Devonshire's copy of *Hamlet* Q1, then the only known copy, had been printed in 1825 at the Shakespeare Press for Payne & Foss, page for page and line for line, but in a modern type. In 1860, the Devonshire quartos of *Hamlet* featured yet again, in a typeset edition that presented the two texts of 1603 and 1604 in parallel, based on the pagination of the Second Quarto, and 'offered to the literary world as a careful and accurate reprint of the two scarce and valuable original editions'. The edition was printed in an old-face type by Josiah Allen, in Birmingham, and was edited by Samuel Timmins of Edgbaston.

The flurry of editions of the first two quartos of *Hamlet*, some in type and some printed lithographically, the competitive claims of photography to accuracy, and the interest in the differing texts that the books offered represent a microcosm of much greater and more general changes in the study and appreciation of early English printed books. In simultaneously presenting texts as accurate facsimiles, and in presenting new, much lower, price structures for this kind of literature, book collecting and scholarship could be made to seem accessible to much wider audiences. They were far from a mass audience. That was for modern editions. Between the late 1830s and the 1860s, Robert Tyas, J. C. Moore, Alexander Macmillan, John Dicks and others drove down to a shilling the cost of a complete Shakespeare, in a modern edition. By July 1868, Dicks claimed that he had sold 700,000 copies of his shilling edition. It was a far cry from the precious facsimiles issued by Halliwell, Ashbee and others.[64]

The fashion for Shakespeare was carefully managed. The tercentenary of his birth fell in 1864, and the newspapers were fed stories to foster interest. There was a 'tercentenary number' of *Punch* on 23 April. A cardboard model of the birthplace could be had for the price of a few stamps. That spring, Garibaldi visited London, to be met by enthusiastic crowds. A leader in *The Times* hailed the two men together as heroes in their different spheres. In Stratford-on-Avon, arguments over responsibility for the festivities provided a stream of entertaining scandal. Conscious of Garrick's inspired orchestration of the jubilee in 1769, and of the further celebrations in 1828 and 1830, the literary and artistic world was determined now to do even better.[65] The celebrations proved a mixed success, but by the end of the summer two dozen collected editions were available, including two expurgated.

Shakespeare was only the most successful. He was not unique in the ways that publishers sought to make profits from different printing techniques. For the market between small limited editions and mass printings, the most successful and resilient publications of this kind proved to be so-called type facsimiles. These imitated, to a greater or lesser extent, the archaic appearance of early books. They ranged from the edition of Caxton's *Game and play of the chesse*, for which an experimental casting of his type by Vincent Figgins was used (Figs. 6.3, 6.4), to books that sought effect more than verisimilitude. As type-founders paid increasing attention to old-face types, and sought out models from the past, so the opportunities for publishers and printers grew.[66] In the 1870s and 1880s there appeared from Elliot Stock type-facsimile editions of Herbert's *The temple*, Milton's *Paradise lost* (Figs. 6.5, 6.6), Bunyan's *The pilgrim's progress*, Walton's *The compleat angler* and Defoe's *Robinson Crusoe*, all more or less claiming to be true representatives of the

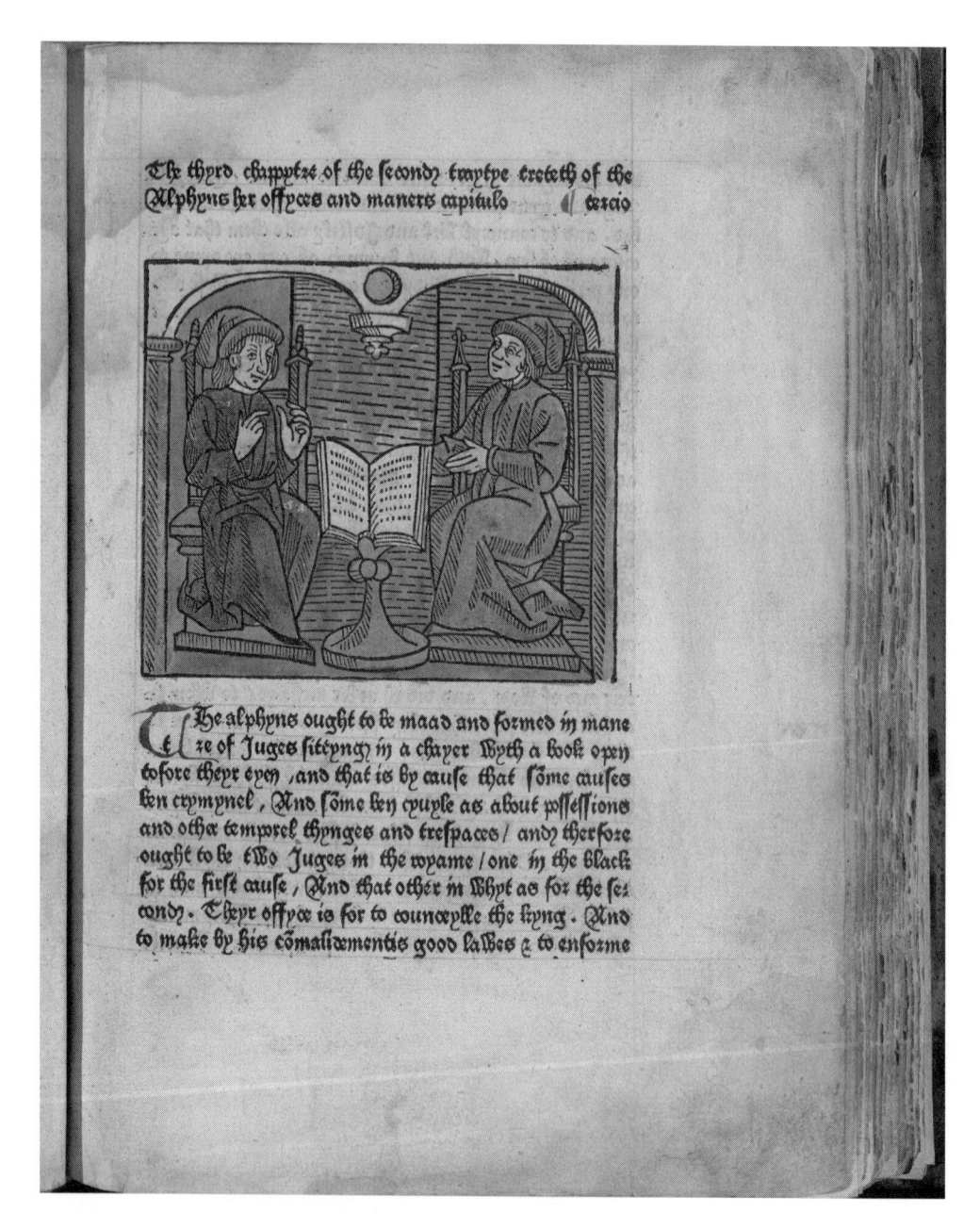

Figure 6.3 Jacobus de Cessolis, *The game of chess* (London: Willam Caxton [1483]). The woodcut has been coloured by hand, and the text has been marked in red and blue, with light underlinings and bounding lines in red. Trinity College, Cambridge VI.18.3.

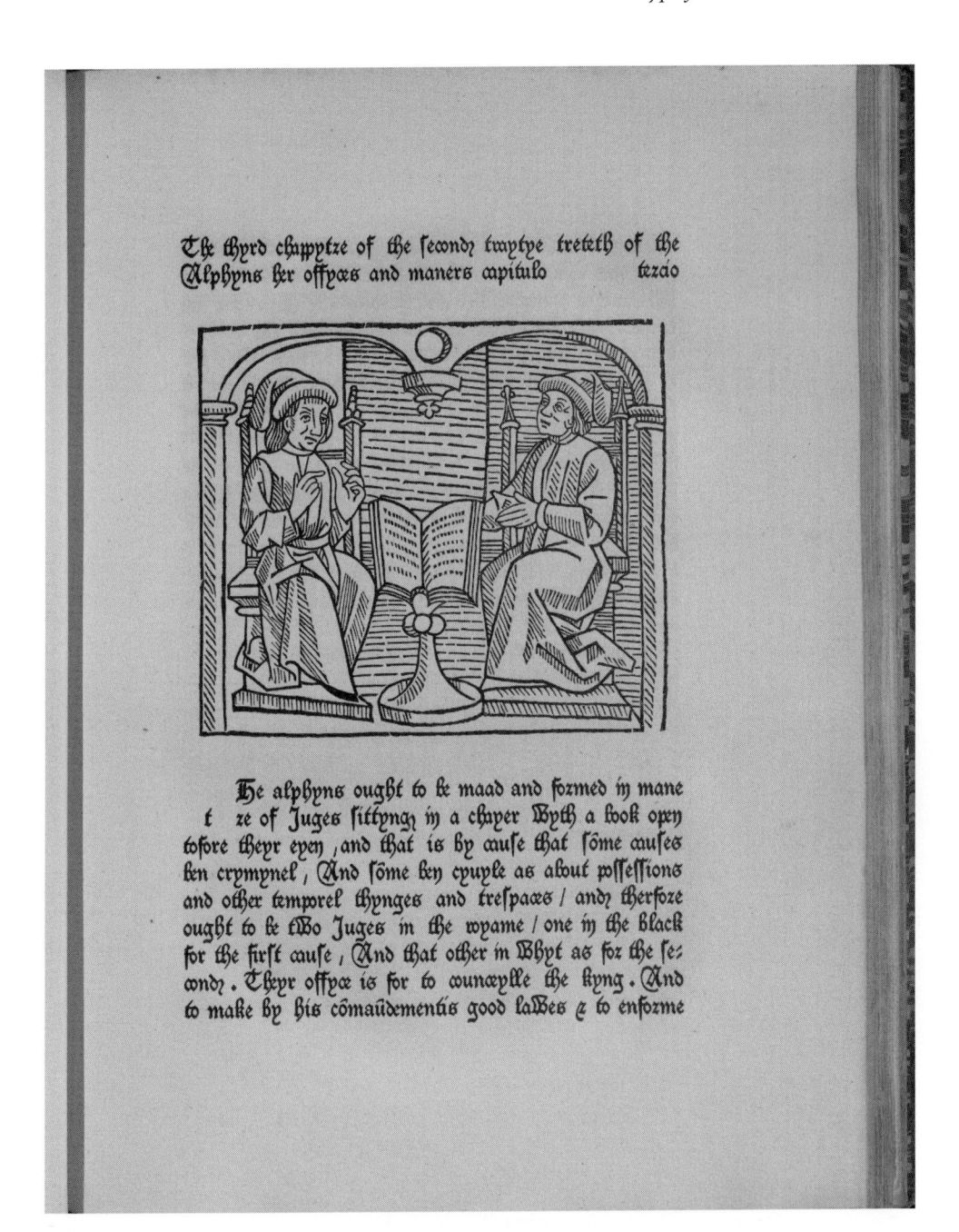

Figure 6.4 *The game of the chesse*, by William Caxton. Reproduced in facsimile by Vincent Figgins (London: J. R. Smith, 1855). Type facsimile.

PARADISE LOST.

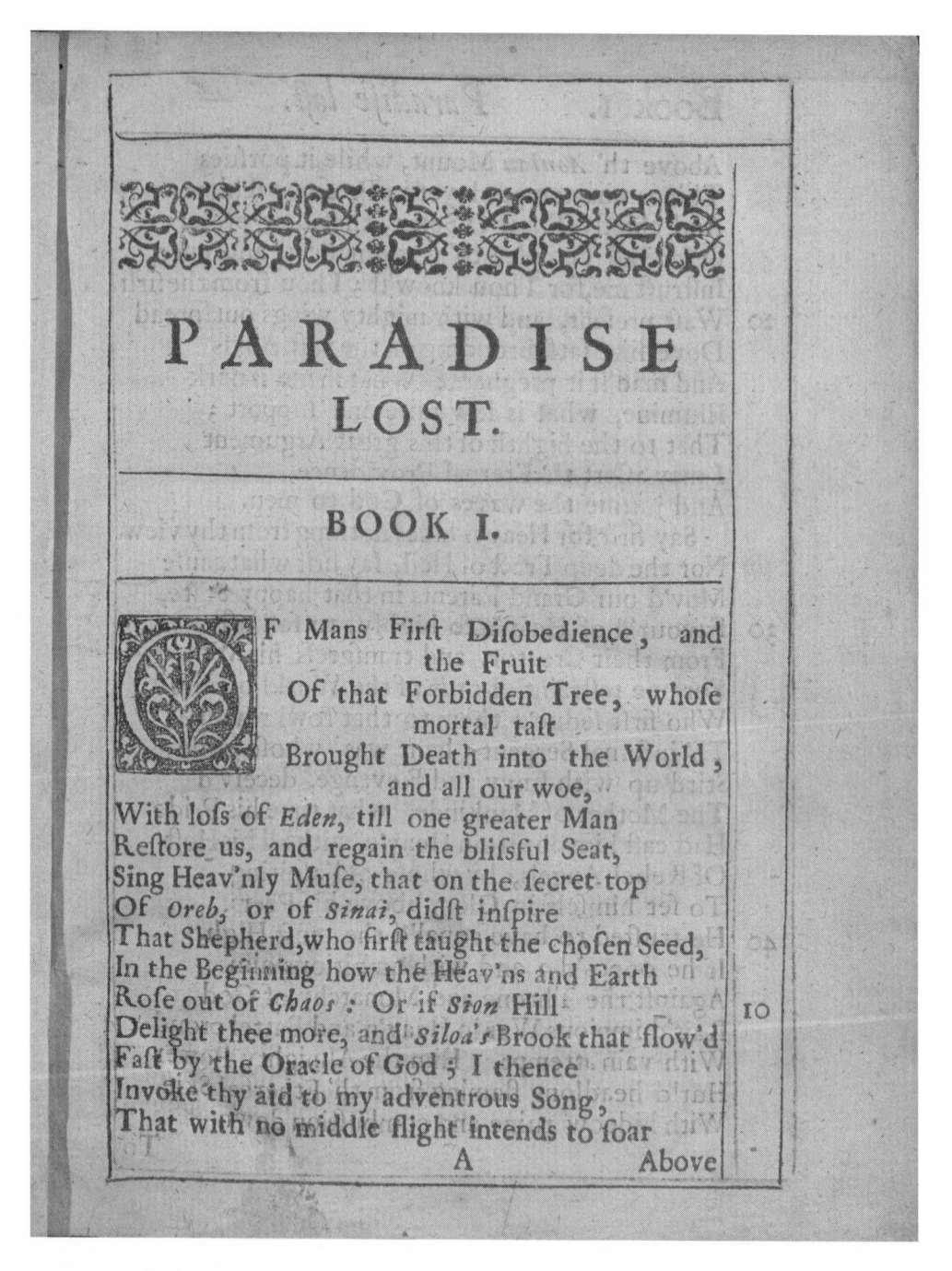

BOOK I.

OF Mans First Disobedience, and the Fruit
Of that Forbidden Tree, whose mortal taſt
Brought Death into the World, and all our woe,
With loſs of *Eden*, till one greater Man
Reſtore us, and regain the bliſsful Seat,
Sing Heav'nly Muſe, that on the ſecret top
Of *Oreb*, or of *Sinai*, didſt inſpire
That Shepherd, who firſt taught the choſen Seed,
In the Beginning how the Heav'ns and Earth
Roſe out of *Chaos*: Or if *Sion* Hill   10
Delight thee more, and *Siloa's* Brook that flow'd
Faſt by the Oracle of God; I thence
Invoke thy aid to my adventrous Song,
That with no middle flight intends to ſoar

A   Above

Figure 6.5 John Milton, *Paradise lost* (1667). Trinity College, Cambridge Capell S.10.

PARADISE
LOST.

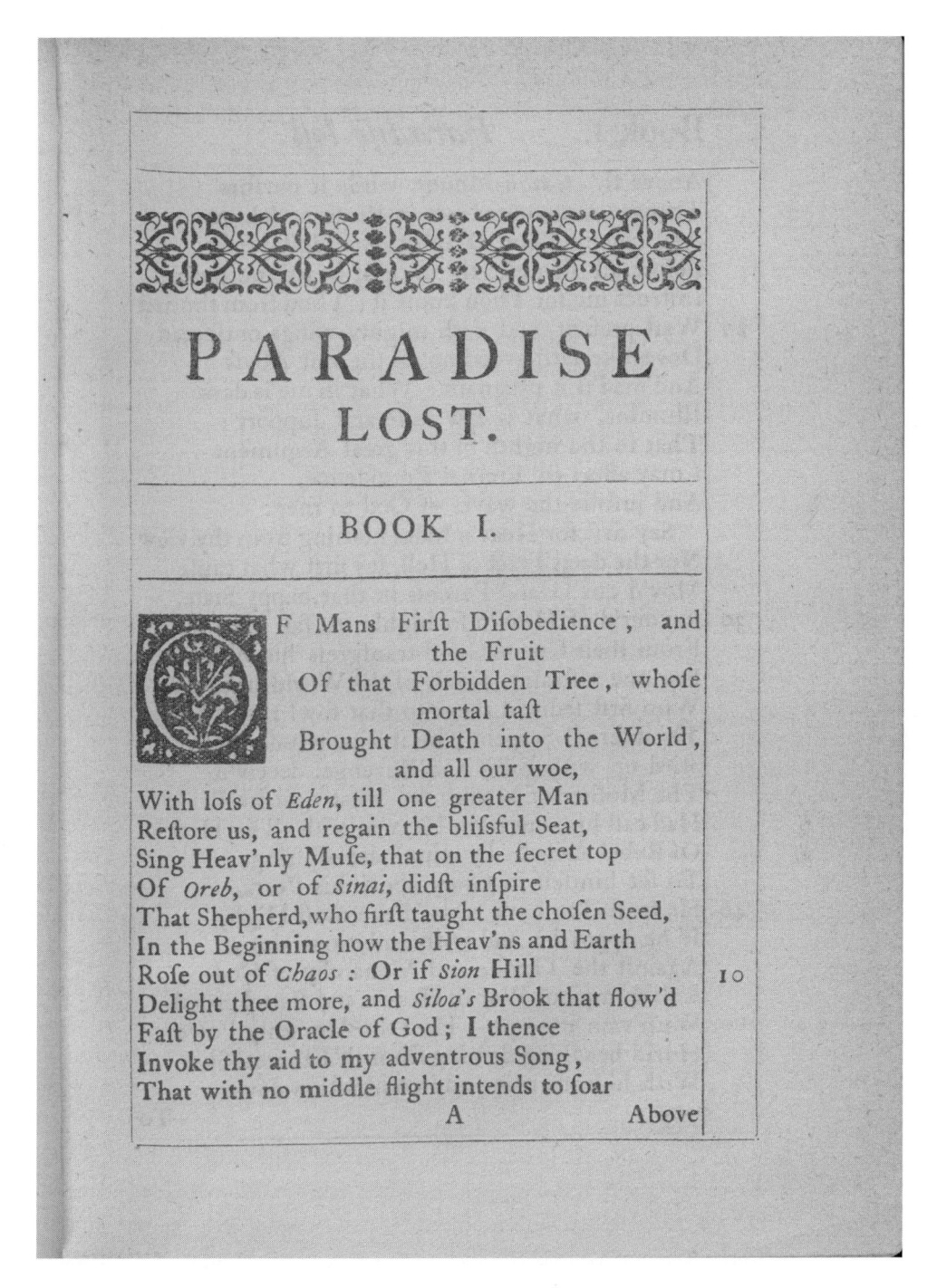

BOOK I.

F Mans Firſt Diſobedience, and the Fruit
Of that Forbidden Tree, whoſe mortal taſt
Brought Death into the World, and all our woe,
With loſs of *Eden*, till one greater Man
Reſtore us, and regain the bliſsful Seat,
Sing Heav'nly Muſe, that on the ſecret top
Of *Oreb*, or of *Sinai*, didſt inſpire
That Shepherd, who firſt taught the choſen Seed,
In the Beginning how the Heav'ns and Earth
Roſe out of *Chaos* : Or if *Sion* Hill   10
Delight thee more, and *Siloa's* Brook that flow'd
Faſt by the Oracle of God; I thence
Invoke thy aid to my adventrous Song,
That with no middle flight intends to ſoar
          A   Above

Figure 6.6 John Milton, *Paradise lost, being a facsimile reproduction of the first edition* (London: Elliot Stock, 1877). Trinity College, Cambridge Adv.c.18.91.

seventeenth- and eighteenth-century editions. Elliot Stock had begun in 1860 as a publisher of religious books, but his interests had shifted to bibliographical antiquarianism: in 1881 he was to launch a periodical *The Bibliographer*, the first of several ventures aimed at a new generation of book collectors keen to be educated; and by his death in 1911 he had accumulated a considerable library of his own.[67] In his type facsimiles, again there was an emphasis on verisimilitude and accuracy. The type facsimile of *Paradise lost* appeared in 1877, introduced with an explicit promise.

For the look of page after page of the ten books of the text in that original edition, down to the minutest detail of typography and stationery, the reader is referred to the present facsimile. It is so accurate a reproduction, even to the printer's errata, that a person having it in his hands may, for that matter, imagine himself one of the first purchasers of the original, in October or November, 1667, who has just left Mr. Parker's shop, near Aldgate, or Mr. Boulter's, in Bishopsgate Street, or Mr. Walker's, in Fleet Street, with a fresh copy.

The type facsimile of *The pilgrim's progress*, published by Elliot Stock in 1875, was much less responsible. It was advertised on the title-page as 'a facsimile reproduction of the first edition'. Only a single copy of the original was known, in the library of R. S. Holford, 'a compact volume, printed on yellowish grey paper, from, apparently, new type' (a second copy emerged soon after publication). For the facsimile, it was explained that the type used had been cast from moulds made in 1720, a phrasing that suggests that the anonymous person who wrote the preface to this reprint had limited understanding of type-founding. The treatment of the illustrations was rather less excusable. Nothing was said in the preface about it, but a number of reproductions of full-page illustrations were inserted into the text that had nothing to do with the first edition. As was soon pointed out, these illustrations had been introduced into the eighth edition and later. Elliot Stock had stretched the idea of facsimile beyond breaking point, and he was to do so again. In 1883 he published Sir Thomas Browne's *Religio medici* (1642), 'being a facsimile of the first edition'. 'Many persons,' remarked the editor W. A. Greenhill, 'like to see the actual type and paper and binding in which it was first given to the world.' The paper was a machine-made laid stock, but the binding was unlike almost all early seventeenth-century English work. It was of glazed wood, bevelled and blind-stamped with a panel inspired by the sixteenth century. Acceptable as it no doubt was for the 1880s gift market, it could not claim to have any connection with the seventeenth century. Percy Fitzgerald, who worked with Elliot Stock in searching out old books, was more accurate when he wrote that 'It is much the fashion now to simulate the old editions, mimicking, as it were, the paper, type, and general air of a favourite work.'[68]

The Elliot Stock type facsimiles were marketed not just as 'facsimile reproductions'. As in other parts of the gift market, they were offered in various bindings and sizes, in cloth, in old style calf and in morocco. Prices for *Paradise lost* in the ordinary quarto size varied from 10s.6d. ('antique binding') through to a guinea (antique cloth), to £1.11s.6d. (polished morocco). Large paper copies started at 15s., with Roxburghe style bindings at a guinea or, most expensively, Turkey morocco antique at £2.10s. Rather confusingly, a photographic facsimile of the autograph manuscript of the *Imitation of Christ* was offered in a 'contemporary leather binding' – presumably an allusion to the style rather than the date.

Though he dominated this niche market, Elliot Stock was not alone. He sold plates of the edition of *The temple* to Baker & Taylor in New York, who replaced the plain brown paper binding of London with an incongruous decorative embossed paper binding featuring Cupid sitting on a lion in the centre of the front cover. In London, Elliot Stock had also been beaten to publication of his type facsimile by a smaller publisher, W. Wells Gardner in nearby Paternoster Buildings. As an antiquarian exercise, the Gardner edition had much to commend it: the format was closer to the original than Stock's large octavo; the paper binding successfully mimicked seventeenth-century panelled calf; the type was in better condition; and the paper was of better quality. It had been printed by the Gresham Press, whose ability to set period typography was to be of advantage to many other customers over the coming years.[69]

Amidst all the excitement about the application of photography to facsimiles of printed books and manuscripts, and the ways in which it was changing the study of works of art, there were a few cautious voices. Once again, it is useful to recall work in media other than printed books. In his work on Caxton, William Blades chose to employ tracings after other methods were available. In the art world, John Ruskin preferred to employ a skilled watercolourist as a copyist, rather than photographs. The brief exhibition of a group of Turner's watercolours at the National Gallery, where they were over-exposed to light, convinced Ruskin of the need for some other method to be found of showing them. Photographs were inadequate, and instead he turned to William Ward, whom he met through the Working Men's College in London. *The Times* quoted Ruskin in 1876, as he referred to most precious drawings, which can only be represented at all in engraving by entire alteration of their treatment and abandonment of their finest purposes. I feel this so strongly that I have given my best attention during upwards of ten years to train a copyist to perfect fidelity in rendering the work of Turner, and have now succeeded in enabling him to produce *fac-similes* so close as to look like replicas – *fac-similes* which I must sign with my own name and his, in the very work of them, to prevent their being sold for real Turner vignettes.[70]

But customers who viewed these copies at the Fine Art Society in New Bond Street could not buy them. Instead, they were offered copies of copies, also autographed by Ruskin. For *The Times* this was doubly unsatisfactory. 'Surely they could not gratify any one who had a true insight for Mr. Turner's work, and, as copies, they are not much better than many chromolithographs?'[71]

The publishing programme of Elliot Stock, and the resort to watercolour copies of Turner's originals, are reminders not only that the technology of late nineteenth-century photography could not meet all the demands of the book trade or of galleries. It was not simply that colour photography was still in its infancy, or that it could be cheaper and more suited to market demand to set so-called facsimiles in type, rather than print them lithographically. In a period that witnessed dozens of innovations in photography and its application to print, old and new technologies sat side by side. The photograph brought new reproductive possibilities. It did not entirely demolish old ones, whose particular advantages remained, for some purposes, no less strong than they had been. But the photograph made people look again, and – more importantly – see with new eyes.

7 | Public exhibition

The idea of universal access, referred to in the first chapter, is an inherently attractive one, whether to health care or to old books. It lies at the centre of UNESCO activities: 'to promote the free flow of all forms of knowledge in education, science, culture and communication'. The launch of the World Digital Library in 2010 embodied some of the best of this.[1] But how far is it a new idea; and how, in an environment specifically of old books, was access increased for different parts of the population in the past? In this and the following chapter, we shall explore how the public face of old printed books was extended, modified and presented to a world where a high measure of literacy was anticipated. The computer-based ambitions of those who strive today for universal access involve a reconsideration of what is meant by the phrase; but ideas of universality and access were by no means alien to the nineteenth century. In 1861 Edmond Werdet, former publisher of Balzac, reflected on the great shift in the sizes and formats of new books of non-fiction, and on the new accessibility so often to be found in their contents: 'Notre époque n'est plus celle des in-folio, à l'usage restraint de quelques vénérables doctes, mais celle des traités substantiels et précis, à l'adresse de tous.'[2] The growth of a large-scale newspaper industry, the determined search for cheap printing that should be available to all, the establishment of a cheap postal system to make the exchange and increase of knowledge easy, the building of national and international railway networks that heralded mass travel, and the invention of the telegraph and telephone to add media that were entirely new all reflected and extended ways of thinking. In a non-electronic world, we need to look at some of these kinds of communication, and in particular for our purposes the ways in which cheaper printing, the newspaper and periodical trades, and the concept of the public exhibition contributed to changed understandings.

In the last chapter, we began to move towards a world where – thanks to cheap photographic processes and the arrival of new publishers who, using these and other methods, were looking for new audiences – it was possible for people of quite ordinary means to acquire representations of rare and old books. Nonetheless, so far in this enquiry we have been mostly concerned with élite reactions to early printed books, by a minority of people who had access to an increasing wealth of published bibliographical knowledge. They dealt in and owned the kinds of books that for the majority, insofar as they addressed the matter, held only the most general value. It was a privileged world of scholarship, leisure and connoisseurship. In between the extremes of privileged awareness and unconcerned ignorance lay an increasing number of people for whom some of the famous names in the history of printing were gradually made more familiar.

We noted in the first chapter some of the difficulties in making generalisations about what is meant by 'the public'. In the nineteenth century this becomes acute. While the century saw the development of such terms as the 'general public' and the 'reading public' (the latter used, not in a complimentary way, by Coleridge in his *Biographia literaria*), in practice it was diffuse in its interests and in its groupings. It sometimes, and sometimes did not, distinguish a large group of people from educational, political or social élites. It did not necessarily signify everyone, and it did not equate with universality. It signified a large body of the population, and it was not always clear what was meant, but it is a term that is useful nonetheless. Across western Europe, the museum- and exhibition-going public was not the same in the years after the Napoleonic wars as it was fifty years later, and it was different again by the end of the century in the wake of national provision for elementary education.[3]

Public galleries for the display of art could be traced back to the ancient world. In Rome. the Capitoline museum opened in 1734, and the pinacoteca followed in 1749. The Ashmolean Mueum in Oxford had been open to researchers since 1683. But none of these expected to admit everyone: in practice, the public was restricted by wealth, class, social connections and education.[4]

However much people might have heard through newspapers, journals or other publications of some of the major books or major names, there were few public opportunities for seeing examples of early printing. Printed books and manuscripts lagged behind paintings, for although the opportunities for public access to collections of paintings were restricted, a few existed. In Paris, the royal collection in the Palais du Luxembourg had been open to the ordinary public since 1750.[5] Opening was limited to three hours on two days a week – but this was six hours more than anywhere in London. For the handful of places in early nineteenth-century London, the ordinary public was in effect restricted by the formidable social and physical exclusivity of the private houses containing works of art. Not everyone, for example, had the courage to approach Cleveland House, home of the Marquis of Stafford, though the collection was open to view. Other owners, such as Sir John Leicester, the Earl of Grosvenor and John Julius Angerstein, provided more limited access. A contemporary guidebook commented on the lack of galleries in a city that had become so rich in paintings since the French Revolution, and how few private collections were in fact open to strangers. 'We shrink,' it remarked, 'from the ostentation of shewing to strangers our private possessions, forgetting that the productions of genius belong to the world, and that their proprietors are but trustees for the public.'[6] This was only partly true, for there was a long tradition of servants' showing off houses to interested visitors, if the family was not at home.[7] But the attitude may have influenced the long delay before libraries and books became common viewing and things to be lent publicity. There was also considerable caution about the divide between private and public, and the desirability or otherwise of admitting to what was supposedly or ostensibly public those who were sometimes termed 'improper persons'.[8] The details of auction sales, including prices and buyers' names, were public property, matters of record and gossip. Once out of the sale rooms and bookshops, books became private property, only to be shared with people of like persuasion or social standing. Even in public collections, books were not for show; they were for use. The early guidebooks to the British Museum, founded in 1753, made much of antiquities and curiosities, but books themselves were for consultation in the limited seating of the old reading room, a space reserved from the ordinary or casual visiting public. There was no public exhibition of books, at least on any scale, until the mid-nineteenth century. Books, like paintings, were reserved to those who had some special claim.

Access by display

This situation began to change in the second and third decades of the century. Books deemed to be old or rare were becoming museum objects as well as tools to be used. Charles Lamb (1775–1834), thinking in the early 1830s not about books but about contemporary works of art, wrote of the 'humour of exhibiting' having begun about fifty years since.[9] In 1830, Galignani's *New Paris guide* described the exhibition in the Bibliothèque Royale. Under Romanelli's ceiling of 1651, painted for Mazarin, there were glass cases containing *inter alia* manuscripts of Galileo, letters from Henri IV, the prayer book of Anne of Brittany and the memoirs of Louis XIV. There were also 'some prayer books' of the fifth and sixth centuries. The emphasis was firmly on manuscripts. Autographs were an obvious focus, as private collectors were discovering how quite modest amounts of money could buy a link with history, and little space would be taken up at home.[10] Galignani's guide drew particular attention to the lithographed anthology of facsimiles *Isographie des hommes célèbres*, edited by Simon Bérard and others. Manuscripts held an established appeal. The evolution of interest in very old printed books was a much more tardy process. Their appeal lay partly in themselves, as physical objects; partly in their literary content; and partly in what they represented: printing as the means of disseminating and establishing religious, political, social, ethical, financial or other values.

In view of these different attributes, it was not surprising that when in 1840 Gall Morel, librarian and archivist from the Benedictine abbey of Einsiedeln, came to review a pioneering exhibition of printing at Leipzig, he wrote first of the tensions between the aesthetic appeal of some books, and their more important purposes as vehicles for texts.[11] By that year, Gutenberg was a public figure, his statue towering over passers-by in Mainz since 1837 (Fig. 7.1). The Leipzig exhibition of 1840, organised by German booksellers as part of the quatercentenary celebrations of Gutenberg, seems to have been the first – at any rate on a large scale – concentrating on the printed book and on printing. After a handful of manuscripts, visitors were introduced to early printed books from Mainz, Cologne and other towns, to the press at Subiaco in Italy in 1466, to Paris and to Zamora. There followed the major printers – Aldus, Froben, Kerver, the Wechels, Plantin and others, with names such as Wechel and Trechsel signalling a move away from the traditional bibliophile market towards some of the important workaday presses. In modern printing, there were the familiar names of bibliophily, but also Tauchnitz and Wigand from Leipzig. A section on woodcuts was followed by books so illustrated, by maps and music, and by modern *Kunstdrucke*. By no means least interesting, albeit towards the end of the 500 or so exhibits, was a section on printing techniques and equipment, including recent electrotyping.

In 1840, it seems as if Gutenberg was difficult for German speakers to escape. An exhibition was not the only hazard. 'Wherever you go, Gutenberg busts and Gutenberg's pictures stare you in the face, and the papers are filled with advertisements alluding in some way or other to the engrossing subject.'[12] If the exhibition of autographs and valuable early manuscripts in the French national library, and the 1840 celebration at Leipzig and elsewhere, represented one end of the spectrum, the other was to be found in much more humble surroundings. In 1839 the Mechanics' Institution at Derby organised an exhibition of various articles lent by local owners. It was of the most miscellaneous kind, including an old custard

Monthly Supplement of
THE PENNY MAGAZINE
OF THE
Society for the Diffusion of Useful Knowledge.

[369.]   November 30 to December 31, 1837.

PRINTING IN THE FIFTEENTH AND IN THE NINETEENTH CENTURIES.

DURING the summer of the present year, a statue of John Gutenberg, the inventor of printing by moveable types, was erected at Mayence, his native city; and on the 14th August, and the two following days, a festival was held there upon the occasion of the inauguration of this monument. In the volume of the 'Penny Magazine' for 1833 (No. 101, p. 422), we have given a brief history of the contending claims of Mayence and of Haarlem for the honour of having produced the invention of printing; and, if the opinion which we there expressed in favour of Mayence were thought inconclusive, abundant evidence has been since brought forward to show that Gutenberg deserves all the honours of having conceived, and in great part perfected, an art which has produced the most signal effects upon the destinies of mankind. It is unnecessary for us to repeat these proofs. At the late festival of Mayence, at which many hundred persons were assembled, from all parts of Europe, to do honour to the inventor of printing, no rival pretensions were put forward, although many of the compatriots of Coster, of Haarlem, were present. The fine statue of Gutenberg, by Thorswalsden (of which we present an engraving), was opened amidst an universal burst of enthusiasm. Never were the shouts of a vast multitude raised on a more elevating occasion;—never were the triumphs of intellect celebrated with greater fervour. The statue of Gutenberg, who had won for his city the gratitude of the world, was opened with demonstrations of popular feeling such as have been wont only to greet the car of the conqueror.
VOL. VI.

[Statue of Gutenberg, at Mayence.]

The poor printer of Mayence indeed achieved a conquest; the fruits of his bloodless victory are imperishable; but it is honourable beyond comparison to the present generation of the citizens of Mayence to have felt that this victory of mind, which has made all future victories of the same nature permanent, was deserving of a trophy as enduring almost as the invention which it celebrates.

Mighty as are the benefits mankind have derived from the art of printing during the space of nearly four centuries during which it has been in operation, they probably amount to but a small portion of the whole sum of good which in its ultimate extension it is destined to confer upon our race. Literature and books, even before the era of this great invention, were the chief sources from which the moral light of the world was drawn. We can hardly conceive a form of civilization without them. Even while books could only be multiplied by the slow process of transcription by the hand, although direct communication with them was necessarily confined to a few, still their indirect influence was extensive. The book which was actually read only by a hundred individuals, through these transmitted at least a portion of its light to many thousands. The first circumscribed impulse was reproduced and spread abroad by all the modes of oral intercourse between man and man—by the sermons of the priest—by the addresses of the popular lecturer, often in those days attended by listening thousands —by the mysteries and moralities of the stage—by the recitations of wandering minstrels —by popular songs and ballads —by common conversation.
3 T

Figure 7.1 Statue of Gutenberg erected at Mainz, August 1837. *Penny Magazine* monthly supplement, 30 November 1837.

> Never were the shouts of a vast multitude raised on a more elevating occasion; – never were the triumphs of intellect celebrated with greater fervour. The statue of Gutenberg, who had won for his city the gratitude of the world, was opened with demonstrations of popular feeling such as have been wont only to greet the car of the conqueror.

dish, an early Derby posset cup and two 'ancient wash basins'. It also included printed books. John Moss, a local lawyer, lent a copy of Justinian (Mainz, 1475). Another collector lent an English Bible of 1576, Guillim's *Display of heraldry* (1611) and two books on artillery. Another lent Speght's edition of Chaucer (1602) and another an illuminated missal. Two exhibits were each described in the catalogue simply as 'an old Bible'.[13] In the following year a similar exhibition was held at Nottingham. Again it presented a sometimes disorganised assortment. One case, described in the catalogue as containing 'manuscripts and curiosities', included ancient books, 'Indian and Egyptian idols' and illuminated manuscripts. Peter Brooke of East Bridgeford, just outside the town, and William Sculthorpe, a local attorney, lent what were described as illuminated missals. Various other enthusiasts lent a calendar of horses entered for the Nottingham races a hundred years previously, fragments of early English printed Bibles, and specimens of American money. A mixture of old swords, pieces of tessellated pavement and objects from New Zealand added to the occasion.[14]

These exhibitions, and others like them, typically included machinery, paintings, modern sculpture, stuffed animals and other natural history specimens. They did not necessarily include books. At Norwich in 1840, the emphasis was not only on the usual mixture of natural history, but also, and especially, on machinery. There was a working steam train, and steam boats plied in the water round the fountain. A local printer and bookseller Josiah Fletcher lent an old common press, to join a lithographic press and a rolling press. One of the guidebooks to the exhibition devoted several pages to printing and type-founding, describing the operations involved in each.[15]

Access by print

Much of the impetus for the interest specifically in the processes of printing sprang from the sometimes almost messianic enthusiasm of a group of men more or less loosely behind the movement for mechanics' institutes. By far the most vocal, persistent and most influential proved to be Charles Knight, printer, publisher and tireless advocate of a cheap press that would bring knowledge (rather than mere cheap entertainment) and social cohesion among classes for whom skilled literacy was not universally familiar. In a succession of books, he promoted the history of printing alongside its modern equivalents, constantly emphasising the modern virtues of cheapness and universality. He used his *Penny Magazine* to support his beliefs, which in turn underpinned the reform movements of the 1830s. The cult of

Caxton began before then, but it was extended from the auction rooms of the wealthy to the homes of the middle and working classes. In the late 1820s the new Society for the Diffusion of Useful Knowledge, a body chaired by Lord Brougham and thus closely linked to the mechanics' institute movement, issued a series of sixpenny pamphlets as a 'library of useful knowledge'. The series began with works on hydrostatics, hydraulics and other scientific matters, before moving to biographies of Cardinal Wolsey and Christopher Wren, and the history of Greece. By August 1828 it was the turn of Caxton. In price, the pamphlet was a far cry from Hansard's recently published *Typographia*, a fat volume by a professional printer combining a history of the subject with a full manual on its modern practice and costing 3 guineas, yet both came from the same publishers, Baldwin & Cradock. Caxton was presented not just as England's first printer, and hence the originator of the means to modern knowledge: 'Through his zeal, industry, and perseverance, the art of printing was introduced into England.' As a consequence,

> At present, in our country, there could not, most probably, be found a single hovel in the most lonely and remote district, in which some books would not be found – not treasured as a great rarity and of high value, but, on the contrary, accessible to all.[16]

The combination of personal industry and public benefit was irresistible. Caxton was created as a popular hero, the subject not just of learned monographs but also of cheap literature. The transition specifically via Caxton from old and expensive books to modern and cheap ones required some historical elision, but it proved a potent one. The fact that by the nineteenth century his own books commanded exceptional prices as old books was not an issue in the context of Knight's intended readership.

While it is difficult to judge accurately the relationship between the number of any book or periodical printed and the number of people or type of person who read it, Knight himself claimed that in his first year the *Penny Magazine* was printed in editions of 160,000 copies.[17] He was proud of its national circulation: by the end of the first year, the wholesalers named in the imprint ranged from Falmouth to Glasgow and Edinburgh, besides Dublin and even New York. And because the whole of the magazine was stereotyped[18] from the first, it was possible to reprint it for yet further sales sometimes years after initial publication.

In 1844 Knight launched another series of books, Weekly Volumes for All Readers. As the initial volume he offered his own account of Caxton.[19] In small format, but running to 240 pages and with a frontispiece portrait that was wholly imaginary, it was the first extended biography of Caxton since that of John Lewis in 1737, and it had the benefit of several generations of collectors and writers since. At the head of his list of authorities were the successive revisions of Joseph Ames's *Typographical antiquities* by William Herbert and Dibdin. Then came Andrew Kippis's article in *Biographia Britannica* (1784). There was little available of a primary nature, other than Caxton's own words. Like others before and since, Knight quoted them extensively. Then, as an afterword, he added a summary history of printing in England from the fifteenth century to the present. Much of this was taken – often long sections and suitably updated as to the statistics – from his more general account published in the *Penny Magazine* in 1837. Knight frequently re-used his work, but in his constant insistence on the relationship of the achievements of the press in the distant past to the practices and opportunities of the present, he offered a simple historical moral.

Remarkably, though his book was extensively illustrated with wood engravings, he offered scarcely any representation of any book printed by Caxton. While Dibdin, writing for an entirely different market – wealthy and highly educated – tended almost to over-illustrate to the point where his books became highly expensive, Knight all but ignored the issue.[20] Despite having at his command plenty of highly trained artists, he scarcely used them. The thousands of blocks prepared for the *Penny Magazine*, all of them stereotyped, offered a mine for this and his other publications. But the magazine had produced all too little to help in this cheap shilling volume, where costs were pared to a minimum. So, apart from eight lines showing 'Caxton's type' and a copy of a woodcut from the Canterbury tales, there was nothing. Rather oddly, though perhaps few readers will have noticed, he included without comment or caption an engraving of one of the scenes from the pediment of the Mainz statue of Gutenberg and originally published in the *Penny Magazine* in 1837; the assumption for most readers will have been that this was Caxton.

As was repeatedly emphasised, printing was one of the cornerstones of modern civilisation. It was also a technical triumph, both in the fifteenth century and in the developments of the nineteenth: the application of steam power to newspaper printing and the development of stereotyping were repeatedly cited as accomplishments at least equal to the other inventions of the industrial revolution. But whereas (for example) railways, steam navigation and the electric telegraph were recent inventions, printing could be fêted as something at once much older, and just as modern. These dual values, celebrated by Charles Knight, found their way into more general popular literature about modern discoveries. John Timbs (1801–75) was one of the century's most prolific authors: between 1821 and 1874 he produced almost three books a year. He had edited the *Mirror of Literature* from 1827 to 1838, and in 1837 he founded the *Year Book of Science and Art*. For seventeen years he was sub-editor of the *Illustrated London News*. Whether his subject was topographical, historical or social, he had few equals as a populariser. His targeted readership was not that of Knight, who aimed the *Penny Magazine* and some of his other publications at those who had little spare money. Instead, Timbs wrote for those who were able – by education, inclination or income – to afford books costing a few shillings. He opened his *Stories of inventors and discoverers* (1860) with Archimedes, followed by the magnet, and then a chapter on 'Who invented printing, and where?' Here he began with the impressed clay of ancient Babylon, with the discoveries exhibited in the British Museum. From this, after a few dismissive sentences about the Coster legend,[21] he moved to Gutenberg, drawing on earlier accounts by Hansard, Lambinet and others, and then Caxton. Historically, he was only occasionally reliable, before he approached modern times with the by now obligatory account of innovations in printing at *The Times* and the astonishing speeds of which recent machines were now capable.

As a production, James Hamilton Fyfe's *Triumphs of invention and discovery* (1860) was more ambitious than Timbs's book. The two were in direct competition, and in place of Timbs's plain brown cloth and lack of illustration, Fyfe (1837–80) had the resources and ambitions of the Edinburgh printers and publishers Thomas Nelson: dressed up in gilt cloth, and with full-page illustrations, his book was also a little cheaper. In 1860, he was not yet a barrister (he became so in 1863), and he made his living as a reporter. Like Timbs, he was a journalist – later to become assistant editor of the *Pall Mall Gazette* and then of the *Saturday Review*. Printing was given pride of place, not just in the ordering of the chapters but also on the gilt-blocked spine, with a depiction of a hand-press; in the title-page picture of Gutenberg; and in the romanticised frontispiece, unsupported by any historical evidence, also depicting Gutenberg, 'in the depths of the cloisters, in a dark secluded place'. But he began with the fiction of Coster and how he, not Gutenberg, was the inventor of printing. Here he drew on sixteenth-century tradition, embellishing it further from his own imagination. He told how Gutenberg had gone to Haarlem and met Coster; how, like Coster, he carved letters out of pieces of wood; and then his discovery of metal letters. It was a tale that had only recently been refreshed in the enthusiastic celebrations of Coster at Haarlem in 1856.[22] From here, Fyfe made the familiar journey through Caxton to the modern equipment installed to print *The Times*. Fyfe's book became well known, an obvious present for anybody with a latent interest in inventions, and some attempt was made to reflect changing public emphases. As revised editions appeared, his name as author was dropped, and by 1885 the images on the binding, in the frontispiece and on the title-page had all been changed. In the pages on printing, now including a passage on stereotyping, Coster was dismissed, the accounts of him being 'evidently deficient in authenticity'. The section on Gutenberg was substantially revised, and the invented medieval room in a monastery was replaced with an inept illustration of Caxton's printing house. Still, however, there were no illustrations of any examples of early printing, and despite the titles of their books both men had little to say about the nature of what they thought had been invented.

Whatever their weaknesses as historians, and whatever their bibliographical innocence, popularisers such as Knight, Timbs and Fyfe not only made some of the early names of printing more widely familiar. They also set printing in the context of other everyday activities, a recognised part of common knowledge. As historians, they were unpredictable, liable to flights of fancy and frequently misleading. Their books lacked the kinds of illustrations that would have made the processes of printing clearer. As journalists, Timbs and Fyfe depended for their daily wages on the press, yet neither man took the time to grasp what he was writing about. But it was in the work of such authors that the general public, untuned to the appearance of early books, ignorant of the advances that were being made in bibliographical knowledge and unfamiliar with exhibitions, learned something of chains of values that were not dominated by sale-room prices or the whims, interests and passions of wealthy collectors.

It remained that while the moral and heroic attributes of early printers were extolled both in biographies and in commemoratory volumes, it was remarkably difficult to discover what many of their publications looked like. Small sections of pages were shown, depicting type, printers' devices or illustrations. Full-size illustrations were much rarer. Partly it was a question of size. Knight's shilling volume provided a page size about one-quarter of Caxton's books, which were mostly printed on chancery-size paper. The Gutenberg Bible, on its larger sheets of paper, was even more demanding, even for expensive publications. Though Falkenstein's celebratory *Geschichte der Buchdruckerkunst* (Leipzig, 1840) was printed in a large quarto format, and was thus able to accommodate the page size of early block-books, he had to employ fold-out pages for some of his bigger illustrations. Even so, he was unable to show a full page of the Gutenberg Bible.

It was left to Eugène Duverger in his *Histoire de l'invention de l'imprimerie par les monuments* (Paris, 1840) to come nearer to achieving this, with a page size large enough to reproduce original dimensions. But though the page size was achieved, the reproductions of Gutenberg's work were far from being facsimiles. As we noted in Chapter 5, they were resettings, in type copied from the original.

Some of this visual desert was the result of misfortune. In the mid-1830s William Young Ottley prepared an illustrated volume on the controversies surrounding the earliest years of printing. But he died before it was completed, the sheets so far printed off lay forgotten, and his work was finally brought to completion only in 1863 as *An inquiry concerning the invention of printing*. It contained little on the early Mainz press, and was largely concerned with arguments over the earliest Dutch printing. Similarly, Samuel Sotheby's *The typography of the fifteenth century* (1845) was a gathering together of plates commissioned but still not published at their editor's death. It was followed by the more important three-volume *Principia typographica* in 1858. Both were the work of Sotheby's son. All of these were expensive, and published in very limited editions; just 220 copies were available to the public of *Principia typographica*.[23] It was not until the publication in 1867 of Henry Noel Humphreys's much more extensive *History of the art of printing* that there was anything of any length available at a reasonable price. This book cost 3 guineas, compared with £8.10s. asked by Quaritch in 1868 for Sotheby's 3 volumes,[24] and it took advantage of the still new process of photolithography; a second edition followed a year later. Dibdin's heavily illustrated works, relying on woodcuts and engravings, had appeared forty and more years previously, and the middle market had had to wait all this time to see more than occasional reproductions of the works of early printers. There was a sufficiency of prose on the subject, but it was accompanied by a general bibliographical invisibility.

The lack of cheaply available reproductions of the work of early printers is all the more remarkable in that it contrasts with activity in circles more concerned with the history of painting, drawing and manuscript book illumination. Increasingly, publications on the history of art were expected to be illustrated. In such illustrations it was inescapable that there was a large element of interpretation, whether in the medium or method chosen, or in the skills or preoccupations of the copyist involved. These reproductions were often far from accurate even in their most basic delineations. Whether a work of art was copied by eye, by measured drawings or by tracing, the resulting version could never be more than that: a version. But the existence even of versions manifestly distant from originals was transforming the study of the history of painting and the graphic arts.[25] Knight himself included several woodcut reproductions of paintings from the new National Gallery (founded in 1824 in a building in Pall Mall, and opened in its new building in 1839) in the later issues of the *Penny Magazine*, and in 1843 published a series of illustrated articles by Mrs Jameson on the lives of Italian painters.[26] In 1839, the magazine included eight articles on the history of medieval illuminated manuscripts, with reproductions from the Lindisfarne Gospels and other volumes in the British Museum. The series was partly inspired by what was referred to as Henry Shaw's 'elegant and accurate' delineations of ornament, published in 1830–3 and introduced by Frederic Madden.[27] As Knight repeatedly pointed out in his autobiographical *Passages from a working life*, wood engravings were expensive. And, as the engraving of the Lindisfarne Gospels showed all too clearly, it was impossible to render an illuminated manuscript convincingly in wood. Lithography offered further possibilities, including cheap colour.

The curious result was that the history of painting could be studied either in books or in the freely available riches of the National Gallery,[28] while the representative masterpieces in the history of printing – the very subject by which politicians, theologians and social reformers set such store – eluded public view. On the other hand, the printed book was not a work of art in the same sense. It was a manufactured article. So, too, were most book illustrations, which were generally treated as inferior to separate prints, despite the fact that in the past artists including Dürer, Holbein, Barlow, Hollar and William Blake had been periodically employed to produce woodcuts, etchings or engravings for inclusion in books. If the reproductive illustration, copying the work of an artist, was understandably considered inferior, not to say irrelevant, to a view of art history that set most store by individual genius, the same could not in truth be said of the usually anonymous work offered in hundreds of printed books.

Library exhibition

It was one matter to make books (or paintings, or other works of art) available to the public. It was quite another to persuade broader sweeps of the public than hitherto to come and see them. Knight's purpose – and mission – was to share knowledge as cheaply as possible. That was not the same as encouraging excursions to exhibitions, museums or libraries. Though there were table exhibition cases in the Radcliffe Camera in the

Bodleian Library at Oxford in the 1830s,[29] the most obvious place of all made no provision for the regular public display of either manuscripts or printed books until the middle of the nineteenth century. The wider public had to be persuaded, partly by education and partly by advocacy and openness. But not everyone was necessarily welcome. While the British Museum had been open to the general public since 1759, and it was possible to see everything from classical antiquities to stuffed animals, the reading room was an area reserved for study.[30] Admission was by application, and there was no associated public exhibition devoted to manuscripts or printed books. In the early 1820s, when it was still in the old Montagu House and visitors still had to be taken round in guided parties, the Museum was open for six hours a day on three days a week.[31] George Samouelle, an entomologist, joined the staff of the Museum in 1821, to look after part of the natural history collection. He had no doubts as to the virtues of admitting the public: 'The ignorant are brought into awe by what they see about them, and the better informed know how to conduct themselves.'[32] His only fear was of drunkenness on bank holidays. Smirke's new building was begun in 1823, starting with the King's Library. In the 1820s the annual numbers of visitors veered between 62,500 (1820–1), 127,600 (1824–5) and 71,300 (1829–30). Then they began to climb. By 1832–3 there were 210,000 visitors, the number having more than doubled in 2 years. By 1843–4 there were 546,000, and in 1848–9 there were 979,000. Use of the ever more overcrowded reading room increased fast as well, from about 1,950 visits in 1810 to over 70,000 in 1849.[33] By then, it was possible to visit the King's Library, though still only if escorted. Antonio Panizzi, as Keeper of Printed Books, was keen for the public to see more, but he was hampered by the buildings, partly by the inconveniences of arrangements for fetching and consulting manuscripts via the King's Library and partly because the shelves in the King's Library were unglazed: he feared that more general access would raise dangerous amounts of dust. But if, proceeding from the entrance hall, the Grenville Library, the manuscript room and the King's Library were opened, 'the public would thus go through three splendid rooms, containing some of the finest collections of books in the world'.[34]

As London prepared for the opening of the Great Exhibition in summer 1851, the question became pressing, and the Trustees of the Museum agreed to open an exhibition of books on five days a week. Glazed cases were provided, both table-height and tall standing ones, and guides were prepared to the printed books and the manuscripts exhibited.[35] The experiment lasted from May to October that year, when the exhibitions closed. Much to the irritation of Sir Frederic Madden, Keeper of Manuscripts,

Panizzi ('Dirty blackguard!') also had printed a twopenny guide to the printed books on display; Madden's own equivalent followed in August. The books were exhibited in a mixture of table cases and gable cases, the latter having large glazed fronts at knee level – hardly the most convenient arrangement for viewers, but allowing much to be crammed into a small space.[36] The emphasis was constantly on quantity. In 1850 the number of visitors to the Museum was about 1.1 million. In 1851 it was 2.5 million. At the National Gallery, where many people expressed fears of overcrowding, numbers rose from about 0.6 million to a little over a million.[37] Although this brief experiment at the Museum ended so quickly, the point had been made. But with books double- or even triple-shelved, and stored in parcels on the floor behind the scenes, space for both books and readers was at a premium until the opening of the new round reading room in 1857. In autumn that year, amidst more complaints from Madden, the public was at last provided with a permanent exhibition of books and manuscripts.[38]

While the selection and the arrangement of the exhibits were eclectic, this was the only substantial permanent exhibition of its kind in Britain. Over the coming years it was to be supplemented with special exhibitions to mark anniversaries, beginning with Luther in 1883. And gradually the number of books in the new showcases for the permanent exhibition was extended. By 1870, the penny guide to the exhibits from the Department of Printed Books listed over 250 items, beginning prominently, just off the entrance hall in the Grenville Library, with a group of *Biblia pauperum* block-books and concluding with a generous selection of bookbindings – several of them from the recent bequest of Felix Slade. The books selected for exhibition were very different from the kinds selected for international exhibitions, where the emphasis was on modern achievements in printing and bookbinding. With two or three exceptions, here it was historic, not just with the earliest printing but with a wide selection from the sixteenth century, books with autographs of the famous, and items valued for their curiosity. The arrangement was designed as much to show a chronology as themes. This meant that a printed Book of Hours, 'a specimen of minute size and type', was displayed next to one of the earliest books printed in Mexico, in 1543–4 (bought in 1869), followed by the 1549 *Book of Common Prayer* (bought in 1848) and the second book printed in Goa, 1563 (bequeathed by Thomas Grenville in 1846). *Robinson Crusoe* (1719) was followed by 'The first printed description of a steamboat' (1737) and Ged's stereotyped edition of Sallust (1744). Of the most recent, curiosity was rewarded with a theatre programme printed on chamois leather on board H. M. S. Assistance, off Griffiths Island during the winter of 1850–51. The other very recent books, also of the 1850s, were both drawn from the Paris exhibition of 1855. First was a book printed by the specialist oriental printers Stephen Austin of Hertford, with decorations derived from manuscripts in the British Museum and East India House. The other was abbé Jean Jacques Bourassé's sumptuously produced *La Touraine* printed at Tours in 1855, said to have cost upwards of £6,000 in its production. It had featured both in the jury's report for the exhibition and in the *Journal des Débats*, and had been bought by the Museum in 1856.[39]

This large, extensive, permanent and freely available exhibition placed the Museum's library firmly before a wide public gaze. It reflected policies that had been slowly and sometimes painfully worked out within little more than a generation.[40] For readers, the new round reading room brought new freedoms and comfort. The collections of early and more recent printed books alike had been systematically improved, both filling in gaps and extending the scope. Visitors were no longer required to be conducted round the Museum in parties, and the sight of early books was no longer restricted to those who could gain admission as readers. For anyone who wished and could get to the Museum, it was easy to see what early books looked like. Facsimiles, reproductions, newspaper reports and hearsay about auction sales all had their place, but they were all eclipsed by the books themselves.

While the exhibitions in the British Museum commanded public attention, the decision to innovate in this way was part of conversations about access and display taking place across Europe. It was possible for non-readers to arrange to be conducted round many large libraries, as in the royal library in Berlin ('It is shown to strangers on application to the Librarian, Wed. and Sat., 9–12'),[41] but other libraries were making their treasures more easily accessible to a world increasingly made up of curious tourists and local inhabitants alike. In Rome, The Vatican Library was open during the early 1840s only for part of the year, to both readers and tourists, but by the 1860s visitors were admitted every afternoon; a gratuity to the *custode* was expected.[42] Several years before the British Museum mounted even a temporary exhibition, other cities had seen both temporary and long-term ventures.[43] We have already seen how the Deutsche Buchhändlerbörse at Leipzig celebrated the anniversary of printing in 1840 with a loan exhibition, seemingly the first on the subject on any scale and notable for being organised by the book trade; there was a parallel exhibition in the university library, including the Gutenberg Bible.[44] In Berlin, the tercentenary of the death of Luther was marked at the Königliche Bibliothek.[45] In 1844 the Munich Staatsbibliothek (which had exhibited parts of its collections since the 1820s) arranged an exhibition of its treasures.[46] At St Petersburg, the appointment in 1849 of Count Modest Andreevich Korff to the imperial library led to the transformation of that library into a publicly accessible institution. Under his energetic and ingenious leadership, within a few years it was restored and modernised, and an extensive permanent exhibition of manuscripts, printed books, prints and bindings was installed. The exhibits were both western and oriental; the printed books were from the fifteenth century onwards. More than many people in countries to the west and closer to the major literary centres, Korff realised that a well-organised library was a vehicle for civilisation. Most importantly, libraries existed for the public, not the public for libraries. The distinction did not escape notice.[47]

In Paris, there had been displays of manuscripts and treasures in the Bibliothèque Nationale since revolutionary times, usually on a very modest scale. Apart from manuscripts, there were displays of prints, and of antiquities from the Département des Médailles. There was little organisation.[48] In 1852, and far more ambitiously, the bookseller Jacques-Joseph Techener published an article in his *Bulletin du Bibliophile* advocating a 'musée bibliographique', to be installed in the new galleries planned for the Louvre. Techener, ever searching out rarities for his customers, was a frequent visitor to England, and it is not impossible that conversations in London turned to public exhibitions of books. He remarked that his article had been ready two years previously – that is, before the events of 1851 in the galleries of the British Museum – but that unnamed circumstances had delayed its appearance. He pointed out that the Louvre was the cradle of the Bibliothèque Nationale, and that the royal collections had been dispersed since the Middle Ages. A new gallery in the Louvre would bring the opportunity to assemble the surviving libraries of Jean II, Charles V, Jean duc de Berry and Philippe de Bourgogne. Manuscripts could be arranged chronologically, from Charlemagne down to the invention of printing and the 1457 Psalter – the first dated printed book. He further envisaged a world where the other large Parisian libraries such as the Arsenal would contribute to this national celebration. The Bibliothèque Nationale itself owned duplicates of books published by Vérard and others from the sixteenth century. Techener placed his emphasis firmly, in an old-fashioned way (harking back to van Praet's priorities at the start of the century), on books printed on vellum,[49] and he drew attention to the importance of expensive bindings. He even suggested how the volumes might be displayed, on sloping shelves covered in velvet, well lit and in glass cases to preserve them from dust.

There was a further advantage, beyond the obviously bibliophile ones of materials. A display such as Techener envisaged would encourage study from a new point of view: the history of man, of arts and of the progress of *sciences humaines*:

Voice le plus ancien manuscrit qui soit en France; sa date remonte au cinquième siècle; les miniatures dont il est orné sont de l'école bysantine, et les lettres initiales rappellent l'école romaine. – Ce livre est le Missel de Charlemagne. – Celui-ci est le Missel de Saint-Louis: admirez la richesse encore sans égale des ornements en or bruni dont ce volume est surchargé. – Cette Bible est celle que lisoit Charles V. – Ce Missel appartenoit à Louis XII; il fut donné par François 1er à Diane de Poitiers. – Henri II fit relier ce volume, et l'on peut remarquer sur les plats ce chiffre historique que les uns attribuent à Diane de Poitiers et les autres à Catherine de Médicis. – Marie Stuart portoit ce livre en marchant au supplice. – La lecture de ce Bréviaire consoloit Louis XVI dans sa prison. – Voilà le volume que l'empereur Napoléon lisoit et annotoit à Sainte-Hélène.[50]

Unlike the ideas that had been developed in England since the early 1830s, Techener's were focussed on the past. Not only did he omit to suggest any kind of relationship between past and present. He also suggested that the Bibliothèque Nationale should be divided at the year 1850, and that a Bibliothèque Nouvelle should be founded. Those bent on serious study of the past could thus pursue their work unencumbered by the frivolities of modern times, and in better space. He was one among many who complained of overcrowding by those who came into the Library simply to keep warm. People seeking merely 'lectures superficielles' could have their own reading room. The suggestion was unrealistic, but it contained one of the germs of what was to become the *Réserve des imprimés*: it grew partly from a concern for the safety of the past, and partly for the convenience of readers.[51]

In his editorial policy, Techener reported frequently on matters of interest in Britain. Organs such as the *Revue Britannique* further enabled events and ideas to be followed over the English Channel. The ties formed during the Napoleonic wars remained: in exiled families; in the experience of prisoners of war; in political entente; and in the book trade: Bossange was the largest and best connected of the French firms in London, but it was not alone. In 1844, the *Revue Britannique* devoted a long article by Adrien Le Roux de Lincy on Caxton – longer than any article on him in the contemporary English periodical press. It coincided with the publication of Knight's biography, the first substantial volume devoted to him since Lewis's study in 1737. For those who sought strategy, it was a reminder of the accord reached between Lord Aberdeen and Guizot: Queen Victoria visited France in 1843, and Louis-Philippe returned the visit the next year.

While France struggled through her mid-century political turmoil, in the Netherlands a different kind of political campaign was being played. Local, national and linguistic loyalties all demanded that the credit for the invention of printing should be given not to Gutenberg, but to Laurens Coster, of Haarlem. Sixteenth-century traditions would not die out. A statue had honoured him ever since the early eighteenth century, and then in 1856 the town mounted a much greater fête. Public buildings were decked out in national flags, a small statue of him was placed, as if a religious image, at the front of a horse-drawn wagon that also carried a working press. A new statue was erected in the Grote Markt, there were merry-go-rounds and other diversions, and suitably festive music. Haarlem was not to be out-done by German celebrations of a few years earlier. More seriously, there was an exhibition including early block-books, early printing from type (including so-called Costeriana), early printing from Dutch towns, a long series of books published between the sixteenth and the nineteenth centuries and a technical exhibition of printing equipment (Fig. 7.2). It was an opportunity for celebration, propaganda and instruction. In England, the *Norfolk Chronicle* – the nearest newspaper, for a region with strong Dutch traditions and trade links to the Netherlands – noted the festivities. But it was, on the whole, a Dutch occasion.[52]

So far as early printing was concerned in England, one anniversary eclipsed all others. The Gutenberg celebrations of 1840, celebrated so eagerly in parts of France and Germany, passed with barely a notice. For Caxton and the anniversary of the introduction of printing into England, several dates presented themselves. When John Lewis published his account of Caxton in 1737, he alluded to sixteenth- and seventeenth-century authority: that this had happened in 1471. The sixpenny life of Caxton published by the Society for the Diffusion of Useful Knowledge in 1828 took matters little further, in evident ignorance of the doubts expressed in 1810 in Dibdin's edition of Joseph Ames's *Typographical antiquities*:[53] 'The common opinion is, that the "Game of Chess" was the first book printed by Caxton at Westminster.'[54] Readers were then reminded that Dibdin considered the *Romance of Jason* to have been the first – both books supposed to have been printed in 1474. This was a date that seemed to have the authority of none other than Caxton himself, for with a little imagination it was possible to see this date in his woodcut printer's device. The same date was repeated in Charles Knight's *Penny cyclopaedia* in 1836. Writing in 1844, Knight quoted first Edward Gibbon: 'It was in the year 1474 that our first press was established in Westminster Abbey.' Then he reverted to the seventeenth-century bookseller and collector John Bagford, who had said that Caxton's first book in the Abbey was *The game of chesse*.[55] Ever

Figure 7.2 The printing exhibition at Haarlem, 1856, in honour of the memory of Lourens (or Laurens) Janszoon Coster. Views of the machinery section and of the book exhibition: note the shelves of seventeenth- to nineteenth-century books for public consultation along one side, opposite the glazed cases for more valuable examples. From J. J. F. Noordziek, *Gedenkboek der Costers-feesten* (Haarlem, 1858).

economical and ready to recycle what he had previously written, Knight repeated this in his more general book published in 1854, *The old printer and the modern press*. Few people had access to Dibdin's expensive edition of Ames, so these various popular sources were in effect the principal and accepted authorities for most.

No-one writing about the history of printing enjoyed a wider circulation than Knight. His opinions permeated the literate working classes as well as those with more money to spend on books for leisure. The British Museum lent its authority to this date in its printed guide of 1870 to the exhibition of books. The idea that the anniversary would therefore fall in 1874 seemed to be well based in long-standing authorities. But, quite apart from the mistaken belief that Caxton had actually set up his press in the Abbey itself (again the Museum stated as much), the date was wrong by several years. So, with Caxton established as a national hero, the enabler of political and religious freedom, it remained that most members of the public knew neither where nor exactly when he had worked. Nor – save in the British Museum – had they seen any of his books. In the following chapter we shall see how, for the first time in England, a large exhibition on the history of printing and its modern development was presented to the London public.

8 | The Caxton exhibition of 1877

Nations on display

Temporary exhibitions of works of art and of industry had been a familiar part of national aspirations since the end of the eighteenth century, and in France the first salon had been held as long ago as 1667. National exhibitions of industry were held in Paris every few years from 1798 onwards.[1] Other national exhibitions were held at Barcelona in 1844, Mechelen in Belgium in 1849 and elsewhere. In London, the Great Exhibition of 1851 marked a change in that it was international – 'International, certainly', in the words of Prince Albert reported by Henry Cole.[2] It was followed at Paris with international exhibitions in 1855 and 1867, both of them featuring paintings as that in London had not. London hosted further exhibitions in 1862 and 1874.

The 1867 exhibition at Paris suggested another opportunity, for in that year a museum of national archives from the early Middle Ages to recent times was opened in the hôtel Soubise. It complemented the archaeological displays at the Musée des Antiquités Nationales that had opened at Saint-Germain-en-Laye in 1862, which in turn had been partly inspired by the purchase and development in the 1840s of the Thermes de Cluny as a more general museum of medieval art.[3] The destructions and losses of the 1790s were barely a generation past, and the memory of them was instrumental in the creation of publicly visible museums in France between the 1830s and the 1860s. There was no such particular sense of loss in Britain, and public interest in the past was for many years less institutionalised, characterised more by the founding of local antiquarian societies than by major museums or other permanent displays. The Museums Act of 1845, permitting local councils to maintain museums, had at first only a limited effect.[4] Paris stood contrasted with London, where various suggestions had been advanced that the Public Record Office (equivalent of the Archives Nationales) should have a small public museum – to no avail. In 1861, Thomas Duffus Hardy, just appointed Deputy Keeper, wrote to the more public-conscious Henry Cole: 'I am sure that the Master of the Rolls would not like to turn the office into a show place.'[5]

In 1874, Paris witnessed an ambitious exhibition of a different kind: one of works of art drawn from private collections and stretching from the Italian renaissance to modern times, with tastes for Dutch and Flemish artists particularly well represented. The exhibition, organised in the Palais Bourbon in aid of refugees from Alsace-Lorraine, also included illuminated manuscripts from the Didot collection and Grolier bindings from the marquis de Ganay. For at least one commentator it was an occasion for national reflection, as he thought also of the collection so recently assembled in France by Sir Richard Wallace but sent to England in 1871 because of his fears of the Commune, and now on loan to the Bethnal Green Museum in London. While on the one hand the survival of France's patrimony had depended so often on private collectors, on the other so much had been lost:

Nos archives, nos bibliothèques, passaient en Russie, nos voisins d'outre-Manche emportaient nos galeries, et la révolution travaillait avec désintéressement à rendre encore plus facile ce partage de la richesse et de la vieille gloire de notre patrie. C'est ainsi que l'Europe s'est fait peu à peu une éducation dont nous payons presque toujours les frais.[6]

The themes were different, the organisations were different and the countries were different. But the inspiration was the same. These major exhibitions were occasions for national reflection and education as well as for national aggrandisement. The work of painters ancient and modern, machinery, the spoils of empire and contemporary manufacturing achievements – all were placed at different times before the public. For Londoners, the years 1851 and 1862 in particular remained features of popular memory into the next generation and beyond. But as the guidebook to the South Kensington exhibition of 1874 remarked, 'It must always be remembered that the main object of this series of exhibitions is not the bringing together of great masses of works, and the attraction of holiday-making crowds, but the instruction of the public in art, science and manufacture, by collections of selected specimens.'[7]

There was, however, a considerable difference, both conceptually and contextually, between these general exhibitions and the developing taste in the third quarter of the century for exhibitions devoted to individuals. This was most apparent in the world of paintings. At Paris, a succession of single-artist retrospective exhibitions from the late 1850s onwards included figures such as Paul Delaroche (1857), Ingres (1861, 1867) and Delacroix (1864). Some were presented by institutions, some by dealers.[8] In London at the Royal Academy, the winter exhibitions from 1870 onwards provided a more regular, if still select, opportunity to pursue both the past and the present. In 1870, old masters were exhibited alongside C. R. Leslie and Clarkson Stanfield, and in 1886 another selection of old masters was shown with Joseph Wright of Derby and watercolours by J. M. W. Turner. None of these, in Paris or London, was addressed to the general populace. They were for audiences who were already defined by their social standing and their knowledge.

There had never been in Britain an exhibition devoted entirely either to medieval manuscripts or to printing. At the Manchester exhibition in 1857, the 'museum' of ornamental art included a section on bookbindings lent by Felix Slade and others,[9] including among the modern work an unusually ambitious example by the firm of Bedford; this had won a silver medal at the Paris exhibition of 1855. As for older bindings, the shilling catalogue summarised one way of appreciating these objects that had been so venerated by wealthy collectors but were so unfamiliar to the bulk of visitors:

Amongst other branches of decorative art illustrated in this portion of the building [the central hall], one especially deserves more than passing attention – that of ornamental bookbinding, which, during all ages until our own, has frequently been of a truly artistic character; thus, amongst the works in metal, ivory, and enamel of the present Collection may be seen very beautiful examples of the application of those arts to the decoration of book-covers. Most of those exhibited in the Museum are of the Renaissance period; during which, embroidery, metal-work, and leather, tooled, stamped, pounced, gilded, and coloured, and sometimes an inlay of different coloured leathers, are of frequent occurrence.

The greatest patron of the art of leather bookbinding, in the early part of the 16th century, was the Chevalier Grolier, who generally employed Gascon, specimens of whose workmanship, choice even at a time when the arts were at their acmé, are now eagerly sought for by connoisseurs. A volume printed by Aldus, and bound by Gascon, with the name of Grolier himself inscribed on it, is a treasure of great price.[10]

With no details about Grolier, nothing to identify the mysteriously intruding Aldus and nothing (this in a large manufacturing town) even about the kinds of leather used, this was not the kind of writing likely to help visitors unfamiliar with sixteenth-century history. The misinformation about Le Gascon and Grolier (who died in 1565, long before Le Gascon was active) merely repeated contemporary misunderstandings; but quite apart from this, the general exhibition-going public deserved better if they were to be brought to understand the values of the past effectively. For all its much lauded inclusiveness, the extraordinary generosity of lenders, the organisation that dealt with vast numbers of visitors and the sheer size of an enterprise that was pioneering in its concentration on works of art rather than on works of manufacture and design, the Manchester exhibition was often little more than amateurish. In the way it was presented, it did not provide a framework on which education could be constructed. The bindings, as they were described here, were no more than curiosities. The descriptions revealed nothing of the reasons for their making, and nothing of their historical contexts. They were, in the words of the catalogue itself, merely 'decorative art'. It was an attitude that was to prove difficult to shift. In 1932 the same opinion was expressed by none other than W. W. Greg in his presidential address to the Bibliographical Society.[11]

When in 1862 the South Kensington Museum organised a loan exhibition of medieval, renaissance and more recent works of art, printed books slipped in literally under cover. Sections of this typically sprawling exhibition (it contained over 8,000 exhibits) were devoted to illuminations and illuminated manuscripts, and to decorative bookbindings.[12] The latter, featuring some 140 exhibits, was the largest exhibition of such work ever to have been shown in London. The list of lenders was headed by the Earl of Gosford, Felix Slade, Lord Spencer and R. S. Turner, and dates ranged from the fifteenth to the eighteenth centuries. In his brief descriptions of the exhibits, James Beck, rector of Parham in Sussex, was careful to note author and title, and place and date of publication, besides the materials of the bindings. Provenances were also essential, as part of the justification for including several of the volumes displayed. Beyond this section, a few books were admitted as 'historical relics', including a prayer book prepared for Elizabeth I in a gold enamelled cover, lent by George Field. But with the exception of a woodblock and an impression from it, lent by Lord Spencer, there was scarcely a mention of printers. These were books for decoration, to be seen on the outside. At least for exhibition-goers, they were not books to be read, nor was there any suggestion that they had ever been used.

In South Kensington the books were openly exhibited to the public. It was less easy to penetrate the rooms of the Royal Archaeological Institute in Burlington House, off Piccadilly, where in May 1871 an exhibition of early printed books was arranged. The loans were mostly from members of the Institute's committee, and it was a private affair, with an opening address by J. Winter Jones, Principal Librarian of the British Museum.[13] After some general remarks about early printing, he turned to some of the exhibits: to the half-dozen lent by the Queen, including copies of the 1457 Psalter, the Caxton French *Recueil* and Coverdale's Bible of 1535. There were several books of hours, two copies of the *Hypnerotomachia Poliphili* (1499), a copy of the *Theuerdanck*, various further Bibles and a scattering of English literature. To a great extent, the choice seems to have been driven by opportunism, and thus inevitably reflecting contemporary taste in bibliophily, rather than by any organised theme. But, for those able to attend, it was an unusual chance to see these books together. The exhibition also reflected something that was becoming ever more clear: that the earliest history of western book printing was a subject for casual discussion on social occasions. One of those most involved in the exhibition was W. J. Loftie, who a few months later contributed to the Institute's *Journal* a review of the English edition of Antonius van der Linde's controversial demolition of the Coster legend.[14] It was a tale as hard to suppress as it was a guarantee of abiding public curiosity.

The quatercentenary in 1870 of the introduction of printing into France passed off without display. This was not a time for celebration. War with Prussia broke out in July that year, and proved disastrous. Napoleon III surrendered on 1 September, and four weeks later Strasbourg surrendered after being heavily attacked. The city's library was destroyed. In the same month Paris was besieged. The city was bombarded with considerable losses in January, and France was forced to capitulate in February. The contrast with London could hardly have been greater. Emphasising German imperialism, in January 1871 Wilhelm I of Prussia was proclaimed Emperor of Germany in the Hall of Mirrors at Versailles; the *Illustrated London News* carried a large illustration of the occasion as soon as an engraving could be made, and it appeared on the front page of the issue for 4 February. But then, as news of the siege of Paris became more serious, and the Commune ended in the destruction not only of the Tuileries and the Palais Royale but also the libraries of the Louvre and the Hôtel de Ville, the *Illustrated London News* carried picture after picture of the last events of the Commune. Amidst them, as if in silent comment, it also published a spread showing the well-behaved crowds in the casts gallery of the South Kensington Museum on the Whit Monday bank holiday.[15] As for France, it was a particular affront that the specialist military library at Metz, built up over three centuries, was taken away by the Prussians to Berlin; the fact that in the early years of the century, under Napoleon, far more had been pillaged or confiscated and removed from their homes to France (much had never been returned) did not prevent cries of dismay now the same was visited on France in a much smaller degree. Losses to libraries continued with the burning of those at Nancy in July 1871 and, in a separate incident, over in the west at Saintes in November.[16]

These various events, with the celebrations surrounding Gutenberg of a few years earlier, formed one part of the background to the impetus for an exhibition to celebrate printing in England in particular. While Britain had no claim to Gutenberg, there was at last sufficient self-confidence to organise and finance a celebration of the beginning of printing in London. Moreover, thanks to a rather disorderly mixture of popular books, stage-plays and everyday journalism, there was also a wider (if not always better informed) curiosity about the history of printing among a public whose education was limited. The stories told by Loftie in his small-format 100-page handbook *A plea for art in the house* were derivative and formulaic: the person who made a fortune by selling an old book (it was usually black-letter) whose true importance he had not recognised; the binder who wrecked books by ploughing edges, or throwing vital leaves away; the owner who made imperfect volumes perfect by assembling from different copies. Loftie's book was reprinted four times within four years of publication. He wrote for a kind of reader whose hope was always improvement, whether in old books or in collecting old furniture or old china. With a smattering of knowledge, there was always such hope. Old books were not just for the rich; with a little luck, valuable examples could still be found. It was to this dual public – the one drawing on education and wealth, the other bent on self-improvement – that the anniversary designed to celebrate England's own printer-hero was addressed.

The Caxton anniversary

Celebrations of anniversaries of literary figures were not new. In their very different ways, Robert Burns and Schiller dominated the year 1859 for many people in Scotland and Germany, and were turned to popular and political use.[17] But it required further imagination to convey complex tales such as the relationship between national interest, changing historical perspectives and priorities, individuals, literature and printing. While – for some parts of the population – exhibitions had become part of national and local life, there was a difference between those having some general import, those dealing with particular trades or manufactures and those celebrating individuals. The inspiration for the centenary exhibition concerning Sir Walter Scott in the summer of 1871 lay in the Dante celebrations at Florence in 1865, where a mixture of manuscripts, printed books and related works of art had been assembled under the auspices of the Tuscan Archives. A statue of him was erected in the Piazza Santa Croce at the same time. Scott already had his monument, but the Scott exhibition followed the same pattern, with a lavish illustrated commemorative catalogue; this time it was a private enterprise, presided over by Sir William Stirling Maxwell, book collector as well as public figure.[18]

As a national hero, by the mid-century Caxton had acquired a status well beyond what he had enjoyed a hundred years earlier. His reputation was not like that of Sir Walter Scott, whose memory derived from best-selling novels, a romantic view of Scotland's past and a biography parts of which were well known. He had died only recently, in 1832. The immense and elaborate Scott memorial in Edinburgh, over 200 feet high and with a huge statue of him in Carrara marble, was completed in 1844. There was nothing like it anywhere else in Europe. Caxton's was a more measured reputation. As an author and translator he figured in popular histories of English literature. He had become a name familiar in the newspapers as well as to bibliophiles and literary scholars. Though he enjoyed a powerful measure of support, he was far out-distanced by Shakespeare, who was the subject of repeated biographies and whose tercentenary was celebrated in 1864 with miscellaneous souvenirs and curiosities. In 1863 a public campaign led by James Orchard Halliwell-Phillipps resulted in the purchase of New Place at Stratford-on-Avon. An exhibition at Stratford-on-Avon in 1864 included a death mask alleged to have been taken of him, as well as his walking stick and a jug said to have belonged to him.[19] No such boasts could be made of Caxton, but there was a story to be told every inch as commanding as that conveyed in the hundreds of paintings large and small recording actors and stage productions relating to Shakespeare. In Caxton, modern printing achievements appeared as the natural successors of his own modest press in the precincts of Westminster Abbey, and they carried with them the benefits that printing had brought, whether political freedom, freedom of the press, education, freedom with specifically Protestant religion or knowledge more generally. As we have seen, Charles Knight repeatedly emphasised such links as he moved from one to the other in successive paragraphs of his journalism, and especially in his biography of Caxton published in 1844. It pleased some writers such as Andrew Marvell in the 1670s and the radical William Hone in the post-Napoleonic era to claim that the invention of printing was at much the same time as the Reformation. In a book reprinted in the 1860s, Hone also quoted a history of England concerning Caxton's bringing printing to England: 'These proceedings for the advancement of learning and knowledge, especially in divine matters, alarmed the ignorant and illiterate monks.'[20]

His reputation was not only a part of Protestant myth. For some, he was the person who brought books to a world beyond court and church. George Lillie Craik was much influenced by Charles Knight, and in 1844–5 he contributed *Sketches of the history of literature and learning in England* to Knight's series of cheap weekly volumes. His work was republished in 1861, in a more lavish format, as *A compendious history of English literature and of the English language*, and in this format it was much reprinted. Caxton had his own place, and was now cast as the person who, in effect, created the 'general reader'.

On the whole, the first books that were printed in England were, for the most part, we see, books for the general reader: none of them were works of recondite learning or science; if they were not all equally edifying, they were as much as possible addressed to the great body of the reading public – the only audience that was then sufficiently numerous to call into profitable exercise the multiplying powers of the press.[21]

Caxton was several different people, depending on social, political or religious viewpoints. Craik's assessment was only one, incomplete, ill-considered and ill-informed. But it was widespread, and sat alongside that of a greater bestseller, Macaulay. In 1848 the first volume was published of Macaulay's The *history of England*. It proved an instant success. To Macaulay, the first benefit of printing was that it brought Bibles down to a price 'which every cottager may now command'. It provided the Reformers, 'the assailants of the Church', 'with a mighty weapon which had been wanting to their predecessors'.

The study of the ancient writers, the rapid development of the powers of the modern languages, the unprecedented activity which was displayed in every department of literature, the political state of Europe, the vices of the Roman court, the exactions of the Roman chancery, the jealousy with which the wealth and privileges of the clergy were naturally regarded by laymen, the jealousy with which the Italian ascendency was naturally regarded by men born on our side of the Alps, all these things gave to the teachers of the new theology an advantage which they perfectly understood how to use.[22]

In such ways, history was adapted to contemporary anxieties about Roman Catholics. It was also the case that support for commemorating Caxton in 1877 was to come mostly from the Established church and its political allies, led by Westminster Abbey itself.

William Blades's biography of Caxton was published in two volumes in 1861–3.[23] It thus came in the wake of writers like Craik and Macaulay, and it presented a very different picture. It was the first modern account of him to be based on a re-examination of his books as well as of such documents as could be discovered in the archives of London and Bruges. Blades was a printer, and he brought a professional eye to the technicalities of type design, categorising the successive faces introduced by Caxton in a scheme that has been adapted only a little in the years since. In a series of lithographed plates after highly skilled tracings by G. I. F. Tupper[24] depicting passages and illustrations in facsimile, he also analysed each character and thus showed properly for the first time the nature of Caxton's typographical equipment. Soon after publication he sent a copy to Henry Bradshaw, on the staff of Cambridge University Library. Bradshaw's own interests were diverse, including medieval manuscripts, Irish printing and the history of the liturgy. They also lay particularly in the fifteenth-century printing of the

Low Countries and the lower Rhine valley, the region where Caxton had worked. He was quickly becoming the leading incunabulist of his day, and he read Blades avidly, annotating heavily and sometimes breaking off to exclaim against something that he thought wrong or misguided. Blades had no more careful, or more constructive, reader, and the two men complemented each other effectively over the next few years.[25]

London was not the first to mark the anniversary. Australia had stolen a march on Europe in 1871 by idiosyncratically commemorating in that year the quatercentenary of the first printing in the English language. Blades, writing only a few years before, had dated the *Recuyell of the historyes of Troy* to 'shortly after' 1471, probably in 1472–4, with a question mark. But his book did not immediately reach everywhere. The *Recuyell* had been translated in 1471, and this in turn was quickly translated by the Melbourne *Argus* into a celebration of the introduction of printing into England. The purpose in Melbourne was to raise funds for distressed printers, a project tackled enthusiastically by organising a cricket match and then arranging some highly successful public lectures on subjects having nothing to do with Caxton.[26] After this premature excitement, Caxton was better timed in Victoria in 1877, when a series of sculptures depicting episodes in his printing career was included on the front of the office of a local newspaper in Williamstown, near Melbourne. Back in England, the year 1874, widely and for many years considered the anniversary of the first book printed in English, had not been observed in London or Westminster. This was the date given by John Power, who also named *The game of chess* as 'the first book printed in England' in his respected general book on book collecting published in 1870.[27] The date was repeatedly referred to even after the publication of Blades's life. Even in 1883 the bibliophile and lawyer J. Herbert Slater, following others than Blades in his guide for book collectors, recorded *The game of chess* (1474) as 'the first book printed in England'.[28] Thanks to Blades the celebrations took place a little later, based on the first dated book known to have been printed in England. Blades himself suggested that Caxton had left Bruges and was already back in England 'about the latter half of 1476'.[29] It was to emerge only in the twentieth century that in fact Caxton was already at work in his printing house beside Westminster Abbey well before the end of that year.

At London in 1877 there was an air almost of afterthought. Bradshaw played little public part in the London celebrations, which owed much to Blades and were rushed together in a hectic few weeks in the first part of 1877 – that is, with the anniversary year already arrived. In February, a meeting was held in the Jerusalem Chamber of Westminster Abbey to consider how the Printers' Pension, Almshouses and Orphan Asylum Corporation should celebrate the event in the coming June.[30] The meeting was presided over by the Dean of Westminster, and apart from various senior members of the printing trades and a smattering from the Church, the Belgian and American ambassadors both attended. A long list of members of the royal family and House of Lords sent apologies and regrets, and a resolution was moved by Sir Charles Reed, the type-founder, that the most appropriate course would be 'a loan collection of the works of Caxton, and of other antiquities, appliances, &c. connected with the art',[31] and that the offer of space by the Stationers' Company should be gratefully accepted. Reed had already been at work with a small group, and he proved effective. A wider public meeting followed in March, this time in the Mansion House in the City, chaired by the Lord Mayor. By then the Queen had indicated her willingness to contribute towards a project intended to be at once attractive and instructive and also to contribute to the Printers' Pension Fund. Anthony Trollope, Sir Charles Dilke and the Deputy Governor of the Bank of England were among those who spoke in support.[32]

By mid-May, preparations were well advanced but still indeterminate in large part. It was hoped to open the exhibition on 9 June – three weeks earlier than proved to be possible. It was not clear that all requests for loans would be met; it was assumed that the manuscript translation of *Ovide moralisé* in the Pepys Library at Magdalene College, Cambridge, would be lent; and it was expected that there would be no fewer than three wooden presses. Imaginatively but impractically, Blades planned that in as many instances as possible there would be two copies of each of Caxton's works on display, one showing the beginning and the other the end.[33] But even Blades's energies could not accomplish the impossible. Time was against him, and in the case of the Ovid so was Samuel Pepys's will, which forbade the loan of the manuscript from the college.

The celebrations opened in Westminster Abbey with a special service at the beginning of June. Musically, the service was dominated by a performance of Mendelssohn's *Lobgesang*, composed in honour of Gutenberg in 1840.[34] The message remained the same, with its closing words from St Paul: 'Let us therefore cast off the works of darkness, and let us put on the armour of light.' Dean Stanley took up the theme in his sermon. Columbus, Erasmus, the Reformation and the Battle of Barnet (1471) – all were grist to his historical mill. He also had a more foreboding message, in his hope that the world might be saved from 'the dissipation of promiscuous reading, and from the overweening presumption of public opinion'. The printing press was not in itself a guarantee of light.[35] But that did not prevent other writers lauding its achievements, or noting the ways in which modern communications had added their own possibilities to those of print: as the *Newcastle Courant* remarked, most newspapers of standing now had a private wire to London so that news could be reported quickly.[36] These wires made it possible to syndicate news reports easily, and so Stanley's sermon and the opening of the exhibition a little later were widely and quickly reported in detail.[37]

The exhibition opened on 30 June. It had outgrown the Stationers' Company near St Paul's Cathedral and was instead in the sprawling exhibition galleries of the Royal Horticultural Society at South Kensington[38] – a location that some thought inconveniently distant from the centre of printing and publishing in the City. With a flourish of trumpets and a prayer from the Archbishop of York, the opening ceremony was performed by Gladstone, whose speech was reported at length in *The Times* as well as in provincial newspapers. He too sounded a note of caution:

Although we are proud of being Britons, we must recognize this, that our position in relation to the early period of the art of printing is a rather humiliating position. It is not only that we did not invent it, but for a long time we seemed hardly to take to it at all. It ought to be understood that we were not quite so civilized a people at that period as we are fond of considering.[39]

Caxton was a person to be admired, but that did not mean also admiring the intellectual world in which he moved. For most people, there was little reason to worry about this larger view. English achievements were quite sufficient. The *Illustrated London News* carried pictures of Gladstone in front of a wooden common press, and of the statue in Germany of Gutenberg, Fust and Schoeffer – reminder of the origin of the skill of printing.[40] *The Graphic* published a full-spread wood engraving representing Caxton showing his press and his work to Edward IV and his queen – the last looking every inch a Victorian lady.[41]

Meanwhile, all was not quite ready. There was still no showcase to receive the Queen's copy of the 1457 Psalter. There was nowhere to sit down other than on the stairs. At the end of July – the exhibition having been now open to the public for a month – *The Times*, which printed a series of detailed summaries of the exhibits, remarked on the 'leisurely manner' in which arrangements were being completed. There was only a 'preliminary edition' of the catalogue, and many exhibits remained un-numbered. The catalogue finally appeared in mid-August, and the labels for the Bible section were then set in place. But complaints continued. While a long report in *The Academy* was enthusiastic,[42] the *Saturday Review* complained at the end of July not only about the unfinished state of the exhibition but also of its distance from London, and (perhaps more pertinently) of the lack of working men, journeymen printers and apprentices among the visitors.[43] In fact the exhibition was open in the evenings precisely to allow people to come at the end of a working day. The closing date was extended to the end of August, as meanwhile other members of the public responded more enthusiastically, by offering further exhibits – offers that understandably could not be accepted.

Exhibitions could be vast, of sizes that it is now difficult to comprehend and that even at the time must have called on unusual reserves of energy, stamina and perseverance for anyone wishing to see most of what was on display. The riches of the 1851 exhibition took many people by surprise, but its magnitude astonished everyone. In 1857 the guide to the Manchester Art Treasures exhibition listed over 1,100 paintings by 'ancient masters', 689 by their modern equivalents and 386 British portraits, besides sculpture, 969 watercolours and a comprehensive museum of ornamental art. In 1872 the Guildhall in London arranged an exhibition of antiquities and works of art, and its catalogue ran to over 600 pages.[44] If the organisers of the Caxton exhibition hoped for the kind of national excitement – even on a smaller scale – that had caused people to flock to London in the summer of 1851, they may have found reason for their hope in the coverage accorded the events of 1877 by local newspapers. Like the service in Westminster Abbey, the opening ceremony was reported across the country, and even the Welsh-language *Baner ac Amserau Cymru* in Denbigh carried a lengthy report at the time of the opening. Numbers would never be as large, but the range of responses was satisfying.

For the first time, the history of printing, and with it a better understanding of old books, was presented as surviving artefacts before a wide public who – guided by carefully directed selections, arrangements of exhibits, labels and catalogues – could now also see for themselves. Printing was provided with a continuous history linking the past to the present. In this continuity the link was at last properly demonstrated in physical objects rather than in ideas, between the concerns of age-old bibliophily and the world of modern communication. Meanwhile Caxton himself became difficult to escape, whether on stage or in children's books (*The earl printer; a tale of the time of Caxton* was published by J. F. Shaw that summer)[45] or in *Punch*. Both *Punch* and (less enthusiastically) *Fun* published verses about him, *Punch* reminding its readers that this was also the anniversary of Wycliffe (1377).[46] Maclise's celebrated painting of Caxton showing the first specimen of his printing to Edward IV had been painted twenty years earlier, and when it was engraved in 1858 it was in the possession of John Forster (d. 1876). In 1877 it was on loan from its new owner, Lord Lytton, to the South Kensington Museum. The central part of the engraving was reissued in April 1877, as a contribution to the festivities (Fig. 8.1).[47] Reproductions were available at reduced prices to readers of *Young Folks* and *Young Folk's Weekly Budget*.[48] As the original copies of the steel engraving had cost 4 guineas and upwards, the special offer price of a shilling plus vouchers from the magazines was a considerable bargain.

The exhibition at South Kensington was cast on a scale that matched expectations encouraged by others. Admission prices were set at a shilling, or sixpence on Mondays.[49] With a catalogue containing 4,734 entries, covering well over 5,000 exhibits, it invited selective viewing. No doubt many who came concentrated on early printing, but many others sought out the later literature on the subject, the large collection of assorted memorabilia or the exhibits relating to contemporary work. It was an exhibition addressed to several different audiences. Apart from the predictable antiquaries, bibliographers and book-lovers, it also attracted (in the words of its Honorary Secretary, writing after its close) 'a vast number of artisans employed in the printing business', so that it had fulfilled 'all the most sanguine anticipations of its promoters'.[50] But while the title-page of the catalogue mentioned the 'loan collection of antiquities, curiosities, and appliances connected with the art of printing', the excuse was Caxton. Blades's recent biography was paraded in the first paragraph of the introduction to the catalogue, and the list of lenders made clear the principal intent: early books from the Queen, Lord Spencer (who lent no fewer than fifty-seven Caxtons), the Duke of Devonshire, the Earl of Jersey and other collectors. Cambridge University Library lent eighteen Caxtons. In all, there were 190 copies of books printed by Caxton, representing 104 different works.

Caxton filled the first part of the exhibition, but then the subject was enlarged: early printing from Scotland, block-books, early oriental printing, Bibles and liturgies, a section of 'specimens noticeable for beauty and excellence of typography', steam and newspaper printing, music printing, illustration processes and more again. The selection was far from solely bibliophilic. It marked a clear break with the past in that though the exhibits of early books were necessarily drawn from long-established libraries, there was a deliberate and sustained policy of presenting printing in many more of its branches. Of the more bibliophilic books not by Caxton, the organisers borrowed not only the long-famed Valdarfer Boccaccio that had figured in the Roxburghe sale in 1812 and that Lord Spencer had later bought for one-third of the price paid then. Now it lay in the case beside the Fust and Schoeffer Cicero, *De officiis* of 1465 in a section that continued through to

Figure 8.1 Daniel Maclise, *Caxton shewing the first specimen of his printing to King Edward IV and the royal family in the abbey of Westminster, 1477*. Steel engraving by Frederick Bromley, 1877. Size of original: 560 x 420 mm.

the Kilmarnock Burns and the first edition of Johnson's *Dictionary*. Among the earliest books, Lord Spencer also lent his copy of the 42-line Bible, now firmly labelled as 'the earliest book known'. Both the Queen and Lord Spencer lent their copies of the 1457 Psalter, and both Lord Leicester and Lord Spencer lent theirs of the 1459 Psalter. The survey of early English printing did not end with Caxton but continued through Wynkyn de Worde, Pynson and others well into the sixteenth century, also taking in the first provincial presses at Tavistock, Ipswich, Worcester and Norwich.

Pride of place was given to the Duke of Devonshire's copy of the *Recuyell of the historyes of Troy*, described by Blades as having been printed at Bruges and dated here to about 1474.[51] As the first book printed in the English language, it was placed in a case by itself on a velvet cushion, a distinction shared by the *Dictes and sayings of the philosophers*, printed in 1477, the first book from Caxton's press at Westminster with both place and date of printing – and thus the justification for the whole exhibition. No mention was made of the unique frontispiece in the *Recuyell* showing what is presumably its presentation by Caxton to his patron Margaret of York, but the fact that it had once belonged to Edward IV's queen Elizabeth was explained in a catalogue note. If the notes to this part of the exhibition were unstructured, there was nonetheless a sufficiency to suggest something both of Caxton's work and also of the history of interest in him by libraries and bibliographers. A loan from Göttingen provided an opportunity for comment on the price of Caxtons in the eighteenth century as well as an allusion to Göttingen's purchases from the Harleian Library in the 1740s. A loan from Corpus Christi College, Cambridge, had been recognised by Bradshaw as Caxton's work only in 1861. A loan from Bedford of an indulgence occasioned a note that it and its companion had been preserved in a binding. In such ways, visitors to the exhibition were provided with clues to bibliographical and historical dimensions beyond the merely decorative. No fewer than seven copies of the Coverdale Bible (1535) had been borrowed, including the copy uniquely possessing its title-page and belonging to the Earl of Leicester. The procession of Bibles stretched from the fifteenth to the late nineteenth centuries including both cheap examples and ornate editions such as one recently published by Longman, overseen by Henry Shaw and illustrated with wood-engravings after early Italian painters.

The catalogue was late – and was criticised for it. But when it appeared it was evident that it was far more than the kind of checklist sold for a shilling or so at other large exhibitions. A cheap 32-page guide was available,[52] but the standard catalogue was pioneering in its comprehensiveness. It cost the somewhat high price of 2s.6d. and it was bound in cloth. Here, in other words, was a book that was expected to have a life as a reference book as well. A few copies, not for sale, were printed on large paper.[53] The contents were also different in style. While successfully conveying appropriate enthusiasm, each section was prefaced not simply by some generally vague effusions but by several pages of firm historical facts. It was a work of shared authorship in the selection and organisation of the exhibits, and in the writing. Blades had been responsible for the early English books. The London-based American bookseller Henry Stevens had been responsible for the Bibles, and also produced a separate catalogue of these exhibits. Lord Charles Bruce had contributed to the descriptions of early overseas printing, helped by notes supplied by Henry Bradshaw in Cambridge. Others expert in their fields had contributed to the modern parts, including Talbot Baines Reed on type-founding and Andrew Tuer, printer, stationer and founder in 1877 of the *Paper and Printing Trades Journal*,[54] on steam printing. In sum, it was a collaboration of experts.

In the Caxton section, Blades set out the bare facts known of Caxton's life, and then provided a list of his books divided up according to typeface. Thus, he explained, it was possible to assign dates to undated books. It was a bibliographical exercise of the kind he had already applied to these books in his own biography, and which Bradshaw was applying at Cambridge to books from many other presses. It had not been presented to a popular audience before. For the Bibles, Stevens provided an even longer note, in a bravura section that fully reflected the generation's intense attention to the subject; his enthusiasm was to be carried forward into the following year, when he published a separate 151-page catalogue of *The Bibles in the Caxton exhibition*. When visitors opened the catalogue at the entry for Bibles they found a profusion of annotation. Several entries had notes of well over a page of small type. While by no means all exhibits were provided with even a brief comment beside their summary descriptions, the section introductions provided contexts and background. Towards the end of the exhibition, matters turned from books to equipment and methods. Type-founding equipment was borrowed from Oxford University Press, the firm of Caslon and others. There were type-casting machines, music plates and various presses, including a toy one said to have been used by Charles I and (less improbably) a wooden one said to have been used by the eighteenth-century punch-cutter J. M. Fleischman at Haarlem. Space was even found for a series of modern machine presses. By no means the least interesting exhibits in these last parts were in a long section including founders' and printers' type specimens from Britain, the Netherlands (mostly Haarlem),

Germany, France, Russia and elsewhere. The whole exhibition concluded with sections on lithography and on paper.

While many people expressed irritation at the various delays, and others found themselves confused by the need to thread a way past a jumble of school furnishings belonging to the Science and Art Department, followed by a collection of stuffed fishes,[55] there was only one extended negative review, remarkable for the animus directed against Stevens, in the persistently hostile *Saturday Review* for 18 August. It concentrated its bad temper on the Bibles section, complaining of omissions and inaccuracies, and it finished by first welcoming and then complaining about the machinery section, which might have been better treated to a separate exhibition that might also have included bookbinding: 'The staid bibliographers above stairs complain much of the noise and smell.'[56] The author of this piece missed the point: this was an exhibition specifically about printing, not about books in general. The subject of bookbinding indeed deserved an occasion, but one that would be to itself.

Although it failed to raise any great sum for the printers' almshouses, the Caxton exhibition had proved a success in the end, in other ways. It had attracted a reported 24,684 visitors. The almost inevitable question arose: How could such a subject be shown more permanently? Obviously the loans had to be returned, but the subjects and scope had been established. Back in July, the *Western Mail*, published at Cardiff, had pointed out that barely a tithe of the people who were flocking to the exhibition would have bothered to read about the subject in books.[57] In September, Hodson wrote to *The Times* suggesting that there should be a longer-term exhibition. He found no immediate answering and effective enthusiasm. Instead, the *Northern Echo* used Caxton as a prompt to reflect on northern England in the late fifteenth century ('little more than a desolate waste');[58] and in its summary of the past year the *Liverpool Echo* sandwiched a sentence between gossip about the church and statistics of lives lost in accidents: 'The Caxton exhibition came and went without adding much to the sum of human knowledge or human satisfaction.'[59] But the point had been made. Even if it was not practicable to show old books and new machinery together, there was a clear public interest. The public, malcontent or not, had to rest content with the exhibition galleries in the British Museum. By the 1890s, these could be complemented in the South Kensington Museum by an exhibition of printing machinery.[60]

The public was reminded once again of the exhibition when in 1878 Henry Stevens at last produced the catalogue of the Bibles section for which there had been neither time nor space the previous summer. 'During those nine short weeks,' he wrote, 'the public had a rare opportunity afforded it of having some of its old popular notions respecting printing dissipated, others corrected, and not a few new ones inculcated.'[61] To that extent, the exhibition was a turning point, though Stevens was occasionally inclined to over-enthusiasm in his expressions. He also took the opportunity of rounding on the *Saturday Review*, first printing its criticisms *in extenso*, counting 141 mis-statements and then answering them point by point.

The exhibition at South Kensington was by far the largest, and by far the longest open, of a small group of shows related to Caxton. Apart from the Australian celebrations already mentioned, there were two exhibitions in Canada: one in Toronto for a few days in June and the other later in the month in Montreal. Toronto made do without any work printed by Caxton, and reached from the twelfth century via China and Japan to incunables, good showings from the sixteenth and seventeenth centuries, and an important section demonstrating the spread of printing in Canada itself, including work from Toronto, Quebec, Montreal, Niagara, Kingston and Halifax. The lenders, institutional and private, were all local.[62] Montreal was both larger and more venturesome in its loans, attracting the Brinley copy of the 42-line Bible, brought up from Connecticut for the occasion. At the last minute two books printed by Caxton were offered and accepted from New York collectors.[63] As a record of Canadian bibliophily, the Montreal exhibition was remarkable. Caxton was an excuse, and the section displaying 'books from 1650 having merit in the development of the Art' was a catch-all for an assortment of enthusiasms. The four Shakespeare folios, Audubon's *Birds of America* (borrowed from McGill College) and (as at Toronto) a spread of Canadian printing were further reminders of a truth that was as obvious in London as it was in Toronto or Montreal: that while Caxton provided the occasion, the tradition that he was made to represent, and the variety and spread of printing, in books memorable for all kinds of reasons, were of much greater importance. For those unable to get to an exhibition in person, newspaper reports and illustrations were reminders of the past and its links with the present. Early printed books, for all their usual appearance in expensive sales rather than at public exhibition, were not necessarily unrelated to the nineteenth century.

The Caxton celebrations demonstrated a need, and they were a reminder. Despite all the exhibitions that had been organised in recent decades, the history of the printed book and of printing had been ignored. For all their beauty, their historical interest and their readily admitted relevance to arguments about the modern world, old printed books were not merely *refusés* so far as large general exhibitions were concerned. They were orphans. What was usually no more than implicit in the English press's reports of the Caxton celebrations was made explicit in France. There the *Bulletin du Bibliophile* included a report on preparations for the exhibition. It had to admit that for once the English had the initiative.

Heureux Pays, où l'on sait, dans les réunions publiques, s'occuper d'autre chose que de déblatérer contre le pouvoir et contre Dieu même, de réformer ou de déformer la societé![64]

France, even richer than England in its printed inheritance, should take the first opportunity to present a similar exhibition. The next universal exhibition would present one opportunity, and no-one could forget the impression gained from the manuscripts, jewels and other works of art at the 1867 exhibition or at the more recent exhibition in aid of Alsatian refugees. The coming exhibition in 1878 presented an obvious opportunity to show the wealth of the French printed inheritance. It would be an invaluable way of restoring national pride, so recently damaged by the Prussian war.[65] Comparisons with Germany were inescapable, not just concerning the history of printing but also in policy, and especially concerning the treatment by occupying powers. In 1872, baron Ernouf sought moral high ground by comparing the Prussian invasion with the much better behaviour of the French during their occupation of northern Germany in the first years of the century:

moins pénible, moins répugnante, que n'a été la récente occupation prussienne... On y chercherait en vain la rapacité systématique, réfléchie, des vahisseurs de 1870.[66]

In considering public occasions, one might also have added that the double centenary of the deaths of Voltaire and Rousseau in 1788 would serve as a national focus. In fact, although these two anniversaries were to be celebrated throughout France,[67] in the last quarter of the century France turned not to the Enlightenment but to her earlier history and literature: to the Chanson de Roland, to Joan of Arc and to adaptations of medieval art. In themselves, early printed books and the history of printing – a German's invention, and with Strasbourg now in German hands – had little to offer a nation facing the shame of defeat by her German neighbours. The tensions were no less apparent in 1900, when Anatole Claudin (1833–1906), one of the principal Paris booksellers, produced the first thoroughly authoritative account of the early French presses. It was printed on the very grandest scale by the Imprimerie Nationale, and as was explained in the preliminaries,

en imprimant cet ouvrage, notre Etablissement national a surtout pour but d'offrir aux bibliophiles les spécimens les plus curieux et les moins connus de la typographie essentiellement française, et d'établir la prééminence de nos artistes par l'influence qu'ils exercèrent sur leurs émules des nations voisines lorsque se propageait l'art de Gutenberg à l'époque de la Renaissance.[68]

Facsimiles of Caxton's work

For those who had no wish or were unable to own a book printed by Caxton, there were a few illustrations of his work in cheap literature, while for those able to afford an edition of Ames's *Typographical antiquities*, the successive revisions and expansions provided a growing gallery of reproductions, albeit of poor quality.

We have already seen how the fashion for type facsimiles and imitations took root in the early nineteenth century. It was by no means a solely British phenomenon. In Geneva, Jules-Gustave Fick achieved a considerable reputation during the mid-century for his use of typefaces derived from the sixteenth century, and a stock of woodcuts dating back to the de Tournes press in the same period. When in 1866 he printed an edition of a book published in 1552, his patron Gustave Revilliod wrote of its being 'un fac-simile exact'. It was nothing of the kind, but a re-setting in new type.[69]

It is noticeable that amongst all the type facsimiles and other imitations, hardly any were devoted to the work of Caxton. The Caxton exhibition of 1877 was, however, too obvious an opportunity to miss, and one publisher resurrected a project from earlier in the century. In September that year – that is, after the exhibition had closed – Quaritch issued a prospectus for *A new Biblia pauperum*. The text, taken from Wycliffe's translation of the New Testament, was to be set in Figgins's Caxton type. The stimulus was a group of woodcuts apparently dating from 1470, depicting scenes centred on the life of Christ. According to Quaritch's publicity, these blocks had been acquired at Nuremberg in about 1832 by a Mr Sams of Darlington; they were now owned by Unwins, the printers. In the words of the prospectus, they 'appear never to have been used in any printed book', and it was suggested that they presented an opportunity for a memento of the Caxton exhibition. The edition was to be limited to 250 copies, price one guinea to subscribers. If all was true that was claimed, here was a most unusual opportunity to acquire not just a memento, but pulls from fifteenth-century blocks at a price far below those commanded by original editions.[70] In December, the book was noticed in *The Times* among 'Christmas books'.[71] It was a brave effort, but the blocks had in fact been printed before. Quite apart from questions that have since arisen about their early date, they had been printed several times in the nineteenth century, first on paper watermarked 1815. While the date of the blocks has been doubted, and it is therefore unclear what exactly was achieved, the project illustrated yet another means of resurrecting the past, and reinterpreting it in a modern publication. Meanwhile purchasers were left in no doubt that they were acquiring neither a facsimile nor a remodelling, but as close as a low price could get to an illustrated book of the fifteenth century.[72]

The impetus to publish Caxton's work in facsimile came not so much from literary interest as from the needs of bibliophiles and booksellers. Imperfect books could be perfected only with considerable labour. But if a type was available in which imitations of missing pages could be set and printed, there was a considerable potential for savings. It was perhaps this, as well as technological curiosity, that the London type-founder Vincent Figgins had had partly in mind when in the early 1850s he cut an imitation fount of the type used for the second, illustrated, edition of the *Game of chess*. As a typefounder, Figgins took particular interest in the metal composition of the type used by Caxton, and believed that the evidence of damage suggested that it was of pewter. Figgins found particular difficulties in cutting punches in imitation of the originals when it involved some judgement of when types were broken. His labours were compounded because (not surprisingly) he was not permitted to remove a copy of the original from the British Museum:

The fact that the original is printed from cut metal types, and is a mixture of black letter and the character called secretary, with all the shades of modification and approximation to each other of which the two styles are capable, makes the work of reproducing by cast types from a single cut punch somewhat difficult; but as I found the black letter and its approximations predominate, I have endeavoured, while keeping between the two styles, to adhere more closely to the black letter. Could I have had a copy of the original beside me during my progress, I should have succeeded more to my own satisfaction, and completed my work in one-fourth of the time. As it is, I hope it will not be esteemed a bad imitation of Caxton's book; and as few persons, except those who have decidedly antiquarian tastes, and the curious who take the trouble to seek for these old works in their present solitude, have any idea of their appearance, or even of any black-letter book, this may not be without use in conveying a knowledge of these things into quarters which the originals can never reach.[73]

He emphasised the efforts made to reproduce the original, even to the specially made paper with watermarks imitating those of Caxton. Meanwhile, profits from the book were to go to the printers' almshouses at Tottenham, and Figgins went on to market the typeface as Caxton two-line long primer; it enjoyed a following amongst printers' sets of display types well into the twentieth century.

Figgins's pioneering work was quickly followed by others. In 1858, William Blades used the Dysart copy of the original to produce an edition of the *Governayle of helthe*, using types 'very similar to those employed by Caxton, to give this reprint something of the appearance of the original'. Using the Christie-Miller copy, he then produced a type facsimile of Cristine de Pisan's *Morale proverbes* in 1859, and this time added further to the effect by arranging for the paper to be stained by damp as if it had suffered in the same way as the original. When Henry Bradshaw discovered a unique copy of the *Ars moriendi* in the Bodleian, Blades made a type facsimile of this as well. These books, all printed from type cast in pewter, were produced in very small quantities: just fifty-five were printed of the *Governayle of helthe*. The type was too soft to allow larger impressions. Of necessity, they were circulated privately, and they therefore had little impact on public opinion. Blades's biography of Caxton published in 1861–3, with its carefully drawn lithographic facsimiles, was a very different project, no longer a laboratory experiment for a few friends but a commercial publication on a large scale. It transformed the subject, and provided a stimulus to further efforts. In 1869 a Kent antiquary, John Rae, had a facsimile (not a type facsimile) made from his own copy of the Statutes of Henry VII.[74] It was a considerable advance on its predecessors, but that did not prevent other less successful attempts on further books.

All these imitations and copies required a suspension of ordinary judgement. They appeared to be exact copies. In fact, few were. The same claims to verisimilitude and accuracy tended to be made about them as were made about the facsimiles of Shakespeare and others, produced at about the same time. The facsimile of Caxton's *Fifteen Oes* produced by Stephen Ayling in 1869 was a noticeable failure. Considerable liberties were taken in reproducing it by photolithography from the only complete copy, in the British Museum, and it was described in the preface as an 'exact fac-simile'. This was mendacious, for where the original had a passage about pardon crossed through, the facsimile restored it. The Museum's accession date stamped on the last page was also removed. But at least Ayling was able to claim truthfully that his was a cheaper method than that used by others.

It might be supposed that such books would have been reproduced more frequently by photographic means. This was not the case. Those involved in the production of reprints of these and other early printed books preferred the more laborious process of tracing for some time after cheaper methods were available. It was only in 1877 that Blades turned to photolithography for the facsimile of *The dictes and sayings of the philosophers*, to mark the Caxton celebrations of that year. Just 250 copies were printed, at a subscription price of a guinea, rising to half as much again after publication. The publisher was Elliot Stock,[75] and thus for the first time Blades was in the hands of an ordinary publisher for his work on Caxton. His earlier type facsimiles had been published privately, and his study of 1861–3 had been published by Joseph Lilly, whose main business lay in antiquarian bookselling. At a guinea and a half (£1.11s.6d.), the *Dictes* was exactly the price of a three-decker novel, and it is worth pausing over the two markets. The price of novels was maintained by publishers' convention and by the profits from the very large orders placed for new novels by circulating libraries. Comparatively few people bought new novels in this form, preferring instead to wait for the one-volume reprints that appeared within a few months. The price of the *Dictes* likewise reflected a limited market, but one unsupported by extensive library demand. Even after the publicity that had attended the Caxton exhibition, it was still thought not worth printing more than a small number – larger than the fifty or sixty copies of earlier facsimiles produced privately by Blades, but still well short of most ordinary commercial editions. Caxton was far from a heavy seller when his books were presented in facsimile. The demand was for studies of his life and printing. Blades's pioneering two-volume study of 1861–3 had been priced at 5 guineas; 255 copies were printed. In 1877, on the occasion of the exhibition, it was republished for a more popular market in a slightly revised form to bring it up to date and to take account of the observations of Henry Bradshaw. This one-volume edition sold sufficiently well for a further revision to be published in 1882. It remained the last scholarly monograph to be published on Caxton until Edward Gordon Duff's study published by the Caxton Club in Chicago in 1905.

Bibliophily apart, the cutting of types in imitation of Caxton had its inexorable effect. The types proved to be a valuable asset to jobbing printers for publicity, as well as to book printers and printers of periodical publications. By 1879 an American forgot his own country's earliest printing history when he felt moved to write that 'now we are so Caxtonian in our tastes that tradesmen's circulars are issued by the thousand in type which is an excellent imitation of that used by our first printer'.[76] If Caxton's work and reputation had spread to the southern and western hemispheres, at least to the USA, Canada and Australia, there remained the question of exactly on what his reputation relied. To a degree this had not changed since Charles Knight had promoted it in the 1830s and 1840s. For bibliophiles, his work was more sought out than ever. This was to be amply demonstrated in the excitement generated by the Osterley Park sale in 1885, including eleven Caxtons that had belonged to Bryan Fairfax in the eighteenth century. Five, including the *Recuyell*, were bought by Quaritch for

Lord Amherst. Quaritch also bought the only complete *Morte d'Arthur* for Abby Pope, in America. For most people – and most people were not book collectors, let alone bibliophiles – Caxton's name was now inescapable for other reasons: in street names, in the names of office buildings, in the names of proprietary goods, in the names of companies, in the titles of the periodical press. His work was to be seen, consciously or no, in typefaces derived from those he had used 400 years previously and that were now paraded in handbills, newspaper advertisements and ephemeral printing of all kinds. Unlike Gutenberg in Strasbourg and Mainz, Scott in Edinburgh and Dante in Florence, there was still no commemorative statue. He never dominated a townscape, to be looked up to (literally) by passers-by. As for books, if the antiquarian book itself had not become omnipresent, then its derivatives most certainly had, whether in facsimiles or in the everyday experience of reading. They raise once again the questions underpinning this book: how the past related to the present, and how past technology related to contemporary change.

9 | A bibliographical and public revolution

The Caxton exhibition of 1877 was more than a commemoration of old books or of English history. It was more than a celebration of the relationship of technical achievement to political, religious, intellectual and social advancement. In seeking to educate a wider public, it echoed a persistent divergence between popular antiquarianism – soon to be expressed in the work of publishers such as Elliot Stock and in magazines such as *The Bookworm* – and the emergent bibliographical scholarship of a new generation. Yet it also looked forward. On the one hand it drew on the collections assembled by wealthy collectors over the past 200 years. On the other, it turned its back on much of the literature that had sustained a kind of collecting that was passing from fashion. Ames and Dibdin had been expressly rejected by Blades in his new study of Caxton's life and works. But on yet another hand, and more discreetly, it looked forward to a new generation of scholarship, even a complete change of direction. This period has been described as a bibliographical revolution,[1] and when in 1963 Stanley Morison wrote his acutely wide-ranging introduction to a series of facsimiles of early type specimens from the Netherlands and Germany, he paid particular attention to Blades, Bradshaw and Reed.[2] It was also a period of change in another way, revolutionary for much of the wider public who claimed no bibliographical expertise but who had greater access than ever previously to view the collections of early printing assembled in the libraries and museums of Europe.

The conception, planning and much of the execution of the 1877 exhibition owed almost everything to William Blades. In the words of his obituarist, his study of Caxton and his work had

marked a new epoch in bibliography, and disposed finally of the lax methods of the old school. With a work like the Life of Caxton on record, it would be impossible in future to write with authority about the old printers and their books, without approaching the study from the point of view of the typographical expert.[3]

The words were by Talbot Baines Reed, the person perhaps most readily sympathetic to Blades's combination of practical printer and historian. The two men's understanding of industrial methods that had changed little in principle over four centuries enabled them respectively to see how many of the enigmas in Caxton's printing could be solved, and how an understanding of the history of type-founding could contribute to a firmer understanding of the history of printing itself. Reed, whose professional life centred on the Fann Street Letter Foundry, owner of one of the most extensive collections of old typefaces in the country, was in 1887 to write his own pioneering and still (in a revised form) standard history of type-founding in Britain.[4] Both men worked together with Henry Bradshaw, and all three learned much from each other. In these three – printer, type-founder and librarian – were laid the foundations of modern bibliographical method in Britain. No-one henceforth could write seriously about old books without recourse to their methods, either explicitly or at a remove. Of the three, only Bradshaw did not write a full-scale monograph on any of the subjects with which he was familiar. But in his correspondence and in a handful of memoranda that he had printed at his own expense he did more than anyone to alter the course of the subject, and provide its modern identity.

Most importantly, all three recognised the essential materiality of print. Old books were more than high-priced curiosities. If they were to be understood, and therefore if their contents were to be understood, then it was necessary to understand their making. Bradshaw insisted on the importance of codicological questions, the physical structure of books and how this related to the texts they contained. In setting out the different typefaces used by Caxton, and addressing an engraved plate of them to the type-founder William Caslon, Joseph Ames had in the eighteenth century not understood the implications of what he was offering to the reader.[5] In his elaborate recreations of Caxton's types in the early nineteenth century, Whittaker had equally misunderstood what he was working with. It remained to Blades not only to analyse the typefaces more closely and thus modify Ames's classification, but also to arrange for them to be reproduced accurately and set out letter by letter, figure by figure, and ligature by ligature. Blades thought as a printer, faced with a pair of type-cases, filled with letters cast in metal, to be printed.

Reed was aged only twenty-five when he contributed to the Caxton exhibition. He was still only thirty-five when he published his carefully detailed and full national history of type-founding. Like so many others, he emphasised the similarities rather than the differences in the methods of fifteenth- and nineteenth-century printers. But unlike others he included a substantial account of English type bodies and the various families of faces. He was the first to use Moxon's *Mechanick exercises* (1683–4) as a source not so much for printing (Moxon's work had been repeatedly raided by subsequent writers of printers' manuals) as for type-founding, and hence as a contribution to the history of a trade that had an obvious and direct relevance to the appearance of books. He was further a pioneer in stressing the importance of founders' and printers' type specimen books, of which there was a substantial selection in the 1877 exhibition. These provided documentation concerning both the development of the trade and the history of type design, including the demands made on type-founders.

What, however, of books other than those from Caxton? Much of this study has had reference to the growth and development of concern with England's first printer. It has been partly further concerned with other fifteenth-century books, and with the growing interest in English literature down to the early seventeenth century. These were the areas where most wealthy or influential collectors in Britain were to be found. These were also, therefore, the areas where most comment was made in print. But these kinds of evidence drive their own story. They do not necessarily reveal very much about the ways in which other kinds of books were regarded. In particular, they ignore many varieties of cheaper books, sometimes but not always more recent. They encourage attention to literature and history rather than to the sciences and mathematics. They undervalue subjects as disparate as theology and architecture. They neglect book illustration. They direct attention to books in English or in Latin or ancient Greek, not to those in other modern languages. We may speculate on the reasons for this, but one in particular suggests itself. Members of the influential collectors' world had a shared education which placed the classical historical and literary traditions at its centre. Other subjects, whether theology, history, topography or voyages and travels, were a mixture of interests always supplementary to training received at school.

One example may be taken, though there were many earlier examples of collectors. The history of science as a field for collecting was a phenomenon that can be dated from the 1830s. It was encouraged not only by polymaths such as Augustus de Morgan (1806–71) but also by the writings of men such as William Whewell (1794–1866), whose *History of the inductive sciences* appeared in 1837. One of the first to take an interest in scientific manuscripts was J. O. Halliwell-Phillipps, whose reputation never recovered from his being associated with thefts from Trinity College Library in Cambridge when he was a young man.[6] But these manuscripts, mostly given to the College in 1738 and dating from a collection formed in the late seventeenth century, were themselves witnesses to an older interest, long before the nineteenth century. For printed books, the absence of bibliographical guidance meant that it was only after the 1830s and 1840s that the subject developed popularly for collectors.[7] Halliwell-Phillipps's own attempt to found a society for the publication of older scientific works, modelled on the Camden Society, came to nothing.[8]

More usefully, Augustus de Morgan's *Arithmetical books from the invention of printing to the present time* (1847) was valuable and accessible thanks to its bibliographical details and annotations, besides being restricted to those books that the author had seen personally. Again, there was a distinction in the meaning of bibliography between encyclopaedic compendia of lists and attention paid to the details of the making of books.[9] The emphases in Quaritch's early catalogues suggest that historical study of the subject hardly existed: the catalogues repeated what had always been stressed – that, for example, in botany many of the standard works had been issued in extremely limited editions because of the high expense of illustration. In the many absentees among standard works and early editions of important figures, both of which were readily available, the catalogues also reveal how little Quaritch, who was to become indisputably the greatest bookseller in the country and arguably so in Europe, was prepared to invest in older books in scientific subjects. He bought early printed books, and he acted as agent for many learned societies, including scientific ones. But the middle ground of the seventeenth, eighteenth and early nineteenth centuries was represented with less than his usual thoroughness.

Meanwhile, when in 1867 Henry Noel Humphreys turned to the new process of photolithography for his heavily illustrated *History of the art of printing*, published by Quaritch, he managed the more general story only down to the 1560s, and the last years were extremely skimpily covered. Three years later, the London antiquarian booksellers Sotheran published his further work, *Masterpieces of the early printers and engravers*. These books remained standard collections of large-scale pictures for a generation and more. But Humphreys spoke for more than his own:

> The energetic successors of Koster and Gutenberg carried their art to a degree of perfection, as regards the beauty of their various kinds of type, the excellence of their illustrative devices, and of such decorative features as beautiful initial letters and fine ornamental borders, which has not been surpassed, if even equalled, by the finest books of the present day. It is, indeed, those ornamental features and the truly artistic feeling with which they were developed, that impart to some of the choice volumes of the fifteenth and sixteenth centuries that picturesque character which has rendered them so attractive, and caused them to be so keenly sought by collectors, at prices which occasionally seem almost fabulous.[10]

The attractions of many old books lay more in their visual qualities than their content. It generally remained – as it generally remains today – that early books with pictures were more expensive than those without. For more recent ones, where prices were not so high and copies were more widely available, prices were lower.

By the 1880s, there were well-articulated though always overlapping divisions in the world of old books, in attitudes to them, in their treatment, in the various groups of people who took an interest in them, and in the definitions people chose to apply. There were further problems. By the end of the century the differences were still more marked. For the sake of convenience and clarity in a complicated world, these may be partially summed up under six heads: booksellers and their catalogues; the literature concerning book-collecting; reference works on the subject; the bibliographical study of books; the importance attached to provenance; and finally the social world of old books. Such a summary is by no means complete, but it does indicate the different ways in which people approached old books. Though such books increasingly became a subject for academic study, some of the most influential and knowledgeable voices came from outside the circles of wealthy collectors and long-established booksellers. They also came from outside academia. Nor was their study restricted to the rich, or even the well-to-do. In the previous chapters, we have been concerned mostly with early printed books that were at any one time regarded as either rare or of particular interest. As these grew in value, and became more and more difficult to find outside large libraries or the private collections of the wealthy, so interest in cheaper and formerly neglected books increased. The applications of 'old' and 'rare' changed, to encompass much that had not so long since been thought to be commonplace.

For their part, second-hand and antiquarian booksellers sought to create new enthusiasms and new markets. Established firms like Quaritch, Sotheran[11] and Ellis[12] remained. Among the newcomers, in London, Bertram Dobell (1842–1914) installed himself in Charing Cross Road, and began to issue catalogues of seventeenth-century English literature. George Harding opened his shop off Great Russell Street in 1884, specialising in topography. In Camden Town, Haigh Hartley opened his business in 1884 and specialised in children's books. Frank Hollings (1892) dealt in old occult books as well as more general literature. Walter Spencer, who founded his business in 1884, specialised in modern first editions and in books with humorous illustrations at his shop in New Oxford Street, and claimed to have the largest collection of such material in the world.[13] There were several other bookshops across the country which advertised a similar interest in first editions of modern authors. In Birmingham, Edward Baker dealt in early railway books; in Sheffield Thomas Miles (founded 1879) dealt in old sporting books; in Weymouth, Sherren & Son dealt in Egyptology. Besides such booksellers, large and small, where a stock of

100,000 volumes was by no means unknown, there were plenty of others who chose not to advertise, as did Forbes in Hill Street, Birmingham, that they specialised in bric-a-brac.[14]

The catalogues issued by booksellers ranged from the elaborately detailed to the simplest summary of a book in one or two lines. Those of Quaritch were a touchstone in their extent, and in the detailed presentation of many of the books that they contained. His aggressive buying at auctions, supported by credit and by special arrangements with the auction houses, was celebrated frequently in the newspapers and magazines. It enabled him to dominate the market, and to dominate prices. He was far from being the only major London antiquarian bookseller, but he was the largest, and his was the name on people's lips. In 1884, his catalogue of English literature offered three copies of the Shakespeare First Folio, at prices ranging from £136 for one with the verses and the title-leaf replaced in facsimile, to £880, with the preliminary leaves, usually missing to more or less extent, intact: 'untouched by the hand of any modern renovator'. This last copy was bound in red morocco by Bedford, and came with a matching box with a key. Confident of his foresight, Quaritch also announced in capital letters that it was the only completely sound copy which could come into the market 'for probably another quarter of a century'. For those not fortunate enough to possess complete copies, the same catalogue offered facsimiles of the title-page of the 1623 and 1664 folios for 4 guineas and £2.10s. respectively. Apart from the several pages of English incunables, Shakespeare was accorded most attention, in a catalogue that also included a 1667 *Paradise lost* offered in four lines, Henry Glapthorne's plays (1639–40) offered in eighteen and Ashmole's *Theatrum chemicum* in the same. Unusually, Quaritch provided a detailed collation of the 1532 Chaucer, on the grounds that no bibliographical description could be found. But many English books of the sixteenth and seventeenth centuries were simply too common to be worth extended descriptions. As usual, Quaritch divided his catalogue up by subject groups. Even so, there were odd bedfellows in the alphabetical order, such as the copy of the Greville memoirs (1875) between *Greene's groatsworth of wit* (1637) and Michelangelo Florio's account in Italian of Lady Jane Grey, which Quaritch mistakenly believed to have been printed by Richard Paynter (Pittore) at London in 1607.[15] As for the Shakespeare First Folio, he quickly proved himself wrong, for by 1889 he was offering a further perfect copy – 'genuine, sound, fine, and very large', bound in the 'Veneto-English style of Queen Elizabeth's time' by Bedford, price £1,200.[16] The incongruity of a supposedly Elizabethan-style binding on a book of 1623 seems not to have been a worry.

Quaritch handled more fifteenth-century printed books than anyone else in Britain, and he was supremely successful in courting collectors in both Britain and America. But he remained curiously out of touch with the methods used on the continent. He rarely referred to the obvious foreign authorities even in what was in some ways the summit of his career as a dealer in such books, his catalogue of *Monuments of typography and xylography* issued in 1897. This came at the end of his life, for he died in 1899. He prefaced it with a note of his own:

The collection is the fruit of assiduous gathering during twenty years, and although made by a mere bookseller, is one which many museums might be proud of. It illustrates with sufficient clearness and fulness the early history of the Art which has been the most powerful agent in the work of Civilisation. From the brain of the inventor, it sprung fully armed into existence, and founded the empire of the Press, a mightier and wider sovereignty than has ever been wielded by conqueror or statesman. When we think that in 1450, Gutenberg was only negotiating for aid in money to convert his airy fancies into realities, and to give them a local habitation and a name; when we know that the enormous forty-two line Bible (the fruit of years of labour) was ready for distribution and sale before 1456; when we see in it a work of such typographical magnificence as the proudest printer of our own time could not hope to excel; – that first book in movable types seems to be the result of Magic.[17]

If printing, once thought of as God-given, was magic to Quaritch, to others it was the result of technical, financial and personal effort and ingenuity. Genius, but not magic.

Quaritch hoped to sell the whole of this catalogue as a collection, for £32,500 or a little less if necessary, but he did not achieve this ambition. The 42-line Bible on vellum, bought recently from the Earl of Ashburnham, went to the American collector Robert Hoe, and the 1459 Psalter from the Thorold sale back in 1884 went to Pierpont Morgan. The collection of specimens of early printing assembled by Ames, Herbert and latterly Sir John Fenn went via New York first to Tasmania and then to the Public Library of Victoria in Melbourne.[18] As some of the most celebrated monuments in the history of printing, the earliest books commanded the space given to them in the catalogue. But many lesser books, third- and even fourth-rate in that they were not of absolute rarity or of key importance in literary or typographical history, were also systematically described as to their extent and typography, their condition and their bindings, often together with their decoration. As usual, Quaritch frequently also gave their recent provenance – thus recording his successes at London auctions – and he often provided details of the more obvious past owners. In what amounted to a swan-song, readers of the catalogue were left in no doubt that he had commanded the London trade in early books for the past several decades.

Bibliographically it was a testimonial to an era when early printed books had still received comparatively little systematic study outside a small scholarly circle. While from time to time it alluded to Henry Bradshaw (always with respect), and to others such as Jean Philibert Berjeau (a believer in the fiction of Laurens Coster as the first printer, though 'his opinions had no vitiating effect upon his powers of reproduction' of early books)[19] and W. H. J. Weale on liturgical books, the catalogue displayed little of the change that was evolving even as it was being circulated. It cited Brunet's long-established *Manuel du libraire* (often to correct him) and Hain's *Repertorium* (still the standard reference book for all incunabula, if clearly very far from comprehensive), but Campbell's *Annales de la typographie Néerlandaise au XVe siècle* barely at all. Quaritch and his staff found no occasion to mention the recent work by Pellechet on the incunabula at Lyon or Voullième on Bonn, nor the posthumously published catalogue of those at Besançon by Auguste Castan – 'undoubtedly... at the head of any catalogue of Fifteenth Century books yet issued in France', in the words of W. A. Copinger reviewing it in the *Transactions of the Bibliographical Society* in 1894.[20] In 1898, too late for Quaritch, the first part was to appear of Robert Proctor's listing of the incunabula in the British Museum and the Bodleian Library.[21] The effect of Proctor's work, building on that of Henry Bradshaw, was to be revolutionary, leading in turn to the series of catalogues of fifteenth-century printing in the British Museum, of which the first volume was published in 1908. For early printing in France, Anatole Claudin began to gather up some of the articles he had published in the *Bulletin du Bibliophile*, and published the first of his volumes on Paris in 1900.[22] In his 1897 catalogue, Quaritch alluded periodically to watermarks, but it was in a vacuum: their study had scarcely advanced since Sotheby had included reproductions in his *Principia typographica* in 1858. Again this was a field of study that was shortly to be transformed, with the publication of Briquet's systematically documented albums of dated and located reproductions, *Les filigranes*, in 1907.[23]

The existence of a growing number of reliable reference works in some respects made it possible to present catalogues in a much more staccato as well as better informed manner. While the changing demography and educational backgrounds of collectors required more extended notes, of rarity, of literary and bibliographical matters and of personal details of authors, much space could be saved by reference to the descriptions of books accessible in a growing number of standard sources. This was especially true of incunabula. It was not, yet, true of sixteenth- or seventeenth-century English literature, or of the growing interest being paid to books of travel, or of the great bulk of later books printed on the continent. There was never any question of the major booksellers retreating for their better books to the single-line summaries standard in their predecessors' catalogues of the seventeenth and eighteenth centuries. Instead, there was a shift of emphasis in the use of space in catalogues. And space could be at a premium. While a few booksellers, such as Quaritch in London or Muller in Amsterdam,[24] felt able to use large type, good paper and ample margins in their catalogues, the vast majority preferred to save space and money, with small, close-set type, poor paper and minimal annotation. It was not simply that some were selling mostly to the knowledgeable, and others were pioneering with new kinds of customers. Whether in London, Leipzig, Paris or Munich, booksellers had a single purpose: to sell books as economically as possible within their own sphere and customer base.

If Quaritch did not make use even of what was available, he did more than other London booksellers. His principal rival in the last few years of his life was Ellis & Elvey, whose large *General catalogue of rare books and manuscripts* issued in 1894 contained a First Folio, 'perfect throughout and free from facsimile leaves', for £460, besides works from the presses of Caxton and Wynkyn de Worde. A more telling comparison with Quaritch in respect of bibliographical and other more miscellaneous detail is the catalogue of incunabula issued by the Munich firm of Jacques Rosenthal in 1900. The differences could hardly have been greater.[25] This catalogue was, again, the accumulation of several years, assembled to mark the turn-of-the-century anniversary of Gutenberg that was widely celebrated in Germany. Copies of books were summarised in two or three lines, together with remarks on their rarity that did not depend so much on allegations as on facts, such as the now easily documented absence of copies in the British Museum, the Bodleian, Paris and other large libraries; advertising was thus made much more precise, and focussed. Furthermore, where Quaritch, who regularly supplied indexes to his larger catalogues but was somewhat selective in them, Rosenthal provided a concordance to Hain's *Repertorium* as well as indexes of printers and of places of printing.

The last decade of the nineteenth century proved a further turning point in the ways that old books were to be studied, and so also the ways in which they were presented to the public. Various reasons might be adduced for why this surge of interest occurred at this time. They were not necessarily all connected with books, and in any case the newspapers had been publishing details of sales of early books for decades. William Morris was as interested in old buildings as old books. Once again it is necessary to begin at the wealthier end of the spectrum. The books from his Kelmscott Press, founded in 1891, drew on fifteenth-century models, and the types he designed owed their origins to his own study of early books combined with advice from modern practitioners.[26] But whereas Bradshaw, Blades and others concentrated on the history of the use of printing types, art historians were concerned with the study of illustration. Morris died in 1896, and in the following year Sydney Cockerell drew together some of the Press's unused material to have printed a slim album of *Some German woodcuts of the fifteenth century*. Although slight in its way, it influenced a change of focus apparent well beyond Morris, overtaken by William Maxwell's bequest to the British Museum in 1895 of early German woodcuts and superseded by Campbell Dodgson's catalogue of German and Flemish woodcuts. W. H. Willshire's much more substantial catalogue of these prints in the British Museum had shown something of the strengths of the national collection when published in 1879. As Sidney Colvin, writing as Director of the Museum, later pointed out, Willshire knew little of continental collections. He was also working before the appearance of W. L. Schreiber's more general studies. This double disability – writing shortly prior to a major and transforming benefaction, and writing in ignorance – weakened the long-term significance of Willshire's catalogue, but it did not diminish its significance when it was first published.[27] Much of this attention to early printing, typography and illustration came as momentum building up over several decades reached a critical point.[28]

For the mostly English-speaking scholarly world, the foundation of the Bibliographical Society in 1892 expressed the aspirations of a group of people of mixed backgrounds, drawn from universities, libraries, printing, publishing, bookselling and private collecting. Its first secretary was Talbot Baines Reed, a type-founder as well as historian of his trade.[29] Its first President, W. A. Copinger, was a lawyer and author of the standard book on copyright. His primary interest was in incunabula, and in his inaugural address he spoke mostly of their cataloguing.[30] Like other learned societies, it embarked on a series of publications, with a journal and a series of monographs. The contents of the earliest issues of the journal reflected its more general interests, at first in papers by Morris, the printer C. T. Jacobi and others linking present ideas of book design and production with the past. Soon, under the leadership of A. W. Pollard of the British Museum, they took a clearer direction in the study specifically of older printed books.

While the society represented fresh work, its immediate influence was limited by the decision to restrict personal membership to just 210 people.

Membership became unlimited only in 1915.[31] Its publications, a mixture of opportunism and new research, were naturally closely focussed: it was hardly to be expected that the general public would hasten to buy monographs on Erhard Ratdolt in fifteenth-century Venice, or Jan van Doesburgh at Antwerp, or an iconography of Don Quixote.

Commercial publishers were quite different, and it is in these that the most obvious public changes were to be seen. In 1893 Kegan Paul launched a cheaply priced series of *Books on books*, edited by his friend A. W. Pollard.[32] Among the first to appear were Edward Gordon Duff on early printed books (dedicated to the memory of Henry Bradshaw), Pollard himself on early illustrated books and Falconer Madan from Oxford on *Books in manuscript*. We shall return to Duff's important book below. Herbert Horne followed in 1894 on bookbinding; he dedicated his book to Cobden-Sanderson. The series was sufficiently popular for revised editions to be published later. Pollard, persuasive, evangelical, learned, commandingly placed in the British Museum and endlessly forward-looking, followed this series of short books with another project, deliberately circumscribed, the three bulky volumes of the more specialist *Bibliographica* published between 1895 and 1897.

The decoration and illustration of books applied equally to modern ones and old ones. The old and the contemporary merged in popularly priced and highly influential works such as Walter Crane's *Of the decorative illustration of books* (1896, price 10s.6d.) and Edward F. Strange's *Alphabets* (1895; 2nd edn 1896, price 5s.), both published by Bell. Public preference was for decoration, and much of the purpose of a series of expensively produced and highly priced albums of pictures of bindings was to meet this interest: William Salt Brassington on the Bodleian Library, Sir Richard Holmes on the Royal Library at Windsor, and first Henry B. Wheatley and then W. Y. Fletcher on the British Museum.[33] These had their foreign equivalents at Dresden and Paris, while Quaritch's special catalogue of bindings appeared in 1889.[34] For the less serious-minded, or less wealthy, there was a long shelf of books of popular bibliophily, imparting knowledge in an easily digestible and gossipy style.[35] Joseph Cundall had written about the ornamentation of bindings as long ago as 1848,[36] and his more substantial book *On bookbindings ancient and modern* (1881) sustained his lifelong emphasis in decoration; its publication at a price well below that of the expensive albums on the British Museum or the royal library guaranteed it a wider influence. More generally again, there were bibliophile magazines, mostly of an antiquarian nature and mostly short-lived in a market that was not quite certain of itself. In all this, if there were few books quite as commandingly and generally authoritative on their subjects as some of those in Pollard's series, or Edward Maunde

Thompson's magisterial *Handbook of Greek and Latin palaeography*, first published in 1893 at the accessible price of 5 shillings,[37] it remained that provision for general public assessment of old books had been fundamentally changed within a decade.

To these various publications was joined an increasing interest in exhibitions, usually temporary, on themes connected with books. The purchase of Plantin's printing house by the city of Antwerp in 1876, and its opening to the public as a museum in 1877, was greeted with international enthusiasm. Under the enlightened curatorship of Max Rooses it became a major tourist attraction as well as a centre of scholarship.[38] In London, the British Museum drew on several departments to mark the fourth centenary of Luther's birth with a special exhibition in 1883 (supported by a twopenny guide), and followed with Wycliffe in 1884. Luther had been suggested as a subject by the Old Testament authority and collector of Bibles C. D. Ginsburg, in emulation of the celebrations in Germany, but visitors were left in little doubt as to the real context, as they passed the final cases containing portrait medals of Thomas More and Henry VIII – 'Fidei defensor et in terra ecclesiae Anglicanae et Hibernicae sub Christo caput supremum'. As so often, the impetus for commemoration was given a national purpose.

Art exhibitions were long established. As we have seen, exhibitions of manuscripts and early printed books, for show rather than for sale, remained much less so, in Britain as in France. During the 1880s both countries saw if not a revolution then at least a substantial expansion in taste for public exhibitions, as they became a requisite part of social life, sitting among the more familiar – and much more plentiful – exhibitions of works of art. In 1877 the *Bulletin du Bibliophile* – still the best measure of French public interest in old books – noted the presence of works by Anna Maria van Schurman in an exhibition of Frisian books at Leeuwarden, in the Netherlands.[39] This was seemingly a far cry from Paris; but her association with Descartes and the beliefs of the former Jesuit priest Jean de Labardie made her a figure of French interest as well. As we have seen, the Caxton exhibition of that year aroused interest and some jealousy in France. Only in 1878 did the Bibliothèque Nationale introduce permanent exhibitions of many of its treasures, accompanied by three catalogues. At the time it was unclear, at least to the public, whether these would remain permanently or were just temporary.[40] In 1883 the Bibliothèque Mazarine lent its copy of the Gutenberg Bible to an exhibition mostly from private collections. Beyond Paris, Caen held an exhibition of printing in 1883,[41] and in the summer of 1884 a major exhibition at Rouen organised by the Société Archéologique et Historique de l'Orléanais presented a theme linking the history of the university and the history of local printing.[42] Limoges had an exhibition of manuscripts and printed books in 1886.[43] An exhibition at Rouen in the following year placed especial emphasis on Corneille.[44]

These epitomised the well-established tradition of studies of local printing in France, a tradition that was difficult to follow in Britain thanks to the comparatively brief history of printing in most places.[45] In London in 1860, the Society of Antiquaries had organised a loan exhibition of illuminated manuscripts, described by its progenitor as 'probably the most extraordinary display of the kind ever witnessed'. This was followed by one of early printed books, described similarly as not only perhaps never equalled but also as unlikely to be so in the future.[46] Members of the public were admitted to both, as guests of Fellows of the Society; these were not occasions for all and sundry. Sir William Tite used the occasions to offer commentaries on those of his own early, mostly English, books that were included, and outlined the distinctions between the principal liturgical manuscripts. This was well before the Caxton celebrations. Although in some ways the exhibition of printed books, offered as representing 'the progress of humanity',[47] may have provided an example, in others its much more restricted view of its subject remained in past traditions of bibliophily. The Burlington Fine Arts Club added its own activities to those of the British Museum, in a series of loan exhibitions at Burlington House in Piccadilly that mingled topics in the history of painting and print-making with a major exhibition on bookbindings in 1891, introduced by two specialists, Sarah Prideaux and Edward Gordon Duff.[48] The New Gallery in Regent Street in London assembled paintings, coins, medals and books, in exhibitions on the Stuarts in 1889 and on the Tudors in 1890. As confidence in the appeal of printed books grew, so did the numbers of them that were exhibited. They scarcely appeared in the Stuart exhibition. The Tudor exhibition gave them prominence, with many lent by Lord Spencer. In the winter of 1893–4 the gallery presented an exhibition of Italian art, including early Italian printed books borrowed from Fairfax Murray, Lord Crawford and others.

It could not be pretended that such exhibitions, whether in France or in London's West End, were necessarily more than diversions mingling entertainment with education for people enjoying spare cash and spare time. In England, they were also self-evidently limited to London. There further remained a perennial and little-acknowledged question. Exhibitions, and booksellers' catalogues, tended to highlight books that were more obviously attractive, whether because of their appearance or because of their subject or because of their author. And yet, the vast majority of books that had survived from the past could claim to possess none of these essential attributes. They looked dull: 'no books', as Bernard Quaritch described them in 1889, taking up Charles Lamb's phrase 'biblia abiblia'. This had several consequences. In the trade, there was a constant temptation to remove the outsides of bindings from the less interesting to the more interesting – and saleable – volumes.[49] A decorative binding on a well-known work always sold better than a plain one. For the study of the history of bookbinding, the real situation was obscured in other ways, as almost everyone concentrated their attention on the more finely decorated volumes. Not for nothing did Quaritch include the words 'artistic' in his album of reproductions published in 1889. In his introduction he was more forceful about the generality of early bindings:

The finest examples are unfortunately found associated with books that are 'no books', dull tomes of divinity and philology, or of annals as written by Latinists insensible to style and to the spirit of history. The dry and dismal nature of such books has caused their preservation; while the frequent handling of those which belong to true literature has led to the almost complete destruction of well-bound copies.[50]

So much for bindings.[51] As for the subjects of printing and early printed books, these found a more national and socially widespread appeal. For the Edinburgh Exhibition in 1886 there was an exhibit of 'printing as in the olden time' at the Ballantyne Press. In the following year, the Royal Jubilee Exhibition at Manchester in 1887 featured an 'ancient printing office' provided by the Deansgate Press.[52] In 1893 the public library at St Helens in Lancashire organised an exhibition of rare and valuable books.[53] A more select group of people in Manchester were admitted to an exhibition of early printing in 1893.[54]

Snapshots though these are, with all the randomness and selectivity they imply, such occasions in Scotland and in London represented fundamental social and educational changes that took the subject to new audiences. Apart from them, national libraries were beginning to discover new and further responsibilities to the general public, showing their books and manuscripts as the national galleries showed their pictures. Loan exhibitions elsewhere, sometimes but not necessarily involving national collections, were not of assortments of local antiquarian taste such as had characterised so many of the provincial exhibitions earlier in the century, but of major books, carefully selected, from a structured world of wealthy bibliophiles. Between the 1860s and the 1890s the world of antiquarian books was reorganised socially, financially and bibliographically. It was easier to see some kinds of old books – those that were chosen for exhibition – even as it became more difficult to see the much greater number that had been gathered up – often literally from the streets – into the antiquarian trade, sold to libraries, sorted into retrospective bibliographies, listed publicly and made available only on application in reading rooms.

Special occasions and special arrangements for security signalled more than curiosity or antiquarian values. They also signalled rarity, but where the implications of the word could be very different for the exhibition-going public and for the antiquarian book trade. The term 'excessively rare' was a term well established in the trade by the mid-nineteenth century, and it remains in use even today despite the fact that it is utterly meaningless. At the Renouard sale of Aldines in 1828, the 1501 Virgil, much sought after partly because it was the first book to be printed in italic type, had been termed 'excessively rare', and it was bought by Thorpe for 19 guineas. Renouard himself had described it more soberly as 'extrêmement rare'.[55] As if to reassure the world that rarity and price were not necessarily linked, Thorpe also bought the next lot, the more important edition of 1514, for slightly more. The term was used much too frequently by Quaritch: as John Carter was later to point out, rarity can hardly be excessive.[56] Quaritch could confuse even himself. The St Albans chronicle (c. 1486) is indeed rare,[57] but it is hardly 'excessively rare', as Quaritch alleged in his 1888 *Catalogue of the monuments of the early printers*; in any case, he was offering three copies, all imperfect (no perfect copy was known) and the third little more than a fragment. In the same catalogue he offered for £155 the genuinely rare Aldine Virgil of 1501, noting that neither Beckford nor the Duke of Hamilton had managed to obtain a copy. Only a little earlier in the catalogue, on the other hand, readers had been told that the 1494 Musaeus was 'excessively rare', despite Quaritch's being able to offer two copies at £36 and £42. 'This choice and beautiful book,' he remarked as he broke into capital letters for emphasis, 'is the first and rarest production of the Aldine press.' Nonsensical allegation was endemic in some parts of the trade, for Quaritch was by no means the only one to exhibit the disease. It was contagious. There was of course a difference in meaning, since a book could be rare in the trade if not rare in the total of known surviving copies. But Quaritch seldom made that distinction. In the same Aldine section of this catalogue he offered a copy of Catharine of Siena (1500), by no means a rare book and priced accordingly at £6.10s. Here he was more careful in his ambiguous phrasing, describing it as 'very scarce and much sought after in Italy'.

The catalogues of Quaritch were a far remove from most people, even most people who professed some interest in antiquarian books. The British Museum was in London, a city vastly larger than others yet visited by most people only very occasionally, if at all, in the course of their lives. But, thanks to the development of public libraries, there were scattered around the country places where old books could be looked at, if not in their originals, then at least in facsimile. This was the proposal put forward by A. W. Pollard of the Museum when he was invited to address the Library Association in 1893. He revealed to his audience that the exhibition in the Museum already included two facsimiles, which he thought were rarely spotted by visitors. Thanks to the quality of photographs now available, it was possible to mount exhibitions that would range over the entire history of printing, with no regard for scarcity.[58] He did not take his argument a step further, and suggest touring exhibitions for facsimiles of printed books of the kind already organised for other materials by the South Kensington Museum.

Meanwhile further ideas were in circulation. Many public libraries contained collections of books, more or less old and of more or less interest because of their age. While most energy and money from the local rates was spent on books that could be borrowed, the major libraries also assembled reference collections. These also served as repositories for collections of local history and assortments of books donated by well-wishers. But they sometimes presented a difficulty, in that the reference collections attracted relatively few readers, and fewer still who were interested in exploring the collections in depth. One way was to offer exhibitions, a proposal sufficiently unusual to be explained to the Library Association in 1893. Alfred Lancaster of St Helens described how he had organised two exhibitions, one by simply laying about 200 books out on long tables spread with crimson cloth. The exhibition was only open for the afternoon and evening of an Easter Sunday, but it attracted about 1,200 people. Library staff and volunteers were on hand to help in turning over the pages. For the second, which lasted two months, he put the more valuable books in borrowed glass cases, and placed less important books on stands round the room so that visitors could turn the pages if they wished. About 4,000 people came.[59] These were ideas welcomed by Thomas Greenwood, author of a standard manual on public libraries as well as of an influential professional yearbook. From the St Helens experience he concluded that 'the older practice of showing a few curiosities in glazed cases after the Museum plan has been found to attract but few readers'. Instead, he thought, it was better to follow a more liberal method, and lay books out on tables for people to examine more easily.[60]

Bibliography and cataloguing

But what, in all this, was understood by bibliography? That it was more than the listing of books had been clear since the early years of the century. Other words were tried. The French, following Peignot, spoke of *bibliologie*.

Robert Southey, of the same generation as Peignot, wrote of bibliology but meant something different.[61] The term did not catch on. Instead, and initially most successfully at the hands of students of fifteenth-century printing, the older word, and the term that described the person who practised it as a bibliographer, were extended.

If books were understood, appreciated and approached in so many different ways, how were they to be described? The long history of cataloguing was concerned primarily with access to their contents. This was the burden of the arguments over the catalogues of the printed books in the British Museum conducted by Antonio Panizzi and his critics in their evidence to the British Museum Commission in 1850,[62] in newspaper correspondence and in pamphleteering. For some, the unfinished eighteenth-century catalogue of the Biblioteca Casanatense in Rome seemed to offer an answer, with its multitude of analytical entries referring to appearances of texts in large collections.[63] Others spoke for the Bodleian Library, others again for what for a time was known as the Cambridge system. The British Museum's ninety-one rules acquired their own authority de facto. When Charles A. Cutter published another set of rules, appended to the report on public libraries in the United States in 1876, he in turn found his adherents. Discussions spilled over from professional to popular literature. In 1889 Elliot Stock's Book-Lover's Library included a volume by the general editor Henry B. Wheatley on *How to catalogue a library*. It dealt much with the British Museum's catalogue, with the merits of different kinds of catalogues (author, dictionary and so forth), with Cutter, the forms of names and arrangement. It summarised rules for the cataloguing of a small library.

Yet all of this barely addressed the question of what was meant by a book, let alone an old book. Wheatley acknowledged the difference when he came to a question that vexed several senior members of the emergent library profession in the second half of the nineteenth century: size notation. How should the size of a book be measured? Charles Jewett, of the Smithsonian Museum in Washington, had suggested in 1850 that the type area was the most relevant. Others suggested the size of the printed page, others the size of the bound volume.[64] The older assumption, that folio, quarto and octavo sufficiently represented size, was always inadequate, since it ignored the size of the sheets of which books were made. It remained to Henry Bradshaw in an address to the recently founded Library Association to point out that these terms were what he called form notation, and not size notation; and that books made of machine-made paper, printed on large machines, could not be properly described by the use of terms applicable to those applied to books made from separate sheets of hand-made paper. Accordingly, size notation was appropriate to modern books, and form notation to older ones.[65] He was an influential voice; but how exactly was the boundary between hand-made and machine-made to be established? E. W. B. Nicholson, at Oxford, thought he had the answer in the detailed rules drawn up for cataloguing books in the Bodleian: 'The size of a book printed on water-marked paper is to be described in accordance with Table I ... On unwater-marked paper ... with Table II.'[66] Extensive and detailed though these tables were, they were self-confessedly not comprehensive. Meanwhile, Bradshaw concluded on a slightly sour note:

I am bound to say that I have not found, during the last twenty years, five Englishmen, either librarians or booksellers, who knew how to distinguish a folio from a quarto, or an octavo from a 12° or a 16°. It is surely high time, then, that we should make a serious effort to arrive at some common understanding as to a matter of such purely practical concern; seeing that we are all agreed that it is desirable to convey some idea of the size of a book by the notation we use to describe it.[67]

The size of a book, and the relationship of a finished book to the choices and processes of its manufacture, are two key factors in the understanding of the book as an artefact. So, too, is the question of its make-up. But here too there was disagreement and misunderstanding: the concept of a collational formula existed, but it was not worked out either logically or consistently, let alone in sufficient detail to avoid all incompleteness or ambiguity. As late as 1889, Wheatley referred his readers to a 'model bibliography', William Upcott's *Bibliographical account of the principal works relating to English topography* (3 vols., 1818).[68] But Upcott's method, admittedly more than a mere counting of leaves, did not fully reflect the physical composition of books, the codicological relationship of text to paper, the insertions and cancellations that characterised so many volumes not just from the earliest period but also in modern times. Bradshaw, again, sought over several years to settle on a method that would demonstrate how a book was made up, and how by a proper collation of its leaves the stages of printing, compilation and even authorship could be determined. He recognised the relationship between structure and composition.[69]

Quite apart from the inadequacy of the computer screen in representing most of these essential elements in describing the size or make-up of a book, some issues concerning the bibliographical description of the physical features of books remain unresolved more than a century later, most notably concerning volumes with inserted plates. This is the result of the general concentration on the mechanics of letterpress and its printing, coupled with the fact that letterpress involves entirely different skills from those for intaglio printing or lithography. The resulting conceptual void has retarded the study of many illustrated books.[70] But Bradshaw's recognition of the importance of representing the manufacture of books was in its way revolutionary. It sought to recover the creative sequences of making books. Rather than focus on the most obvious externals, it sought out the reasons why books looked as they did – the decisions, choices and (sometimes) changes of mind in their making. As a historian, he employed his bibliographical and codicological skills to unravel the history of printed artefacts. In doing so, he sought to follow matters forward, not backwards. To describe a book was also to explain its creation, and accordingly to set it within bibliographical and textual contexts. This called upon a knowledge and understanding of the history, techniques, possibilities, limits and relationships of each element that made up a printed artefact. Bradshaw died in 1886, prematurely. But in his legacy, this extended series of requirements, and in the work of his contemporaries such as Blades and Talbot Baines Reed, there was defined a late nineteenth-century bibliographical revolution on whose practices and ideas Pollard, R. B. McKerrow, W. W. Greg, Fredson Bowers and others subsequently built.[71]

Edward Gordon Duff, born in 1863 (the year of Blades's completing his biography of Caxton), was an undergraduate at Oxford when Bradshaw died in 1886, but even as an undergraduate he took an interest in the Bodleian incunables.[72] In 1893 he became librarian to Mrs Rylands, and hence also responsible for the library formed by Lord Spencer earlier in the century. In the same year he dedicated his small manual on *Early printed books* to the memory of Bradshaw: 'Only,' he wrote, 'by writing from facts can we help to keep bibliography in the position to which Henry Bradshaw raised it, of scientific study.'[73] There has been much misunderstanding and dispute about what may be claimed or meant by scientific study, but Duff's emphasis, echoing Bradshaw,[74] on the importance of facts was critical. As for the nature of those facts, though he provided only a partial answer in that he did not attempt to enlarge on their foundations or their implications, it is one that is helpful as far as it goes. Apart from his historical chapters taking the story of printing through from its invention to its early application in the countries of Europe, with a more generous treatment of Britain, Duff added two concluding chapters. The first was on the study of bookbinding. The second, and by far the more important, was 'the collecting and describing of early printed books'. Inspired by Bradshaw, whom he quoted at length, he placed his emphases on understanding their original condition, on the integrity of volumes, on understanding their physical make-up, on provenance and on the individuality of copies: 'The individual history of a book is of the utmost importance, and should never be ignored.'[75] In other words, books were to be studied bibliographically not just as figures in a list but as the creations both of those who manufactured and those who used them. It was a process that by implication insisted on the importance of the evidential value of multiple copies. By these means their writers and their reputations could be better understood. Duff wrote not as a pioneer but in response to current and past practice; and yet in following Bradshaw he set an agenda for much of what was to follow, whether for historical and literary studies in their broadest senses or in the responsibilities and processes of those whose task it was to create and manage the research collections of libraries.

While in some ways it was a distinctively British revolution, that was to lead to an Anglo-American school of bibliography, in many other ways it was also a European one. J. W. Holtrop, Konrad Haebler, C. M. Briquet, Léopold Delisle, Anatole Claudin, W. L. Schreiber and Karl Dziatzko all worked closely with British colleagues on projects that reshaped their subjects, whether in the study of incunabula, of woodcuts, of paper or of manuscripts. Cross-channel collaborations were expressed both in professional work and in friendships. The early membership of the London Bibliographical Society included collectors such as the duc d'Aumale, Count Apponyi and the Prince d'Essling, booksellers such as Honoré Champion, Jacques and Ludwig Rosenthal and Martinus Nijhoff, and bibliographers such as Konrad Burger and Marie Pellechet.[76]

When W. W. Greg, friend and admirer of A. W. Pollard and one of the most influential of all twentieth-century bibliographers, sought later to find the origins of this revolution, he turned to the catalogue of fifteenth-century printed books in the British Museum. The first volume of this project appeared only in 1908, but it was planned in the last years of the nineteenth century.

> In an undertaking such as this the duties of the cataloguer lead him beyond the record of superficial data, beyond even the identification and classification of types. They embrace the complete investigation of the material construction of the books enumerated and the whole history of their production. And so the cataloguer, beginning with enumeration and description, is forced by the nature of his work to become the student of everything that affects either the original fashioning or the subsequent fortunes of the books that come within his purview; and if he is philosophically minded he must come in the end to realize that it is this life-history of books that is the true study of the bibliographer, and that actual enumeration and description are only incidental.[77]

Greg wrote forty or fifty years after the event, and he wrote from his own point of view, as one who had learned most about the printing of books and the management of the book trade through his interest in Elizabethan and Jacobean plays. He had, for example, little interest in book illustration or (as we saw earlier) in bindings, 'another subject that has particularly appealed to the dilettante'. But in his linking the 'original fashioning' and the 'subsequent fortunes' of books, he encapsulated the importance of understanding manufacture and use: that the two are in effect inseparable; that, therefore, each copy of each book has its own importance whether in what it can tell us about the vagaries and processes of manufacture, or about the individual and cumulative evidence of books in use. The origins of these ideas are to be found in the seventeenth century. They were worked out not only by bibliographers, professional or amateur, but by a mixture of printers and publishers, booksellers and collectors, librarians and scholars, whose demands of each other shaped what could eventually be described as a discipline. Their implications, and the importance for understanding what it is that we mean by the printed book, remain with us even as we face the various forms of paper and electronic surrogates through whose aid and through whose interpretive mechanisms we now face the past.

10 | Conclusion

In recovering the past, and choosing how to remember its particular features, ever since the fifteenth century we have depended very largely (if, emphatically, only partly) on print – not just in the printed word but also on images. This book has been mostly concerned with the printed word as it has been packaged according to the tastes, preoccupations, skills and opportunities of several centuries. In seeking to understand some of the practices and implications in understanding the past that is now generated by a shift from paper to screen, we have focussed on two principal themes. First, attitudes to old books, rather than new ones, though it is by no means either easy or indeed desirable always to distinguish between the two. Artefacts from the past have their own curiosity values, and require criteria by which to judge them that are often alien to those applicable to books hot off the press. Second, it has been concerned with books, not just with printing. Writers and readers, theologians and politicians, printers and booksellers have been debating and recording their views about printing and the printed word ever since the fifteenth century. It was '*sancta ars*', a divine art.[1] It brought fame to authors. It meant that books could be cheaper. It was a means of spreading learning, at every level. It could be an aid to discovery. It brought a new reliability to texts. It offered support to religious belief and practice. It resulted in a larger reading public. On the other hand, printing made it more difficult to control knowledge, political opinion or religious belief. It involved sometimes challenging questions about its financing and management. It raised new questions about property and copyright. For some books, the market became over-stocked. And those very qualities that to some seemed most desirable were to others the very opposite. Widespread education was not necessarily for the good of everyone. The availability of the Bible in vernacular languages was not necessarily to be welcomed. Cheap books did not necessarily mean better ones, or even texts of adequate quality. And as printing bred ever more printed books, so there was an ever-increasing danger of being overwhelmed.[2] Often joined to this debate were questions not just about printing but also about other aspects of books. We have seen how such issues as paper, bindings and previous ownership could all also affect the ways in which books were regarded, and valued. The processes of manufacture and of use, reshaping and re-use complement printing, and they add their own criteria.

By examining changing priorities, changes in the physical treatment of what is inherited and the search for ways of preserving the past whether in conservation or by the making of copies and facsimiles, it is possible also to discover important aspects of how the past has been valued, interpreted and selected for physical preservation. The variability of previous practices and priorities, represented and explored in the previous chapters, should alert us to some of the issues lying behind the much more recent shift to what is now for many people the primary experience, on screen. In a world of print and manuscript that has always been definable by shifts in practices and values, the computer screen not only presents further variables. In doing so, it likewise draws selectively from the past. And that is not a novelty.

The revolution in the dispersal and sharing of words, images and ideas that is today developing on screen in ever more diverse ways has provoked further complicated debates about the accompanying technological and social changes: how these in turn have altered, and will further alter, the ways in which we act, write and share knowledge or experience. They change the ways in which we behave within our human and natural environments. It has long been clear that the latest so-called revolution of the book has brought several revolutions, more quickly and more far-reaching than any of the earlier ones – including those as fundamental as the shift from scroll to codex, and the invention of printing.[3] This further revolution is also different in kind. It transcends literacy, and its implications are affecting the world very much faster than any previous revolution in communication.

If, in thinking about books (as individual objects, not as organised in libraries),[4] we restrict ourselves to discussions about the relationship of the new electronic world to the world of printing (or, indeed, of writing) and its nature, then we miss some of the most important issues involved in even the most basic features of this revolution. Most obviously, the flat screen of an electronic delivery mechanism, be it desk computer, laptop, tablet or pocket device, is designed to deliver texts and images as speedily and efficiently as possible. If we express its purpose like that, then the similarities with printing on paper or other matter are self-explanatory. Because reading alpha-numeric signs is a deeply conservative process, dependent on conventions expressed as series of agreed shapes and agreed orderings, there is an essential convergence between manuscript, print and screen. To that extent, the revolutions they have undergone on screen are strictly circumscribed. The differences arise once we consider the details of delivery, the ways and orders in which text can be accessed and searched, the ways in which texts and images from utterly different sources can be drawn together for comparison or to supplement what was initially before us, the ways in which databases can be drawn down and scanned, the ways in which video and sound can be introduced, the possibility (eventually) of universal access – with all the challenges of organisation that implies.

The changes that books undergo are of at least comparable scale. Once we move away from most people's primary and most obvious concern, to see text in some conveniently legible form, then further complexities in the change become clearer. In bibliographical terms, and to return to the beginning of this book, forms effect meaning. McKenzie's dictum,[5] succinctly linking bibliographical to literary criticism, requires some elaboration. Our understanding of any text is not only affected by the physical means and the circumstances of its delivery and reception. It is actually created and established – effected – by them.[6] In other words, and to repeat, it is insufficient just to consider the relationship of screen to print. Much more is lost in the translation than is immediately obvious. The previous chapters have been concerned both with the obvious, and with some features that are less so. In order to avoid distraction, and to find ways of measuring how change happens, we have focussed not on new books but on changing attitudes to old ones over the course of more than four centuries. We have sought to discover what features were valued, how they came to be valued and why they were valued. The answers are not the same for all generations, though a measure of development can frequently be seen in the parallel proceedings of changes in knowledge and of taste. Amongst many others, they involve questions about the typographical appearance of the page, about the materials of books such as their paper, about their bindings. We might have explored several other features, and we would have found different answers in matters of detail. The principles would not have been different. Not surprisingly, tastes and concerns with older books can frequently be shown to be related to the same in new, contemporary, publications.

Relationships between the present and the past can manifest themselves in imitations: hence our concern with facsimiles and copies. This is not a world of sharp divisions. As we have seen, it involves varying degrees of mimicry, falsification, repairs, fakes, replacements, exchanges and transfers. Bibliographical integrity is undermined, but only if it is defined in particular ways. Beyond this lie concerns about the nature of the relationship between multiplicity and individuality. This can be expressed as a desire to know degrees of rarity, how many copies of a book survive. It can also relate to the particular features of a book to hand, be it the binding or repairs or annotation or marks of past ownership. As we have seen, these have not always been of much interest save to distinct, select and often self-defining discrete groups of people, and they certainly cannot be counted as universally held concerns save insofar that they may affect the value, and hence often the price, of a given copy. More generally, we have reminded ourselves of the most obvious means of assessing the age of one book relative to another, and the ways in which books can be physically located: hence our interest in true and false dates and imprints.

The focus of this study has been on books – that is, mostly on bound volumes. Yet issues about change, about the relationship of the past to the present and about the interpretation of the past, and the means by which we may pursue it, are equally applicable to other forms of print, most obviously but not exclusively newspapers, periodicals, pamphlets and advertising matter. In such sometimes more ephemeral matter there emerges a further issue, for which there is no room on this occasion. Most of what is printed is thrown away within a very short period, in the case of newspapers within a few hours. Equally, most of what has been printed in the past has been lost, deliberately or accidentally. Much of the survival of the past depends on choice, decisions on what to keep. Much more of the surviving record, the majority of what we now possess, depends on accident. The books that have formed the subjects of this study are those that have been kept, or those that were kept for some reason in the past. We know and understand far too little about how distinctions were reached at various times and in various circumstances. Much was accidental. Much was deliberate.

At the beginning of this book we noted some of the questions that can pose themselves when we face books and other printed matter that have been digitised. We noted how for many people such questions are unseen. We also noted that the delivery mechanisms of texts and images can affect meaning, and the very limited extent to which surrogates make it possible to understand contexts whether of the past or the present. The intervening chapters have examined aspects of how books have at various times been changed and re-presented according to the needs and aspirations of differing audiences. The changes wrought by digitisation are indeed proving revolutionary, but they need also to be seen in the longer history of printing, bookselling, bookbinding and reading.

As we have already remarked, much of the evidence for these changes cited in the past chapters has inevitably been drawn from books that, whatever their original price, now have a sometimes high antiquarian value. That is unavoidable, given the fluid nature of what is considered old or valuable at any one time. But it raises two questions: first, the extent to which these books have in the past been seriously regarded by more than quite small groups of people; and second, the extent to which these same questions can be applied to the wider generality of old books as that term is now understood.

The first question concerns what we mean by public response. How far did different groups of people care? Until quite recently, the vast majority of books that might now be classed as antiquarian had little interest or value. The incunabula that have attracted bibliophile and scholarly attention are far outnumbered by the thousands of books from the same period that have roused little curiosity even amongst specialists. Many eighteenth-century books remain common and readily obtainable in the open market even today. In a world where so much was common and consequently ignored, and where the number and nature of books offering substantial bibliophile, scholarly, financial or other benefit was in effect restricted to a few thousand titles and editions, general public interest was commensurately circumscribed. These limitations are reflected in the dozens of guides to rarity and to the choice of old books that became such a feature of publishing from the eighteenth century onwards. Moreover, whatever the numbers of people who read about early printing in Charles Knight's *Penny Magazine* in the 1830s, whatever the numbers who visited the Caxton exhibition in 1877, whatever the numbers who bought the new popularising guides to book collecting in the 1880s and 1890s, their attention remained almost always directed to a limited selection of acknowledged rarities. There was no over-arching general message about books, whose ubiquity disguised most gradations in scales of values.

Today, with the promise of all but universal digitisation, it is no longer so easy to speak of gradations of value. The computer screen is a much greater leveller, for content and for readers alike, than the printed page or the cheque book.

The second question is related directly to scarcity and value, and here we return to changes in the book trade, a subject already alluded to in the first chapter. Books that are difficult to find attract more attention than those that are common. For example, until after the Second World War, and indeed for some years after that, British eighteenth-century books were mostly cheap, readily found and stocked in quantity and variety by large shops. Among the reasons for their increasing scarcity were wartime destruction, and the gargantuan appetites of north American research libraries.[7] Within about two decades, competition among established institutions and ambitious newcomers or those with a new focus or new funds, all striving for size and status, transformed the English-speaking market. In the words of an American bookseller turned librarian, 'University libraries... [went] completely berserk in their sudden frantic attempts to achieve "status," or something, by appallingly ignorant mass purchases of rare books.'[8] The gradually increasing scarcity of British books published before the mid-seventeenth century had been countered by microfilm programmes; but there was in the 1950s and 1960s no such programme for the eighteenth century, and copies could only be obtained by purchasing the originals. Programmes to make early continental books available have been much slower. For British books, the eighteenth century was followed by the nineteenth, and then by the twentieth, in a progression that could further be seen in the dwindling numbers of second-hand booksellers with more than small stocks. It perhaps needs to be emphasised that this phenomenon of wholesale buying was readily observable long before some of the factors that have more recently been blamed for the decline of antiquarian and second-hand bookshops. The spread of antiquarian book fairs beyond the largest[9] became a reflection of the trade's contraction and fragmentation as well as of its ambitions. Bookselling on the Web is a further reflection of this transmutation in a more extreme form.

With scarcity comes challenge. Some eighteenth-, nineteenth- and twentieth-century books have become as liable to changes and alteration as older ones were in the past. We have already noted how a made-up copy of the first edition of Fielding's *Tom Jones* became celebrated thanks to a bookseller's passing the book off to a collector who was of a naturally tenacious turn of mind.[10] Most of the resourcefulness, variations and contrivances that we have noted for earlier books (and our survey has been very far from comprehensive) can be paralleled in more recent periods. The demand for nineteenth-century novels by Dickens and others in the original monthly parts, as they were published, and the concomitant shortage of perfect examples of the fragile originals, has led to innumerable sets whose individual parts are made up from different sources.[11] The more recent interest in copies of twentieth-century books in dustwrappers, and the considerable difference in price between a first edition of a well-known book with or without its wrapper, has led to the practice of moving wrappers from a copy of the second or later printing, and placing it on a first printing.[12] In the old tradition of making facsimile pages to complete books, dustwrappers are also available for many books in facsimile, from specialist suppliers. Less nefariously, and vastly more usefully, thousands of books that were once thought to be of negligible interest or value, but that have now become scarce, have been reprinted in facsimile. The scholarly and the book-collecting markets alike have both benefited immeasurably from this. But the extent to which these facsimiles are necessarily true or complete copies has been rightly challenged.[13] Many of them, from their new large and small publishers alike, do not reproduce the entire original, omissions including information such as original imprints and dates of publication, and even entire sections.

These practices, of mixed copies, facsimiles and unannounced incompleteness, not only lie in a continuing tradition that can be traced back for generations. In their ambiguities and omissions, they are also the immediate precursors of the values that now accompany the reproduction of books in electronic environments and in the world of print-on-demand. One difference is that, as we saw in the first chapter, some of the more recent digitisation and reprint programmes acknowledge their faults, albeit in imprecise and therefore unhelpful ways, and sometimes in a manner that smacks of special pleading.

A related question concerns relative values not of cash but of perceived importance. It is statistically possible that more editions have been completely lost from the fifteenth century than those that now survive.[14] Whatever the period, losses are attributable to many factors, but they share one frequent characteristic: what is lost was deemed – for whatever reason – to have lost its value in some way. The same feature applies to all periods and all places. It explains – at least in the most general terms – the loss of thousands of pamphlet titles from every century since the fifteenth, the loss of entire editions of much-printed bestsellers, the disappearance of eighteenth-century novels whose existence is well documented,[15] the loss of entire runs of periodicals and newspapers[16] and the loss of unknown quantities of printed matter that has come to underpin almost very aspect of everyday life.[17] By no means all of this last was ephemeral, though the destruction of so much that was never intended to be of more than passing use has limited our understanding of what we might mean by a 'world of print'.[18] The importance set on previously little regarded forms of literature increases with the constant quest by book collectors for new fields, with new paths of enquiry by historians, and with better understanding of the implications of retrospective bibliographies. In all this, again, there is a continuous line of descent that can be traced back through attention in past centuries to the earliest printing, and to emphases on some kinds of books rather than others. While different kinds of publications have always possessed different status, and their relative status usually changes over the centuries, they do not change bibliographically. They remain artefacts, possessing physical properties that contribute to their meanings. The questions that pose themselves today, about access, bibliographical and historical values, and re-presentation in new electronic environments, are no different for the great mass of ordinary printed matter than they are for books that have been more consistently valued since publication.

It is appropriate in these last pages to recall also some more specific aspects of what has been lost or destroyed. Ever since the fifteenth century, the world of print and paper has seemed to be not merely plentiful but even over-supplied. While (at least until the early nineteenth century) it was almost always costly to manufacture, paper was also so abundant that once it had been used it could be treated as waste, even if by some criteria it had not yet reached that stage. To castigate figures such as John Bagford, who in the late seventeenth and early eighteenth centuries not only collected scraps but also removed parts of books to illustrate his accumulations on the history of printing and of paper, is to miss the point.[19] What seems to be abundant varies with each generation. We have noticed how different kinds of books have been treated as a consequence, and how for different reasons it was acceptable to destroy books in order to create new bibliographical concoctions sometimes bearing little relation to the editions they purported to represent. In a world where there were plenty of imperfect copies on which to draw, and to make up 'complete' copies, there seemed no reason to be ashamed of such artificialities. When in 1911 Pollard objected to this bibliographical dishonesty, he was writing at the end of a period of super-abundance that can be traced to the aftermath of the Napoleonic wars. Other practices can be traced in the same way to periods of plenty and disorder. Maps stripped from atlases, colour plates cut from books, and the more general destruction wrought by the creation of leaf books all have their origins in worlds where destruction seemed to signify little bibliographical or scholarly loss, but where the financial gains could be substantial. Unsaleable incomplete books and incomplete sets of books are turned into objects having a market demand. The dismemberment of 'breakers', the trade name for imperfect books where (usually) the plates have a greater value as individual objects than as a collection, creates rarity and gives a new meaning to the vestiges of history. While many of the more responsible booksellers (scholars must also bear part of the blame) now deplore such practices, old books continue to be destroyed. It is at the expense of one kind of historical evidence. That is as true of imperfect books and odd volumes as of complete copies. The inexorable effect is a diminution of history, where the value of evidence so often lies in its multiplicity. In a world of apparent plenitude, it is easy to justify the breaking up of a book into its constituent leaves, and dividing them more democratically among a large number of new owners. By this method, scholars otherwise as reputable as Falconer Madan at Oxford and Konrad Haebler in Germany created what were in effect works of reference.[20] But they were works of reference having a value limited to what was seen or attempted by their compilers. Madan was interested in the history of printing at Oxford, not with the divergent fortunes of books from there. Haebler was most concerned with type design, and with the spread of printing. He was not concerned with ownership or the spread of reading. As increasing weight is placed on the differences between individual copies of books (in their printing, in their ownership, in their use, in their annotation, in their decoration, in their bindings, in their presentation to readers and their use by readers), so the importance of multiplicity, of context and of variability is recognised. We noted this in the first chapter.[21] The single representative copy available on a database is not a sufficient representation of past creation or of past experience; and the single leaf has still more limited value.

Each generation values antiquarian books for different reasons. That should have become clear in the course of this study. The process continues, now in dramatically new ways. Yet the surviving corpus of these books is being reduced. At the beginning of this book we observed how increased dependence on scanned copies of books on screen tends for inescapable reasons to obscure one of the most obvious features of printed editions: that they consist of multiple copies. The larger the number of old books that survive, complete or incomplete, the better each individual volume can be understood. In a world increasingly populated with surrogates, this places a burden on libraries that requires a change of outlook, one not the same as formerly. At every level, from school libraries to public libraries to university libraries to learned societies and to national libraries, books are being discarded and destroyed at an unprecedented rate. Electronic surrogates are readily available, and for most readers they will answer most purposes perfectly well. But libraries also have a duty of care, both to the needs of their readers and as trustees of the printed and manuscript past. This does not require that every book must be kept. It does require that those responsible for their care should be alert to what readers of all kinds expect, now and in the foreseeable future.

On the other hand, we now face an electronic world where it is difficult to throw some kinds of data away. Yet, confusingly, we are also faced with a world where the long-term safe future of data cannot be confidently foreseen. The bases on which we make value-decisions, and the priorities we attach to different records or activities, have thereby to be moderated. This further affects our attitudes to the past, the extent to which we wish or are able to preserve it, and hence the ways in which it can be understood.

At least for the present, only a very few aspects of our bibliographical inheritance, books that have survived in their physical forms, can be captured in computer memory or on screen. For all its many advantages over books – both printed and manuscript – in some respects, the screen can thus present only a very imperfect and incomplete view of the past. By itself, the study of attitudes to printing alone will not provide us with a sufficient history either of the book or even of texts. Nor will it enable us to understand properly what is involved in the transition from printed to electronic environments. As bibliographers have become well aware, the contextual physical properties of the vehicle on which a text is printed or written, or in which it is contained, the circumstances of its manufacture, circulation and sale, and the nature of the history of multiple individual copies, all contribute to understanding the purposes, hopes and compromises integral to the relationship between writing and reading. They are prerequisites in the transmission of knowledge. And such bibliographical observations have repercussions for all disciplines that claim some historical base. As the electronic environment grows, and common experience shifts emphasis from page to screen, so experience develops into assumptions. So the challenge in the future for understanding the nature of both recent and older books will become all the greater.

Notes

1 The past in pixels

1. See for example Tanselle, 'Reproductions and scholarship' and 'The future of primary records'.
2. McKenzie, 'Computers and the humanities'.
3. Stevens, 'Photobibliography'.
4. Harrison circulated a dossier of reproductions prepared by the printers Percy Lund Humphries, proprietors of the Replika process: *Facsimile reprints*.
5. Eugene B. Power, 'An American filming service in Europe'; Lawrence S. Thompson, 'Facsimiles and the antiquarian trade'. Thompson includes a brief summary of a meeting organised by the Bibliographical Society in 1926, a date well beyond most confines of this book. See further below, pp. 9–10.
6. Jackson, 'Some limitations of microfilm'.
7. This is far too large a subject to be represented adequately here. But for some of the issues, see W. J. West, *The strange rise of semi-literate England*; Tanselle, 'The latest forms of book-burning'; Singer, 'Missed opportunities dept.'; Nicholson Baker, *Double fold*; Darnton, 'The great book massacre'; McKitterick (ed.), *Do we want to keep our newspapers?*; Flood, 'Varieties of vandalism'.
8. For late twentieth-century work, see for example Hutt, *Newspaper design*; Evans, *Newspaper design*; Evans, *Pictures on a page*; Mirsky and Tropea (eds.), *The news aesthetic*. Many of the issues raised in these books apply to the earlier development of newspaper typographic and editorial conventions of which they are the descendants.
9. See for example Deegan and Sutherland, *Transferred illusions*.
10. Thomson, *The publishing business in the twenty-first century*; Striphas, *The late age of print*. For the management and exploitation of the Harry Potter phenomenon see for example Blake, *The irresistible rise of Harry Potter*; Gupta, *Re-reading Harry Potter*; and Gunelius, *Harry Potter*.
11. *The Bookseller*, 29 January 2010.
12. *The Bookseller*, 23 February 2011.
13. See http//creativecommons.org.
14. Google has been thought to have a target of 15 million titles: see Heather Jackson's review of Darnton's *The case for books* in *Times Literary Supplement*, 29 January 2010.
15. http://britishperiodicals.chadwyck.co.uk/journals. Consulted 23 November 2009.
16. Marketing section for the ProQuest series of EEBO: www.proquest.co.uk/assets/literature/products/databases/eebo.pdf. Accessed 25 August 2011. On the

following, see also Kichuk, 'Metamorphosis'; and Gadd, 'The use and misuse of Early English Books Online'.

17 'About this reprint' notice giving the address of 'betterreprints@bookprep.com'. The volume from which this is taken, a reprint (dated 15 July 2011) of one of the titles in the nineteenth-century *Encyclopédie Roret*, omits several scattered pages where they should be, and instead prints them together at the end without further comment.

18 Note prefixed to ECCO Print Editions, 2010.

19 www.digital-collections.de/index.html?c=faecher_index&l=en&kl=191 (27 August 2011).

20 Madan, '"The duplicity of duplicates"'. His words were delivered at a meeting of the society in 1911. More generally, see Gaskell, *A new introduction to bibliography*, pp. 353–4.

21 McKitterick, *Print, manuscript and the search for order*, pp. 132–4.

22 See for example Barnes, *A bibliography of Elizabeth Barrett Browning*.

23 For a summary of some of this, see for example Pearson, *Provenance research in book history* and his *Books as history*. The literature on this subject is now substantial. Gingerich, *An annotated census of Copernicus' De revolutionibus* provided a world-wide survey of surviving copies and their histories. For other similarly inspired surveys, see for example de Ricci, *A census of Caxtons*; Anthony J. West, *The Shakespeare First Folio*; and Rasmussen and West (eds.), *The Shakespeare First Folio*. For another approach to a corpus of surviving copies, see Liesen and Sorgeloos, *Le rayonnement des Moretus*, which charts copies of books from the Moretus press in Antwerp according to their bindings.

24 Cf. Weitenkampf, 'What is a facsimile?'. Weitenkampf was in charge of the prints at the New York Public Library, and much of this article is concerned with facsimiles and other imitations of images.

25 Roberts and Skeat, *The birth of the codex*; Blanchard (ed.), *Les débuts du codex*; Mercier (ed.), *Les trois révolutions du livre*; Barbier (ed.), *Les trois révolutions du livre*.

26 Many books are conceived as accompaniments to websites, or are sometimes derived from them. But the fundamental conceptions remain generally conservative.

27 For a treatment of some of these issues, see Sordet, *L'amour des livres au siècle des lumières*, especially pp. 219–61.

28 See for example Raymond (ed.), *The Oxford history of popular print culture*.

29 Lewis, *Printed ephemera*; Lewis, *Such things happen*, pp. 160–7. Cf. also two pioneering exhibitions: Bodleian Library, *The John Johnson collection* and Labarre and Gasnault, *Le livre dans la vie quotidienne*. More comprehensively in some respects, see Rickards, *The encyclopedia of ephemera*.

30 http://ebba.english.ucsb.edu/page/ballad-facsimiles, consulted 30 May 2012.

31 See below, pp. 42–4, 88–93.

32 Impey and MacGregor (eds.), *The origins of museums*; Lugli, *Naturalia et mirabilia*; di Gregorio, "Le coselline di un ometto curioso".
33 Balayé, *La Bibliothèque Nationale des origines à 1800*. For the legal deposit of books in the royal library, see Estivals, *Le dépôt légal sous l'ancien régime de 1537 à 1791*. For some of the English-speaking world, see Partridge, *The history of the legal deposit of books*.
34 Philip, *The Bodleian Library*.
35 See for example Richard Bentley, *A proposal for building a royal library*.
36 Fabian, 'An eighteenth-century research collection'; Fabian (ed.), *Handbuch der historischen Buchbestände in Deutschland* II.I, pp. 140–266.
37 *Printing and the mind of man*. The subsequent volume, Carter and Muir (eds.), *Printing and the mind of man*, was concerned solely with a selection of influential books. For Knight, see below, pp. 144–8.
38 Meanwhile, cf. Beckwith, *Victorian bibliomania*; Hindman and others (eds.), *Manuscript illumination in the modern age*; Coomans and de Maeyer (eds.), *The revival of medieval illumination*.
39 For one example, see Kuitert, 'De secondhand handel'. This takes a more analytical approach than works such as Stern, *Antiquarian bookselling in the United States*; Buijnsters, *Geschiedenis van het Nederlandse antiquariaat*; Hertzberger, *Boek, veel boeken – en mensen*. For a variety of views and approaches, see Mandelbrote (ed.), *Out of print and into profit*.
40 Cf. Stobart and van Damme (eds.), *Modernity and the second-hand trade*.
41 Ford, 'Importation of printed books into England and Scotland'. For a longer and wider view of the international European trade in new books, see Barbier and others (eds.), *L'Europe et le livre*.
42 Amidst a substantial literature on this, see van Deursen, *Professions et métiers interdits*; Swift, 'The French booksellers in the Strand'; Swift, 'Dutch penetration of the London market for books'.
43 Jefcoate, 'German immigrants and the London book trade'.
44 See for example Hassall, *The Holkham library*, pp. 9–24; Mortlock, *Holkham library*, especially (for printed books acquired in Italy by or for Thomas Coke, 1st Earl of Leicester (1698–1759)) pp. 36–64.
45 While this book is primarily concerned with the English, French and Dutch trades, for aspects of the nineteenth-century German antiquarian market see for example Sarkowski, 'Das wissenschaftliche Antiquariat in Leipzig und die Ueberproduktion deutscher Verlag'. For individual firms see for example Carlsohn, *Lebensbilder Leipziger Buchhändler*; Jäger and Wittmann, 'Der Antiquariatsbuchhandel' (for the international nature of the trade, see especially pp. 214–18); and McKitterick, *A changing view from Amsterdam*.
46 *Archives du Bibliophile* no. 7 (July 1858), pp. 187–9; no. 8 (August 1858), pp. 219–20. For Johnson's letter to Frederick Barnard, see Samuel Johnson, *Letters* I, pp. 307–14.

2 Restoration and invention

1. Pollard and Potter, *Early bookbinding manuals* is concerned with binding rather than repair.
2. Cf. Tanselle, 'The textual criticism of visual and aural works'.
3. Kristian Jensen, *Revolution and the antiquarian book*, ch. 5: 'Commemorating and obliterating the past'.
4. Pepys Library 2365: see Nixon, *Catalogue of the Pepys Library*, p. xiii and plate 2.
5. Pepys Library 2257: see Nixon, *Catalogue of the Pepys Library*, p. xxv and plate 28.
6. In 1970 this was deposited in Cambridge University Library.
7. Keynes, *John Evelyn*; Coron, '"Ut prosint aliis"'.
8. Amidst the considerable literature on the history of decorated bookbindings, a useful overall picture can be most readily obtained in some of the catalogues of major collections, such as Nixon, *The Broxbourne library*; Foot, *The Henry Davis gift*; Needham, *Twelve centuries of bookbindings*.
9. For Marsh's Library, see McCarthy, *All graduates and gentlemen*; McCarthy and Simmons (eds.), *Marsh's Library*; Foot, *The decorative bindings in Marsh's Library*. For Worth, see Coakley, 'Edward Worth and his library'.
10. Davenport, *Roger Payne*, p. 69.
11. Davenport, *Roger Payne*, p. 71.
12. Advertisement in the *Public Advertiser*, 17 June 1769. For Dymott, see also Barber, 'Richard Dymott, bookbinder'.
13. Hecquet, *Catalogue des estampes gravées d'après Rubens*.
14. 'Rapport d'un mémoire de M Chaptal', at p. 71. See also Crosland, *In the shadow of Lavoisier*, pp. 201–2.
15. Berthollet, *Essay on the new method of bleaching*.
16. Berthollet, *Essay on the new method of bleaching*, pp. 119–20.
17. Imison, *Elements of science and art* II, pp. 162 and 589–90.
18. Peignot, *Dictionnaire raisonné de bibliologie* I, pp. 108–10.
19. [Renouard] *Catalogue de la bibliothèque d'un amateur* I, p. 2.
20. Namur, *Manuel du bibliothécaire*, p. 237.
21. Lenormand, *Nouveau manuel complet du relieur*, p. 231.
22. Rhodes, 'Hell's own brew'.
23. Balston, *The Whatmans and wove paper*, pp. 224–7; McKitterick, *A history of Cambridge University Press*, pp. 252–4.
24. See for example Koops, *Historical account of the substances*. For further selections, see *Vegetable substances*, pp. 129–54.
25. See for example *The World*, 12 December 1787. For another view of 'the book as waste', see Price, *How to do things with books in Victorian Britain*, pp. 219–57.
26. *The World*, 24 February 1790. Cheesemongers (like others) used quantities of waste paper as wrapping: see for example the evidence of John Jessop, a cheesemonger, to the House of Commons, *Select Committee on printing and stationery*, pp. 47–9.

27 Ingpen, 'Decorated papers'; Easton, *Marbling*, pp. 74–5.
28 *The Sun*, 14 June 1800.
29 *Albion and Evening Advertiser*, 18 July 1800.
30 *The Sun*, 26 June, 21 July 1800.
31 Coleman, *The British paper industry*, p. 203.
32 De Ricci, *A catalogue of the early English books*, no. 864.
33 McKitterick, *Print, manuscript and the search for order*, pp. 107–8.
34 Cicero, *Epistolae ad Atticum*, etc. (Venetiis: Paulus Manutius, '1548'.) Trinity College, Cambridge M.12.178. Adams C1917.
35 Namur, *Manuel du bibliothécaire*, p. 236.
36 For Le Clabart, see Muzerelle, '"Cet Esclabart avait une belle main"'.
37 Waddesdon Manor, 'Recueil d'adresses' (a collection in four large volumes of printed ephemera relating to the French eighteenth-century book trade, accession no. 3686.2.72.183. For the collection, see Plock, 'Advertising books in eighteenth-century Paris'.
38 *Catalogue de la bibliothèque de M. L*****, lots 2587, 708. The copy of *Orlando furioso* is now in Trinity College, Cambridge, Grylls 11.325.
39 Dibdin, *The bibliographical decameron* II, pp. 414–16. For Nicol's subsequent description of the 42-line Bible in 1825, see Folter, 'The Gutenberg Bible in the antiquarian book trade', p. 295.
40 McKitterick, *Print, manuscript and the search for order*, pp. 139–63.
41 Lindenbaum, 'Publishers' booklists in late seventeenth-century London'. See more generally Pollard and Ehrman, *The distribution of books by catalogue from the invention of printing to A.D. 1800*.
42 McKitterick, *Print, manuscript and the search for order*, pp. 97–138.
43 Johnson to Frederick Barnard, 28 May 1768, in Samuel Johnson, *Letters* I, pp. 307–14, at p. 314.
44 Quinn (ed.), *The Hakluyt handbook* II, pp. 490–6.
45 For a summary of the bibliographical complications and their historical background, see the notes to STC 13569. For a fuller assessment of surviving sheets and their printing, see Clegg and McLeod, *The peaceable and prosperous regiment of blessed Queene Elizabeth*. For the facsimiles, see Maslen, 'Three eighteenth-century reprints'; Maslen and Lancaster (eds.), *The Bowyer ledgers*, pp. 77, 80, 127; Clegg, *Press censorship in Elizabethan England*, pp. 138–69. A copy of the Mears-Gyles-Woodman sheets, *The castrations of the last edition of Holinshed's Chronicle*, is in Trinity College, Cambridge, shelf-mark X.4.8.
46 The history of the so-called leaf book, frequently involving the destruction of incomplete copies of rare books, and where individual leaves are presented to the accompaniment of sometimes nugatory commentaries, is a further development of this phenomenon; it is worth noting that one of the first of the genre, a collection of leaves taken from early editions of the English Bible and assembled by Francis Fry (1865), coincides with heavy demand for made-up copies of these same books. For the development of this genre, see de Hamel and others, *Disbound and dispersed*.

47 Page, *Matthew Parker and his books*, pp. 46–55; Leedham-Green and McKitterick, 'A catalogue of Cambridge University Library in 1583'.
48 Craig, 'The earliest Little Gidding concordance'; Ransome, 'Monotessaron'; Dyck, '"A new kind of printing"'.
49 [J. -J. Rive] *La chasse aux bibliographes et antiquaires mal-avisés*.
50 See for example Bernard Quaritch Ltd, catalogue 1027, *English poetry before 1701* (1982), offering fragments of books from their own stock and from the former firms of Dobell and Pickering & Chatto.
51 A. W. Pollard, 'Bibliography and bibliology'.
52 Trinity College, Cambridge, Grylls.11.414 (1545: Adams C2414): leaves π2 and g6 are inserted from the edition of 1499.
53 Quaritch, *A general catalogue of books arranged in classes*, p. 974.
54 Quaritch, p. 1065.
55 Francis Fry, *A description of the Great Bible*. Many attempts have been made to unravel the 1611 and 1613 Bibles, a task that A. W. Pollard considered had been rendered 'almost hopeless' by the activities of collectors and booksellers in transferring sheets from one copy to another: A. W. Pollard, *Records of the English Bible*, p. 70. For a fuller account based on several copies, see Herbert, *Historical catalogue of printed editions of the English Bible*, pp. 130–3, 136–8. A proper bibliographical study has yet to be done.
56 Rothschild (ed.), *The history of Tom Jones*.
57 *Catalogue of manuscripts and early printed books* III, pp. 112–13; de Ricci, *A census of Caxtons*, nos. 3b.3–4: George III's copy is now at Windsor. For Caxton, Mansion and this book see now Hellinga, *William Caxton and early printing in England*, pp. 50–1.
58 White, 'Newly discovered fragments'.
59 BMC XI, pp. 107–8.
60 Oates, *Catalogue of the fifteenth-century printed books*, nos. 3837 (exchanged with H. P. Kraus for a copy of Caxton's French vocabulary) and 3838 (retained): see *Fifty-five books printed before 1525*, pp. 3–4 and Kraus, *A rare book saga*, pp. 246–8.
61 For one detailed example, see Dane, 'The Huntington Apocalypse blockbook'.
62 Tuer, *Bartolozzi and his works* II, ch. 2, pp. 91–5.
63 On the other hand, some examples are easily detected. For example, a copy now in the Houghton Library, Harvard University, of the English Bible, *Book of common prayer*, and metrical psalms, all printed at London in 1628, was supplied with a gilt calf binding bearing the arms of James I (d. 1625).
64 See most recently Anthony Hobson, 'Some deceptive bookbindings'.
65 Anthony J. West, *The Shakespeare first folio* II, pp. 226–7.
66 The Zaehnsdorf company, one of the leading binders and restorers in London, whose reference books were sold by Oak Knoll Books of New Castle, Delaware, in 2008–10, possessed copies of both the French and German editions, the latter with a partial interleaved translation into English.

67 For examples of the extensive literature on this, see Mark Jones, *Fake?*; Mark Jones (ed.), *Why fakes matter*. For illuminated manuscripts, see for example Alexander, 'Facsimiles, copies, and variations'. For a more general perspective, see Nagel and Wood, *Anachronic renaissance*, especially chs. 22 and 23. For furniture, see for example Wainwright, *The romantic interior*, pp. 58–9.

68 For practice and taste in the restoration of sculpture, and its bearing on attitudes to book restoration, in the late eighteenth and early nineteenth centuries, see also Kristian Jensen, *Revolution and the antiquarian book*, especially pp. 167–70.

69 Christian, *Empire without end*, pp. 174–5. See also Barkan, *Unearthing the past*, especially pp. 173–89, 210–31.

70 Haskell and Penny, *Taste and the antique*; Vaughan, 'The restoration of classical sculpture'; Ramage, 'Restorer and collector'; Grossman and others (eds.), *History of restoration of ancient stone sculpture*.

71 Marvin, *The language of the muses*, p. 97.

72 Conti, *Storia del restauro e della conservazione delle opere dell'arte*, pp. 114–20.

73 Michel, *Mazarin, prince de collectionneurs*.

74 Haskell and Penny, *Taste and the antique*, pp. 246–7; Bober and Rubenstein, *Renaissance artists and antique sculpture*, pp. 164–8.

75 Reitlinger, *The economics of taste* II, p. 62, with further references; Jenkins and Sloan, *Vases and volcanoes*, pp. 220–2. For Piranesi's 'genius for transporting the past to serve modern tastes', see the essay by John Wilton-Ely in Wilton and Bignamini, *Grand tour*, p. 207.

76 Quatremère de Quincy, *Letters to Miranda and Canova*, p. 84.

77 Winckelmann, *Raccolta d'antiche statue*; Howard, *Bartolomeo Cavaceppi*; Bignamini and Hornsby, *Digging and dealing in eighteenth-century Rome* I, pp. 226–8, 252–4, 305–7. More generally, see Pinelli, 'Artisti, falsari o filologhi?'

78 For an example of deliberate damage done to an antique piece in order to render it more attractive, see Angelicoussis, 'An Olympiad's portrait'. With the help of some judicious chiselling, a bust of Hermes found at Tivoli in about 1770 was transformed into a 'bust of a conqueror of the Olympic games', anciently crowned with wild olive.

79 Ravaisson, *La Vénus de Milo*; Curtis, *Disarmed*, pp. 99–106.

80 Coltman, *Classical sculpture*, pp. 87–91.

81 Coltman, *Classical sculpture*, pp. 111–14.

82 Haskell and Penny, *Taste and the antique*, p. 103. For Denon's work in organising and arranging the Musée Napoléon at this time, see Denon, *Correspondance*.

83 Details from www.britishmuseum.org (February 2011).

84 Haskell and Penny, *Taste and the antique*, p. 103. For Denon's work with sculptors more generally, see Lemaistre, 'Les commandes de sculptures'.

85 E. D. Clarke, *Greek marbles*, pp. ii–iii. See also Budde and Nicholls, *A catalogue of the Greek and Roman sculpture*, pp. 46–9, identifying the statue as a caryatid

from the Inner Propylaea at Eleusis. For the Apollo Belvedere, see Haskell and Penny, *Taste and the antique*, pp. 148–51.

86 A seventeenth-century smaller copy in the National Gallery by Gerrit Lundens (1622–1683?) records its appearance before this.

87 For example the Noveliers family in Brussels in the early seventeenth century: see Campbell, 'The conservation of Netherlandish paintings', at p. 21.

88 Conti, *A history*, pp. 39, 66–8, 120–34; Jaffé, *Rubens and Italy*, p. 68; Talley, 'Miscreants and hotentots'.

89 Reynolds, *A journey to Flanders and Holland*, index, s.v. 'cleaned pictures', 'restored pictures'.

90 Conti, *A history*, pp. 181–220.

91 Massing, 'Restoration policy in France in the eighteenth century'; Massing, *Painting restoration before la restauration*.

92 Emile-Mâle, *Pour une histoire de la restauration des peintures en France*, pp. 39–227: 'Contribution à l'histoire de la restauration des peintures en France sous la Révolution'.

93 Conti, *A history*, p. 51.

94 Conti, *A history*, p. 58.

95 Quoted in Conti, *A history*, p. 93. 'Mi è capitato un quadro che mi è parso per gli animali, e il restante, di buon gusto; solo manca nella figura, quale vorrei mi ricoprisse di una tinta di gran gusto, però nella stessa medesima attitudine. E il panno, e camicia, e acconciatura di testa rifatela a vostro gusto; come anche vorrei che le due testi di morto, sì di femmina che di uomo le ricoprisse ma tutto vorrei, che vedesse dal vero, perché con questo che vi avviso facciate che si riduce un buon quadro' (*Storia del restauro*, p. 88).

96 Hommes, *Changing pictures*. For a concise overview of this and some of the other issues mentioned here, see for example the catalogue of the *Exhibition of cleaned pictures*.

97 *The Spectator* 83 (5 June 1711).

98 Hogarth, *The analysis of beauty*, especially pp. 91–4, 135–6. Some of these issues are concisely discussed in Gombrich, 'Dark varnishes'.

99 Talley, 'Miscreants and hotentots', at p. 39.

100 For contemporary influences and needs, and their relationship to the restoration of earlier works, see for example *Middeleeuwse muurschilderingen in de 19de eeuw*.

101 BBC News, 18 November 2010. A hand was restored to Venus and a penis to Mars, at a reported cost of 73,000 euros.

102 For aspects of these understandably much debated themes, see for example Phillips, *Exhibiting authenticity*. Like almost all writers on the subject, he ignores questions concerning the treatment of books and manuscripts.

103 Quatremère de Quincy, *Letters to Miranda and Canova*, p. 146.

3 Conservation, counterfeiting and bookbinding

1. The increasingly familiar software used for 'turning the pages' is a compromise, and the illusion is a very limited one.
2. Willis and Clark, *The architectural history of the University of Cambridge*. For Willis, see especially Pevsner, *Some architectural writers of the nineteenth century*, pp. 52–61 and the notice by Ben Marsden in the *Oxford dictionary of national biography* (ODNB).
3. Enschedé, *Fonderies de caractères et leur matériel dans les Pays-Bas*. Translated and revised by Harry Carter and others as *Typefoundries in the Netherlands*.
4. William Morris to *The Athenaeum*, 10 March 1877: Morris, *Letters* I, p. 352.
5. *Manifesto of the Society for the Protection of Ancient Buildings*.
6. Miele (ed.), *From William Morris*, pp. 30–65: 'Morris and conservation', at pp. 42–3.
7. Lubbock, 'On the preservation of our ancient national monuments', at p. 257. For Lubbock's long battle in Parliament, from 1873 onwards, to pass legislation for the preservation of ancient monuments, see for example G. B. Brown, *The care of ancient monuments*, pp. 152–4.
8. Loftie, 'Thorough restoration'; George G. Scott, 'Thorough anti-restoration'. For Loftie, see the ODNB article by W. B. Owen and Bernard Nurse.
9. Choay, *The invention of the historic monument*, pp. 96–108.
10. See below, Chapter 8.
11. Cobham and Wood (eds.), *Report of the committee on leather for bookbinding*.
12. P. R. Harris, *A history of the British Museum Library*, p. 427.
13. See Breslauer, *The uses of bookbinding literature*.
14. Needham, 'William Morris', at p. 25.
15. Tidcombe, *Bookbindings of T. J. Cobden-Sanderson*.
16. Morris to A. C. Swinburne: Morris, *Letters* II, p. 110.
17. *Catalogue of manuscripts and early printed books* II, pp. 202–4.
18. Cf. the essay by Morris on fifteenth-century woodcuts from Ulm and Augsburg, prefixed to Cockerell, *Some German woodcuts of the fifteenth century*.
19. See p. 70.
20. Quaritch, *Catalogue of works on the fine arts*, p. 1217. See also Wheatley, 'Mr Quaritch's catalogue of bookbindings'.
21. *Bibliotheca Sunderlandiana; Hamilton Palace libraries*. For the Sunderland library, see Swift, 'Bibliotheca Sunderlandiana'. For Beckford's, see Gemmett, *Consummate collector*; and Ostergard (ed.), *William Beckford*. Both Sunderland and Beckford are discussed in W. Clarke, *Repertorium bibliographicum*, pp. 316–24, 203–30; Quaritch, *Contributions towards a dictionary of English book collectors*; and de Ricci, *English collectors of books and manuscripts*, pp. 38–40, 84–7.
22. Quaritch, *Contributions towards a dictionary of English book collectors*, part II.
23. *The Times*, 1 July 1882.

24 For a contemporary, and suitably enthusiastic, portrait of this library, see Janin, 'Le duc d'Aumale et la bibliophilie'; for an account mainly of his earlier years, see Barker, 'Henri d'Orléans, Duc d'Aumale'.
25 *The Times*, 18 July 1882.
26 This copy is now at Princeton. For details of this and other of Beckford's Blakes, see G. E. Bentley, *Blake books*.
27 Quaritch, *Catalogue of works on the fine arts*, pp. 1167–8.
28 *The Times*, 13 December 1881. According to the same report, 1,500 copies of the sale catalogue were printed. Large-paper copies were printed of both the Sunderland and the Beckford catalogues.
29 For Bryant, see Munby, 'Jacob Bryant and the Sunderland library'.
30 Quaritch, *Catalogue of English literature*, p. 2117.
31 Quaritch, *Catalogue of romances of chivalry*, pp. 696–7. The Sunderland copy was bought by W. H. Crawford, and then in 1891 by the British Museum.
32 See above, p. 29.
33 De Conihout and Ract-Madoux, *Reliures françaises du XVIIe siècle*.
34 See above, p. 49.
35 [Claudin] 'Les faussures de livres', at p. 513. For further concerns about forgeries, see for example Harrisse, 'Falsifications bolognaises'.
36 See pp. 129–30.
37 McKitterick, *Cambridge University Library*, pp. 690–9.
38 Cambridge University Library MS Add.4081 and SSS.36.22. Burlington Fine Arts Club, *Exhibition of bookbindings*, nos. A57 (with plate) and F10. For the manuscript, see Ringrose, *Summary catalogue of the additional medieval manuscripts*, pp. 131–2; for the forged Grolier binding by Monte and Vittorio Villa, see Nixon, 'Binding forgeries'.
39 On this, see in general Nixon, 'Binding forgeries'. Nixon is concerned here largely with I. F. Joni, who in the first half of the twentieth century produced large numbers of paintings ostensibly of the renaissance, including boards seemingly from the bindings of account books in the Sienese archives; Joni's selectively revealing autobiography was published as *Memorie di un pittore di quadri antichi*. See also Mazzoni (ed.), *Falsi d'autore*.
40 For Hagué, see Eudel, *Le truquage*. For his work with Quaritch and sales to the collector John Blacker, see Foot, 'Double agent'. See also Foot, Blacker and Poole-Wilson, 'Collector, dealer and forger'; and Foot, 'Binder, faker and artist'. In due course, Hagué's work was to be celebrated and advertised as desirable in itself, as modern imitations of old bindings: for later recognition of his skills see for example Sotheran's catalogue no. 97 (1928), which offered two bindings copying work for Henri II and Diane de Poitiers: items 137 (Bartolus de Saxo Ferrato, 1527, 'a beautiful imitation of a very fine binding', with photograph) and 201 (Fuchs, *Commentaires de l'hystoire des plantes*, 1549).
41 Joseph van Praet had published a list of some of his books in his *Catalogue des livres imprimés sur vélin*.

42 Laffitte, 'Faux ou pastiches'.
43 See above, p. 67.
44 Quaritch, *A collection of facsimiles from examples of historic or artistic bookbinding*, p. 15: 'Introduction'.
45 Coleridge, *Biographia literaria*.

4 Representation and imitation

1 Knight, *Passages of a working life* I, p. 80. Assuming that Knight was telling the truth, this copy is not known to have survived. For a copy once owned by him, but made up with sheets from Wright's facsimile, see *The library of William Foyle*, part III (Christie's, 12–13 July 2000), lot 453; and Rasmussen and West (eds.) *The Shakespeare First Folio*, pp. 699–702. The editors report that the present owner 'has sought to replace facsimile leaves with originals' – an innovative reversal.
2 Lowry, *The world of Aldus Manutius*, pp. 154–8. Aldus's rejoinder to the counterfeiters is printed in Renouard, *Annales de l'imprimerie des Alde*, pp. 321–3: for the privileges, see H. G. Fletcher, *New Aldine studies*, pp. 143–7. For early sixteenth-century italic types, see Tinti, *Il corsivo nell tipografia del cinquecento*; Balsamo and Tinti, *Origini del corsivo nella tipografia italiana del cinquecento*; and Shaw 'The Lyons counterfeit of Aldus's italic type'.
3 See for example Harry Carter, *A view of early typography*, pp. 86–7: 'What look like Garamond's faces in our Elizabethan books often turn out on closer acquaintance to be Haultin's.' On these two type-founders in this context, see especially Vervliet, *The palaeotypography of the French renaissance*; and Vervliet, *French renaissance printing types*.
4 For *contrefaçons* of *Tartuffe* and *L'avare* see for example Brunet, *Manuel du libraire* III, cols. 1805–6; see also Riffaud, *Répertoire du théâtre français imprimé*. For fake imprints more generally, see Parenti, *Dizinario dei luoghi di stampa falsi, inventati o suppositi*; and Moureau, *Les presses grises*.
5 McKitterick, *Print, manuscript and the search for order*, pp. 97–138.
6 STC 19120.7. For the various fortunes of Henry Fitzalan, 12th Earl of Arundel (1512–80), see the account by Julian Lock in ODNB.
7 Foxon, *English verse*, nos. S253–4. For Settle's use of special presentation bindings prepared to enhance his chances of success in seeking patronage or other reward, and his practice of having them altered if the attempt with one person was unsuccessful, see G. D. Hobson (ed.), *English bindings* pp. 92–6 and Nixon, *Five centuries of British bookbinding*, pp. 130–1. See also the British Library database of bookbindings: www.bl.uk/catalogues/bookbindings (accessed 20 May 2012).
8 See for example Goff, 'Falsifed dates in certain incunabula'; Hellinga, '"Less than the whole truth"', with further references; Treadwell, 'On false and misleading imprints'.
9 ISTC is00634000; see also Anderson, 'A variant specimen of Anton Sorg's "Bücheranzeige"'.

10 The copy in Cambridge University Library (Sel.4.5) was bought by James Clarke at Venice on 23 May 1732.
11 Haym, *Notizia de' libri rari nella lingua italiana*, p. 172.
12 A. W. Pollard, 'Bibliography and bibliology'.
13 Carter and Pollard, *An enquiry into the nature of certain nineteenth century pamphlets*; Barker and Collins, *A sequel to an enquiry*.
14 Graham Pollard, 'The scope for further typographical analysis'.
15 For a method to discover whether paper had been made to appear old by being exposed to smoke and soot, see Horne, *An introduction to the study of bibliography* I, p. 123, quoting Achard, *Cours élémentaire de bibliographie*.
16 Enschedé, *Type-foundries in the Netherlands*; *Schriftproben der Offizin Haag-Drugulin A. G.*; Imprimerie Nationale, *Le cabinet des poinçons de l'Imprimerie Nationale*; Stephenson, *Caslon old face, roman and italic* (but see also Howes, 'Caslon's punches and matrices'); Rooses, *Index characterum architypographicae Plantinianae*; *Inventaris van de stempels en matrijzen van et Museum Plantin-Moretus*; Hart, *Notes on a century of typography*; Axel-Nilsson, *Type studies*.
17 *Proef van letteren, welke gegooten worden in de nieuwe Haerlemsche lettergietery van J.Enschedé.*
18 Mores, *A dissertation upon English typographical founders*.
19 *The most ancient and famous history of the renowned prince Arthur King of Britaine* (1634). STC 806.
20 For Passenger, or Passinger, see Spufford, *Small books and pleasant histories*.
21 N. A. Smith, *Catalogue of the Pepys Library*. Pepys had his 'Vulgaria', fifty-one pamphlets c. 1637–93, bound up into three volumes (now nos. 1190–3). For the titles of these, see his own catalogue: McKitterick (ed.), *Catalogue of the Pepys Library*, part II, pp. 299–305.
22 *A collection of articles, injunctions, canons . . . of the Church of England* (1661), preface by Anthony Sparrow (later Bishop of Exeter). Further editions appeared in 1671 and 1675.
23 The original is STC 16044.
24 [Fisher] *The funeral sermon of Margaret*.
25 Now Cambridge University Library Syn.7.63.399. See Case, *A bibliography of English poetical miscellanies*, nos. 84, 84b.
26 For some other libraries, see Hazen, 'Type-facsimiles'.
27 'The *English Mercurie* will remain an incontestible proof of the existence of a printed news-paper in England, at an epoch, when no other nation can boast a vehicle of news of a similar kind.' Chalmers, *The life of Thomas Ruddiman*, pp. 107–9.
28 Watts, *A letter to Antonio Panizzi, Esq.*, p. 7. For Caslon's specimen of 1766 see Caslon, *A specimen of printing types by William Caslon*.
29 See the notice by G. M. Ditchfield in ODNB.
30 For Wyatt, see J. M. Robinson, *The Wyatts*; and Colvin, *A biographical dictionary of English architects*. For Soane, see his *Designs in architecture*; Stroud, *Sir John*

Soane as architect; Watkin, *Sir John Soane*; and Colvin, *A biographical dictionary*. For Abbotsford, see Wainwright, *The romantic interior*, pp. 147–207; and Iain Brown, *Abbotsford and Sir Walter Scott*. The Gothic revival was of course only one aspect of ways of viewing and reinterpreting the past.

31 Hitchcock, *Architecture*; Chenesseau, *Sainte-Croix d'Orléans*.
32 Milner, *A dissertation on the modern style of altering ancient cathedrals*.
33 STC 11088.5. There are fragments in three other libraries. See also Oates, 'The Trewe encounter'.
34 For modern faces, fat faces and other typographical innovations, see for example Edmund Fry, *Specimen of modern printing types*. The most convenient summary, though one now somewhat dated, remains A. F. Johnson, *Type designs*.
35 Hazen, 'J. Sturt, facsimilist'; see also Macdonald, 'Note'.
36 STC 22895–22895a; Kyd, *Works*, p. lv; Jackson, *The Carl H. Pforzheimer library*, no. 953; Greg, *A bibliography of the English printed drama*, no. 109; Hazen, 'Type-facsimiles', at pp. 209–12.
37 For these and other publishing societies, see Hume, *The learned societies and printing clubs*. Further lists of publications are given in Bohn, *Appendix to the bibliographer's manual of English literature*. For the Bannatyne Club, see Laing (ed.), *Bannatyne Club*.
38 Warren, *The Charles Whittinghams*; Keynes, *William Pickering*; Buechler, '"Adapted from an old book"'; Buechler, *Charles Whittingham*.
39 Barker, *The publications of the Roxburghe Club*; Barker, *The Roxburghe Club*.
40 *Six bookes of metamorphoseos in whyche ben conteyned the fables of Ovyde. Translated out Frensshe into Englysshe by William Caxton* (1819).

5 From copying to facsimile

1 Twyman, *Lithography, 1800–1850*; Twyman and others, *Images en couleurs*.
2 'The Shakespeare tercentenary', *Ladies' Treasury*, 1 April 1864, p. 121.
3 Review of his *Handbook to autographs* (1862) in *Saturday Review* 14 (1862), p. 453. For this and other examples, see the *Oxford English Dictionary*. Among his other work, Netherclift prepared the plates for the *Autograph miscellany* (1855), the *Autographic album* (1866) and the *Autograph souvenir* (1867).
4 *The Times*, 7 July 1866.
5 See for example Kurtz, *The reception of classical art in Britain*.
6 See for example Davies, 'The Albacini cast collection'; Vaughan, 'Albacini and his English patrons'; Spier and Kagan, 'Sir Charles Frederick and the forgery of ancient coins'.
7 Hughes and Ranfft (eds.), *Sculpture and its reproductions*; Knox, 'Sir Francis Dashwood'; Coltman, *Classical sculpture*; Friedman and Clifford, *The man at Hyde Park Corner*. The manufacture, appreciation and use of plaster casts are considered from several viewpoints in Frederiksen and Marchand (eds.), *Plaster casts*.

8 Malcolm Baker, 'The portrait sculpture', pp. 110–37; Clarke and others, *Stowe landscape gardens*.

9 *A catalogue of the entire collection of that ingenious artist Mr. Ishmael Parbury, late of Salisbury Court, in Fleet-Street, watch-chaser, deceas'd. consisting of his most excellent models and casts ... his collection of prints, drawings, books, coins and medals, limnings and pictures ... Which will be sold by auction, by Mr. Cock, on Wednesday and Thursday the 17th and 18th of this instant, December, 1746* [1746]; *A catalogue of the genuine and entire collection of Italian and other drawings, prints, models, and casts, of the late eminent Mr. Jonathan Richardson, Painter, deceas'd. which will be sold by auction, by Mr. Cock, at his house in the Great Piazza, Covent-Garden, on Thursday the 22d of January, 1746-7, and the seventeen following nights, (Sundays excepted)*[1747]; *A catalogue of the genuine and entire collection of Italian and other drawings, prints, models, and casts, of the late eminent Mr. Jonathan Richardson, painter, deceas'd. which will be sold by auction, by Mr. Cock, at his house in the great piazza, Covent-Garden, on Thursday the 22d of January, 1746-7, and the seventeen following nights* ... [1747].

10 *A descriptive catalogue of a very extensive and capital collection of anatomical preparations, original casts of the gravid uterus ... Which will be sold by auction, by Mr. Hutchins ... on Monday, December the 10th, 1787* [1787].

11 38 Geo.III.c.71, *An act for encouraging the art of making new models and casts of busts, and other things therein mentioned*.

12 8 Geo.II.c.13.

13 *A copy of the documents, &c. respecting an Act of Parliament, intitled. "An act to encourage the art of making new models and casts ..." To which is added a copy of a letter of thanks from the Royal Academy to Mr. Garrard, who ... obtained this law for the benefit of the arts* (1799).

14 For a German summary of the materials available for casts, see Ringelhardt, *Die Kunst alle Arten Abgüsse und Abdrucke*. See also Engelmann, *Bibliotheca mechanico-technologica*.

15 *Synopsis of the contents of the British Museum*.

16 Thomas Spencer, 'An account of some experiments'; Thomas Spencer, 'Voltaic engravings'.

17 Advertised, for example, in the *Morning Chronicle* from 10 January 1840.

18 Several papers at this time include Jacobi, 'Ueber die Inductions-Phänomene'; Lenz and Jacobi, 'Ueber die Gesetze der Electromagnete'.

19 De Demidoff, 'Sur le procédé de galvanoplastique découvert par M. Jacoby'.

20 Glasgow: Richard Griffin and Co. for Thomas Tegg, London. Reviewed in the *Liverpool Mercury*, 18 December 1840.

21 *John Bull*, 25 November 1843, p. 750.

22 Solly, 'Observations on the precipitation of copper'; Smee, 'On the production of electrotypes'.

23 A further edition appeared in 1851.

24 Advertisement by Kemp & Co., *Aberdeen Journal*, 9 March 1842.

25 *Price list of reproductions of works of art*. A briefer list, without the account of the Raphael cartoons, was published in the same year. Some of the inter-relationships among different media are discussed in Malcolm Baker, 'The reproductive continuum', pp. 485–500.
26 Trajan's column was created from metal casts held in the Louvre, made under the direction of Napoleon III (reigned 1852–70). See the notes by Diane Bilbey: www.vam.ac.uk/res_cons/conservation/behind/trajan; and Bilbey and Trusted, '"The question of casts"'. See also Physick, *The Victoria and Albert Museum*, pp. 156–60 etc. More generally, see Anthony Burton, *Vision and accident* and Elizabeth James, *The Victoria and Albert Museum*.
27 *Notes of objects in Italy suitable for reproduction by various methods* (1870).
28 See below, pp. 120–1.
29 Elkington & Co., *Inventory of reproductions in metal*.
30 *Catalogue of the casts, busts, reliefs, and illustrations* , p. xii.
31 J. C. Robinson, *Catalogue of 'the circulating collection' of works of art*.
32 *Price list of mounted photographs*.
33 For a summary guide, see Bridson and Wakeman, *Printmaking and picture printing*.
34 See for example Verhoogt, *Art in reproduction*. Haskell, *The painful birth of the art book* is largely concerned with eighteenth-century reproductive engravers, especially in Pierre Crozat's *Recueil d'estampes*. More generally, see Lloyd, *Art and its images*. See also p. 99.
35 Chaudonneret, 'Le statut et la réception de la lithographie en France'.
36 The Aratea manuscript is now Leiden UB MS Voss. lat.Q.79. Cf. Hugo Grotius (ed.), *Syntagma Arateorum: opus antiquitatis et astronomiae studiosis utilissimum* (Leiden, 1600).
37 The plates are in the Museum Plantin-Moretus, Antwerp. See Cockshaw, 'A propos de [sic] plus ancien fac-similé'. For a reproduction, see Godding and others, *Bollandistes*, p. 50. One of the original copper plates is depicted in de Nave and Voet, *Plantin-Moretus Museum*, p. 66.
38 See *Trois cents chefs-d'oeuvre en fac-similé*; Nordenfalk, *Color of the middle ages*; Lemaire and Cockx-Indestege (eds.), *Manuscrits et imprimés anciens en fac-similé*; Klamt, 'Zur Reproduktionsgeschichte mittelalterlicher Schriftformen und Miniaturen in der Neuzeit'; Klamt, 'Als die Photographie noch nich erfunden war'; Worm, 'Reproducing the middle ages'; Zotter, *Bibliographie Faksimilierter Handschriften*.
39 Meerman, *Origines typographicae*, plate III; Sotheby, *Principia typographica*.
40 Sotheby, *Principia typographica* I, p. 153.
41 Sotheby, *Principia typographica* II, plate LVI*. This is not in Gernsheim, *The Incunabula of British photographic literature*.
42 In the second volume, Dibdin thanked John Nesbit, M. J. Byfield and Mary Byfield. In the third, Ebenezer Byfield received profuse thanks.

43 [J. van Praet] *Notice sur Colard Mansion*; Wetter, *Kritische Geschichte der Erfindung der Buchdruckerkunst.*

44 *Albert Durer's designs of the prayer book* (1817). Many of the marginal drawings had already been reproduced by lithography by J. N. Strixner in 1808: *Albrecht Dürers christlich-mythologische Handzeichnungen* (Munich, 1808). See Twyman, *Lithography*, pp. 15–16, 21.

45 *Confessionale ou Beichtspiegel nach den zehn geboten*, p. 16.

46 *Revue Française*, 1839, pp. 130–4.

47 See also Dupont, *Essais pratiques d'imprimerie*; Delamotte, *On the various applications of anastatic printing and papyrography*; Jordan, *A treatise on anastatic printing*; Cowell, *A brief description of the art of anastatic printing*; Harris, 'Experimental graphic processes in England'.

48 *Exhibition of the works of industry of all nations* III, p. 882. The jury for the relevant section, under the chairmanship of Ambroise Firmin Didot, noted that 'Il est fâcheux que les imprimeurs anglais n'aient pas cru envoyer le produit de leurs presses . . .; la comparaison de leurs belles impressions aurait été honorable et même profitable à eux-mêmes et autres concurrents des divers pays. (Didot, *L'Imprimerie*, p. 14.)

49 *Exhibition of the works of industry of all nations* III, p. 895.

50 *Exhibition of the works of industry of all nations* III, pp. 890, 986–7.

51 *Exhibition of the works of industry of all nations* IV, p. 1542.

52 *Exhibition of the works of industry of all nations* IV, p. 1559. For Appel, see Wakeman, 'Anastatic printing for Sir Thomas Phillipps'. Appel's other work included *Fifteen views of Australia* (c. 1853). He was still working in Ipswich in 1848.

53 Although by far the most celebrated, John Harris, father and son, were not the only ones in their profession. For example, apart from Frederick Netherclift (see above. p. 94), cf. Hazlitt, *The confessions of a collector*, p.166, referring to 'Mr Burt the facsimilist'. For Harris, father and son, see also Weimerskirch, 'John Harris, Sr.'

54 For a summary account of Harris, see Janet Ing Freeman in ODNB, with further references.

55 Wyman W. Parker, *Henry Stevens of Vermont*, p. 183. See also Stevens, *Recollections of Mr. James Lenox of New York*.

56 *Exhibition of the works of industry of all mations* III, pp. 891–2. For Whittaker, see also above, p. 37.

57 *Catalogue of a very important collection of early English Bibles and Testaments* (Sotheby & Wilkinson, 20 August 1857). The anonymous owner of the first part of the sale was the American bookseller Henry Stevens. Harris's facsimiles occupied lots 665–766, at the end of the sale.

58 Now British Library C.132.h.46.

59 Eudel, *Le truquage*, pp. 253–4; Samaran, 'Adam Pilinski'. The facsimile leaves and ornamentation in the vellum copy of the Gutenberg Bible in the Pierpont Morgan Library have been attributed to him.

60 His work is to be seen, for example, in the British Library copy of the *Golden legend* (Wynkyn de Worde, 1493: BMC XI, p.186), facsimiles dated 1866 and 1870 and in two copies of the third folio of Shakespeare (1664), now in the Folger Shakespeare Library: (1) formerly the property of Francis Brown Hayes (1819–84) and, with a penned note 'F. S by H junr.' on the third leaf; (2) formerly the property of Sidney Smith Rider (1833–1917), with similar notes.
61 Murphy, *Shakespeare in print*, p. 196.
62 Spevack, *James Orchard Halliwell-Phillipps; the life and works*, pp. 275–8, 358–9. Halliwell destroyed nineteen of each of the editions of fifty copies.
63 Myers, 'George Isaac Frederick Tupper'.
64 Preface, p.vi.
65 Myers, 'George Isaac Frederick Tupper'; Myers, 'William Blades's debt to Henry Bradshaw'.
66 *The first New Testament printed in the English language ... reproduced in facsimile*. Introd. Francis Fry (Bristol, 1862), p. 17.
67 See below, pp. 131–2.
68 *Bulletin du Bibliophile*, 1840, pp. 343–5.
69 See for example Koestler, *The act of creation*, pp. 121–4.
70 In 1862, ninety-seven punches passed to the Imprimerie Nationale: see Imprimerie Nationale, *Le cabinet des poinçons de l'Imprimerie Nationale*: 'Latin de forme gothique', corps 24.

6 The arrival of photography

1 Pollard and others, '"Facsimile" reprints of old books'.
2 Busch (ed.), *Die acht Schalkheiten*.
3 *Ars moriendi*, pp. 2–3.
4 *Speculum humanae salvationis*, p. lxxi.
5 Bradshaw, *Henry Bradshaw's correspondence on incunabula* II, pp. 310–11 etc.
6 Just 155 copies were printed of the facsimile of the *Speculum humanae salvationis*, price 4 guineas.
7 For publication details, see Bradshaw, *Henry Bradshaw's correspondence on incunabula* II, pp. 492–3.
8 *Confessionale ou Beichtspiegel nach den zehn geboten*. The volume had been described by F.K. Ruppel in the catalogue of the von Stengel library of Bamberg in 1823; Dibdin included a facsimile of one of the blocks and several lines of text in his *Reminiscences* II, pp. 962–5; Falkenstein included a facsimile in his *Geschichte der Buchdruckerkunst*, p.43; and Sotheby included a copy from Dibdin in his *Principia typographica* II, plate 86. It was bought by Samuel Butler at the Kloss sale in 1835, and then passed to Payne & Foss, who sold it to Baron van Westreenen van Tielandt for 8 guineas.

9 In 1866 Holtrop fretted about the facsimiles in the new catalogue of the incunables at Hannover. See Bradshaw, *Henry Bradshaw's correspondence on incunabula* I, pp. 82 and II, pp. 327–8.
10 Hamber, 'The use of photography'; Hamber, *"A higher branch of the art"*; Hamber, 'Facsimile, scholarship, and commerce'.
11 See for example the long passage on the subject, quoting Delisle at length, in Birch, *The history, art and palaeography*, pp. vi–xvi.
12 Thompson, *Handbook of Greek and Latin palaeography*, p. viii. In this first edition it is the more noticeable that though he drew extensively on published collections of facsimiles, Thompson did not include any photographs among the dozens of illustrations in his book, which was part of a popular series in the sciences.
13 For this well-known statement, see for example Therrien, *L'histoire de l'art en France*, p. 398 and Ouwekerk, 'Met kunst geïllustreerd'.
14 For the following, see Gernsheim, *The origins of photography*, pp. 28–59 and Schaaf, *Out of the shadows*.
15 Gernsheim, *L. J. M. Daguerre*.
16 Talbot, *Some account of the art of photogenic drawing*.
17 Gernsheim, *Incunabula of British photographic literature*, pp. 85–6.
18 Talbot, *Some account of the art of photogenic drawing*.
19 For further discussion, see Hamber, *"A higher branch of the art"*; Helene Roberts (ed.), *Art history through the camera's lens*; Isabelle Jammes, *Blanquart-Evrard*; McCauley, 'Art reproduction for the masses', pp. 265–300; De Font-Réaulx and Bolloch, *The work of art and its reproduction*.
20 Talbot, *The pencil of nature*, caption to plate XI. For Talbot's earlier experiments in copying prints, see Schaaf, *The photographic art of William Henry Fox Talbot*, pp. 182–3.
21 This process required that the reverse of the leaf was blank. The copy used of the *Statuta Angliae* (William de Machlinia, 1485?), STC 9264 is now in the Law Library at Harvard: see Schaaf, *William Henry Fox Talbot*, no. 4.
22 Schaaf, *Out of the shadows*, p. 66.
23 Talbot, *The pencil of nature*, caption to plate IX.
24 *Photographic facsimiles of the remains of the Epistles of Clement of Rome*, note. For earlier facsimiles of Biblical manuscripts, see Stresow, 'Meisterwerke typographischer Faksimilierung früher Bibelkodizes'. For bibliographical surveys of early history of photographs in books, see Heidtmann, *Wie das Photo ins Buch kam* and Gernsheim, *Incunabula of British photographic literature*.
25 Helene Roberts (ed.), *Art history through the camera's lens*, pp. 104–5; Haworth-Booth, 'Camille Silvy'.
26 *Fac-simile delle miniature contenute nel Breviario Grimani*; 'Au lecteur'. Perini referred to his procedure as Galvanoplastie, or galvano-plastica.
27 Hinrichsen, *Baedeker's Reisehandbücher*; Lister, *A bibliography of Murray's Handbooks for travellers*.
28 *New York Times*, 4 December 1905.

29 Baudelaire, *The mirror of art*, pp. 230–1. 'Il faut donc qu'elle rentre dans son véritable devoir, qui est d'être la servante des sciences et des arts, mais la très humble servante, comme l'imprimerie et la sténographie, qui n'ont ni créé ni supléé la littérature ... Qu'elle sauve de l'oubli les ruines pendantes, les livres, les estampes et les manuscrits que le temps dévore, les choses précieuses dont la forme va disparaître et qui demandent une place dans les archives de notre mémoire, elle sera remerciée et applaudie' (Charles Baudelaire, 'Salon de 1859', *Oeuvres complètes* 7 vols. 4: *Curiosités esthétiques* (Paris, n.d.), p. 244). The comments were originally published in the *Révue Française*.

30 Hardy; *The Athanasian Creed*; Bond and others, *The Utrecht Psalter*; Birch, *The history art and palaeography*.

31 *The Times*, 10 and 15 July 1872; 2, 5, 11, 18 and 21 February 1873. See also 'Date of the Athanasian Creed', *The Times*, 10 August 1874.

32 See below, pp. 130–8.

33 Hamber, "A higher branch of the art", p. 464. For the Arundel Society, see Hamber, "A higher branch of the art", pp. 303–14 and Maynard, *Descriptive notice of the drawings and publications of the Arundel Society*.

34 Hamber, "A higher branch of the art", pp. 466–70.

35 Blades, *The life and typography of William Caxton* I, pp. ix–x.

36 *Report of the progress of the Ordnance Survey and Topographical Depôt, to the 31st December 1859*, pp. 5–6.

37 Henry James, *Account of the methods*. See also A. de C. Scott, *On photo-zincography and other photographic processes*.

38 Henry James, *Photo-zincography*.

39 Kenyon, 'Photo-lithography'.

40 *Report of the progress of the Ordnance Survey and Topographical Depôt, to the 31st December 1860*, pp. 4–5.

41 The price asked for a set bound in Russia leather in Willis & Sotheran's catalogue of 1862, p. 163.

42 *Norfolk*, preface, dated 31 December 1863.

43 *Facsimiles of national manuscripts, from William the Conqueror to Queen Anne*; *Facsimiles of national manuscripts of Scotland*; *Facsimiles of national manuscripts of Ireland*.

44 Earle (ed.), *Gloucester fragments*, p. vi.

45 For Staunton, see ODNB and Spevack, 'James Orchard Halliwell and friends'.

46 *Report of the progress of the Ordnance Survey and Topographical Depôt, to the 31st December 1863*, pp. 5–6.

47 Advertisement in *The Publishers' Circular*, 2 November 1863, p. 576.

48 *The Times*, 14 April 1864, p. 15.

49 Willis & Sotheran, *Catalogue* (1862), p. 475. A finely bound copy of Samuel Purchas *Purchas his Pilgrimes* with the fourth edition of *Purchas his Pilgrimage* (1625–6) was priced at £68.10s in the same catalogue.

50 Advertisement in *The Publishers' Circular*, 8 December 1863, illustrations section, p. 34. Though the three parts were dated 1862–4, the first part was published in December 1861. They were designed to be bound up with a general title-page; in fact most surviving copies were left in the three parts as issued. Photographs pasted to the several title-pages represented the engraved title-page portrait to the original, the monument in Stratford parish church and the birthplace.
51 Advertisement in *The Times*, 9 December 1870. The edition was of 1636, altered in manuscript by Convocation in 1661. For the sealed copies, see James Parker, *An introduction to the history of successive revisions*, pp. 510–26.
52 *Publishers' Circular*, 15 April 1864, p. 205.
53 *Fac-simile of the autograph score of* Messiah. Compare the Bärenreiter facsimile, in full colour and with commentary by Donald Burrows (Kassel, 2008).
54 *The Times*, 1 August 1868. See also Bennett, 'The autograph of Handel's "Messiah"'.
55 *Reports on the Paris Universal Exhibition* I, p. 174.
56 Gernsheim, *Incunabula of British photographic literature*.
57 Arber (ed.), *The first printed English New Testament*, p. 70.
58 *Frederick James Furnivall*; Benzie, *Dr. F. J. Furnivall*. The ODNB article is by William S. Peterson.
59 Spevack, *James Orchard Halliwell-Phillipps; a classified bibliography*, p. 86.
60 For Greg's criticism of the Griggs facsimile of *The merry wives of Windsor*, see Murphy, *Shakespeare in print*, pp. 194–5. William Aldis Wright's annotated copy of the facsimile of the First Quarto is in Cambridge University Library, Syn.6.88.175.
61 See for example Major, *The bibliography of the first letter of Christopher Columbus*.
62 Major, *The bibliography of the first letter of Christopher Columbus*, p. 60.
63 Randolph G. Adams, *The case of the Columbus letter*; Payne (ed.), *The Spanish letter of Columbus*.
64 Murphy, *Shakespeare for the people*, pp. 78–86.
65 Robert E. Hunter, *Shakespeare and Stratford-on-Avon*.
66 McKitterick, 'Old faces and new acquaintances'.
67 Pantazzi, 'Elliot Stock'.
68 Fitzgerald, *The book fancier*, p. 158.
69 *Unwin Brothers*; Unwin, *The printing Unwins*.
70 *The Times*, 22 April 1876. For Ward, see Wise (ed.), *Letters from Ruskin to William Ward*.
71 *The Times*, 22 April 1876.

7 Public exhibition

1 www.wdl.org/en. See also Abid, 'The world digital library'.
2 Werdet, *Histoire du livre en France* I, p. vii. For Werdet's varying success as a publisher, see Felkay, *Balzac et ses éditeurs*, pp. 219–49.

3 For one recent study, with further references, see Nys, *De intrede van het publiek*. She is, however, little concerned with local exhibitions.
4 Bock, 'Collections privées et publiques'; Bjurström, 'Les premiers musées d'art en Europe et leur public'; Alsop, *The rare art traditions*, pp. 170–211; Klemm, *Zur Geschichte der Sammlungen für Wisssenshaft und Kunst*.
5 McClellan, 'The museum and its public', p. 62.
6 *The picture of London*, 22nd edn (1824), p. 285.
7 Tinniswood, *The polite tourist*. This led, of course, to a key occasion in Jane Austen's *Pride and prejudice* (1813), when Elizabeth Bennet and her party visited Pemberley, believing that its owner, Mr Darcy, was not at home.
8 See for example Hoock, *The King's artists*, pp. 206–15.
9 Lamb, 'Barrenness of the imaginative faculty'.
10 Munby, *The cult of the autograph letter* focusses on the late eighteenth century and later.
11 Morel, 'Ueber die Ausstellung'. For this and other celebrations of anniversaries associated with Gutenberg, see Estermann, *"O werthe Druckerkunst / Du Mutter aller Kunst"* and Flood, 'On Gutenberg's 600th anniversary'. For reviews of various German books marking the 1840 anniversary, see the summary account by [Mohnike], 'Review of German books'.
12 [Mohnike] 'Review of German books', p. 446.
13 *Catalogue of articles*. Though not concerned with exhibitions of books, Fawcett, *The rise of English provincial art* offers much on the provincial background.
14 *A descriptive catalogue of the Nottingham mechanics' exhibition*.
15 *Catalogue of the Norwich polytechnic exhibition*; Mrs Barwell, *A companion to the Norwich polytechnic exhibition*.
16 *The life of William Caxton* (1828). This biography was later reprinted between biographies of Lord Somers and Admiral Blake in the volume of *Lives of eminent persons* (1833).
17 *Penny Magazine* 1832, preface to the bound annual volume.
18 For stereotyping (the casting of metal plates from pages of type), see Dooley, *Author and printer in Victorian England*, pp. 55–68.
19 Knight, *William Caxton, the first English printer*. For a general account of Knight, see Valerie Gray, *Charles Knight*.
20 Jackson, *Annotated list of the publications of the Reverend Thomas Frognall Dibdin*; Windle and Pippin, *Thomas Frognall Dibdin*. On the reproduction of early books in some of Dibdin's publications, see Dane, *Out of sorts*, pp. 164–90.
21 See also below, p. 163.
22 See also below, p. 156.
23 *Specimen of Mr. S. Leigh Sotheby's Principia typographia*.
24 In 1858 Quaritch had paid 9 guineas each – the standard price – for 13 copies: see *Specimen of Mr. S. Leigh Sotheby's Principia typographia*, 'List of purchasers'.
25 In a very large literature, see for example Rebel, *Faksimile und Mimesis*; Lilien, *Jacob Christoph Le Blon*; Grasselli, *Colorful impressions*; Bähr, *Repräsentieren, bewahren,*

belehren; Schwaighofer, *Von der Kennerschaft zur Wissenschaft*; Brakensiek and Polfer (eds.), *Graphik als Spiegel der Malerei*; Vermeulen, *Picturing art history*.

26 Later published as Jameson, *Memoirs of the earlier Italian painters*. John Murray published a new and much illustrated edition in 1858.
27 Henry Shaw, *Illuminated ornaments*. See also McLean, *Victorian book design and colour printing*, pp. 64–70.
28 Conlin, *The nation's mantelpiece*; Robertson, *Sir Charles Eastlake and the Victorian art world*; Avery-Quash, *The travel notebooks of Sir Charles Eastlake*. Whitehead, *The public art museum* is concerned primarily with debates about architecture and display.
29 Depicted in the *Oxford Almanack*, 1836; see Petter, *The Oxford almanacks*.
30 For a summary of arrangements for visitors and readers until the mid-nineteenth century, see the preface by J. Winter Jones to *A list of the books of reference in the reading room*.
31 *London and its environs*, p. 105.
32 House of Commons, *Report from the Select Committee (of the House of Commons) on the ... British Museum*, Evidence, para.3915.
33 House of Commons, *Report from the Select Committee (of the House of Commons) on the ... British Museum*, Appendix, pp. 324, 356; *Account of the income and expenditure of the British Museum for the year 1849*, p. 4.
34 *Report of the Commissioners*, Minutes, p. 262.
35 A watercolour by Eugene Armand Roy (c. 1820–84) depicts the tribune of the King's Library at this time, with the showcases: British Museum Dept of Prints and Drawings 2003, 0227.1. Reproduced in Sloan, *Enlightenment*, fig. 42.
36 Backhouse, 'Manuscripts on display'. Plates 2–3 show Madden's sketches of how the exhibition of manuscripts was arranged.
37 Summary in House of Commons, *Report from the Select Committee on the National Gallery* (1853), Appendix, p. xviii.
38 Harris, *A history of the British Museum library*, pp. 195–7. The personal and professional disagreements between Panizzi and Madden have been told many times: see for example Miller, *Prince of librarians*.
39 *British Museum; A guide to the printed books exhibited to the public* (1870).
40 P. R. Harris, *A history of the British Museum library*, p. 197.
41 *A handbook for travellers on the continent: being a guide to Holland, Belgium, Prussia ...*, 11th edn (1856), p. 343.
42 Murray, *Handbook for travellers to central Italy*, p. 422; Murray, *A handbook of Rome and its environs*, p. 241.
43 Kaltwasser, *Die Bibliothek als Museum*, pp. 215–28, 237–40.
44 See above, p. 142.
45 *Die Luther-Austellung der Königlichen Bibliothek*.
46 Reviewed in *Serapeum* 6 (1844), pp. 81–6.
47 Rastaptchine, 'La Bibliothèque Impériale'.

48 Balayé, 'Les publics de la Bibliothèque Nationale', at p. 331. See also Sarmant, *Le Cabinet des Médailles de la Bibliothèque Nationale*, pp. 292–4. Foreign visitors to the *cabinet* were predominantly English.
49 Van Praet, *Catalogue des livres imprimés sur vélin de la Bibliothèque du Roi*; Van Praet, *Catalogue des livres imprimés sur vélin, qui se trouvent dans les bibliothèques*.
50 T[echener], 'Un musée bibliographique'.
51 But see Veyrin-Forrer, 'Les Réserves (livres imprimés)', pp. 369–92.
52 *Gedenkboek der Costers-feesten van 15, 16 en 17 Julij 1856*; *Catalogus van voorwerpen*; *Norfolk Chronicle*, 19 July 1856; Hellinga-Querido and De Wolf, *Laurens Janszoon Coster was zijn naam*.
53 'That it was executed in this country there is no kind of evidence upon the face of the book itself' (Ames and Herbert, *Typographical antiquities* I, p. xciv).
54 *The Life of William Caxton*, p. 24.
55 Knight, *William Caxton, the first English printer*, pp. 149, 155.

8 The Caxton exhibition of 1877

1 Viaux, 'Les expositions des produits de l'industrie'; Mainardi, *Art and politics of the Second Empire*, pp. 17–21.
2 Quoted in Mainardi, *Art and politics*, p. 22.
3 Poulot, *Une histoire des musées de France*, pp. 135–9.
4 Early museums included Sunderland (1846), Warrington (1848), Leicester (1849) and Salford (1849): see the details of foundation dates summarised in the Standing Commission on Museums and Galleries, *Survey of provincial museums and galleries*.
5 Quoted in Cantwell, *The Public Record Office*, p. 219. For an earlier airing, see Cantwell, *The Public Record Office*, p. 78.
6 Ch. Timbal, review of the exhibition at the Palais Bourbon, *Revue des Deux Mondes* 44 (1874), pp. 444–64, at p. 464. See also Trenchard Cox, *A short illustrated history*.
7 London International Exhibition 1874, official guide (1874), quoted in Greenhalgh, *Ephemeral vistas*, p. 19.
8 Robert Jensen, *Marketing modernism in fin-de-siècle Europe*, p. 118.
9 For Slade, see the account by David M. Wilson in ODNB. He left a collection of fine bindings to the British Museum, with a considerable collection of other works of art.
10 *Catalogue of the art treasures*, p. 165. For the exhibition more generally, see Pergam, *The Manchester Art Treasures Exhibition of 1857*.
11 'Ornamental binding is certainly less important in the history of book production and preservation, and the fact that it has received a vastly greater amount of attention is a tribute rather to its artistic attraction than to its bibliographical importance. As illumination belongs to fine art, so decorated bookbinding belongs to fine craft' (Greg, 'Bibliography – an apologia', p. 244).

12 *Catalogue of the special exhibition of works of art*, pp. 591–613. The accompanying album, J. C. Robinson, *The art wealth of England*, includes an early photograph of the early medieval binding of the Stonyhurst Gospel. See also Anthony Burton, *Vision and accident*, pp. 66–8. For further details of the South Kensington Museum exhibitions in this period, see Elizabeth James, *The Victoria and Albert Museum*.
13 J. Winter Jones, 'Early printed books'.
14 *Archaeological Journal* 28 (1871), pp. 341–2.
15 *Illustrated London News*, 3 June 1871. In a voluminous literature on these months, see for example Tombs, *The war against Paris, 1871*. For a contemporary report on the Hôtel de Ville and the Bibliothèque du Louvre, see Baudrillart, 'Les pertes éprouvées par les bibliothèques de Paris' (especially on the Bibliothèque du Louvre), extracted from the *Bulletin Administratif* of the Ministère de l'Instruction Publique. See also Baudrillart, 'Rapport sur les pertes éprouvées par les bibliothèques publiques'.
16 For Strasbourg, see Roth, 'Sources et grandes lignes des bibliothèques publiques'. For Saintes, see Desgraves, 'Les bibliothécaires', pp. 285–6.
17 Noltenius, 'Schiller als Führer und Heiland'; Quinault, 'The cult of the centenary'; Rigney, 'Embodied communities'.
18 *The Scott exhibition, MDCCCLXXI.*
19 *Catalogue of pictures and drawings.* Predictably, loyalties were divided between Stratford and London, the former sensing that London had stolen the thunder. See James Cox (Mayor of Stratford-upon-Avon), *The tercentenary*.
20 Hone, *Ancient mysteries described*, p. 228.
21 Craik, *A compendious history of English literature* I, p. 385.
22 Macaulay, *The history of England* I, ch. 1.
23 Blades, *The life and typography of William Caxton*.
24 Myers, 'George Isaac Frederick Tupper'. For the following, see also Myers, *Caxtoniana*.
25 For Bradshaw and Blades, see Prothero, *A memoir of Henry Bradshaw*, pp. 73–5; Myers, 'William Blades's debt to Henry Bradshaw'; and Needham, *The Bradshaw method*, pp. 14–16.
26 Carmody, 'Mirror of a world'. The offices of the *Williamstown Advertiser* still survive, now as a chandler's shop.
27 J. Power, *A handy-book about books*, p. 29.
28 Slater, *The library manual*, p. 14.
29 Blades, The *life and typography of William Caxton* I, p. 63.
30 *The Times*, 19 February 1877.
31 *The Times*, 19 February 1877.
32 *The Times*, 27 March 1877. For a further view of the Caxton exhibition, see Myers, 'The Caxton celebration of 1877'.
33 Blades, 'The Caxton celebration'.
34 For a recent analysis, see Minor, *Choral fantasies*, pp. 33–67.

35 *The Times*, 5 June 1877.
36 *Newcastle Courant*, 1 June 1877.
37 For Stanley, see also for example the *Liverpool Mercury*, 4 June 1877 and the *Hampshire Telegraph*, 6 June 1877.
38 Jevons, 'The use and abuse of museums'.
39 *The Times*, 2 July 1877. See also for example *Saturday Review*, 7 July 1877, pp. 9–10; *Northern Echo and Leeds Mercury*, 2 July 1877; *Derby Mercury*, 4 July 1877; and *Bristol Mercury*, 7 July 1877.
40 *Illustrated London News*, 30 June 1877.
41 *The Graphic*, 30 June 1877. The press as depicted was extraordinarily impractical.
42 *The Academy*, 30 June 1877, pp. 581–2.
43 'The Caxton exhibition', *Saturday Review*, 28 July 1877, p. 109. For other individuals, see for example a visitor from south London, *The Times*, 27 August 1877 and the apologetic letter from J. S. Hodson, Honorary Secretary of the exhibition, *The Times*, 31 August 1877.
44 Overall (ed.), *A catalogue of engraved portraits*.
45 Reviewed briefly in *The Graphic*, 14 July 1877.
46 *Punch*, 7 April 1877, p. 149; 14 April 1877, p. 157; and 23 June 1877, p. 149; *Fun*, 20 June 1877. *Fun* also published a sketch of a conversation in a city chop-house, 11 July 1877.
47 The original engraving (1858) of the full painting was by Frederick Bromley, and was published jointly by Henry Graves & Co in London and Knoedler in New York. The central part of Bromley's engraving, 'Dedicated by permission to the Caxton Celebration Committee', was published on 2 April 1877 by James Henderson of Red Lion Court, by permission of Graves.
48 *Young Folks*, 21 April 1877; *Young Folk's Weekly Budget*, 30 June 1877.
49 See for example the advertisement in *The Times*, 6 August 1877.
50 *The Times*, 6 September 1877.
51 It is now dated 1473, and most recently has been suggested to have been printed at Ghent: see Hellinga, *William Caxton and early printing in England*, pp. 49–51 and Hellinga, 'William Caxton, Colard Mansion and the Printer'.
52 *A guide to the objects of chief interest in the loan collection of the Caxton celebration* (1877).
53 Blades's copy, bound in eight volumes and much extended with contemporary documentation, is in the British Library, shelf-mark C.61.e.8.
54 Young, *Field & Tuer, the Leadenhall Press*.
55 Jevons, 'The use and abuse of museums'.
56 Quoted at length in *The Bibles in the Caxton exhibition*, pp. 8–10.
57 *Western Mail*, 2 July 1877.
58 *Northern Echo*, 28 September 1877.
59 *Liverpool Mercury*, 31 December 1877.
60 *Catalogue of machinery, models etc*. Another edition was published in 1897.

61 Stevens, *The Bibles in the Caxton exhibition MDCCCLXXVII*.
62 Canadian Institute, *Caxton celebration, Toronto*.
63 Virr, 'Behold this treasury of glorious things'.
64 'L'exposition des livres de Caxton en Angleterre', at p. 234; Emery and Morowitz, *Consuming the past*.
65 'L'exposition des livres de Caxton en Angleterre'.
66 Ernouf, *Les Français en Prusse*, p. 304. See also his *Souvenirs de l'invasion prussienne en Normandie*.
67 Goulemot and Walter, 'Les centenaires de Voltaire et de Rousseau'; Dalisson, *Célébrer la nation*, pp. 235–7; Bird, *Reinventing Voltaire*.
68 Claudin, *Histoire de l'imprimerie en France*. I, Avant-propos. For Claudin, see De Ricci, *Bibliographie des publications d'Anatole Claudin*.
69 *Les censures des théologiens de Paris; avec la réponse* (Geneva, 1866), reprinted from the edition of 1552. 'Nous réproduisons ici d'après l'unique édition selon nous connue, celle de 1552, dont notre habile typographe, M. Fick, s'efforce d'offrir au lecteur un fac-simile exact' (concluding note by Gustave Revilliod). For the Ficks, see Weigelt, 'Les Fick imprimeurs du XIXe siècle'.
70 In his *Catalogue of works on the fine arts*, Quaritch was to offer a block-book *Apocalypse* for £200 and an imperfect *Biblia pauperum* with 8 leaves in facsimile for £300.
71 *The Times*, 28 December 1877.
72 The divisions of opinion among various experts are summarised in Buchanan-Brown, 'A forged series of woodcuts?'; see also Feather, 'Thirty-eight old woodcuts'.
73 William Caxton, *The game of the chesse, reproduced in facsimile by Vincent Figgins* (1855), 'Remarks', p. 7.
74 *The statutes of Henry VII*.
75 See Pantazzi, 'Elliot Stock'.
76 Beedham, *A list of the reproductions*, p. 2.

9 A bibliographical and public revolution

1 Morison, *Talbot Baines Reed*, p. 45.
2 Morison, 'On the classification of typographical variations'.
3 Reed, 'Memoir of the late William Blades', in Blades, *The Pentateuch of printing*, p. xii. For Blades's writings, see also *Catalogue of an exhibition*.
4 Morison, *Talbot Baines Reed*. A new edition of Reed, *A history of the old English letter foundries* was published in 1952, revised by A. F. Johnson. As the book includes a chapter on the Scottish type-founder Alexander Wilson, the title is slightly misleading.
5 See above, p. 102. Ames, *Typographical antiquities*, engraved plate: 'A specimen of Caxton's letter'. The engraving, a poor copy of the typefaces that failed to recognise the manufacturing characteristics of type-founding, was by the writing master

George Bickham. Ames also reproduced watermarks found in paper stocks used by Caxton, but again without realising their potential importance in dating books and the structure of the book trades – only fully understood in the late twentieth century. See BMC XI, pp. 311–34 and, for background, Stevenson, 'Paper as bibliographical evidence' and Needham, 'The paper supply of the Gutenberg Bible'.

6 Winstanley, 'Halliwell Phillipps and Trinity College library'; Spevack, *James Orchard Halliwell-Phillipps; the life and works*, pp. 125–43.
7 Munby, *The history and bibliography of science in England*.
8 Spevack, *James Orchard Halliwell-Phillipps; a classified bibliography*, index, s.v. 'Science – history'; Spevack, *James Orchard Halliwell-Phillipps; the life and works*, pp. 27–8, 40–1; De Morgan, *Memoir of Augustus de Morgan*, p. 124.
9 Brock, 'Scientific bibliographies and bibliographers'.
10 Humphreys, *Masterpieces of the early printers and engravers*, p. v.
11 Victor Gray, *Bookmen*.
12 Smith and Benger, *The oldest London bookshop*.
13 Walter T. Spencer, *Forty years in my bookshop*.
14 J. H. Burton, *The book hunter*; William Roberts, *The book hunter in London*. James Clegg's *Directory of second-hand booksellers* was first published at Rochdale in 1886, and was subsequently enlarged many times.
15 The book was in fact printed by R. Schilders, at Middelburg.
16 Quaritch, *A catalogue of fifteen hundred books*, no. 1323.
17 Quaritch, *Monuments of typography and xylography*, Preface, p. v. For once, Quaritch signed this. Most of his catalogues are written anonymously, and were largely the work of his chief assistant Michael Kerney (c. 1832–1901), joined later by F. S. Ferguson (1878–1967) and Edmund H. Dring (1864–1928): see the account of Quaritch by Arthur Freeman in ODNB and the articles in the special number of the *Book Collector*, 1997. For printing as God-given, see Needham, '"Haec sancta ars"'.
18 Foxcroft, *A catalogue of English books and fragments*; Foxcroft, *Catalogue of fifteenth-century books and fragments in the Public Library of Victoria*.
19 Quaritch, *Monuments of typography and xylography*, Preface, p. v.
20 Copinger, 'Notes by Dr. Copinger on catalogues of incunabula', p. 87.
21 For Proctor, see especially his *Bibliographical essays*; Johnson, *Lost in the Alps*; Barbieri, *Haebler contro Haebler*, pp. 25–46; Bowman (ed.), *A critical edition of the private diaries of Robert Proctor*.
22 Claudin, *Histoire de l'imprimerie en France*.
23 Cf. Briquet, *The new Briquet*.
24 McKitterick, *A changing view from Amsterdam*.
25 Angermair and others, *Die Rosenthals*, pp. 91–135. For a list of the catalogues from Antiquariats Jacques Rosenthal, see Angermair and others, *Die Rosenthals*, pp. 240–4.
26 Dreyfus, 'William Morris, typographer'; Peterson, *A bibliography of the Kelmscott Press*; Peterson, *The Kelmscott Press*.

27 Willshire, *Descriptive catalogue of early prints in the British Museum*; Dodgson, *Catalogue of early German and Flemish woodcuts*.
28 Some of the literature down to 1895 is conveniently listed in Reed, 'A list of books and papers'.
29 *The Bibliographical Society, 1892–1942*; R. J. Roberts, 'The Bibliographical Society as a band of pioneers'.
30 Copinger, 'Inaugural address'.
31 Francis, 'The Bibliographical Society'.
32 Paul, *Memories*; Howsam, *Kegan Paul*. Though it takes no account of his exceptional personal influence, Pollard's exemplary work in promoting bibliographical studies is summed up in *A select bibliography of the writings of Alfred W. Pollard*; see also the obituary notice of him by J. Dover Wilson, 'A. W. Pollard', and A. W. Pollard, *Alfred William Pollard; a selection of his essays*.
33 Brassington, *Historic bindings in the Bodleian Library*; Holmes, *Specimens of royal, fine and historical bookbinding*; Wheatley, *Remarkable bindings in the British Museum*; Fletcher, *English bookbindings in the British Museum*; Fletcher, *Foreign bookbindings in the British Museum*; Zimmerman, *Bucheinbände*; Bouchot, *Les reliures d'art de la Bibliothèque Nationale*. For a summary of some of this, see Breslauer, *The uses of bookbinding literature*.
34 Quaritch, *A collection of facsimiles*.
35 Lang, *The library*; Slater, *The library manual*; Fitzgerald, *The book fancier*; Wheatley, *How to form a library*; William Roberts, *The book hunter in London*. In France, similar markets were met by works such as Rouveyre, *Connaissances nécessaires à un bibliophile* and 'Jules Richard', *Art de former une bibliothèque*.
36 Cundall, *On ornamental art*.
37 Subsequently much revised and expanded, in a larger format and with photographs instead of line illustrations, as Edward Maunde Thompson, *An introduction to Greek and Latin palaeography*.
38 Rooses, *Le Musée Plantin-Moretus*; Voet, *The golden compasses* I, pp. 407–10; Nys, *De intrede van het publiek*, pp. 184–6, 200–2, etc.
39 *Bulletin du Bibliophile* (1877), p. 568.
40 *Bulletin du Bibliophile* (1878), p. 549.
41 *Bulletin du Bibliophile* (1883), p. 504.
42 *L'Université et la typographie*.
43 Ducourtieux, *Les manuscrits et imprimés à l'exposition de Limoges*.
44 *Bulletin du Bibliophile* (1887), pp. 300–2; Sauvage, *Souvenirs de l'exposition typographique de Rouen*.
45 For antiquarian studies more generally in provincial France, see Parsis-Barubé, *La province antiquaire*. Much of this way of thinking stemmed from the enquiries organised by départements into libraries from 1790 onwards.
46 Tite, *An address*, pp. 3, 26.
47 Tite, *An address*, p. 3.

48 Burlington Fine Arts Club, *Exhibition of bookbindings*; 'The exhibition of bookbindings at the Burlington Fine Arts Club'. For more recent comment, see Anthony Hobson, 'Early binding studies and chimaeras'.
49 See above, pp. 49, 67.
50 Quaritch, *A collection of facsimiles*, p. 16.
51 This was, however, only five years before the first volume appeared of Weale's pioneering *Bookbindings and rubbings of bindings*: for Weale's multifarious interests as an antiquary in Britain and Belgium, see Van Biervliet, *Leven en werk van W. H. James Weale*. The study in Britain of early stamped bindings developed among a small group of enthusiasts, notably in the work of Gibson (*Early Oxford bindings*) and in the collections assembled by Edward Gordon Duff (later dispersed at Sotheby's) and by the bookseller and collector E. P. Goldschmidt, whose far-seeing *Gothic and renaissance bookbindings* was published in 1928.
52 *Printing as in the olden time at the Ballantyne Press*; *Ancient printing office exhibited by G. Faulkner and Sons, the Deansgate Press*.
53 *The Library* 1st ser. 2 (1890), p. 165, and 1st ser. 6 (1894), pp. 19–22.
54 J. P., *An essay on books and printings*.
55 Renouard, *Annales de l'imprimerie des Alde*, p. 27.
56 John Carter, *ABC for book collectors*, p. 87.
57 Duff, *Printing in England in the fifteenth century*, no. 101, recording twenty-two copies, many imperfect.
58 Pollard, 'On the exhibition of facsimiles'.
59 Lancaster, 'On the advantage of occasional exhibitions'.
60 Greenwood (ed.), *Greenwood's library year book*, pp. 92–3.
61 'A sort of title-page and colophon knowledge – in one word, bibliology': Southey (ed.), *The life and correspondence of Robert Southey* III, p. 108.
62 *Report of the Commissioners*, Index, s.v 'Catalogues'.
63 *Bibliothecae Casanatensis catalogus librorum typis impressorum*; Serrai, *Storia della bibliografia* VII, pp. 663–714.
64 Wheatley, *How to catalogue a library*, pp. 169–73. For a pioneering example of the size of the page as a measurement, see Maxwell, *An essay towards a collection of books*. Earlier practices are described briefly in Norris, *A history of cataloguing and cataloguing methods*.
65 Bradshaw, 'A word on size-notation'. This was first presented as a paper to the Library Association in 1882: Thomas (ed.), *Transactions and proceedings*, pp. 238–40.
66 Bodleian Library cataloguing rules, paraphrased in Wheatley, *How to catalogue a library*, pp. 177–8. The rules, including the size tables, were later included in annual editions of the Bodleian Library *Staff-Kalendar*.
67 Bradshaw, *Collected papers*, p. 409.
68 Wheatley, *How to catalogue a library*, pp. 178–9.

69 See for example his remarks on the subject in his paper on 'The printer of the Historia S. Albani', first published privately in 1868 and reprinted in his *Collected papers*, pp. 148–63. For a more extended discussion of the development of his ideas, and the later development of collational formulae, see Needham, *The Bradshaw method*, pp. 24–33. See also Tanselle, 'Title page transcription'.

70 For some pertinent recent work, see for example Griffiths, *Prints for books* and Bowen and Imhof, *Christopher Plantin and engraved book illustrations*. Some thoughtful remarks concerning the description of illustrated books with inserted plates are to be found in Stevenson, 'A bibliographical method'.

71 McKerrow, *An introduction to bibliography for literary students*; Greg, 'Ronald Brunlees McKerrow'; Greg, *Collected papers*; F. P. Wilson, 'Sir Walter Greg'; Tanselle, *The life and work of Fredson Bowers*.

72 Obituaries include *The Library* 4th ser. 5 (1924–5), pp. 264–6 and the *Library Association Record* 26 (1924), pp. 226–8. See also the article by Arnold Hunt in ODNB.

73 Duff, *Early printed books*, p. vii.

74 'Arrange your facts vigorously and get them plainly before you, and let them *speak for themselves*' (Bradshaw to F. J. Furnivall, 7 August 1868, quoted in Prothero, *A memoir of Henry Bradshaw*, p. 349 (Bradshaw's emphasis)).

75 Prothero, *A memoir of Henry Bradshaw*, p. 211.

76 See also Vicaire, 'Les Incunabula Biblica de M. W. A. Copinger'.

77 Greg, 'Bibliography – a retrospect', p. 27.

10 Conclusion

1 Needham, '"Haec sancta ars"'.

2 For some of these questions, see for example Richardson, 'The debates on printing in renaissance Italy'.

3 Mercier (ed.), *Les trois révolutions du livre*. See also Barbier (ed.), *Les trois révolutions du livre*.

4 Compare Summit, *Memory's library*, p. 234: 'This reading of the library's pre-modern past began as a reflection on its digital future.'

5 McKenzie, *Bibliography and the sociology of texts*, p. 4.

6 See above, p. 6.

7 For two mostly anecdotal accounts, one by an Englishman and the other by an American, see John Carter, 'Sidelights on American bibliophily' and Vosper, 'Books for libraries'. Two illuminating accounts of American booksellers, both concentrating on the high end of the market rather than the thousands of books shipped by their contemporaries, are Wolf and Fleming, *Rosenbach* and Kraus, *A rare book saga*.

8 Randall, *Dukedom large enough*, p. 29.

9 The first book fair organised in London by the Antiquarian Booksellers' Association was in 1958.

10 See above, p. 47.
11 Hatton and Cleaver, *A bibliography of the periodical works of Charles Dickens*.
12 Tanselle, *Book-jackets*.
13 Tanselle, 'Reproductions and scholarship'.
14 Green and others, 'The shape of incunable survival'.
15 Garside and others (eds.), *The English novel, 1770–1829* I, pp. 20–1: 'Not a single copy appears to survive of 133 or almost a tenth of the total novels published between 1770 and 1799' (James Raven's 'Historical introduction', at p. 21).
16 A question brought to general attention by Nicholson Baker, *Double fold*. See also McKitterick (ed.), *Do we want to keep our newspapers?*
17 See also above, p. 14.
18 For this term, see for example Hall, 'The world of print and collective mentality'.
19 For an index to part of Bagford's collection, with further references, see Wolf, *Catalogue and indexes*.
20 Madan, *The early Oxford press*, including several leaves from books printed in 1587–1638, 'selected from works which are cheap and common'; Haebler, *Der deutsche Wiegendruck in Original-Typenbeispielen*; Haebler, *West European incunabula*. Haebler presented several further collections in 1927–8. For some of these issues seen from the viewpoint of a critical bookseller, see André Jammes, 'De la destruction des livres'. So far as I know, this phenomenon has escaped discussion in the most obvious recent monographs and collections of essays on the destruction of libraries ancient and modern.
21 See above, p. 13. Apart from the examples noted there, see also Fahy, *L'"Orlando furioso" del 1532*. Pearson, *Books as history*, pp. 184–94, offers a case study of five copies of Francis Bacon, *The historie of the raigne of King Henry the Seuenth* (1622).

Select bibliography

Books are published in London unless stated otherwise.

Abid, Abdelaziz, 'The world digital library and universal access to knowledge'. Available at: www.unesco.org/new/fileadmin/MULTIMEDIA/HQ/CI/CI/pdf/programme_doc_wdl.pdf

Achard, Claude François, *Cours élémentaire de bibliographie*, 3 vols. (Marseille, 1806–7)

Adams, H. M., *Catalogue of books printed on the continent of Europe, 1501–1600, in Cambridge libraries*, 2 vols. (Cambridge, 1967)

Adams, Randolph G., *The case of the Columbus letter* (New York, NY, 1939)

Alexander, J. J. G., 'Facsimiles, copies, and variations; the relationship to the model in medieval and renaissance European illuminated manuscripts', in Kathleen Preciado (ed.), *Retaining the original; multiple originals, copies and reproductions* (Washington, DC, 1989), pp. 61–72

Alsop, Joseph, *The rare art traditions; the history of art collecting and its linked phenomena wherever these have happened* (New York, NY, 1976)

Ames, Joseph, *Typographical antiquities* (1749)

Ames, Joseph and William Herbert, *Typographical antiquities*, rev. T. F. Dibdin, 4 vols. (1810–19)

Ancient printing office exhibited by G. Faulkner and Sons, the Deansgate Press (Manchester, 1887)

Anderson, S. F., 'A variant specimen of Anton Sorg's "Bücheranzeige" of 1483–1484', *Papers of the Bibliographical Soc. of America* 52 (1958), pp. 48–52

Angelicoussis, Elizabeth, 'An Olympiad's portrait', *Apollo* (May 2012), pp. 40–5

Angermair, Elisabeth and others, *Die Rosenthals; der Aufstieg einer jüdischen Antiquarsfamilie zu Weltruhm* (Wien, 2002)

Arber, Edward (ed.), *The first printed English New Testament. Translated by William Tyndale. Photo-lithographed from the unique fragment, now in the Grenville Collection* (British Museum, 1871)

Ars moriendi, preface by George Bullen (Holbein Soc., 1881)

Avery-Quash, Susanna (ed.), *The travel notebooks of Sir Charles Eastlake*, 2 vols. (Walpole Soc., 2011)

Axel-Nilsson, Christian, *Type studies; the Norstedt collection of matrices in the typefoundry of the Royal Printing Office* (Stockholm, 1983)

Backhouse, Janet, 'Manuscripts on display; some landmarks in the exhibition and popular publication of illuminated books', in Lynda Dennison (ed.), *The legacy of M. R. James; papers from the 1995 Cambridge symposium* (Donnington, 2001), pp. 37–52

Bähr, Astrid, *Repräsentieren, bewahren, belehren; Galeriewerke (1660–1800). Von der Darstellung herrschaftlicher Gemäldesammlungen zum populären Bildband* (Hildesheim, 2009)

Baker, Malcolm, 'The portrait sculpture', in David McKitterick (ed.), *The making of the Wren library* (Cambridge, 1995), pp. 110–37

'The reproductive continuum; plaster casts, paper mosaics and photographs as complementary modes of reproduction in the nineteenth-century museum', in Rune Frederiksen and Eckart Marchand (eds.), *Plaster casts; making, collecting and displaying from classical antiquity to the present* (Berlin, 2010), pp. 485–500

Baker, Nicholson, *Double fold; libraries and the assault on paper* (New York, NY, 2001)

Balayé, Simone, *La Bibliothèque Nationale des origines à 1800* (Genève, 1988)

'Les publics de la Bibliothèque Nationale', in Dominique Varry (ed.), *Histoire des bibliothèques françaises. Les bibliothèques de la Révolution et du XIXe siècle, 1789–1914* (Paris, 1991), pp. 329–33

Balsamo, Luigi and Alberto Tinti, *Origini del corsivo nella tipografia italiana del cinquecento* (Milano, 1967)

Balsamo, Luigi and Pierangelo Bellettini (eds.), *Anatomie bibliologiche; saggi di storia del libro per il centenario de "La Bibliofilia"* (Firenze, 1999)

Balston, John, *The Whatmans and wove paper; its invention and development in the west* (West Farleigh, 1998)

Bann, Stephen (ed.), *Art and the early photographic album* (New Haven, CT, 2011)

Barber, Giles 'Richard Dymott, bookbinder', *The Library* 5th ser. 19 (1964), pp. 250–4

Barbier, Frédéric (ed.), *Les trois révolutions du livre; actes du colloque international de Lyon/Villeurbanne, 1998. Révue Française d'Histoire du Livre* 106–9 (2000 [2001])

Barbier, Frédéric and others (ed.), *L'Europe et le livre; réseaux et pratiques du négoce de librairie, XVIe-XXe siècles* (Paris, 1996)

Barbier, Frédéric and others (eds.), *Le livre et l'historien; études offertes en l'honneur du Professeur Henri-Jean Martin* (Genève, 1997)

Barbieri, Edoardo, *Haebler contro Haebler; appunti per una storia dell'incunabolistica novecentesca* (Milano, 2008)

Barkan, Leonard, *Unearthing the past; archaeology and aesthetics in the making of renaissance culture* (New Haven, CT, 1999)

Barker, Nicolas, 'Henri d'Orléans, Duc d'Aumale; a French bibliophile in England', in Antoine Coron (ed.), *Actes, Association Internationale de Bibliophilie, 1991* (Paris, 2003), pp. 126–48

The publications of the Roxburghe Club, 1814–1962 (Roxburghe Club, 1964)

The Roxburghe Club; a bicentenary history (Roxburghe Club, 2012)
Barker, Nicolas and John Collins, *A sequel to An enquiry* (1983)
Barnes, Warner, *A bibliography of Elizabeth Barrett Browning* (Austin, TX, 1967)
Bartelings, Nelke and others (eds.), *Beelden in veelvoud; de vermenigvuldiging van het beeld in prentkunst en fotografie (Leids Kunsthistorisch Jaarboek* 12) (Leiden, 2002)
Bartholomew, A. T., *Richard Bentley, D. D.; a bibliography* (Cambridge, 1908)
Barwell, Mrs, *A companion to the Norwich polytechnic exhibition* (Norwich, 1840)
Baudelaire, Charles, *The mirror of art*, transl. and ed. Jonathan Mayne (1955)
Baudrillart, Henri, 'Les pertes éprouvées par les bibliothèques de Paris en 1870–1871', *Le Bibliophile Français* 6 (1872), pp. 82–94, 122–5, 147–50
'Rapport sur les pertes éprouvées par les bibliothèques publiques', *Bulletin du Bibliophile* (1870–71), pp. 525–36
Beckwith, Alice, *Victorian bibliomania; the illuminated book in nineteenth-century Britain* (Providence, RI, 1987)
Beedham, B. H., *A list of the reproductions both imitation and in fac-simile of the productions of the press of William Caxton* (Iowa City, IA, 1879)
Bennett, Joseph, 'The autograph of Handel's "Messiah"', *Macmillan's Magazine* 18 (1868), pp. 328–36
Bentley, G. E., Jr, *Blake books* (Oxford, 1977)
Bentley, Richard, *A proposal for building a royal library, and establishing it by Act of Parliament* [1697]
Benzie, William, *Dr. F. J. Furnivall; a Victorian scholar adventurer* (Norman, OK, 1983)
Berkvens-Stevelinck, C. and others (eds.), *Le magasin de l'univers; the Dutch Republic as the centre of the European book trade* (Leiden, 1992)
Berthollet, C. L., *Essay on the new method of bleaching, by means of oxygenated muriatic acid ... from the French of Mr. Berthollet ...* transl. Robert Kerr ([Dublin, 1790?] Edinburgh, 1790)
Bibliographical (The) Society, 1892–1942; studies in retrospect (Bibliographical Soc., 1945)
Bibliotheca Sunderlandiana. Sale catalogue of the Sunderland or Blenheim library, to be sold by auction by Puttick and Simpson, 5 vols. (1881–2)
Bibliothecae Casanatensis catalogus librorum typis impressorum (Romae, 1761–)
Bignamini, Ilaria and Clare Hornsby, *Digging and dealing in eighteenth-century Rome*, 2 vols. (New Haven, CT, 2010)
Bilbey, Diane and Marjorie Trusted, '"The question of casts"; collecting and later reassessment of the cast collections at South Kensington', in Rune Frederiksen and Eckart Marchand (eds.), *Plaster casts; making, collecting and displaying from classical antiquity to the present* (Berlin, 2010), pp. 465–83
Birch, Walter de Gray, *The history, art and palaeography of the manuscript called the Utrecht Psalter* (1876)
Bird, Stephen, *Reinventing Voltaire; the politics of commemoration in nineteenth-century France* (Oxford, 2000)

Bjurström, Per, 'Les premiers musées d'art en Europe et leur public', in E. Pommier (ed.), *Les musées en Europe à la veille de l'invention du Louvre* (Paris, 1995), pp. 549–63

Bjurström, Per (ed.), *The genesis of the art museum in the 18th century* (Stockholm, 1993)

Blades, William, 'The Caxton celebration', *The Athenaeum*, 19 May 1877, pp. 641–2
    The life and typography of William Caxton, 2 vols. (1861–3)
    The pentateuch of printing (1891)

Blake, Andrew, *The irresistible rise of Harry Potter* (2002)

Blanchard, Alain (ed.), *Les débuts du codex* (*Bibliologia* 9) (Turnhout, 1989)

BMC. *Catalogue of books printed in the XVth century now in the British Museum* [*British Library*], 13 parts, some reprinted with annotations (London and 't Goy-Houten, 1963–2007)

Bober, Phyllis Pray and Ruth Rubenstein, *Renaissance artists and antique sculpture; a handbook of sources*, 2nd edn (Turnhout, 2010)

Bock, Henning, 'Collections privées et publiques; les premices du musée publique en Allemagne', in E. Pommier (ed.), *Les musées en Europe à la veille de l'invention du Louvre* (Paris, 1995), pp. 59–77

Bodleian Library, *The John Johnson collection; catalogue of an exhibition* (Oxford, 1971)

Bohn, Henry G., *Appendix to the bibliographer's manual of English literature* (1864)

Bond, E. A. and others, *The Utrecht Psalter; reports addressed to the Trustees of the British Museum on the age of the manuscript* (1874)

Bouchot, Henri, *Les reliures d'art de la Bibliothèque Nationale* (Paris, 1888)

Bowen, Karen L. and Dirk Imhof, *Christopher Plantin and engraved book illustrations in sixteenth-century Europe* (Cambridge, 2008)

Bowman, J. H. (ed.), *A critical edition of the private diaries of Robert Proctor; the life of a librarian at the British Museum* (Lenniston, NY, 2010)

Bradshaw, Henry, *Collected papers* (1889)
    Henry Bradshaw's correspondence on incunabula with J. W. Holtrop and M. F. A. G. Campbell, ed. Wytze and Lotte Hellinga, 2 vols. (Amsterdam, 1966[1968]–78)
    'A word on size-notation as distinguished from form-notation', in Henry Bradshaw, *Collected papers* (Cambridge, 1889), pp. 406–9

Brakensiek, Stephan and Michel Polfer (eds.), *Graphik als Spiegel der Malerei; Meisterwerke der Reproduktionsgraphik, 1500–1830* (Milano, 2009)

Brassington, W. S., *Historic bindings in the Bodleian Library* (1891)

Breslauer, B. H., *The uses of bookbinding literature* (New York, NY, 1986)

Bridson, Gavin and Geoffrey Wakeman, *Printmaking and picture printing; a bibliographical guide to artistic and industrial techniques in Britain, 1750–1900* (Oxford, 1984)

Briquet, C. M., *The new Briquet*, ed. Allan Stevenson, 4 vols. (Amsterdam, 1968)

British Museum; a guide to the printed books exhibited to the public (1870)

Brock, W. H., 'Scientific bibliographies and bibliographers, and the history of the history of science', in Andrew Hunter (ed.), *Thornton and Tully's scientific books, libraries and collectors*, 4th edn (Aldershot, 2000), pp. 298-332
Brown, G. Baldwin, *The care of ancient monuments* (Cambridge, 1905)
Brown, Iain Gordon, *Abbotsford and Sir Walter Scott; the image and the influence* (Edinburgh, 2003)
Brunet, G., *Manuel du libraire*, 5th edn, 6 vols. (Paris, 1860-5)
Buchanan-Brown, John, 'A forged series of woodcuts?', *The Library* 5th ser. 29 (1974), pp. 165-96
Budde, Ludwig and Richard Nicholls, *A catalogue of the Greek and Roman sculpture in the Fitzwilliam Museum, Cambridge* (Cambridge, 1964)
Buechler, John, '"Adapted from an old book"; some sources for Chiswick Press woodcut initials', *Printing History* 7/8 (1982), pp. 49-54
 Charles Whittingham, printer, 1795-1876, introd. Janet Ing (Burlington, VT, 1983)
Buijnsters, Piet J., *Geschiedenis van het Nederlandse antiquariaat* (Nijmegen, 2007)
Burlington Fine Arts Club, *Exhibition of bookbindings* (1891)
Burton, Anthony, *Vision and accident; the story of the Victoria and Albert Museum* (1999)
Burton, J. H., *The book hunter*, new edn with memoir of the author (Edinburgh, 1882)
Butsch, A. F. (ed.), *Die acht Schalkheiten; xylographisches Product aus der Mitte des XV. Jahrhunderts. Photographisches Facsimile nach dem einzig bekannten Exemplare* (Augsburg, 1873)
Campbell, Lorne, 'The conservation of Netherlandish paintings in the fifteenth and sixteenth centuries', in Christine Sitwell and Sarah Staniforth (eds.), *Studies in the history of painting restoration* (1998), pp. 15-26
Canadian Institute, *Caxton celebration, Toronto, June 13-16, 1877; catalogue of books, etc.* (Toronto, 1877)
Cantwell, John D., *The Public Record Office, 1838-1958* (1991)
Carley, James P. and Colin G. C. Tite (eds.), *Books and collectors, 1200-1700; essays presented to Andrew Watson* (1997)
Carlsohn, Erich, *Lebensbilder Leipziger Buchhändler: Erinnerungen an Verleger, Antiquare, Exportbuchhändler, Kommissionäre, Gehilfen und Markthelfer* (Meersburg, 1987)
Carmody, Shane, 'Mirror of a world; William Caxton at the State Library', *La Trobe Journal* 77 (2006), pp. 5-22
Carter, Harry, *A view of early typography up to about 1600* (Oxford, 1969)
Carter, John, *ABC for book collectors*, 4th edn (1966)
 'Sidelights on American bibliophily', *The Book Collector* 5 (1956), pp. 357-67
Carter, John and Graham Pollard, *An enquiry into the nature of certain nineteenth century pamphlets* (1934); 2nd edn, with an epilogue, ed. Nicolas Barker and John Collins (1983)
Carter, John and Percy H. Muir (eds.), *Printing and the mind of man* (1967)
Case, Arthur E., *A bibliography of English poetical miscellanies* (Oxford, 1935)

Caslon, William, *A specimen of printing types by William Caslon, London 1766*, facsimile edn with introduction and notes by James Mosley, *Journal of the Printing Historical Society* 16 (1981–2)

Catalogue of an exhibition in commemoration of the centenary of William Blades, held in the Saint Bride Foundation Institute (1924)

Catalogue of articles contained in the exhibition of the Derby Mechanics' Institution, 1839 (Derby, 1839)

Catalogue of machinery, models etc. in the Machinery and Inventions Division of the South Kensington Museum, with descriptive and historical notes by E. A. Cowper; paper-making and printing machinery (1890; another edn, 1897)

Catalogue of manuscripts and early printed books... now forming portion of the library of J. Pierpont Morgan, 3 vols. (1907)

Catalogue of pictures and drawings exhibited at the town hall, Stratford-on-Avon, at the celebration of the tercentenary birthday of William Shakespeare (Stratford-upon-Avon, 1864)

Catalogue of the art treasures of the United Kingdom. Collected at Manchester in 1857 [Manchester, 1857]

Catalogue of the casts, busts, reliefs, and illustrations of the school of design and ceramic art in the Museum of Art at the Melbourne Public Library (Melbourne, 1865)

Catalogue of the Norwich polytechnic exhibition (Norwich, 1840)

Catalogue of the special exhibition of works of art of the mediaeval, renaissance, and more recent periods, on loan at the South Kensington Museum, June 1862 (1862)

Catalogus van voorwerpen, ingezonden ter algemeene; typographische tentoonstelling gehouden te Haarlem bij gelegenheid der plectige onthulling van het metalen standbeeld van L. J. Coster [Haarlem, 1856]

Chalmers, George, *The life of Thomas Ruddiman* (1794)

Chaudonneret, Marie-Claude, 'Le statut et la réception de la lithographie en France dans les années 1820–1840', in Sophie Raux and others (eds.), *L'estampe; un art multiple à la portée de tous?* (Villeneuve d'Ascq, 2008), pp. 323–31

Chenesseau, G., *Sainte-Croix d'Orléans; histoire d'une cathédrale gothique réédifiée par les Bourbons, 1599–1819*, 3 vols. (Paris, 1921)

Choay, Françoise, *The invention of the historic monument* (Cambridge, 2001) (originally published as *Allégorie du patrimoine* (Paris, 1992))

Christian, Kathleen Wren, *Empire without end; antiquities collections in renaissance Rome, c. 1350–1527* (New Haven, CT, 2010)

Clarke, E. D., *Greek marbles brought from the shores of the Euxine, Archipelago, and Mediterranean and deposited in the vestibule of the public library of the University of Cambridge* (Cambridge, 1809)

Clarke, George and others, *Stowe landscape gardens* (1977)

Clarke, W., *Repertorium bibliographicum* (1819)

Claudin, Anatole, *Histoire de l'imprimerie en France au XVe et au XVIe siècle*, 4 vols. (Paris, 1900–14[20])

'Les faussures de livres', *Bulletin du Bibliophile* (1891), pp. 513–24

Clegg, Cyndia Susan, *Press censorship in Elizabethan England* (Cambridge, 1997)

Clegg, Cyndia Susan and Randall McLeod, *The peaceable and prosperous regiment of blessed Queene Elizabeth; a facsimile from Holinshed's Chronicles (1587)* (San Marino, 2005)

Clegg, James, *Directory of second-hand booksellers* (Rochdale, 1886 and later edns)

Coakley, Davis, 'Edward Worth and his library', in Danielle Westerhof (ed.), *The alchemy of medicine and print; the Edward Worth Library, Dublin* (Dublin, 2010), pp. 36–47

Cobham, Viscount and Sir Henry Trueman Wood (eds.), *Report of the committee on leather for bookbinding* (1905)

Cockerell, S. C., *Some German woodcuts of the fifteenth century* (Kelmscott Press, 1897)

Cockshaw, Pierre, 'A propos de [sic] plus ancien fac-similé', in P. Cockshaw and others (eds.), *Miscellanea codicologica F. Masai dicata*, 2 vols. (Gand, 1979), II, pp. 535–40

Cockshaw, Pierre and others (eds.), *Miscellanea codicologica F. Masai dicata*, 2 vols. (Gand, 1979)

Coleman, D. C., *The British paper industry, 1495–1860; a study in industrial growth* (Oxford, 1958)

Coleridge, S. T., *Biographia literaria* (1817)

Coltman, Viccy, *Classical sculpture and the culture of collecting in Britain since 1760* (Oxford, 2009)

Colvin, H. M., *A biographical dictionary of English architects*, 4th edn (2008)

Confessionale ou Beichtspiegel nach den zehn geboten, réproduit en fac-similé d'après l'unique exemplaire, conservé au Museum Meermanno-Westreenianum, introd. J. W. Holtrop (La Haye, 1861)

Conlin, Jonathan, *The nation's mantelpiece; a history of the National Gallery* (2006)

Conti, Alessandro, *Storia del restauro e della conservazione delle opere dell'arte* (Milano, 2002), transl. Helen Glanville as *A history of the restoration and conservation of works of art* (Oxford, 2007)

Coomans, Thomas and Jan De Maeyer (eds.), *The revival of medieval illumination; nineteenth-century Belgian manuscripts and illuminations from a European perspective* (Leuven, 2007)

Copinger, W. A., 'Inaugural address, with printed sources from which collections towards a supplement to Hain's Repertorium bibliographicum might be compiled', *Trans Bibliographical Soc.* 1 (1893), pp. 29–59

'Notes by Dr. Copinger on catalogues of incunabula', *Trans Bibliographical Soc.* 2 (1893–4), p. 87

Coron, Antoine, '"Ut prosint aliis"; Jacques-Auguste de Thou et sa bibliothèque', in Claude Jolly (ed.), *Histoire des bibliothèques françaises; les bibliothèques sous l'ancien régime, 1530–1789* (Paris, 1988), pp. 101–25

Coron, Antoine (ed.), *Actes, Association Internationale de Bibliophilie, 1991* (Paris, 2003)

Cowell, S. H., *A brief description of the art of anastatic printing* (Ipswich [1858?])

Cox, James, *The tercentenary; a retrospect* (1865)
Cox, Trenchard, *A short illustrated history of the Wallace Collection and its founders* (1936)
Craig, C. Leslie, 'The earliest Little Gidding concordance', *Harvard Library Bulletin* 1 (1947), pp. 311–31
Craik, George Lillie, *A compendious history of English literature and of the English language* (1861)
Crosland, Maurice, *In the shadow of Lavoisier; the Annales de Chimie and the establishment of a new science* (Oxford, 1994)
Cundall, Joseph, *On ornamental art applied to ancient and modern bookbinding* (1848)
Curtis, Gregory, *Disarmed; the story of the Venus de Milo* (New York, NY, 2003)
Dalisson, Rémi, *Célébrer la nation; les fêtes nationales en France de 1789 à nos jours* (Paris, 2009)
Dane, Joseph A., *Out of sorts; on typography and print culture* (Philadelphia, PA, 2011)
  'The Huntington Apocalypse blockbook (Schreiber editions IV/V), with a note on terminology', *Printing History* 42 (2001), pp. 3–15
Darnton, Robert, *The case for books* (Cambridge, MA, 2009)
  'The great book massacre', *New York Review of Books*, 26 April 2001; repr. as 'A paean to paper', in Robert Darnton, *The case for books, past, present, and future* (New York, NY, 2009), pp. 109–29
Davenport, Cyril, *Roger Payne, English bookbinder of the eighteenth century* (Chicago, IL, 1929)
Davies, Glenys, 'The Albacini cast collection; character and significance', *Journal of the History of Collections* 3 (1991), pp. 145–65
Davies, Martin (ed.), *Incunabula; studies in fifteenth-century printed books presented to Lotte Hellinga* (1999)
de Conihout, Isabelle and Pascal Ract-Madoux, *Reliures françaises du XVIIe siècle; chefs-d'oeuvre du Musée Condé* (Chantilly, 2002)
de Demidoff, Anatole, 'Sur le procédé de galvanoplastique découvert par M.Jacoby, de l'Académie des Sciences de Saint-Pétersbourg', *Annales de Chimie et de Physique* 65 (1840), pp. 24–36
de Font-Réaulx, Dominique and Joëlle Bolloch, *The work of art and its reproduction* (Paris, 2006)
de Hamel, Christopher and others, *Disbound and dispersed; the leaf book considered* (Chicago, IL, 2005)
de Morgan, Sophia Elizabeth, *Memoir of Augustus de Morgan* (1882)
de Nave, Francine and Leon Voet, *Plantin-Moretus Museum, Antwerp* (Ghent, 1989)
de Ricci, Seymour, *Bibliographie des publications d'Anatole Claudin (1833–1906)* (1926)
  A catalogue of the early English books in the library of John L. Clawson, Buffalo (Philadelphia, PA, 1924)
  A census of Caxtons (Bibliographical Soc., 1909)
  English collectors of books and manuscripts (1530–1930) and their marks of ownership (Cambridge, 1930)

Deegan, Marilyn and Kathryn Sutherland, *Transferred illusions; digital technology and the forms of print* (Farnham, 2009)
Delamotte, Phillip H., *On the various applications of anastatic printing and papyrography* ... (1849)
Dennison, Lynda (ed.), *The legacy of M. R. James; papers from the 1995 Cambridge symposium* (Donnington, 2001)
Denon, Vivant, *Correspondance (1802–1815)*, ed. Marie-Anne Dupuy and others, 2 vols. (Paris, 1999)
Descriptive (A) catalogue of the Nottingham mechanics' exhibition ... by Mr Barker, of the Nottingham Mercury (Nottingham, 1840)
Desgraves, Louis, 'Les bibliothécaires', in Dominique Varry (ed.), *Histoire des bibliothèques françaises. Les bibliothèques de la Révolution et du XIXe siècle, 1789–1914* (Paris, 1991), pp. 281–93
Di Gregorio, Maurizio, *"Le coselline di un ometto curioso"; l'idea per fare le gallerie universali di tutte le cose del mondo, naturali, artificiali e miste* (Salento, 2008)
Dibdin, Thomas Frognall, *The bibliographical decameron*, 3 vols. (1817)
  Bibliomania, or, book madness (1811)
  Reminiscences of a literary life, 2 vols. (1836)
Didot, Ambroise Firmin, *L'imprimerie, la librairie et la papeterie à l'Exposition Universelle de 1851; rapport du XVIIe jury* (Paris, 1854)
Dodgson, Campbell, *Catalogue of early German and Flemish woodcuts preserved in the Department of Prints and Drawings in the British Museum*, 2 vols. (1903)
Dominique-Vivant Denon, l'oeil de Napoléon (Musée du Louvre, 1999)
Dooley, Allan C., *Author and printer in Victorian England* (Charlottesville, VA, 1992)
Dreyfus, John, 'William Morris, typographer', in Paul Needham (ed.), *William Morris and the art of the book* (New York, NY, 1976), pp. 71–94
Ducourtieux, Paul, *Les manuscrits et imprimés à l'exposition de Limoges en 1886* (Limoges, 1888)
Duff, E. Gordon, *Early printed books* (1898)
  Printing in England in the fifteenth century (1917); expanded edn by Lotte Hellinga (2009)
Dupont, Paul-François, *Essais pratiques d'imprimerie, précédés d'une notice historique. Typographie-lithographie* (Paris, 1849)
Dyck, Paul, '"A new kind of printing"; cutting and pasting a book for a king at Little Gidding', *The Library* 7th ser. 9 (2008), pp. 306–33
Earle, John (ed.), *Gloucester fragments* I: *Facsimile of some leaves in Saxon handwriting... copied by photozincography at the Ordnance Survey Office, Southampton* (1861)
Easton, Phoebe Jane, *Marbling; a history and a bibliography* (Los Angeles, CA, 1983)
Elkington & Co., *Inventory of reproductions in metal* [1887]

Emery, Elizabeth and Laura Morowitz, *Consuming the past; the medieval revival in fin-de-siècle France* (Aldershot, 2003)

Emile-Mâle, Gilberte, *Pour une histoire de la restauration des peintures en France*, ed. Ségolène Bergeon Langle (Paris, 2008)

Engelmann, Wilhelm, *Bibliotheca mechanico-technologica*, 2 vols. (Leipzig, 1844–50)

Enschedé, Charles, *Fonderies de caractères et leur matériel dans les Pays-Bas du XVe au XIXe siècle* (Haarlem, 1908)

   Type-foundries in the Netherlands from the fifteenth to the nineteenth century; a history based mainly on material in the collection of Joh. Enschedé en Zonen at Haarlem, transl. with revisions and notes by Harry Carter and Netty Hoeflake, ed. Lotte Hellinga (Haarlem, 1978)

Ernouf, Baron, *Les Français en Prusse (1807–8) d'après des documents contemporains recueillis en Allemagne* (Paris, 1872)

   Souvenirs de l'invasion prussienne en Normandie (Paris, 1872)

Estermann, Monika, *"O werthe Druckerkunst / Du Mutter aller Kunst"; Gutenbergfeiern im laufe der Jahrhunderte* (Mainz, 1999)

Estivals, Robert, *Le dépôt légal sous l'ancien régime de 1537 à 1791* (Paris, 1961)

Eudel, Paul, *Le truquage; altérations, fraudes et contrefaçons dévoilées* (Paris, 1908)

Evans, Harold, *Newspaper design*, 2nd edn (1976)

   Pictures on a page; photo-journalism, graphics and picture editing (1978)

'Exhibition (The) of bookbindings at the Burlington Fine Arts Club', *The Library* 1st ser. 3 (1891), pp. 251–8, 287–91

Exhibition of cleaned pictures (1936–1947) (National Gallery, 1947)

Exhibition of the Works of Industry of All Nations, 1851. Reports of the juries. 4 vols. (1852)

'Exposition (L') des livres de Caxton en Angleterre', *Bulletin du Bibliophile* 44 (1877), pp. 231–4

Fabian, Bernhard, 'An eighteenth-century research collection; English books at Göttingen University Library', *The Library* 6th ser. 1 (1979), pp. 209–24

Fabian, Bernhard (ed.), *Handbuch der historischen Buchbestände*, 44 vols. (Hildesheim, 1992–2001)

Fac-simile delle miniature contenute nel Breviario Grimani, conservato nella Biblioteca di S.Marco, eseguito in fotografia da Antonio Perini, con illustrazioni di Francesco Zanotto (Venezia, 1862)

Facsimiles of national manuscripts, from William the Conqueror to Queen Anne, chiefly from the Public Record Office. Transl. and notes by W. B. Sanders, 4 vols. (Southampton, 1865–9)

Facsimiles of national manuscripts of Ireland, selected and ed. by Sir John Gilbert, 5 vols. (Dublin and London, 1874–84)

Facsimiles of national manuscripts of Scotland, selected under the direction of Sir William Gibson-Craig (Southampton, 1867–71)

Fac-simile of the autograph score of Messiah… executed in photo-lithography by Vincent Brooks, Day and Son (Sacred Harmonic Soc., 1868)

Fahy, Conor, *L'"Orlando furioso" del 1532; profilo di una edizione* (Milano, 1989)
Falkenstein, Constantin Carl von, *Geschichte der Buchdruckerkunst* (Leipzig, 1840)
Fawcett, Trevor, *The rise of English provincial art; artist, patrons, and institutions outside London, 1800–1830* (Oxford, 1974)
Feather, John, 'Thirty-eight old woodcuts; some notes on an early 19th-century block-book', *The Book Collector* 26 (1977), pp. 371–9
Felkay, Nicole, *Balzac et ses éditeurs, 1822–1837; essai sur la librairie romantique* (Paris, 1987)
Fifty-five books printed before 1525 representing the works of England's first printers; an exhibition from the collection of Paul Mellon (Grolier Club, 1968)
Fitzgerald, Percy, *The book fancier, or the romance of book collecting* (1886)
Fletcher, H. George, *New Aldine studies* (San Francisco, CA, 1998)
Fletcher, W. Y., *English bookbindings in the British Museum* (1895)
Foreign bookbindings in the British Museum (1896)
Flood, John L., 'On Gutenberg's 600th anniversary; towards a history of jubilees of printing', *Journal of the Printing Historical Soc.* N.S. 1 (2000), pp. 5–36
'Varieties of vandalism', *Common Knowledge* 8 (2002), pp. 366–86
Folter, Roland, 'The Gutenberg Bible in the antiquarian book trade', in Martin Davies (ed.), *Incunabula; studies in fifteenth-century printed books presented to Lotte Hellinga* (1999), pp. 271–351
Foot, Mirjam M., 'Binder, faker and artist', *The Library* 7th ser. 13 (2012), pp. 133–46
The decorative bindings in Marsh's Library, Dublin (Aldershot, 2004)
'Double agent; M. Coulin and M. Hagué', *The Book Collector* special number for the anniversary of Quaritch (1997), pp. 136–50
The Henry Davis gift; a collection of bookbindings, 3 vols. (1978–2010)
Foot, Mirjam M. (ed.), *Eloquent witnesses; bookbindings and their history* (2004)
Foot, Mirjam M., Carmen Blacker and Nicholas Poole-Wilson, 'Collector, dealer and forger; a fragment of nineteenth-century binding history', in Mirjam M. Foot (ed.), *Eloquent witnesses; bookbindings and their history* (2004), pp. 264–81
Ford, Margaret Lane, 'Importation of printed books into England and Scotland', in Lotte Hellinga and J. Trapp (eds.), *The Cambridge history of the book in Britain* III: *1400–1557* (Cambridge, 1999), pp. 179–201
Foxcroft, A. B., *A catalogue of English books and fragments from 1477 to 1535 in the Public Library of Victoria* (Melbourne, 1933)
Catalogue of fifteenth-century books and fragments in the Public Library of Victoria (Melbourne, 1936)
Foxon, D. F., *English verse, 1701–1750*, 2 vols. (Cambridge, 1975)
Francis, F. C., 'The Bibliographical Society; a sketch of the first fifty years', in *The Bibliographical Society, 1892–1942; studies in retrospect* (Bibliographical Soc., 1945), pp. 1–22
Frederick James Furnivall; a volume of personal record (Oxford, 1911)
Frederiksen, Rune and Eckart Marchand (eds.), *Plaster casts; making, collecting and displaying from classical antiquity to the present* (Berlin, 2010)

Friedman, Terry and Timothy Clifford, *The man at Hyde Park Corner; sculpture by John Cheere, 1709–1787* (Leeds, 1974)

Fry, Edmund, *Specimen of modern printing types, 1828*, facsimile, ed. David Chambers (1986)

Fry, Francis, *A description of the Great Bible, 1539, and the six editions of Cranmer's Bible ... Also of the editions in large folio of the Authorised Version of the holy scriptures, printed in the years 1611, 1613, 1617... Together with an original leaf of each of the editions described* (1865)

Gadd, Ian, 'The use and misuse of Early English Books Online', *Literature Compass* 6 (2009), pp. 1–13

Game (The) of the chesse, reproduced in facsimile by Vincent Figgins (1855)

Garside, Peter and others (eds.), *The English novel, 1770–1829; a bibliographical survey of prose fiction published* in the British Isles, 2 vols. (Oxford, 2000)

Gaskell, Philip, *A new introduction to bibliography* (Oxford, 1972)

Gazda, Elaine K. (ed.), *The ancient art of emulation; studies in artistic originality and tradition from the present to classical antiquity* (Ann Arbor, MI, 2002)

Gedenkboek der Costers-feesten van 15, 16 en 17 Julij 1856 (Haarlem, 1856)

Gemmett, Robert J., *Consummate collector; William Beckford's letters to his bookseller* (Wilby, 2000)

Gernsheim, Helmut, *The incunabula of British photographic literature, 1839–1875* (1984)

The origins of photography (1982)

Gernsheim, Helmut and Alison, *L. J. M. Daguerre; the history of the diorama and the Daguerreotype* (1956)

Gibson, Strickland, *Early Oxford bindings* (1903)

Gingerich, Owen, *An annotated census of Copernicus' De revolutionibus (Nuremberg 1543 and Basel 1566)* (Leiden, 2002)

Godding, Robert and others, *Bollandistes; saints et légendes* (Bruxelles, 2007)

Goff, Frederick R., 'Falsifed dates in certain incunabula', in H. Lehmann-Haupt (ed.), *Homage to a bookman; essays on manuscripts, books and printing written for Hans P. Kraus on his 60th birthday* (Berlin, 1967), pp. 137–45

Goldschmidt, E. P., *Gothic and renaissance bookbindings*, 2 vols. (1928)

Gombrich, E. H., 'Dark varnishes; variations on a theme from Pliny', *Burlington Magazine* 104 (1962), pp. 51–5

Goulemot, Jean-Marie and Eric Walter, 'Les centenaires de Voltaire et de Rousseau', in Pierre Nora (ed.), *Les lieux de mémoire*, 3 vols. (Paris, 1997), I, pp. 351–82

Grasselli, Margaret Morgan, *Colorful impressions; the printmaking revolution in eighteenth-century France* (Washington, DC, 2003)

Gray, Valerie, *Charles Knight; educator, publisher, writer* (Aldershot, 2006)

Gray, Victor, *Bookmen: London; 250 years of Sotheran bookselling* (2011)

Green, Jonathan, Frank McIntyre and Paul Needham, 'The shape of incunable survival and statistical estimation of lost editions', *Papers of the Bibliographical Soc. of America* 105 (2011), pp. 141–75

Greenhalgh, Paul, *Ephemeral vistas; the expositions universelles, great exhibitions and world's fairs, 1851–1939* (Manchester, 1988)

Greenwood, Thomas (ed.), *Greenwood's library year book* (1897)

Greg, W. W., *A bibliography of the English printed drama to the Restoration*, 4 vols. (Bibliographical Soc., 1939–59)

'Bibliography – a retrospect', in *The Bibliographical Society, 1892–1942; studies in retrospect* (Bibliographical Soc., 1945), pp. 23–31

'Bibliography; an apologia', repr. in W. W. Greg, *Collected papers*, ed. J. C. Maxwell (Oxford, 1966), pp. 239–66

Collected papers, ed. J. C. Maxwell (Oxford, 1966)

'Ronald Brunlees McKerrow', *Proc. British Academy* 26 (1940), pp. 488–515

Griffiths, Antony, *Prints for books; book illustration in France, 1760–1800* (2004)

Grossman, Janet and others (eds.), *History of restoration of ancient stone sculpture* (Los Angeles, CA, 2003)

Guide (A) to the objects of chief interest in the loan collection of the Caxton celebration (1877)

Gunelius, Susan, *Harry Potter; the story of a global business phenomenon* (Basingstoke, 2008)

Gupta, Simon, *Re-reading Harry Potter* (Basingstoke, 2003)

Haebler, Konrad, *Der deutsche Wiegendruck in Original-Typenbeispielen. 115 Inkunabelproben* (Munich, 1927)

West European incunabula; 60 original leaves from the presses of the Netherlands, France, Iberia and Great Britain (Munich, 1928)

Hall, David D., *Cultures of print; essays in the history of the book* (Amherst, MA, 1996)

'The world of print and collective mentality in seventeenth-century New England', in John Higham and Paul Conkin (ed.), *New directions in American intellectual history* (Baltimore, MD, 1979), pp. 166–80; repr. in David D. Hall, *Cultures of print; essays in the history of the book* (Amherst, MA, 1996), pp. 79–96

Hamber, Anthony, 'Facsimile, scholarship, and commerce; aspects of the photographically illustrated art book (1839–1880)', in Stephen Bann (ed.), *Art and the early photographic album* (New Haven, CT, 2011), pp. 124–49

"*A higher branch of the art*"; *photographing the fine arts in England, 1839–1880* (Amsterdam, 1996)

'The use of photography by nineteenth-century art historians', in Helene E. Roberts (ed.), *Art history through the camera's lens* (Amsterdam, 1995), pp. 89–121

Hamilton Palace libraries; catalogue of . . . the Beckford library, removed from Hamilton Palace . . . sold by auction by Messrs Sotheby, Wilkinson & Hodge, 4 parts (1882–3)

Handbook (A) for travellers on the continent: being a guide to Holland, Belgium, Prussia . . . 11th edn (1856)

Hardy, Sir Thomas Duffus, *The Athanasian Creed in connexion with the Utrecht Psalter* (1873)

Harris, Elizabeth M., 'Experimental graphic processes in England, 1800–1859', part IV, *Journal of the Printing Historical Soc.* 6 (1970), pp. 53–89

Harris, P. R., *A history of the British Museum library, 1753–1973* (1998)

Harrison, G. B., *Facsimile reprints, being a paper read before the Anglo-American conference of historians, 13–18 July 1931* (1931)

Harrisse, Henry, 'Falsifications bolognaises; reliures et livres', *Bulletin du Bibliophile* (1902), pp. 428–42, 445–666, 505–23; (1903), pp. 449–52

Hart, Horace, *Notes on a century of typography at the University Press, Oxford, 1693–1794*, repr. with additional notes by Harry Carter (Oxford, 1970)

Haskell, Francis, *The painful birth of the art book* (1987)

Haskell, Francis and Nicholas Penny, *Taste and the antique* (New Haven, CT, 1981)

Hassall, W. O., *The Holkham library* (Roxburghe Club, 1970)

Hatton, Thomas and Arthur H. Cleaver, *A bibliography of the periodical works of Charles Dickens, bibliographical, analytical and statistical* (1933)

Haworth-Booth, Mark, 'Camille Silvy; the photography of works of art as record and restoration', in Stephen Bann (ed.), *Art and the early photographic album* (New Haven, CT, 2011), pp. 78–89

Haym, Nicola, *Notizia de' libri rari nella lingua italiana* (Londra, 1726)

Hazen, A. T., 'J.Sturt, facsimilist', *The Library* , N.S. 25 (1944), pp. 72–9

'Type-facsimiles', *Modern Philology* 44 (1947), pp. 209–17

Hazlitt, W. C., *The confessions of a collector* (1897)

Hecquet, R., *Catalogue des estampes gravées d'après Rubens... Avec un secret pour blanchir les estampes & en ôter les taches d'huile* (Paris, 1751)

Heidtmann, Frank, *Wie das Photo ins Buch kam* (Berlin, 1984)

Hellinga, Lotte, '"Less than the whole truth"; false statements in 15th-century colophons', in Robin Myers and Michael Harris (eds.), *Fakes and frauds; varieties of deception in print and manuscript* (Winchester, 1989), pp. 1–27

William Caxton and early printing in England (2010)

'William Caxton, Colard Mansion and the Printer in Type 1', *Bulletin du Bibliophile* (2011), pp. 86–114

Hellinga, Lotte and J. Trapp (eds.), *The Cambridge history of the book in Britain* III: *1400–1557* (Cambridge, 1999)

Hellinga-Querido, Lotte and Clemens de Wolf, *Laurens Janszoon Coster was zijn naam* (Haarlem, 1988)

Herbert, A. S., *Historical catalogue of printed editions of the English Bible, 1525–1961* (1968)

Hertzberger, Menno, *Boek, veel boeken – en mensen* (Nijmegen, 2008)

Hindman, Sandra etc. (eds.), *Manuscript illumination in the modern age; recovery and reconstruction* (Evanston, IL, 2001)

Hinrichsen, Alex, *Baedeker's Reisehandbücher, 1832–1944; Bibliographie der deutschen, französischen und englischen Ausgaben* (Holzminden, 1981)

Hitchcock, Henry-Russell, *Architecture, nineteenth and twentieth centuries* (Harmondsworth, 1958)

Hobson, Anthony, 'Early binding studies and chimaeras', *The Book Collector* 60 (2011), pp. 385–99
  'Some deceptive bookbindings', in James H. Marrow and others (eds.), *The medieval book; glosses from friends and colleagues of Christopher de Hamel* ('t Goy-Houten, 2010), pp. 250–7
Hobson, G. D. (ed.), *English bindings, 1490–1940, in the library of J. R. Abbey* (1940)
Hogarth, William, *The analysis of beauty*, ed. Ronald Paulson (New Haven, CT, 1997)
Holmes, Sir Richard, *Specimens of royal, fine and historical bookbinding, selected from the Royal Library, Windsor Castle* (1893)
Hommes, Margriet van Eikema, *Changing pictures; discoloration in 15th-17th-century oil paintings* (2004)
Hone, William, *Ancient mysteries described* (1823; repr. c. 1860)
Hoock, Holger, *The King's artists; the Royal Academy of Arts and the politics of British culture, 1760–1840* (Oxford, 2003)
Horne, T. H., *An introduction to the study of bibliography*, 2 vols. (1814)
Horodisch, Abraham (ed.), *De arte et libris; Festschrift Erasmus, 1934–1984* (Amsterdam, 1984)
House of Commons, *Report from the Select Committee on the . . . British Museum* (1836)
  Report from the Select Committee on the National Gallery (1853)
  Select Committee on printing and stationery, 1822
Howard, S., *Bartolomeo Cavaceppi, eighteenth-century restorer* (New York, NY, 1982)
Howes, Justin, 'Caslon's punches and matrices', *Matrix* 20 (2000), pp. 1–7
Howsam, Leslie, *Kegan Paul; a Victorian imprint. Publishers, books and cultural history* (1998)
Hughes, Anthony and Erich Ranfft (eds.), *Sculpture and its reproductions* (1997)
Hume, A., *The learned societies and printing clubs of the United Kingdom* (1847), with a *Supplement* by A. I. Evans (1853)
Humphreys, H. N., *Masterpieces of the early printers and engravers* (1870)
Hunter, Andrew (ed.), *Thornton and Tully's scientific books, libraries and collectors*, 4th edn (Aldershot, 2000)
Hunter, Robert E., *Shakespeare and Stratford-on-Avon; a 'chronicle of the times' . . . with a full record of the tercentenary celebration* (1864)
Hutt, Allen, *Newspaper design*, 2nd edn (Oxford 1967)
Imison, John, *Elements of science and art*, 2 vols. (1803)
Impey, Oliver and Arthur MacGregor (eds.), *The origins of museums; the cabinet of curiosities in sixteenth- and seventeenth-century Europe* (Oxford, 1985)
Imprimerie Nationale, *Le cabinet des poinçons de l'Imprimerie Nationale*, 3rd edn (Paris, 1963)
Ingpen, Roger, 'Decorated papers', *The Fleuron* 2 (1924), pp. 99–106
Inventaris van de stempels en matrijzen van het Museum Plantin-Moretus (Antwerpen, 1960)
ISTC. *Incunabula short-title catalogue*. Available at: www.bl.uk/catalogues/istc

Jackson, W. A., *Annotated list of the publications of the Reverend Thomas Frognall Dibdin, based mainly on those in the Harvard College Library* (Cambridge, MA, 1965)

The Carl H. Pforzheimer library; English literature, 1475–1700, 3 vols. (New York, NY, 1940)

'Some limitations of microfilm', *Papers of the Bibliographical Soc. of America* 35 (1941), pp. 281–88

Jacobi, M. H., 'Ueber die Inductions-Phänomene beim Oeffnen und Schliessen einer Voltaschen Kette', Académie des Sciences, Saint-Pétersbourg, *Bulletin Scientifique* no. 86 (1838), cols. 212–23

Jaffé, Michael, *Rubens and Italy* (1977)

Jäger, Georg and Reinhard Wittmann, 'Der Antiquariatsbuchhandel', in Georg Jäger (ed.), *Geschichte des deutschen Buchhandels im 19. und 20. Jahrhunderts* (Berlin, 2010), part I, III, pp. 195–280

James, Elizabeth, *The Victoria and Albert Museum; a bibliography and exhibition chronology, 1852–1996* (1998)

James, Henry, *Account of the methods employed for the reduction of plans by photography, at the Ordnance Survey, Southampton* (1859)

Photo-zincography (Southampton, 1860)

Jameson, Anna, *Memoirs of the earlier Italian painters; and of the progress of painting in Italy, from Cimabue to Bassano*, 2 vols. (1845)

Jammes, André, 'De la destruction des livres', in Frédéric Barbier and others (ed.), *Le livre et l'historien; études offertes en l'honneur du Professeur Henri-Jean Martin* (Genève, 1997), pp. 813–17

Jammes, Isabelle, *Blanquart-Evrard et les origines de l'édition photographique française* (Genève, 1981)

Janin, Jules, 'Le duc d'Aumale et la bibliophilie', *Le Bibliophile Français* 6 (1872), pp. 5–18, 33–44

Jefcoate, Graham, 'German immigrants and the London book trade, 1700–70', in Randolph Vigne and Charles Littleton (eds.), *From strangers to citizens; the integration of immigrant communities in Britain, Ireland and colonial America, 1550–1750* (Brighton, 2001), pp. 503–10

Jenkins, Ian and Kim Sloan, *Vases and volcanoes; Sir William Hamilton and his collection* (1996)

Jensen, Kristian, *Revolution and the antiquarian book; reshaping the past, 1780–1815* (Cambridge, 2011)

Jensen, Robert, *Marketing modernism in fin-de-siècle Europe* (Princeton, NJ, 1994)

Jevons, W. Stanley, 'The use and abuse of museums', in Stanley W. Jevons, *Methods of social reform and other papers* (1883), pp. 53–81

Johnson, A. F., *Type designs, their history and development*, 3rd edn (1966)

Johnson, Barry C., *Lost in the Alps; a portrait of Robert Proctor the 'great bibliographer' and of his career in the British Museum* (1985)

Johnson, Samuel, *Letters*, ed. Bruce Redford, 5 vols. (Princeton, NJ, 1992–4)

Jolly, Claude (ed.), *Histoire des bibliothèques françaises; les bibliothèques sous l'ancien régime, 1530–1789* (Paris, 1988)

Jones, J. Winter, *A list of the books of reference in the reading room of the British Museum* (1859)

   'Early printed books', *Archaeological Journal* 28 (1871), pp. 1–22

Jones, Mark, *Fake? The art of deception* (1990)

Jones, Mark (ed.), *Why fakes matter; essays on problems of authenticity* (1992)

Joni, I. F., *Memorie di un pittore di quadri antichi* (Sancasciano, 1932), transl. as *Affairs of a painter* (1936); ed. Gianni Mazzoni with parallel English translation (Siena, 2004)

Jordan, C. J., *A treatise on anastatic printing* (1853)

Kaltwasser, Franz Georg, *Die Bibliothek als Museum; von der Renaissance bis heute, dargestellt am Beispiel der Bayerischen Staatsbibliothek* (Wiesbaden, 1999)

Kenyon, A. S., 'Photo-lithography; a Victorian invention', *Victoria Historical Magazine* 11 (1926–8), pp. 175–8

Keynes, Geoffrey, *John Evelyn; a study in bibliophily, with a bibliography of his writings*, 2nd edn (Oxford, 1968)

   William Pickering, publisher (1924)

Kichuk, Diana, 'Metamorphosis; remediation in Early English Books Online (EEBO)', *Literary and Linguistic Computing* 22 (2007), pp. 291–303

Klamt, Johann-Christian, 'Als die Photographie noch nich erfunden war; zur Reproduktion mittelalterlicher Miniaturen', *Aus dem Antiquariat* (2003/3), pp. 167–78

   'Zur Reproduktionsgeschichte mittelalterlicher Schriftformen und Miniaturen in der Neuzeit. Teil. 1: Das 17. und 18 Jahrhundert', *Quaerendo* 29 (1999), pp. 169–207; 'Teil 2: Das 19. Jahrhundert', *Quaerendo* 29 (1999), pp. 247–74

Klemm, G., *Zur Geschichte der Sammlungen für Wissenschaft und Kunst in Deutschland* (Zerbst, 1837)

Knight, Charles, *Passages of a working life*, 3 vols. (1864)

   William Caxton, the first English printer; a biography (1844); introd. Kenneth Day (Wynkyn de Worde Soc., 1976)

Knox, Tim, 'Sir Francis Dashwood of West Wycombe Park, Buckinghamshire, as a collector of ancient and modern sculpture', in Nicholas Penny and Eike D. Schmidt (eds.), *Collecting sculpture in early modern Europe* (New Haven, CT, 2008), pp. 397–419

Koestler, Arthur, *The act of creation* (1964)

Koops, Matthias, *Historical account of the substances which have been used to describe events*, 2nd edn (1801)

Kraus, H. P., *A rare book saga* (New York, NY, 1978)

Kuitert, Lisa, 'De secondhand handel; een doorbraak op het gebied van goedkope literatuur', *De Negentiende Eeuw* 15 (1991), pp. 185–202

Kurtz, Donna C., *The reception of classical art in Britain; an Oxford story of plaster casts from the antique* (Oxford, 2000)

Kyd, Thomas *Works*, ed. F. S. Boas (Oxford, 1901)
Labarre, Albert and Pierre Gasnault, *Le livre dans la vie quotidienne* (Paris: Bibliothèque Nationale, 1975)
Laffitte, Marie-Pierre, 'Faux ou pastiches; quelques reliures à "décor rétrospectif" de la collection Barrois', *Revue de la Bibliothèque Nationale de France* 13 (2003), pp. 56–8
Laing, D. (ed.), *Bannatyne Club, Edinburgh; lists of members and the rules, with a catalogue of books printed* (Edinburgh, 1867)
Lamb, Charles, 'Barrenness of the imaginative faculty in the productions of modern art', in Charles Lamb, *Last essays of Elia* (1833)
Lancaster, Alfred, 'On the advantage of occasional exhibitions of the more rare and valuable books in public libraries', *The Library* 1st ser. 6 (1894), pp. 19–22
Lang, Andrew, *The library* (1881; 2nd edn 1882)
Leedham-Green, Elisabeth and David McKitterick, 'A catalogue of Cambridge University Library in 1583', in James P. Carley and Colin G. C. Tite (eds.), *Books and collectors, 1200–1700; essays presented to Andrew Watson* (1997), pp. 153–235
Lehmann-Haupt, H. (ed.), *Homage to a bookman; essays on manuscripts, books and printing written for Hans P. Kraus on his 60th birthday* (Berlin, 1967)
Lemaire, Claudine and Elly Cockx-Indestege (eds.), *Manuscrits et imprimés anciens en fac-similé de 1600 à 1984* (Bruxelles: Bibliothèque Royale Albert Ier, 1984)
Lemaistre, Isabelle Leroy-Jay, 'Les commandes de sculptures', in Pierre Rosenberg (ed.), *Dominique-Vivant Denon, l'oeil de Napoléon* (Musée du Louvre, 1999), pp. 352–64, 385–9
Lenormand, Sébastien, *Nouveau manuel complet du relieur*, nouvelle édn (Paris, 1840)
Lenz, E. and M. Jacobi, 'Ueber die Gesetze der Elektromagnete', Académie des Sciences, Saint-Pétersbourg, *Bulletin Scientifique* no. 86 (1838), cols. 337–67
Lewis, John, *Printed ephemera* (1962)
  Such things happen; the life of a typographer (Stowmarket, 1994)
Liesen, Bruno and Claude Sorgeloos, *Le rayonnement des Moretus* (Bruxelles, 2006)
Life (The) of William Caxton (1828)
Lilien, Otto M., *Jacob Christoph Le Blon, 1667–1741, inventor of three and four colour printing* (Stuttgart, 1985)
Lindenbaum, Peter, 'Publishers' booklists in late seventeenth-century London', *The Library* 7th ser. 11 (2010), pp. 381–404
Lister, W. B. C., *A bibliography of Murray's Handbooks for travellers* (Dereham, 1993)
Lloyd, Christopher, *Art and its images* (Oxford, 1975)
Loftie, W. J., *A plea for art in the house* (1876)
  'Thorough restoration', *Macmillan's Magazine* 36 (1877), pp. 136–42
London and its environs; or, the general ambulator, and pocket companion, 12th edn (1820)
London International Exhibition 1874; official guide (1874)
Lowry, Martin, *The world of Aldus Manutius; business and scholarship in renaissance Venice* (Oxford, 1979)

Lubbock, Sir John, 'On the preservation of our ancient national monuments', *Nineteenth Century* 1 (1877), pp. 257–69

Lugli, Adalgisa, *Naturalia et mirabilia; il collezionismo enciclopedico nelle Wunderkammern d'Europa*, ed. Martina Mazzotta (Milano, 2005)

Luther-Austellung (Die) der Königlichen Bibliothek (Berlin, 1846)

Macaulay, T. B., *The history of England from the accession of James II*, 5 vols. (1849–61)

Macdonald, Hugh, 'Note', *The Library*, N.S. 26 (1946), pp. 307–8

Madan, Falconer, *Books in manuscript* (1893)

    '"The duplicity of duplicates" and "A new extension of bibliography"', *Trans Bibliographical Soc.* 12 (1914), pp. 15–24

    The early Oxford press; a bibliography of printing and publishing at Oxford, '1468'–1640 (Oxford, 1895)

Mainardi, Patricia, *Art and politics of the Second Empire; the universal expositions of 1855 and 1867* (New Haven, CT, 1987)

Major, Richard Henry, *The bibliography of the first letter of Christopher Columbus describing his discovery of the New World* (1872)

Mandelbrote, Giles (ed.), *Out of print and into profit; a history of the rare and secondhand book trade in Britain in the twentieth century* (2006)

Manifesto of the Society for the Protection of Ancient Buildings, repr. in Chris Miele (ed.), *From William Morris; building conservation and the Arts and Crafts cult of authenticity, 1877–1939* (New Haven, CT, 2005), pp. 337–9

Marrow, James H. and others (eds.), *The medieval book; glosses from friends and colleagues of Christopher de Hamel* ('t Goy-Houten, 2010)

Marvin, Miranda, *The language of the muses; the dialogue between Roman and Greek sculpture* (Los Angeles, CA, 2008)

Maslen, Keith, 'Three eighteenth-century reprints of the castrated sheets in Holinshed's Chronicles', *The Library* 5th ser. 13 (1958), pp. 120–4; repr. in Keith Maslen, *An early London printing house at work; studies in the Bowyer ledgers* (New York, NY, 1993), pp. 27–32

Maslen, Keith and John Lancaster (eds.), *The Bowyer ledgers* (1991)

Massing, Ann, *Painting restoration before la restauration; the origins of the profession in France* (Turnhout, 2012)

    'Restoration policy in France in the eighteenth century', in C. Sitwell and S. Staniforth (eds.), *Studies in the history of painting restoration* (1998), pp. 63–84

Maxwell, Sir William Stirling, *An essay towards a collection of books relating to proverbs, emblems . . . being a catalogue of those at Keir* (Privately printed, 1860)

Maynard, Frederic W., *Descriptive notice of the drawings and publications of the Arundel Society* (1869)

Mazzoni, Gianni (ed.), *Falsi d'autore; Icilio Federico Joni e la cultura del falso tra otto e novecento* (Siena, 2004)

McCarthy, Muriel, *All graduates and gentlemen; Marsh's Library* (Dublin, 1980)

McCarthy, Muriel and Ann Simmons (eds.), *Marsh's Library; a mirror on the world; law, learning and libraries, 1650–1750* (Dublin, 2009)

McCauley, Ann, 'Art reproduction for the masses', in Ann McCauley, *Industrial madness* (New Haven, CT, 1994)

McClellan, Andrew, 'The museum and its public in eighteenth-century France', in Per Bjurström (ed.), *The genesis of the art museum in the 18th century* (Stockholm, 1993), pp. 61–80

McKenzie, D. F., *Bibliography and the sociology of texts* (1986)

  'Computers and the humanities; a personal synthesis of conference issues', in May Katzen (ed.), *Scholarship and technology in the humanities* (1991), pp. 157–69

McKerrow, R. B., *An introduction to bibliography for literary students* (Oxford, 1927); introd. D. McKitterick (Winchester, 1994)

McKitterick, David, *Cambridge University Library; a history. The eighteenth and nineteenth centuries* (Cambridge, 1986)

  A changing view from Amsterdam; where next with book history? (Amsterdam, 2010)

  A history of Cambridge University Press II: *Scholarship and commerce, 1698–1872* (Cambridge, 1998)

  'Old faces and new acquaintances; typography and the association of ideas', *Papers of the Bibliographical Soc. of America* 87 (1993 [1994]), pp. 163–86

  Print, manuscript and the search for order, 1450–1830 (Cambridge, 2003)

McKitterick, David (ed.), *Catalogue of the Pepys Library at Magdalene College, Cambridge* VII: *Facsimile of Pepys's catalogue* (Cambridge, 1991)

  Do we want to keep our newspapers? (2002)

  The making of the Wren library (Cambridge, 1995)

McLean, Ruari, *Victorian book design and colour printing*, 2nd edn (1972)

Meerman, Gerard, *Origines typographicae*, 2 vols. (Hagae-Comitum, 1765)

Mercier, Alain (ed.), *Les trois révolutions du livre; catalogue de l'exposition du Musée des Arts et Métiers* (Paris, 2002)

Michel, Patrick, *Mazarin, prince de collectionneurs; les collections et l'ameublement du cardinal Mazarin (1602–1661); histoire et analyse* (Paris, 1999)

Middeleeuwse muurschilderingen in de 19de eeuw; studie en inventaris van middeleeuwse muurschilderingen in Belgische kerken (Leuven, 1998)

Miele, Chris (ed.), *From William Morris; building conservation and the Arts and Crafts cult of authenticity, 1877–1939* (New Haven, CT, 2005)

Miller, Edward, *Prince of librarians; the life and times of Antonio Panizzi of the British Museum* (1967)

Milner, John, *A dissertation on the modern style of altering ancient cathedrals as exemplified in the cathedral of Salisbury* (1798)

Minor, Ryan, *Choral fantasies; music, festivity, and nationhood in nineteenth-century Germany* (Cambridge, 2012)

Mirsky, L. and S. Tropea (eds.), *The news aesthetic* (New York, NY, 1995)

[Mohnike, G. C. F.] Review of German books marking the Gutenberg anniversary, *Foreign Quarterly Review* 25 (1840), pp. 446–57

Montoya, Alice C. and others (eds.), *Early modern medievalisms; the interplay between scholarly reflection and artistic production* (Leiden, 2010)

Morel, G., 'Ueber die Ausstellung auf der deutschen Buchhändlerbörse zu Leipzig während der Feier des Buchdruckfestes 1840', *Serapeum* 15 (1840), pp. 225-37

Mores, Edward Rowe, *A dissertation upon English typographical founders and founderies (1778) with a catalogue and specimen of the typefoundry of John James (1782)*; ed. with introd. and notes by Harry Carter and Christopher Ricks (Oxford Bibliographical Soc., 1961)

Morison, Stanley, 'On the classification of typographical variations', in John Dreyfus (ed.), *Type specimen facsimiles 1-15* (1963)

Talbot Baines Reed; author, bibliographer, typefounder (Cambridge, 1960)

Morris, William, *Letters*, ed. Norman Kelvin, 4 vols. in 5 (Princeton, NJ, 1984-96)

Mortlock, D. P., *Holkham library; a history and description* (Roxburghe Club, 2006)

Moureau, François (ed.), *Les presses grises; la contrefaçon du livre (XVIe-XIXe siècle)* (Paris, 1988)

Moxon, Joseph, *Mechanick exercises on the whole art of printing*, ed. Herbert Davis and Harry Carter, 2nd edn (Oxford, 1962)

Munby, A. N. L., *The cult of the autograph letter in England* (1962)

The history and bibliography of science in England; the first phase, 1833-1845 (Berkeley, CA, 1968)

'Jacob Bryant and the Sunderland library', *The Library* 5th ser. 2 (1947-8), pp. 192-9

Murphy, Andrew, *Shakespeare for the people; working-class readers, 1800-1900* (Cambridge, 2008)

Shakespeare in print; a history and chronology of Shakespeare publishing (Cambridge, 2003)

Murray, John, *Handbook for travellers to central Italy* (1843)

A handbook of Rome and its environs, 8th edn (1867)

Muzerelle, Danielle, '"Cet Esclabart avait une belle main"', *Revue de la Bibliothèque Nationale de France* 13 (2003), pp. 50-55

Myers, Robin, 'The Caxton celebration of 1877; a landmark in bibliophily', in Robin Myers and Michael Harris (eds.), *Bibliophily* (Cambridge, 1986), pp. 138-63

Caxtoniana, or the progress of Caxton studies from the earliest times to 1976; an exhibition at the St Bride Printing Library (1976)

'George Isaac Frederick Tupper, facsimilist, "whose ability in this description of work is beyond praise" (1820?-1911)', *Trans Cambridge Bibliographical Soc.* 7 (1978), pp. 113-34

'William Blades's debt to Henry Bradshaw and G. I. F. Tupper in his Caxton studies; a further look at unpublished documents', *The Library* 5th ser. 33 (1978), pp. 265-83

Myers, Robin and Michael Harris (eds.), *Bibliophily* (Cambridge, 1986)

Fakes and frauds; varieties of deception in print and manuscript (Winchester, 1989)

Pioneers in bibliography (1996)

Myers, Robin and others (eds.), *Books for sale; the advertising and promotion of print since the fifteenth century* (2009)

Nagel, Alexander and Christopher S. Wood, *Anachronic renaissance* (New York, NY, 2010)

Namur, P., *Manuel du bibliothécaire* (Bruxelles, 1834)

Needham, Paul, *The Bradshaw method; Henry Bradshaw's contribution to bibliography* (Chapel Hill, NC, 1988)

"'Haec sancta ars'"; Gutenberg's invention as a divine gift', *Gazette of the Grolier Club* N.S. 42 (1990), pp. 101–20

'The paper supply of the Gutenberg Bible', *Papers of the Bibliographical Soc. of America* 79 (1985), pp. 303–74

Twelve centuries of bookbindings, 400–1600 (New York, NY, 1979)

'William Morris; book collector', in Paul Needham (ed.), *William Morris and the art of the book* (New York, NY, 1976), pp. 21–47

Needham, Paul (ed.), *William Morris and the art of the book* (New York, NY, 1976)

Nixon, H. M., 'Binding forgeries', *VIth International Congress of Bibliophiles, Vienna, 1969. Lectures* (Wien, 1971), pp. 69–83

The Broxbourne library; styles and designs of bookbindings from the twelfth to the twentieth century (1956)

Catalogue of the Pepys Library at Magdalene College, Cambridge VI: *Bindings* (Woodbridge, 1984)

Five centuries of British bookbinding (1978)

Noltenius, Rainer, 'Schiller als Führer und Heiland; das Schillerfest 1859 als nationaler Traum von der Geburt des zweiten deutschen Kaiserreichs', in Dieter Düding and others (eds.), *Öffentliche Festkultur; politische Feste in Deutschland von der Aufklärung bis zum Ersten Weltkrieg* (Reinbek bei Hamburg, 1988), pp. 237–58

Nora, Pierre (ed.), *Les lieux de mémoire*, 3 vols. (Paris, 1997)

Nordenfalk, Carl, *Color of the middle ages; a survey of book illumination based on color facsimiles of medieval manuscripts* (Pittsburgh, PA, 1976)

Norris, Dorothy May, *A history of cataloguing and cataloguing methods, 1100–1850* (1939)

Nys, Liesbet, *De intrede van het publiek; museumbezoek in België, 1830–1914* (Leuven, 2012)

Oates, J. C. T., *A catalogue of the fifteenth-century printed books in the University Library Cambridge* (Cambridge, 1954)

'The *Trewe encounter*; a pamphlet on Flodden Field', *Trans Cambridge Bibliographical Soc.* 1 (1950), pp. 126–9

ODNB. *Oxford dictionary of national biography*, 60 vols. (Oxford, 2004)

Osborn, James M. and Robert Vosper, *Building book collections; two variations on a theme* (Los Angeles, CA, 1977)

Ostergard, Derek E. (ed.), *William Beckford, 1760–1844; an eye for the magnificent* (New Haven, CT, 2001)

Ouwerkerk, Annemiek, 'Met kunst geïllustreerd; de kunstreproductie in de eerste helft van de negentiende eeuw in Nederland', in Nelke Bartelings and others (eds.), *Beelden in veelvoud; de vermenigvuldiging van het beeld in prentkunst en fotografie* (*Leids Kunsthistorisch Jaarboek* 12) (Leiden, 2002), pp. 275–93

Overall, W. H. (ed.), *A catalogue of engraved portraits, topographical drawings and prints, coins, gems, autographs, antiquities and works of art, exhibited at the opening of the new library and museum of the Corporation of London, November 1872* (1872)

P., J., *An essay on books and printing; read to a literary society in 1893 and accompanied by an exhibition of books from the presses of early printers* (Manchester, 1894)

Page, R. I., *Matthew Parker and his books* (Kalamazoo, MI, 1993)

Pantazzi, Sybille, 'Elliot Stock', *The Book Collector* 20 (1971), pp. 25–46

Parenti, Marino, *Dizionario dei luoghi di stampa falsi, inventati o suppositi* (Firenze, 1951)

Parker, James, *An introduction to the history of successive revisions of the Book of Common Prayer* (Oxford, 1877)

Parker, Wyman W., *Henry Stevens of Vermont; American rare book dealer in London, 1845–1886* (Amsterdam, 1963)

Parsis-Barubé, Odile, *La province antiquaire; l'invention de l'histoire locale en France (1800–1870)* (Paris, 2011)

Partridge, R. C. B., *The history of the legal deposit of books throughout the British Empire* (1938)

Paul, C. Kegan, *Memories* (1899)

Payne, Anthony (ed.), *The Spanish letter of Columbus; a facsimile of the original edition published by Bernard Quaritch in 1891* (2006)

Pearson, David, *Books as history; the importance of books beyond their texts* (2008)
  Provenance research in book history; a handbook (1998)

Peignot, Gabriel, *Dictionnaire raisonné de bibliologie*, 2 vols. (Paris, 1802)

Penny, Nicholas and Eike D. Schmidt (eds.), *Collecting sculpture in early modern Europe* (New Haven, CT, 2008)

Pergam, Elizabeth A., *The Manchester Art Treasures Exhibition of 1857; entrepreneurs, connoisseurs and the public* (Aldershot, 2011)

Peterson, William S., *A bibliography of the Kelmscott Press* (Oxford, 1984)
  The Kelmscott Press; a history of William Morris's typographical adventure (1991)

Petter, Helen Mary, *The Oxford almanacks* (Oxford, 1974)

Pevsner, Nikolaus, *Some architectural writers of the nineteenth century* (1972)

Philip, I. G., *The Bodleian Library in the seventeenth and eighteenth centuries* (Oxford, 1983)

Phillips, David, *Exhibiting authenticity* (Manchester, 1997)

Photographic facsimiles of the remains of the Epistles of Clement of Rome made from the unique copy preserved in the Codex Alexandrinus (1856)

Physick, John, *The Victoria and Albert Museum; the history of its building* (1982)

Picture (The) of London, 22nd edn (1824)

Pinelli, O. Rossi, 'Artisti, falsari o filologhi? Da Cavaceppi al Canova. Il restauro della scultura tra arte e scienza', *Ricerche di Storia dell'Arte* 13/14 (1981), pp. 41–56

Plock, Philippa, 'Advertising books in eighteenth-century Paris; evidence from Waddesdon Manor's trade card collection', in Robin Myers and others (eds.), *Books for sale; the advertising and promotion of print since the fifteenth century* (2009), pp. 87–108

Pollard, A. W., *'Bibliography and bibliology', Encyclopaedia Britannica*, 11th edn (1911)

'On the exhibition of facsimiles of rare books in public libraries', *The Library* 1st ser. 5 (1893), pp. 260–4

Records of the English Bible (Oxford, 1911)

Alfred William Pollard; a selection of his essays, ed. Fred W. Roper (Metuchen, NJ, 1976)

Pollard, A. W., G. R. Redgrave, R. W. Chapman, W. W. Greg and others, '"Facsimile" reprints of old books', *The Library* 4th ser. 6 (1926), pp. 305–28

Pollard, Graham, 'The scope for further typographical analysis', in William B. Todd (ed.), *Thomas J. Wise; centenary studies* (Austin, TX, 1959), pp. 64–79

Pollard, Graham and Albert Ehrman, *The distribution of books by catalogue from the invention of printing to A.D. 1800* (Roxburghe Club, 1965)

Pollard, Graham and Esther Potter, *Early bookbinding manuals; an annotated list of technical accounts of bookbinding to 1840* (Oxford, 1984)

Pommier, E. (ed.), *Les musées en Europe à la veille de l'invention du Louvre* (Paris, 1995)

Poulot, Dominique, *Une histoire des musées de France, XVIIIe-XXe siècle* (Paris, 2008)

Power, Eugene B., 'An American filming service in Europe', in M. Llewellyn Raney (ed.), *Microphotography for libraries; papers presented at the microphotography symposium at the 1936 conference of the American Library Association* (Chicago, IL, 1936), pp. 72–6

Power, J., *A handy-book about books* (1870)

Preciado, Kathleen (ed.), *Retaining the original; multiple originals, copies and reproductions* (Washington, DC, 1989)

Price, Leah, *How to do things with books in Victorian Britain* (Princeton, NJ, 2012)

Price list of mounted photographs printed from negatives taken for the Science and Art Department by the official photographer, C. Thurston Thompson (1864)

Price list of reproductions of works of art by means of photography, electrotyping, casting, etc., selected from the South Kensington Museum . . . with a historical sketch of the cartoons of Raffaelle at Hampton Court (1859)

Printing and the mind of man; catalogue of a display of printing mechanisms and printed materials arranged to illustrate the history of western civilization and the means of multiplication of literary texts since the XV century . . . assembled at the British Museum and Earls Court (1963)

Printing as in the olden time at the Ballantyne Press; Ancient printing office exhibited by G. Faulkner and Sons, the Deansgate Press (Edinburgh, 1886)

Proctor, Robert, *Bibliographical essays*, preface by A. W. Pollard (1905)

Proef van letteren, welke gegooten worden in de nieuwe Haerlemsche lettergietery van J.Enschedé (Haarlem, 1768); repr. in facsimile with introd. and notes by John A. Lane (Haarlem, 1993)

Prothero, G. W., *A memoir of Henry Bradshaw* (1888)

Quaritch, Bernard, *Catalogue of English literature* (1884)

  A catalogue of fifteen hundred books remarkable for the beauty or the age of their bindings (1889)

  Catalogue of romances of chivalry (1882)

  Catalogue of works on the fine arts ... and a splendid series of books in historical and remarkable bindings (1883)

  A collection of facsimiles from examples of historic or artistic book-binding (1889)

  Contributions towards a dictionary of English book collectors (1892–8)

  A general catalogue of books arranged in classes (1868)

  Monuments of typography and xylography (1897)

Quatremère de Quincy, Antoine, *Letters to Miranda and Canova on the abduction of antiquities from Rome and Athens*, introd. Dominique Poulot, transl. Chris Miller and David Gilks (Los Angeles, CA, 2012)

Quinault, Roland, 'The cult of the centenary, c. 1784–1914', *Historical Research* 71 (1998), pp. 303–23

Quinn, D. B. (ed.), *The Hakluyt handbook*, 2 vols. (Hakluyt Soc., 1974)

Ramage, Nancy H., 'Restorer and collector; notes on eighteenth-century recreations of Roman statues', in Elaine K. Gazda (ed.), *The ancient art of emulation; studies in artistic originality and tradition from the present to classical antiquity* (Ann Arbor, MI, 2002), pp. 61–77

Randall, David A., *Dukedom large enough* (New York, NY, 1969)

Ransome, Joyce, 'Monotessaron; the harmonies of Little Gidding', *The Seventeenth Century* 20 (2005), pp. 22–52

'Rapport d'un mémoire de M Chaptal sur quelques propriétés de l'acide muriatique oxigéné; fait à l'Académie Royale des Sciences par MM. Lavoisier and Berthollet', *Annales de Chimie* 1 (1789), pp. 69–72

Rasmussen, Eric and Anthony James West (eds.), *The Shakespeare First Folio; a descriptive catalogue* (Basingstoke, 2012)

Rastaptchine, Comte, 'La Bibliothèque Impériale et Publique de Saint-Pétersbourg', *Archives du Bibliophile* 26 (February 1860), pp. 63–7

Raux, Sophie and others (eds.), *L'estampe; un art multiple à la portée de tous?* (Villeneuve d'Ascq, 2008)

Ravaisson, Félix, *La Vénus de Milo* (Paris, 1871)

Raymond, Joad (ed.), *The Oxford history of popular print culture* I: *Cheap print in Britain and Ireland to 1660* (Oxford, 2011)

Rebel, Ernst, *Faksimile und Mimesis; Studien zur deutsche Reproduktionsgraphik des 18. Jahrhunderts* (Mittenwald, 1981)

Reed, Talbot Baines, *A history of the old English letter foundries* (1887); new edn, rev. A. F. Johnson (1952)

'A list of books and papers on printers and printing under the countries and towns to which they refer', *Trans Bibliographical Soc.* 3 (1895), pp. 81–152

Reidy, Denis V. (ed.), *The Italian book, 1465–1800; studies presented to Dennis E. Rhodes on his 70th birthday* (1993)

Reitlinger, Gerard, *The economics of taste*, 3 vols. (1961–70)

Renouard, A.-A. *Annales de l'imprimerie des Alde*, 3rd edn (Paris, 1834)
 Catalogue de la bibliothèque d'un amateur, 4 vols. (Paris, 1819)

Report of the Commissioners appointed to inquire into the constitution and government of the British Museum (1850)

Report of the progress of the Ordnance Survey and Topographical Depôt, to the 31st December 1859

Report of the progress of the Ordnance Survey and Topographical Depôt, to the 31st December 1860

Report of the progress of the Ordnance Survey and Topographical Depôt, to the 31st December 1863

Reports on the Paris Universal Exhibition, 1867 (Parliamentary papers, 1867–8)

Reynolds, Sir Joshua, *A journey to Flanders and Holland*, ed. Harry Mount (Cambridge, 1996)

Rhodes, Barbara, 'Hell's own brew; home book renovation from nineteenth-century receipts to today's kitchen chemistry; its legacy for preservation', *Paper Conservator* 15 (1991), pp. 60–70

Richardson, Brian, 'The debates on printing in renaissance Italy', in Luigi Balsamo and Pierangelo Bellettini (eds.), *Anatomie bibliologiche; saggi di storia del libro per il centenario de "La Bibliofilia"* (Firenze, 1999), pp. 135–55

Rickards, Maurice, *The encyclopedia of ephemera; a guide to the fragmentary documents of everyday life*, ed. Michael Twyman (2000)

Riffaud, Alain, *Répertoire du théâtre français imprimé entre 1630 et 1660* (Genève, 2009)

Rigney, Ann, 'Embodied communities; commemorating Robert Burns, 1859', *Representations* 115 (2011), pp. 71–101

Ringelhardt, Bernhardt, *Die Kunst alle Arten Abgüsse und Abdrücke von Münzen, Medaillen, Cameen, Glaspasten, Käfern, Insekten... auf's sauberste und vollkommenste zu verfetigen* (Quedlinburg and Leipzig, 1834)

Ringrose, Jayne, *Summary catalogue of the additional medieval manuscripts in Cambridge University Library acquired before 1940* (Woodbridge, 2009)

Rive, J.-J., *La chasse aux bibliographes et antiquaires mal-avisés* ('Londres', 1789)

Roberts, Colin H. and T. C. Skeat, *The birth of the codex* (Oxford, 1987)

Roberts, Helene E. (ed.), *Art history through the camera's lens* (Amsterdam, 1995)

Roberts, R. J., 'The Bibliographical Society as a band of pioneers', in Robin Myers and Michael Harris (eds.), *Pioneers in bibliography* (1996), pp. 86–99

Robinson, J. C., *Catalogue of 'the circulating collection' of works of art, selected from the Museum at South Kensington: intended for temporary exhibition in provincial schools of art* (1863)

Robinson, J. M., *The Wyatts; an architectural dynasty* (Oxford, 1979)

Rooses, M., *Le Musée Plantin-Moretus; description sommaire des bâtiments et des collections* (Anvers, 1878)

Rooses, Max (introd.), *Index characterum architypographicae Plantinianae; proeven der lettersoorten gebruikt in de Plantijnische Drukkerij* (Antwerpen, 1905)

Roth, J., 'Sources et grandes lignes des bibliothèques publiques de Strasbourg détruites en 1870', *Cahiers Alsaciens d'Archéologie, d'Art et d'Histoire* 15 (1971), pp. 145–80

Rothschild, Victor (ed.), *The history of Tom Jones, a changeling* (Cambridge, 1951)

Rouveyre, Edouard, *Connaissances nécessaires à un bibliophile* (Paris, 1877; 5th edn 1899)

'Richard, Jules', *Art de former une bibliothèque* (Paris, 1883)

Samaran, Charles, 'Adam Pilinski', *Bibliothèque de l'Ecole des Chartes* 97 (1936), p. 463

Sarkowski, Heinz, 'Das wissenschaftliche Antiquariat in Leipzig und die Ueberproduktion deutscher Verlag', *Aus dem Antiquariat* 1996/2, pp. A67–74

Sarmant, Thierry, *Le Cabinet des Médailles de la Bibliothèque Nationale, 1661–1848* (Paris, 1994)

Sauvage, Abbé, *Souvenirs de l'exposition typographique de Rouen* (Rouen, 1887)

Schaaf, Larry J., *Out of the shadows; Herschel, Talbot, and the invention of photography* (New Haven, CT, 1992)

The photographic art of William Henry Fox Talbot (Princeton, NJ, 2000)

William Henry Fox Talbot; selections from a private collection (Hans P. Kraus, Jr, catalogue 17, *Sun pictures* (New York, NY, 2007))

Schriftproben der Offizin Haag-Drugulin A. G. (Leipzig, 1929)

Schwaighofer, Claudia-Alexandra, *Von der Kennerschaft zur Wissenschaft; Reproduktionsgraphische Mappenwerke nach Zeichnungen in Europa, 1726–1857* (Berlin, 2009)

Scott, A. de C., *On photo-zincography and other photographic processes employed at the Ordnance Survey office* (Southampton, 1862)

Scott, George Gilbert, 'Thorough anti-restoration', *Macmillan's Magazine* 36 (1877), pp. 228–37

Scott (The) exhibition, MDCCCLXXI; catalogue of the exhibition held at Edinburgh, in July and August 1871, on occasion of the commemoration of the centenary of the birth of Sir Walter Scott (Edinburgh, 1872)

Select (A) bibliography of the writings of Alfred W. Pollard (Oxford, 1938)

Serrai, Alfredo, *Storia della bibliografia* VII: *Storia e critica della catalogazione bibliografica*, ed. Gabriela Miggiano (Roma, 1997)

Shaw, David, 'The Lyons counterfeit of Aldus's italic type; a new chronology', in Denis V. Reidy (ed.), *The Italian book, 1465–1800; studies presented to Dennis E. Rhodes on his 70th birthday* (1993), pp. 117–33

Shaw, Henry, *Illuminated ornaments selected from manuscripts of the Middle Ages* (1830–33)

Siegel, Jonah, *The emergence of the modern museum; an anthology of nineteenth-century sources* (Oxford, 2008)

Singer, Mark, 'Missed opportunities dept.', *New Yorker*, 12 January 1998, p. 29

Sitwell, Christine and Sarah Staniforth (eds.), *Studies in the history of painting restoration* (1998)

Slater, J. Herbert, *The library manual; a guide to the foundation of a library* (1883; 3rd edn 1892)

Sloan, Kim, *Enlightenment; discovering the world in the eighteenth century* (2003)

Smee, Alfred, 'On the production of electrotypes', *London and Edinburgh Philosophical Magazine* 16 (1840), pp. 530–2

Smith G. and F. Benger, *The oldest London bookshop; a history of 200 years* (1928)

Smith, N. A., *Catalogue of the Pepys Library at Magdalene College, Cambridge* I: *Printed books* (Cambridge, 1978)

Soane, Sir John, *Designs in architecture* (1778)

Solly, Edward, 'Observations on the precipitation of copper by voltaic electricity', *London and Edinburgh Philosophical Magazine* 16 (1840), pp. 309–15

Sordet, Yann, *L'amour des livres au siècle des lumières; Pierre Adamoli et ses collections* (Paris, 2001)

Sotheby, Samuel Leigh, *Principia typographica*, 3 vols. (1858)

Southey, C. C. (ed.), *The life and correspondence of Robert Southey*, 6 vols. (1849–50)

Specimen of Mr. S. Leigh Sotheby's Principia typographia (1858)

Speculum humanae salvationis, introd. J. Ph. Berjeau (1861)

Spencer, Thomas, 'An account of some experiments made for the purpose of ascertaining how far voltaic electricity may be usefully applied to the purpose of working in metal', *Annals of Electricity, Magnetism and Chemistry* 4 (1839–40), pp. 258–77

'Voltaic engravings' (letter to the editor), *Literary Gazette*, 4 July 1840, p. 433

Spencer, Walter T., *Forty years in my bookshop*, ed. T. Moult (1923)

Spevack, Marvin, 'James Orchard Halliwell and friends IV: Howard Staunton; V: Samuel Weller Singer; VI: Charles Knight', *The Library* 6th ser. 19 (1997), pp. 122–37

James Orchard Halliwell-Phillipps; a classified bibliography (Hildesheim, 1997)

James Orchard Halliwell-Phillipps; the life and works of the Shakespearean scholar and bookman (New Castle, DE, 2001)

Spier, Jeffrey and Jonathan Kagan, 'Sir Charles Frederick and the forgery of ancient coins in eighteenth-century Rome', *Journal of the History of Collections* 12 (2000), pp. 35–90

Spufford, Margaret, *Small books and pleasant histories; popular fiction and its readership in seventeenth-century England* (1981)

Standing Commission on Museums and Galleries, *Survey of provincial museums and galleries* (1963)

Statutes (The) of Henry VII. In exact facsimile from the very rare original, printed by Caxton in 1489, ed. John Rae (1869)

STC. A. W. Pollard and G. R. Redgrave, *A short-title catalogue of books printed in England, Scotland, and Ireland, and of English books printed abroad, 1475–1640*, 2nd edn, rev. William A. Jackson, F. S. Ferguson and Katharine F. Pantzer, with a chronological index by Philip R. Rider, 3 vols. (Bibliographical Soc., 1976–91)

Stephenson, Blake, *Caslon old face, roman and italic; cast entirely from matrices produced from the original punches engraved in the early part of the eighteenth century* (1924)
Stern, Madeleine B., *Antiquarian bookselling in the United States; a history from the origins to the 1940s* (Westport, CT, 1985)
Stevens, Henry, *The Bibles in the Caxton exhibition MDCCCLXXVII, or a bibliographical description of nearly one thousand representative Bibles in various languages ... Special edition revised and carefully corrected with additions* (1878)
  'Photobibliography; a word on catalogues and how to make them', preface to Henry Stevens, *Bibliotheca geographica and historica* (1872)
  Recollections of Mr. James Lenox of New York and the foundation of his library (1886); ed. V. H. Paltsits (New York, NY, 1951)
Stevenson, Allan, 'A bibliographical method for the description of botanical books', *Catalogue of botanical work in the collection of Rachel McMasters Miller Hunt*, 3 vols. (Pittsburgh, PA, 1958–61), III, pp. cxli–ccvi
  'Paper as bibliographical evidence', *The Library* 5th ser. 17 (1962), pp. 197–212
Stobart, Jon and Ilja Van Damme (eds.), *Modernity and the second-hand trade; European consumption cultures and practices, 1700–1900* (Basingstoke, 2010)
Stresow, Gustav, 'Meisterwerke typographischer Faksimilierung früher Bibelkodizes', *Aus dem Antiquariat* 1999/6, pp. A316–27
Striphas, Ted, *The late age of print; everyday book culture from consumerism to control* (New York, NY, 2009)
Stroud, Dorothy, *Sir John Soane as architect* (1996)
Summit, Jennifer, *Memory's library; medieval books in early modern England* (Chicago, IL, 2008)
Swift, Katherine, 'Bibliotheca Sunderlandiana; the making of an eighteenth-century library', in Robin Myers and Michael Harris (eds.), *Bibliophily* (Cambridge, 1986), pp. 63–89
  'Dutch penetration of the London market for books, c. 1690–1730', in C. Berkvens-Stevelinck and others (eds.), *Le magasin de l'univers; the Dutch Republic as the centre of the European book trade* (Leiden, 1992), pp. 265–79
  'The French booksellers in the Strand', *Proc. Huguenot Soc.* 25 (1990), pp. 123–39
Synopsis of the contents of the British Museum, 43rd edn (1841)
Talbot, W. H. Fox, *The pencil of nature* (1844); facsimiles with introductions by B. Newhall (New York, NY, 1969) and by Colin Harding (Chicago, IL, 2011)
  Some account of the art of photogenic drawing (1839)
Talley, M. Kirby Jr, 'Miscreants and hotentots: restorers and restoration attitudes and practices in seventeenth and eighteenth century England', in C. Sitwell and S. Staniforth (eds.), *Studies in the history of painting restoration* (1998), pp. 27–42
Tanselle, G. Thomas, *Book-jackets; their history, forms and use* (New Castle, DE, 2012)
  'The future of primary records', *Biblion; Bulletin of the New York Public Library* 5 (1996), pp. 4–32; repr. in G. Thomas Tanselle, *Literature and artifacts* (Charlottesville, VA, 1998), pp. 96–123

'The latest forms of book-burning', *Common Knowledge* 2 (1993), pp. 172–7; repr. in G. Thomas Tanselle, *Literature and artifacts* (Charlottesville, VA, 1998), pp. 89–95

The life and work of Fredson Bowers (Charlottesville, VA, 1993)

Literature and artifacts (Charlottesville, VA, 1998)

'Reproductions and scholarship', *Studies in Bibliography* 42 (1989), pp. 25–54; repr. in G. Thomas Tanselle, *Literature and artifacts* (Charlottesville, VA, 1998), pp. 59–88

'The textual criticism of visual and aural works', *Studies in Bibliography* 57 (2005–6), pp. 1–37

'Title page transcription and signature collation reconsidered', *Studies in Bibliography* (1985), pp. 45–81

T[echener], J., 'Un musée bibliographique', *Bulletin du Bibliophile* 10 (1852), pp. 595–601

Therrien, L., *L'histoire de l'art en France; genèse d'une discipline universitaire* (Paris, 1998)

Thomas, Ernest C. (ed.), *Transactions and proceedings of the fourth and fifth annual meeting of the Library Association of the United Kingdom, held at London 1881 and at Cambridge 1882* (1884)

Thompson, Edward Maunde, *Handbook of Greek and Latin palaeography* (1893)

An introduction to Greek and Latin palaeography (Oxford, 1912)

Thompson, Lawrence S., 'Facsimiles and the antiquarian trade', *Library Trends* 9 (1961), pp. 437–45

Thomson, John B., *The publishing business in the twenty-first century* (Cambridge, 2010)

Tidcombe, Marianne, *Bookbindings of T. J. Cobden-Sanderson; a study of his work, 1884–1893, based on his time book* (1984)

Tinniswood, Adrian, *The polite tourist; four centuries of country house visiting* (1998)

Tinti, Alberto, *Il corsivo nella tipografia del cinquecento* (Milano, 1972)

Tite, William, *An address delivered before the Society of Antiquaries of London ... December 12th, 1861, at an exhibition of early printed books, to which is subjoined an address delivered ... June 6th, 1861, at an exhibition of illuminated manuscripts* (1862)

Todd, William B. (ed.), *Thomas J. Wise; centenary studies* (Austin, TX, 1959)

Tombs, Robert, *The war against Paris, 1871* (Cambridge, 1981)

Treadwell, Michael, 'On false and misleading imprints in the London book trade, 1660–1750', in Robin Myers and Michael Harris (eds.), *Fakes and frauds; varieties of deception in print and manuscript* (Winchester, 1989), pp. 29–46

Trois cents chefs-d'oeuvre en fac-similé (Paris: Bibliothèque Nationale, 1940)

Tuer, Andrew, *Bartolozzi and his works*, 2 vols. (1881)

Twyman, Michael, *Lithography, 1800–1850; the techniques of drawing on stone in England and France and their application to works of topography* (Oxford, 1970)

Twyman, Michael and others, *Images en couleurs; Godefroy Engelmann, Charles Hullmandel et les débuts de la chromolithographie* (Lyon, 2007)

Université (L') et la typographie; exposition organisée par la Société Archéologique et Historique de l'Orléanais (Orléans, 1885)

Unwin Brothers; a century of progress being a record of the rise and present position of the Gresham Press, 1826-1926 (1926)

Unwin, P., *The printing Unwins; a short history of Unwin Brothers, the Gresham Press, 1826-1976* (1976)

Van Biervliet, L., *Leven en werk van W. H. James Weale een Engels kunsthistoricus in Vlaanderen in de 19e eeuw* (Brussel, 1991)

Van Deursen, Arie Theodorus, *Professions et métiers interdits; un aspect de l'histoire de la révocation de l'Edit de Nantes* (Groningen, 1960)

Van Praet, Joseph, *Catalogue des livres imprimés sur vélin* (Paris, 1813)

Catalogue des livres imprimés sur vélin de la Bibliothèque du Roi, 6 vols. (Paris, 1822-8)

Catalogue des livres imprimés sur vélin, qui se trouvent dans les bibliothèques tant publiques que particulières, 4 vols. (Paris, 1824-8)

Notice sur Colard Mansion, libraire et imprimeur de la ville de Bruges en Flandre (Paris, 1829)

Varry, Dominique (ed.), *Histoire des bibliothèques françaises. Les bibliothèques de la Révolution et du XIXe siècle, 1789-1914* (Paris, 1991)

Vaughan, Gerard, 'Albacini and his English patrons', *Journal of the History of Collections* 3 (1991), pp. 183-97

'The restoration of classical sculpture in the eighteenth century and the problem of authenticity', in Mark Jones (ed.), *Why fakes matter; essays on problems of authenticity* (1992), pp. 41-50

Vegetable substances; materials of manufactures (1833)

Verhoogt, Robert, *Art in reproduction; nineteenth-century prints after Lawrence Alma-Tadema, Jozef Israëls and Ary Scheffer* (Amsterdam, 2007)

Vermeulen, Ingrid R., *Picturing art history; the rise of the illustrated history of art in the eighteenth century* (Amsterdam, 2010)

Vervliet, H. D. L., *French renaissance printing types; a conspectus* (2010)

The palaeotypography of the French renaissance; selected papers on sixteenth-century typefaces, 2 vols. (Leiden, 2008)

Veyrin-Forrer, Jeanne, 'Les Réserves (livres imprimés)', in Jeanne Veyrin-Forrer, *La lettre et le texte* (Paris, 1987)

Viaux, Jacqueline, 'Les expositions des produits de l'industrie, 1798-1849', in Abraham Horodisch (ed.), *De arte et libris; Festschrift Erasmus, 1934-1984* (Amsterdam, 1984), pp. 427-49

Vicaire, Georges, 'Les Incunabula Biblica de M. W. A. Copinger et la "Bibliographical Society"', repr. from *Bulletin du Bibliophile* (1893), pp. 374-82

Vigne, Randolph and Charles Littleton (eds.), *From strangers to citizens; the integration of immigrant communities in Britain, Ireland and colonial America, 1550-1750* (Brighton, 2001)

Virr, Richard, 'Behold this treasury of glorious things; the Montreal Caxton Exhibition of 1877', *Papers of the Bibliographical Soc. of Canada* 30 (1992), pp. 7–20

Voet, Leon, *The golden compasses*, 2 vols. (Amsterdam, 1969–72)

Vosper, Robert, 'Books for libraries; institutional book collecting', in James M. Osborn and Robert Vosper, *Building book collections; two variations on a theme* (Los Angeles, 1977), pp. 17–46

Wainwright, Clive, *The romantic interior; the British collector at home, 1750–1850* (New Haven, CT, 1989)

Wakeman, Geoffrey, 'Anastatic printing for Sir Thomas Phillipps', *Journal of the Printing Historical Soc.* 5 (1969), pp. 24–40

Warren, Arthur, *The Charles Whittinghams, printers* (New York, NY, 1896)

Watkin, David, *Sir John Soane; enlightenment thought and the Royal Academy lectures* (Cambridge, 1996)

Watts, Thomas, *A letter to Antonio Panizzi, Esq. . . . on the reported earliest printed newspaper, "The English Mercurie", 1588* (1839)

Weale, W. H. James, *Bookbindings and rubbings of bindings in the National Art Library*, 2 vols. (1898–4)

Weigelt, Gertrude, 'Les Fick imprimeurs du XIXe siècle', in Beat Weber (ed.), *Cinq siècles d'imprimerie à Genève, 1478–1978* (Genève, 1978), pp. 195–202

Weimerskirch, Philip J., 'John Harris, Sr., 1767–1832; memoir by his son, John Harris, Jr., 1791–1873', *The Book Collector* 42 (1993), pp. 245–52

Weitenkampf, Frank, 'What is a facsimile?', *Papers of the Bibliographical Soc. of America* 37 (1943), pp. 114–30

Werdet, Edmond, *Histoire du livre en France, depuis les temps les plus reculés jusqu'en 1789*, 5 vols. (Paris, 1861–4)

West, Anthony James, *The Shakespeare First Folio; the history of the book*, 2 vols. (Oxford, 2001–3)

West, W. J., *The strange rise of semi-literate England* (1991)

Westerhof, Danielle (ed.), *The alchemy of medicine and print; the Edward Worth Library, Dublin* (Dublin, 2010)

Wetter, Johann, *Kritische Geschichte der Erfindung der Buchdruckerkunst durch Johann Gutenberg zu Mainz* (Mainz, 1836)

Wheatley, Henry B., *How to catalogue a library* (1889)
 How to form a library (1886)
 'Mr Quaritch's catalogue of bookbindings', *The Bibliographer* (August 1883), pp. 65–9
 Remarkable bindings in the British Museum (1889)

White, Eric Marshall, 'Newly discovered fragments from three "made up" Delft Bibles of 1477', *Quaerendo* 37 (2007), pp. 147–61

Whitehead, Christopher, *The public art museum in nineteenth century Britain; the development of the National Gallery* (Aldershot, 2005)

Willis, Robert and J. W. Clark, *The architectural history of the University of Cambridge and of the colleges of Cambridge and Eton*, 3 vols. and plans (Cambridge, 1886)

Willshire, W. H., *Descriptive catalogue of early prints in the British Museum* (1879)
Wilson, F. P., 'Sir Walter Greg', *Proc. British Academy* 45 (1959), pp. 307–34
Wilson, J. Dover, 'A. W. Pollard', *Proc. British Academy* 31 (1945), pp. 256–306
Wilton, Andrew and Ilaria Bignamini, *Grand tour; the lure of Italy in the eighteenth century* (1997)
Winckelmann, J. J., *Raccolta d'antiche statue, busti, teste cognite ed altre sculture antiche restaurate da Cav. Bartolomeo Cavaceppi scultore romano*, 3 vols. (Roma, 1768–72)
Windle, John and Karma Pippin, *Thomas Frognall Dibdin, 1776–1847; a bibliography* (New Castle, DE, 1999)
Winstanley, D. A., 'Halliwell Phillipps and Trinity College library', *The Library* 5th ser. 2 (1948), pp. 250–82
Wise, T. J. (ed.), *Letters from Ruskin to William Ward*, 2 vols. (1892)
Wolf, Edwin, II, and John Fleming, *Rosenbach; a biography* (Cleveland, OH, 1960)
Wolf, Melvin H., *Catalogue and indexes to the title-pages of English printed books preserved in the British Library's Bagford Collection* (1974)
Worm, Andrea, 'Reproducing the Middle Ages; Abbé Jean Joseph Rive (1730–1791) and the study of manuscript illumination at the turn of the early modern period', in Alice C. Montoya and others (eds.), *Early modern medievalisms; the interplay between scholarly reflection and artistic production* (Leiden, 2010), pp. 347–89
Young, Matthew McLennan, *Field & Tuer, the Leadenhall Press; a checklist* (New Castle, DE, 2010)
Zimmerman, Karl, *Bucheinbände aus dem Bücherschatze der Kgl. Öffentl. Bibliothek zu Dresden* (Leipzig, 1887–8)
Zotter, Hans, *Bibliographie Faksimilierter Handschriften* (Graz, 1976)

Index

Abbotsford 88
Academy, The 169
accessibility, universal 6, 16, 139
Ackermann, Rudolph (1764–1834), publisher 91, 102, fig. 4.8
Acta sanctorum 100
Addison, Joseph (1672–1719), essayist 54
advertisements in books 41
Allen, Josiah, printer 130
allusive typography 82–7, fig. 4.7
Ames, Joseph (1689–1759), bibliographer 102, 146, 156, 178, 189, fig. 5.1
Amherst, Lord (1835–1909), politician 182
Anglo-American bibliography 202
Annales de Chimie 97
Aponyi, Count 202
Appel, Rudolph, lithographer 105, 108
Aratea, Leiden manuscript of 100
Arber, Edward (1836–1912), scholar 128
Ariosto, Lodovico 39, fig.2.2
Ars moriendi 114–15
Arundel Society 98–9, 121
Ashbee, Edmund William, editor 109, 111, 128, 129
Auchinleck Press 89
Austin, Stephen, printers 153
Australia, lithographic printing in 105; photolithography in 123, 124
Ayling, Stephen 180

Bachelin-Deflorenne, Antoine 61
Bagford, John (1650–1716), book collector 17, 211
Baker & Taylor, publishers 137
Baker, Thomas (1656–1740), antiquary 84–5
Baldwin & Cradock, publishers 145
ballads 18–19
Ballantyne Press 196
banknotes, forgery of 97
Bannatyne Club 91
Barker, James, printer 89
Barrois, Joseph (1785–1855) 70
Baskerville, John (1706–75), printer 35

Bastard, Auguste, comte de 105
Bateman, Christopher, bookseller 43
Baudelaire, Charles (1821–67), poet 121
Baumgarten, John (d. 1782), bookbinder 28
Beckford, William (1760–1844), collector 62–6, 69
Bedford, Public Library 173
Bedford, Francis (1799–1883) bookbinder 60, 188
Bensley, Thomas (d. 1833), printer 89, 91
Bérard, Simon 142
Beresford-Hope, A. J. (1820–87), politician 59
Berjeau, Jean Philibert (1809–91), bibliographer 115, 190
Berlin, Königliche Bibliothek 153
Berthollet, Claude Louis (1748–1822), chemist 31–2
Bethnal Green Museum 160
Bewick, Thomas (1753–1828), wood-engraver 99–100
Bible, Coverdale 107–8, 162, 173; Dutch Old Testament 47; faked binding 219; and Fry 46; and Henry Stevens 174–6; Tyndale 110–11, 128. *See also* Gutenberg, Johann
Biblia pauperum 115
biblia-abiblia 196
Bibliographical Society 192–3, 202
bibliologie 198–9
Bibliomane, Le 115
Bibliophile, Le 115
Bibliophile Illustré, Le 115
Bickham, George (d. 1769), writing master 102, fig. 5.1
Blades, William (1824–90), printer, and Caxton 58, 104, 110, 137, 166–7, 181; and Caxton exhibition 167–8, 171, 174; and *Dictes and sayings* 180–1; and enemies of books 28–9; and facsimiles 109–10, 122; and *Governayle of helthe* 180; obituary 183–4; and *Recuyell* 173; and Tupper 109–10, 137
Blundell, Henry (1724–1810), collector 51
Boccaccio, Giovanni (1313–75) 65–6, 77, 171, fig. 4.3

278

Bonnardot, Alfred, bookbinder 49–50
Book of Common Prayer 126
bookbinders, as enemies of books 28, 60
bookbindings, in exhibitions 66, 152, 161–2, 195; fakes 66–8, 70–1, 219, fig. 3.1; inappropriate 137; and photography 61, 70; retrospective styles 29, 66. *See also* remboîtage
booksellers' stock 6–7, 187–8
bookselling, changes in 6–8; international 24–6 *see also under individual names.*
Bookworm, The 115, 183, fig.6.1
Booth, Lionel 126
Bosvile, A., bookseller 84
Boswell, Alexander (1775–1822), antiquary 89
Bourassé, Jean Jacques, abbé 153
Bowers, Fredson (1905–91), bibliographer 201
Bowyer, William (1699–1777), printer 43
Bradshaw, Henry, librarian (1831–86) 67, 104; and Berjeau 115; and bibliographical description 199–202; and Caxton 166–7, 173–4, 180; influence of 184
Brassington, William Salt 193
breaking books 211
Brewster, printer 80
Brinley, George, book collector 176
Briquet, C. M. (1839–1918), paper historian 190, 202
Bristol Baptist College 110
British Association 118
British Library and newspapers 4
British Museum 151–3; casts 96; and cataloguing 199; condition of bindings in 60; early years 14, 20; exhibitions in 151–3, 194, 197–8, 235; Harris's work in 106; incunables 202; and photography 119; prints collection 192; and Sunderland sale 66; visitors to 151–2
Bronzino, Il (1503–72), painter 53
Browne, Sir Thomas (1605–82), physician 136
Bruce, Lord Charles 174
Bullen, George, librarian 114
Bulmer, William (1757–1830), printer 93
Bunyan, John (1628–88), author of *Pilgrim's progress* 131, 136
Buonarelli, Matteo 50
Burger, Konrad 202
Burlington Fine Arts Club 66, 195
Burns, Robert (1759–96), poet 164

Caedmon 100
Caen 194
Cambridge, Corpus Christi College 133; Trinity College 96, 119, 185
Cambridge University Library 47, 67, 85, figs. 2.4, 3.1; and cataloguing 199; Caxtons in 171; sculpture in 52
Campbell, M. F. A. G. (1840–90), librarian 190
Canova, Antonio (1757–1822), sculptor 51, 55
Capell, Edward (1713–81), Shakespeare scholar 87
Carter, John (1905–75), bibliographer 197
Caslon, typefounders 79, 87, 89
Caslon, William (1692–1766), typefounder 102, 184, fig. 5.1
Castan, Auguste (1833–92), librarian 190
casts, plaster 95–6
cataloguing in libraries 199–200
Cavaceppi, Bartolomeo (c. 1716–99), sculptor 50–1
Caxton, William (d. 1491), printer, and allusive printing 79–80; and children's books 170; facsimiles 178–82; painting by Maclise 170–1, 238, fig. 8.1; and Paris 24; reputation 165–6
Caxton exhibition (1877) 58, 59–60, 158, 164–78; catalogues 169–71, 173–4; display 171–2, 174–5; and France 24, 177–8, 194; visitor numbers 175; effects 183
Cellini, Benvenuto (1500–71), sculptor 50
Cessolis, Jacobus de, *The game and playe of the chesse* 131, 156, 167, 179, figs 6.3. 6.4
Chalmers, George 85
Champion, Honoré (1846–1913), publisher 202
Chantilly, Musée Condé 23
Chaptal, Jean-Antoine (1756–1832) 31–2, 37
Chatsworth 108–9, 173
Chatto & Windus, publishers 126
Cheere, John (1709–87), sculptor 95
chlorine 31–2
Christina, Queen of Sweden (1626–89) 50
chromolithography 94, 150
Cincinnati Bank 97
Clark, John Willis (1833–1910), antiquary 58
Clarke, Edward Daniel (1769–1822), traveller 52
Claudin, Anatole, bookseller 25, 67, 70, 177–8, 202
cleaning books 29–3
Cobden-Sanderson, T. J. (1840–1922), bookbinder 61, 69, 193
Cock, Christopher 96
Cockerell, S. M. (d. 1987), bookbinder, fig. 2.4
Cockerell, Sydney (1867–1962), secretary to William Morris 192
Codex Alexandrinus 119, 125
Cohn, booksellers (Berlin) 63
coins, forgery of 97

Cole, Sir Henry (1808–82), museum administrator 98, 159
Coleridge, S. T. (1772–1834), poet 71, 140
Collier, John Payne (1789–1883), Shakespearean scholar 108, 128
Colonna, Francesco *Hypnerotomachia Poliphili* 46, 162
Columbus letters 67, 129–30
Colvin, Sidney (1845–1927), curator 192
completeness, importance of 10–12, 44
Cooper, Thomas (d. 1594), lexicographer 43
Copinger, W. A. (1847–1910), lawyer 190, 192
copying, three-dimensional 95–9
Coryate, Thomas (d. 1617), traveller 89
Cosimo, Grand Duke of Tuscany (1642–1723) 53
Coster, Laurens, of Haarlem 147–8, 156, 163, fig. 7.2; statues 156
Coverly, Roger de, bookbinder 61
Cowell, printers 104
Craik, George Lillie (1798–1866), author 165–6
Crane, Walter (1845–1915), artist 193
Crawford and Balcarres, James Ludovic Lindsay, 26th Earl of (1847–1913) 195
Creative Commons 7
Cundall, Joseph (1818–95), publisher 193
Cutter, Charles A. (1837–1903), librarian 199

Daguerre, Louis (1787–1851), pioneer in photography 118
daguerreotypes 97
Dante Alighieri (c. 1265–1321) 164
dates, changes to 76
Davenport, Cyril (1848–1941), historian of bookbinding 66
Davy, Sir Humphry (1778–1829), chemist 31
Day & Son, printers 125
Deansgate Press 196
De la Rue, printers 97
Delisle, Léopold (1826–1910), librarian 117, 202
de Morgan, Augustus (1806–71), mathematician 185–6
Denbigh, Caxton and 170
Denon, Dominique Vivant, baron de (1747–1825), museum administrator 51
Derby Mechanics' Institute 142, 144
Desriez, Charles 112
Destruction (The) of Troy 80, fig. 4.5
Devonshire, Dukes of 108–9, 173
Dibdin, Thomas Frognall (1776–1847), bibliographer, and Ames 146, 156; opinion of Whittaker 37; *Reminiscences* 230
Dickens, Charles (1812–70), novelist 209

Dicks, John, publisher 131
Dictes and sayings of the philosophers 173
Didot, Ambroise Firmin (1790–1876), printer 229
digitisation, pitfalls and challenges of 4–6, 9–12, 16–17, 19–20, 57, 207–10
Dilke, Sir Charles (1810–69), politician 168
D'Israeli, Isaac (1766–1848), author 85
Dobell, Bertram (1842–1914), bookseller 187
Dodgson, Campbell (1867–1948), museum curator 192
Domesday Book 123–4, 126
Dossie, Robert (1717–77) 96
Drugulin, type founders 79
Dryden, John (1631–1700), poet 54
Duff, Edward Gordon (1863–1924), bibliographer 181, 193, 195, 201, 242
Dupont, Auguste (1798–1850), printer 104
Dupont, Paul (1796–1879), printer 104–5
dustwrappers 209
Duverger, Eugène, bibliographer 112, 149
Dymott, Richard, bookbinder 31
Dziatzko, Karl (1842–1903), librarian 202

e-books 8–9
Earle, John 124
Early English Books Online, *see* EEBO
ECCO 12
Edinburgh 196
Edinburgh Review 9
Education Act (1870) 21
Edwards, Pietro (1744–1821), restorer 53
EEBO 3, 10, 15
Eighteenth-Century Collections Online, *see* ECCO
electrotyping 96–9
Elkington & Co. 98–9
Ellis & Elvey, booksellers 130, 187, 191
Ellis, F. S., bookseller 61, 63, 64–5
Elzevir press 76
enemies of books 28
English Mercurie 85
engravings, copyright in 96; of manuscripts 100; of printed books 100–2, fig. 5.1
Enschedé, Charles (1855–1919), type founder 58
Enschedé, type founders 79
ephemera 17–18, 207
Erasmus, Desiderius (1466–1536) 85, fig. 4.7
Ernouf, Alfred-Auguste, Baron (1816–89) 177
Essling, Victor Massiéna, Prince d' 202
Evelyn, John (1620–1706), virtuoso 30
'excessive' rarity 197

exhibitions 150–9, fig.7.2; touring 99, 198; presentation of books in 151–5, 171–2, 174–5, 198

Fabra, Francisco López (d. 1891), scholar 124
facsimile leaves 37; in manuscript 37–40; uses of word 94–5
facsimiles, prices of 123–6, 128–9, 181; and verisimilitude 57
Fairfax, Bryan 181
Falkenstein, Constantin Carl von 148
Fenn, Sir John (1739–94), antiquary 189
Fenton, Roger (1819–69), photographer 119
Fick, Jules-Gustave, printer 178
Fielding, Henry, (1707–54), novelist, *Tom Jones* 47, 209
Fifteen Oes 180
Figgins, Vincent (1766–1844), type founder 131, 178–9; fig. 6.4
Fine Art Society 137
Fitzgerald, Percy (1834–1925), critic 66
Fleischman, J. M., punchcutter 79, 174
Fletcher, W. Y. (d. 1913), historian of book collecting 193
formats 199–200
France, anxiety about patrimoine 160
François I (1494–1547), King of France 53
Fry, Francis (1803–86), book collector 46, 110–11, 128, 218
Fry, John (1792–1822), bookseller, 90–1
Furnivall. F. J. (1825–1910), lexicographer 111, 128–9
Fyfe, James Hamilton (1837–80) 147–8

Galignani, publishers 141–2
Galvani, Luigi (1737–98), physicist 96
Galvanism 96
Gardner, W. Wells 137
Garrick, David (1717–79), actor 131, 152
Gesner, Johann Matthias (1691–1763), librarian 20
Ghent Universiteitsbibliotheek 47
Gheyn, Jacob de, engraver 100
Gibbon, Edward (1737–94), historian 156
Gladstone, W. E. (1809–98), politician 123, 169
Godefroid family, restorers 53
Göttingen, Universitätsbibliothek 13, 20, 173
Governayle of helthe 180
Graphic, The 169
Great exhibition (1851) 105, 106–7, 108, 151–2, 159
Greenhill, W. A. 136

Greenwood, Thomas (1851–1908), advocate of public libraries 198
Greg, W. W. (1875–1959), bibliographer 129, 162, 202–3, 236
Grenville, Thomas (1755–1846), book collector 106
Griggs, William, printer 70, 111, 129
Grimani Breviary 98, 120–1
Grolier, Jean (1479–1565) 67, 69, 160, fig. 3.1
Guercino, Il (1591–1666), painter 52
Gutenberg, Johann, printer 8; Bible 13–14, 23, 148–9, 153, 176, 194; celebrations of 142–3, 156; legends of 147–8; statues of 142, 146, 169, fig. 7.1

Haarlem exhibition (1856) 156, fig. 7.2
Hadrian, emperor, sculpture of 51
Haebler, Konrad (1857–1946), librarian 202, 211
Hagué, Théodore, bookbinder 69–70, 223
Hain, Ludwig (1781–1836), bibliographer 191
Hakluyt, Richard (d. 1616), geographer 42–3
Halliwell-Phillipps, James Orchard (1820–89), bibliographer 109, 111, 126, 165, 185
Hamilton, Sir William (1731–1803), diplomat 50
Handel, Georg Friedrich (1685–1759), *Messiah* 126
Hansard, T. C. (1766–1833), printer 145
Harding, George, bookseller 187
Hardy, Thomas Duffus (1804–78), archivist 159
Harley, Edward, Earl of Oxford (1689–1741), collector 62
Harris, John (1791–1873), facsimilist 105–8, 122
Harris, John, the younger, facsimilist 108, 230
Harrison, G. B., Shakespeare scholar 3, 214
Haslewood, Joseph (1769–1833), antiquary 88
heating, damage by 60
Hecquet, Robert, engraver 31, 37
Heliotype Company 128
Herbert, George (1593–1633), poet 131, 137
Herbert, William (1718–95), bibliographer 102, 146, 189
Heyne, Christian Gottlob (1729–1812), librarian 20
Hibbert, George (1757–1837), book collector 93
History of Jason 47
Hodson, James (1819–99), charity administrator 175
Holbein Society 114–15
Holford, R. S. (1808–92), collector 136
Holinshed, Raphael, chronicler 43, fig. 2.3

Holmes Sir Richard 193
Holtrop, J. W. (1806–70), librarian 101, 102–3, 115–17, 202
Hone, William (1780–1842), bookseller 165
'honest copies' 55
Horne, Herbert (1864–1916), art historian 193
hospital copies 45
Huguenots and the book trade 24–5
Humphreys, Henry Noel (1810–79), numismatist and artist 149, 186

Illustrated London News 163, 169
illustrations, reproduction of 149–50
Imison, John (d. 1788), printer 32, 34
Imprimerie Royale 79
imprints, to be cut off 90
incunables, catalogues of 190
Ives, George Brayton, book collector 130

Jackson, W. A. (1905–64), bibliographer 3
Jacobi C. T. (1853–1933), printer 192
James, Sir Henry (1803–77), Director of the Ordnance Survey 123–5
Jammes, André (b. 1927), bookseller 244
Jewett, Charles Cofffin (1816–68), librarian 199
Johnson, John (1882–1956), printer 17
Johnson, Samuel (1709–84), lexicographer 25, 42
Jones, John Winter (1805–81), librarian 162
Joni, Icilio Federico (1866–1946), painter 223

Kalthoeber, Christian Samuel (1752–1819), bookbinder 28, 63
Kegan Paul, publishers 193
Kelmscott Press 192
Kennett, White (1660–1728), bishop 29
Kerney, Michael, bookseller 62–3, 70, 240
Kerr, Robert, surgeon 32
Kippis, Andrew (1725–95), biographer 146
Kneller, Sir Godfrey (1646–1723), artist 54
Knight, Charles (1791–1873), publisher 22, 144–8, 158; and Caxton 145–6, 150, 165; and early printing 156, 208; and type facsimile 72–3
Korff, Modest Andreevich, Count (1800–76) 154

Lamb, Charles (1775–1834), essayist 141, 196
Lancaster, Alfred, librarian 198
Laocoön 50
La Vallière, Louis-César de La Baume Le Blanc, duc de (1708–80) 45
Lawler, John, cataloguer 65
leaf books 211, 218, 248

leather, poor quality of 60
Leathersellers' Company 60
Lee, Sir Sidney (1859–1926), Shakespeare scholar 49
Leeuwarden 194
Le Fevre, Raoul *Recueil des histoires de Troyes* 47, 162; *Recuyell of the historyes of Troy* 47, 80, 167, 173, 181 figs 2.4, 4.4
Le Gascon, bookbinder 63
Leicester, Lord 108, 173
Leipzig exhibition (1840) 142, 153
Lemercier, printers 128
Lenormand, Sébastien (1757–1837), parachutist 34
Lenox, James (1800–80), book collector 106
Le Roux de Lincy, Adrien 155
Lewis, Charles (1786–1836), bookbinder 63
Lewis, John (1675–1747), antiquary 146, 155, 156
Lewis, John (1912–96), typographer 17–18
libraries, access to 20–1; and bulk buying 208–9; and discarding books 3–4, 212; management 3–4, 10, 14, 212
Library of Congress 4
Libri, Guglielmo (1803–69), book thief 61
Lichfield Cathedral 94
Lilly, Joseph, bookseller 181
litho-typographie 104
lithography 90, 99–100, 101–2, 104–5, 107, fig. 4.8
Little Gidding 45
Liverpool Echo 175
Lofft, Capell (1751–1824), author 87
Loftie, W. J. (1839–1911), historian 59, 163, 164
London, exhibitions of artists 160–1; private galleries in 140–1. *See also under the names of individual institutions*
Lubbock, Sir John (1834–1913), politician 59
Luther, Martin (1483–1546), reformer 152, 153, 194

Mabillon, Jean (1632–1707), palaeographer 23, 100
Macaulay, Thomas Babington, Lord (1800–59), historian 166
Maclise, Daniel (1806–70), painter 170–1
Macmillan, Alexander (1818–96), publisher 131
Madan, Falconer (1851–1935), librarian 13, 193, 211
Madden, Sir Frederic (1801–73), palaeographer 117, 119, 150, 151–2
made-up copies 45–7
Maitland Club 91
Mâle, Emile (1862–1954), art historian 118

Manchester exhibition (1857) 161–2, 170; Royal Jubilee Exhibition 196
manuscripts, and engraving 100
Manutius, Aldus (1449–1515), printer 73, 76, 161
Maratta, Carlo (1625–1713), painter 52
Mari, Baldassare, sculptor 50
Marsh, Narcissus (1638–1713) archbishop 30
Marvell, Andrew (1621–78), poet 165
Maxwell, Sir William Stirling (1818–78), antiquary 164
Maynal, Guillaume (1713–96), author 24
Mazarin, Jules (1602–61), cardinal 50
McKenzie, D. F. (1931–99), bibliographer 2, 206
McKerrow, Ronald Brunlees (1872–1940), bibliographer 201
Mechanics' Magazine 95
Meerman, Gerard (1722–71), bibliographer 101
Melbourne 99, 124, 167, 189
Mendelssohn, Felix (1809–47), composer 168
Mesnager, Charles 112
Michelangelo (1475–1564), sculptor and painter 53
microfilming 3, 9–10
Milan, Biblioteca Ambrosiana 130
Milner, John 88
Milnes, Richard Monckton, Lord Houghton (1809–85) 25
Milton, John (1608–74), poet, *Paradise lost* 87, 131, 136, 188, figs 6.5, 6.6
Mirror of Literature 95
mixing copies 37, 45–7, 72, 209
Montfaucon, Bernard de (1655–1741), palaeographer 100
Montreal 176
Moore, J. C. 131
Morel, Gall (1803–72), O.S.B. 142
Morgand, booksellers (Paris) 63
Morison, Stanley (1889–1967), typographer 183
Morris, William (1834–96), artist 58–9, 60–1, 191–2
Moxon, Joseph (1627–1700), hydrographer 184
Muller, Frederik, bookseller 63, 191
multiple copies, importance of 13–14, 41–2, 212
Munby, A. N. L. (1913–74), librarian 22
Munich, Bayerische Staatsbibliothek 13, 153–4
Museum of Literature 147
Museums Act (1845) 159

Nabu Press 11
Namur, Pie (1804–67), librarian 34, 37
National Gallery 53, 54, 137, 150
Nebrija, Antonio de (1441–1522), grammarian 76–7

Needham, Paul, bibliographer 60–1
Nelson, Thomas, publisher 147
Net Book Agreement 7
Nethercliff, Frederick (1817–92), facsimilist 94
New Biblia pauperum 178–9
New Gallery 195
New Shakspere Society 128
New York, Pierpont Morgan Library 47, 49; Public Library 4, 11, 130
newspapers 4
Nichols, John 85
Nicholson, E. W. B. (1849–1912), librarian 200
Nicholson, John (1730–96), bookseller 41
Niépce, Nicéphore (1765–1833), pioneer in photography 118
Nijhoff, Martinus, bookseller 202
Nodier, Charles (1780–1844), bibliophile 112
Nollekens, Joseph (1737–1823), sculptor 51
Norwich exhibition (1840) 144
Nottingham exhibition (1840) 144

Odemira, Damiano da 89
Osborne, James 124
Ottley, William Young (1771–1836), collector 149
ownership marks 29
Oxford, Ashmolean Museum 140; Bodleian Library, bookbindings 49, 193; Bradshaw and 180; Caedmon manuscript 100; cataloguing 199–200; ephemera 17; exhibition 150–1; English Faculty Library 11
Oxford University Press 174

Padeloup, Antoine Michel (1685–1758), bookbinder 63
paintings and restoration 52–5; woodcut representations of 150
Panizzi, Sir Anthony (1797–1879), librarian 131–2, 199
Papebroch, Daniel (1628–1714), hagiographer 100
paper, cleaning of 29–36, 54; and formats 200; imitations of old 62, 110; old stocks 101; waste 35–7; watermarks 190; wove 35
Parini, Antonio 120
Paris, exhibitions (1855) 161; (1868) 128; Bibliothèque Mazarine 194; Bibliothèque [Royale] Nationale 141–2, 154–5; exhibitions of artists 160–1; Louvre 51, 98, 154; Palais Bourbon 160; Palais du Luxembourg 14; siege of 163; Thermes de Cluny 159
Parker, Matthew (1504–75), archbishop 45
part publications 209

Passinger, Thomas (d. 1688), bookseller 80
Payne & Foss, booksellers 130, 230
Payne, J. T., bookseller 26
Payne, Roger (1739–97), bookbinder 30–1
Peignot, Gabriel (1767–1849), bibliographer 33, 198–9
Pellechet, Marie (1840–1900), bibliographer 202
pen alteration 76; facsimile 37–9, 105–10, 114–5, figs. 2.1, 2.2
Penny Magazine 95, 144–7, 150, 208, fig.7.1
Pepys, Samuel (1633–1703), diarist 17, 29–30, 66, 80, 93, 168
Petrarca, Franceso (1304–74) 47, 64–5
Phelps, John Delafield (1812–42), book collector 91
Philobiblon Society 25
photogenic drawing 118
photography, Baudelaire on 121; beginnings of 117–18; and bindings 61, 70; and facsimiles 101; and manuscripts 98, 120–1, 122–30; and South Kensington Museum 99, 121–2; and woodcuts 101, 114
photolithography 104, 111, 115, 122–30
photozincography 104, 115, 122–6
Picault, Robert (1705–81), restorer 53
Pilinski, Adam (1810–87), facsimilist 108
Piranesi, Giovanni Battista (1720–78), artist 50
Pisan, Cristine de (1364–*c*. 1430) 180
Plantin Museum, Antwerp 194
Plantin-Moretus press 79, 100
Pollard, A. W. (1859–1944), librarian, and Bibliographical Society 192; on exhibitions 198; on improving old books 45; and Kegan Paul 193; and mixed copies 211, 219; on type facsimiles 77
Polytechnic Institute 97
Pope, Abby, book collector 182
Power, Eugene B. (1905–93), publisher 3
Preston, R., photographer 125
Prideaux, Sarah (1853–1933), bookbinder 195
Primer (1546) 83–4
print-on-demand 7, 11–12
printing, alleged consistency of 205; attributes of 204
Printing and the mind of man 22
prints, cleaning and artificial aging 49; collecting 31
Proctor, Robert (1868–1903), librarian 190
ProQuest, publishers 14
public, access to British Museum 153; identities of 140; meaning of 21; reading public 140
pubic interest 4–6, 208

Public Libraries Act (1850) 21
Public Record Office 159
publishing, recent changes in 6–8
Punch 128, 131, 170

quality control, and digitisation 9–12
Quaritch, Bernard (1819–99), bookseller, and American libraries 65; appeals for help in completing books 46; and blockbooks 239; and bookbindings 61–2, 67–9, 196; catalogues 188–91; and Columbus letter 130; on dull books 196; and First Folio 188; and French trade 26; and Hagué 69–70; and history of science 186; *Monuments of typography and xylography* 189; and *New Biblia pauperum* 178; and new books 149; and Osterley Park sale 181–2; as publisher 186; and rarity 197; staff 240; and Sunderland and Beckford sales 62, 63–6
Quatremère de Quincy, Antoine (1755–1849), writer on art 55

Rackham, John, printer 87
Rae, John 180
rarity 65, 141, 197, 208–9, 212
readers, general 165–6
reading, different processes 57
rearrangement of leaves 45
Reed, Talbot Baines (1852–93), type founder 58, 174, 201
remboîtage 49, 67, 196, 219
Rembrandt van Rijn (1606–69), painter, 52
Renouard, Antoine August, bookseller 34, 197
Revilliod, Gustave (1817–90), publisher 178
Reynard the fox 80, fig. 4.6
Reynolds, Sir Joshua (1723–92), painter 52–3
Rive, Jean-Joseph (1730–91), Abbé 45
Rivière, Robert (1808–82), bookbinder 60
Rome, Capitoline Museum 140
Rooses, Max (1839–1914), antiquary 194
Rosenthal, Jacques, bookseller 191, 202
Rosweyde, Héribert (1569–1629), hagiographer 100
Rothschild, Victor, Baron (1910–90), zoologist 47, 209
Rouen 194–5
Rouveyre, Edouard, publisher 66
Roxburghe Club 91–3
Roy, William 91
Royal Archaeological Institute 162
Royal Horticultural Society 169
Royal Institution 95
Royal Society of Arts 60

Index

Rubens, Sir Peter Paul (1577–1640), artist 52
Ruddiman, Thomas (1674–1757), librarian 85
Ruskin, John (1819–1900), art critic 59, 137–8
Russell, John (d.1494), bishop 24

Saint-Germain-en-Laye, Musée des Antiquités Nationales 159
St Helens, Public Library 196, 198
St Petersburg, Imperial Library 154
Salisbury Cathedral 88
Samouelle, George (d. 1846), museum curator 151
Sams, Mr, of Darlington 178
Sandars, Samuel (1837–94), book collector 67–9
Saturday Review 169–70, 175
Scheele, Carl (1742–86), chemist 31
Schiller, Friedrich (1759–1805), poet 164
Schreiber, Wilhelm Ludwig (1855–1932), art historian 192, 202
science, history of 184–5
Scott, Henry 98
Scott, Sir George Gilbert (1811–78), architect 59
Scott, Sir Walter (1771–1832), novelist 88, 91, 164–5
Scrivener, F. H. (1813–91), New Testament scholar 119
sculpture, alterations 51, 55; and restoration 50–2
Seguier, William (1772–1843), picture dealer 54
Settle, Elkanah (1648–1724), poet 76
Shakespeare, William (1564–1616), cheap editions of 12, 131; fashion in 1860s 131; *Hamlet* 108–9, 129, 130–1; *Sonnets* 125; tercentenary 165; *Works* (1623) 72, 188, 191, 233, figs. 4.1, 4.2
Shaw, Henry (1800–73) antiquary 173
Short-title catalogue (Pollard and Redgrave) 85
Sickel, Theodor von (1826–1908), medieval historian 117
Silvy, Camille (1834–1910), photographer 120
Simonin & Toovey, printers 128
Slade, Felix (1790–1868), collector 152, 161, 162
Slater, J. Herbert (1854–1921), bibliophile 66, 167
Smeaton, *see* Smeeton
Smee, Alfred (1818–77), surgeon 97
Smeeton, George, printer 89, 90
Smeeton, Joseph, printer 88–9
Smith, Joseph (1682–1770), consul 47, 77
Société des Bibliophiles François 25
Society for the Diffusion of Useful Knowledge 145, 156

Society for the Protection of Ancient Buildings 58
Society of Antiquaries 195
Sodoma, Il (1477–1549), painter 52
Sorg, Anton, printer 76
Sotheby, Samuel Leigh (1805–61), auctioneer 101, 149, 190
Sotheran, booksellers 187
South Kensington exhibition (1862) 162; (1874) 160
South Kensington Museum and copies 98–9; loan collection 121–2; painting loaned to 171; photography and 99, 121–2; printing machinery in 175; public in 163; publications 98–9; and travelling exhibitions 99, 198
Spanier, E., lithographer 117
Sparrow, Anthony (1612–85) bishop 82–3
Speculum humanae salvationis 101, 115
Spencer, Charles, 3rd Earl of Sunderland (1674/5–1722) *see* Sunderland sales
Spencer, George John, Earl (1758–1834) 28, 65, 106, 162, 171, 173
Spencer, Thomas 96
Spencer, Walter, bookseller 187
Staggemeier, L., bookbinder 63
standards, manufacturing 9
Stanley, Arthur (1815–81), Dean of Westminster 168–9
Stansby, William (1572–1638), printer 79–80
Stationers' Company 168, 169
Staunton, Howard (1810–74), Shakespeare scholar 125–6
steel engravings 100
Stevens, Henry (1819–86), bookseller, and Bibles 106, 174–6; and improving books 43, 106; and microphotography 3; and 1877 exhibition 174–6
Stock, Elliot, publisher 112, 115, 131–2, 136–7, 181, 183,199, figs. 6.1, 6.6
Stockholm, Royal printing office 79
Stowe, gardens 96
Strange, Walter F. 193
Stratford-on-Avon 165
Sturt, J., bookseller 89
Sunderland sales 62–6
Sydney 99

Talbot, W. H. Fox (1800–77), pioneer of photography 117–19
Taylor, R. and A., printers 89, 90
Techener, Jacques Joseph (1802–70), bookseller 61, 63, 154–5
Thomas, Rev. Vaughan, librarian 65

Thompson, Edward Maunde (1840–1929), palaeographer 117, 193–4
Timbs, John (1801–75), journalist 146–8
Times, The 131, 137–8, 147, 169
Timmins, Samuel (d. 1902), Shakespeare scholar 130
Tite, Sir William (1798–1873), architect 195
Toovey, James, bookseller 49, 107
Toronto 176
tourists, and manuscripts 120–1
Towneley, Charles (1737–1805), collector 51
traced facsimiles 109–10, 114–15, 117, 166
Trollope, Anthony (1815–82), novelist 168
Tuckett, John, bookseller 111
Tuer, Andrew (1838–1900), publisher 174
Tupper, G. I. F. T., facsimilist 110, 117, 166
Turner, R. S. 162
Tyas, Robert 131
type facsimiles 19, 42–4, 72–7, 79, 87, 88–93, 109–10, 112, 130–8, figs. 2.3, 4.2, 4.3, 6.4, 6.6
type, recutting 112, 131, 178–9; survivals 79, 93

uniformity, myth of 42
University Microfilms 3, 9, 14–15
University of California, Broadside Ballad Archive 18–19; libraries 12
Unwins, printers 178
Upcottt, William (1779–1845), autograph collector 89, 90, 200
Utrecht Psalter 121

van der Linde, Antonius (1833–97), historian 163
van Dyck, Sir Anthony (1599–1641), painter 52
van Praet, Joseph (1754–1837), librarian 102, 104
Vénus de Milo 51
Vergauwen, Frans, senator 47
Victoria (1819–1901), Queen of the United Kingdom 171, 173
Vienna, Albertina 23
Viollet-le-Duc (1814–79), architect 59
Virgil (Venice, 1501) 199
Vitel, Ludovic 59

Voullième, Ernst (1862–1930), bibliographer 190

Walbancke, Matthew, bookseller 85
Wallace, Sir Richard (1818–90), art collector 160
Walpole, Horace, Earl of Orford (1717–97), antiquary 88
Walther, Henry, bookbinder 28
Ward, William 137
Warwick vase 50
Watts, Thomas, of the British Museum 85–6
Weale, W. H. J. (1832–1917), antiquary 190
Werdet, Edmond (1793–1870), publisher 139
West Wycombe 95
Western Mail 175
Westminster Abbey 166, 167–8
Wetter, Joseph 102
Whatman, James (1702–59), paper-maker 35
Wheatley, Henry B. (1838–1917), cataloguer 66, 193, 199
Whewell, William (1794–1866), Master of Trinity College, Cambridge 185
Whittaker, John, facsimilist 37, 106–7, 184
Whittingham, Charles (1767–1840), printer 89, 91, 105
Williamstown, Victoria 167
Willis, Robert (1800–75), engineer 58
Willshire, W. H., of the British Museum 192
Wilson, John 96
Winckelmann, Johann Joachim (1717–68), art historian, 50
'Wisean' forgeries 77
woodcuts, old 80, 178, fig. 4.6
Worde, Wynkyn de, printer 84
World Digital Library 139
Worth, Edward (1678–1733), physician 30
Wright, John, printer 72–3 4.2
Wyatt, James (1746–1813), architect 88
Wyatt, Sir Matthew Digby (1820–77), writer on art 121
Wycliffe, John (d. 1384), religious reformer 194

Zaehnsdorf, Joseph (1816–86), bookbinder 69